Benefits of Therapeutic Recreation

A Consensus View

Edited by*:

Catherine P. Coyle
W.B. (Terry) Kinney
Bob Riley
John W. Shank

* Editors listed alphabetically. Contributions are considered to be equal.

Published and distributed by:

Idyll Arbor, Inc.
P.O. Box 720
25119 S.E. 262 Street
Ravensdale, WA 98051-0720
(206) 432-3231

A donation will be made to the Bernie Thorne Efficacy Research Fund of the American Therapeutic Recreation Foundation for each book that is purchased.

Library of Congress Number: 93-80023

ISBN 1-882883-06-3

**Printed in the United States of America
Second Edition**

Development and initial dissemination of this report was partially supported by Cooperative Agreement No. H133B80048 funded by the National Institute on Disability and Rehabilitation Research. The opinions expressed herein do not necessarily reflect the opinions of the U.S. Department of Education, and no official endorsement should be inferred.

PREFACE

Terry Kinney, John Shank, & Kathy Coyle

What follows in this conference proceedings is the exciting culmination of a three year research project sponsored by the United States Department of Education (USDOE) and Temple University's Program in Therapeutic Recreation. The conference brought together over 80 of the country's finest researchers, educators, and practitioners in therapeutic recreation to debate and come to agreement on the outcomes, or benefits, of therapeutic recreation in rehabilitation. Undoubtedly, the results of this conference will benefit the discipline tremendously and will guide major research efforts for at least the next decade.

It is important, before proceeding to the content of the report, to place in context the background and impetus that led to this conference; otherwise the reader may conclude, erroneously, that the participants were too narrowly focused on the "therapeutic" aspect over the "recreation" aspect of our services. That, in fact, was exactly the purpose.

In 1988, Temple University's Program in Therapeutic Recreation was awarded a 3-year grant by USDOE's National Institute On Disability and Rehabilitation Research (NIDRR) to conduct research to determine the efficacy of therapeutic recreation in rehabilitation. More specifically, the grant came from the Medical Sciences Division of NIDRR which is particularly interested in medical outcomes and how specific interventions affect medical outcomes. The intent is obvious. NIDRR was anxious to find out if therapeutic recreation, as a medical intervention, deserves support by the medical community. That is, do we impact, in some positive way, on medical outcomes.

As part of the grant award, Temple was to conduct, in the third year, a state-of-the-art National Consensus Conference on the Benefits Of Therapeutic Recreation in Rehabilitation. This was a major part of the grant and involved a complex process that is fully described in the introduction section by Bob Riley.

At the National Conference, we asked the delegates, not necessarily to totally avoid recreation-related benefits, but to attempt to focus on those rehabilitation benefits that could be more closely related to medical outcomes. They were charged with the task of coming to consensus on the theoretical foundations that guide our delivery of interventions; the documented outcomes as identified by the research literature; the outcomes we believe we benefit, but have not yet documented; and, finally, a research agenda to guide efficacy research through the 1990s.

The results are presented in this proceedings and it is for each person to judge how successful the delegates were. Obviously, it was a huge challenge, and impossible to attain in the ideal. With that in mind, we encourage readers to view these proceedings not as the end of a project, but rather as a beginning. Much has been accomplished in identifying our specific benefits; a great deal remains to be done. It is our hope that these proceedings will serve as the motivation for that effort. The research agenda is clear and important; it needs to be accomplished. For any doctoral student readers, we make an urgent plea for you to consider how you can contribute to this agenda through your dissertation as well as future career.

We owe a debt of gratitude to the authors of our position papers. What follows are the chapters: (a) Keynote by Mary Lee Seibert; (b) The Benefits of Therapeutic Recreation in Chemical Dependency by Ann Rancourt; (c) The Benefits of Therapeutic Recreation in Developmental Disabilities by John Datillo and Stuart Schleien; (d) The Benefits of Therapeutic Recreation in Gerontology by Jean Keller and Carol Riddick; (e) The Benefits of Therapeutic Recreation in Pediatrics by Viki Annand and Peggy Powers; (f) The Benefits of Therapeutic Recreation in Physical Medicine by Doris Berryman, Ann James, and Barb Trader; (g) The Benefits of Therapeutic Recreation in Psychiatry by Glen Van Andel, Tom Skalko, and Gino DeSalvatore (h) A Summary of Benefits Common to Therapeutic Recreation by Kathy Coyle, Terry Kinney, and John Shank; and finally, (i) "reaction papers" from each of the consensus groups, written, for the most part, by the group facilitators with input from the group participants.

We also owe a debt of gratitude to Bob Riley for his tireless efforts in coordinating the position paper writing. This was the backbone of this conference and whatever success this conference may have achieved is largely due to his efforts.

December, 1991

Conference Delegates

Chemical Dependency

Facilitator
Mike Rhodes

Group Members
Coco Collins
Cindy Herndon
Colleen Hood
Robin Kunstler
Mark Mattiko
Nancy Navar
Pat O'Dea-Evans
Carol Peterson
Ann Rancourt
Debbie Robbins-Sisco

Developmental Disabilities

Facilitator
Julie Dunn

Group Members
Steve Anderson
Candy Aston-Schaffer
Peg Connolly
Mike Crawford
John Dattilo
Barbara Hawkins
Terry Kinney
Bob Riley
Stuart Schleien
Pat Shank
Patricia Treinen

Conference Delegates

Gerontology

Facilitator
Linda Troyer

Group Members
Rosangela Boyd
Jean Keller
Fran McGuire
Lorraine Peniston
Carol Riddick
Keith Savell
Carla Tabourne
Ted Tedrick
Karen Vecchione

Pediatrics

Facilitator
Linda Caldwell

Group Members
Viki Annand
Andy Chasnoff
Aubrey Fine
Gayle Kanary
Bobbi Kriesburg
Claudette Lefebvre
Peggy Powers
Judy Sottile

Conference Delegates

Physical Medicine

Facilitator
Renee Lyons

Group Members
Doris Berryman
Charlie Bullock
Kathy Coyle
Pam Griffin
Debbie Hutchins
Ann James
Cheri Johnson
Kathy Johnson
Al Kaye
Betsy Kennedy
Chris Lay
Dave Moore
Francie Pagell
Barb Trader
Sue Vernon-White
Ray West

Psychiatry

Facilitator
David Austin

Group Members
David Compton
Ed Crowley
Gino DeSalvatore
John Hall
Karen Luken
Sandy Negley
George Patrick
Carmen Russoniello
John Shank
Thomas Skalko
Glen Van Andel
Jeff Witman

TABLE OF CONTENTS

CHAPTER 1

INTRODUCTION

Bob Riley

For years, the professional literature, as well as the popular press, have provided support for the outcome measurement movement within the general health care industry. The thrust of this movement is twofold in design: (a) to manage health care costs in an effort to keep down spiraling medical expenditures; and (b) to demonstrate treatment efficacy in order to determine which protocols and services are the most effective with respect to given illness, conditions, and/or disabilities. Simply stated, the outcome measurement movement is dedicated to the goal of providing the best quality health care for the least amount of money.

Treatment outcome studies, although difficult to design and implement, are essential to demonstrating the efficacy of therapeutic recreation treatment programs. Given the changing winds surrounding third party payers and the increasing influence of managed care organizations, many therapeutic recreation departments are now being requested to justify their services as "medically necessary" and "active" if such treatment is to be reimbursed. Thus, meeting the resulting challenge set forth for therapeutic recreation is critical. It is clearly time that we devote more resources and attention to the measurement of the results of patient care. In essence, we need to document the measurable benefits of therapeutic recreation through reliable and valid research methods, so that we may unequivocally demonstrate our strategic position within the health care community.

In direct response to the above challenge, a conference entitled "The Benefits of Therapeutic Recreation in Rehabilitation" was conducted in September, 1991. Hosted by the Therapeutic Recreation Program of Temple University via funding provided by the National Institute on Disability and Rehabilitation Research (NIDRR), the conference was designed and conducted as a consensus building workshop. The primary goal of the conference was to facilitate uniform agreement regarding treatment outcomes that should be in association with therapeutic recreation. A secondary goal of the conference was the development of research priorities and strategies which could serve as a guiding research agenda for the discipline during the coming decade. Given the nature of the funding source (NIDRR), and the specific priorities associated with the efficacy grant, emphasis was placed upon research that reflected medical and treatment outcomes as opposed to areas related to the broader issue of recreation and leisure programming.

The "workings" of the conference centered upon six invited position papers, each of which addressed a different disability cluster. These clusters were selected, for the most part, because of the logical grouping of related illness and disabilities. Also, select areas were designated because of the high volume of intervention that therapeutic recreation has historically experienced in these areas of concern. The focused areas of research addressed how therapeutic recreation treatment outcomes are related to the following six population clusters: (a) chemical dependency, (b) developmental disabilities, (c) gerontology, (d) pediatrics, (e) physical medicine, and (f) psychiatry.

The authors of these papers were selected from a group of self-nominated individuals who are leading authorities in one or several of the disability areas as related to therapeutic recreation intervention. Interested individuals were requested to submit a vita and short proposal outlining their strategies for the outcome measurement position paper. From a qualified pool of applicants, six writing teams were selected by jury process to author task papers on treatment outcomes in therapeutic recreation. The authors were charged with the specific task of researching what is currently known and documented regarding the outcomes of therapeutic recreation intervention with respect to their given disability focus. Additionally, authors were also requested to discuss areas that were cited in the literature as proposed outcomes of therapeutic recreation--but for which there was no known related documented research. Lastly, the writers provided a listing of proposed outcome research priorities that they felt should be addressed by the therapeutic recreation discipline.

The time frame for completion of these papers was approximately 1 year. During this time period, the writing teams conducted extensive literature searches and interviewed and surveyed therapeutic recreation practitioners, as well as other allied health practitioners. This was done in an attempt to develop well balanced and unbiased position papers. Additionally, each set of authors worked closely with the project consultant to maintain a certain degree of continuity and uniformity among the six manuscripts.

At the conclusion of this year-long process, the papers were screened, edited, and forwarded to a group of delegates who were pre-selected to attend the "Benefits Conference." Approximately 12 conference delegates were assigned to each position paper. Delegates were selected on a peer-nominated or self-nominated basis and all who were selected possessed indepth knowledge and leadership skill in a specific area of therapeutic recreation via research or practice. The task assigned to these delegates was to review the position paper(s) prior to the conference and arrive prepared to discuss the papers and related research in hopes of reaching consensus regarding the documented outcomes of therapeutic recreation. In anticipation of potential political and philosophical differences, the delegates were requested to view the outcome research issue from a broader, more universal perspective. Individuals attending the conference were asked to put aside their own personal views and to objectively contribute to group discussion by addressing issues and barriers that were related to the universal health care environment.

The conference itself provided an atmosphere of stimulating and fruitful discussion. Incorporating the use of group facilitators, the consensus-building format proved to be an effective method for achieving group cohesion in dealing with many of the issues brought to light in the position papers. From the opening address by Dr. Mary Lee Seibert to the closing comments by consensus group facilitators, delegates were afforded hours of deliberation to discuss outcomes strategies and to reach consensus. Although exhausted and mentally challenged, most delegates left the conference with much more than they brought. The level of commitment and sharing by these delegates was a tribute to the dedication that therapeutic recreation professionals possess for their discipline.

Contained within this volume are the fruits of their labor. This proceedings manual contains several items for critical review. First, there is the conference opening address by Dr. Mary Lee Seibert. Second, the six original outcomes position papers are presented in unabridged form with full references included. Next appears a paper provided by the project staff which serves as a summary chapter interrelating the critical points and related ideas established within the six position papers. Finally, each consensus group drafted a "reaction paper" to summarize the outcomes of the consensus-building process as it occurred at the "Benefits Conference." These papers were, for the most part, written by the facilitators with direct input by the delegates.

In totality, this volume represents the work and ideas of numerous individuals. It is hoped that through this initial and intensive effort, outcome research in therapeutic recreation will reach a new level. It is hoped that all parties who are concerned with the growth and acceptance of therapeutic recreation, academicians and practitioners alike, will reflect very carefully upon the work presented here. It is imperative that we begin to see that a positive view of therapeutic recreation for the future needs to be based upon efficacy studies conducted within the present time period. This project and proceedings manual will have served well if this premise takes a foothold within the therapeutic recreation discipline during the next few years.

CHAPTER 2

KEYNOTE

Mary Lee Seibert

Once upon a time a Sea Horse gathered up his seven pieces of eight and cantered out to find his fortune. Before he had traveled very far he met an Eel, who said,

"Psst. Hey, bud. Where ya goin'?"

"I'm going out to find my fortune," replied the Sea Horse, proudly.

"You're in luck, said the Eel. "For four pieces of eight you have this speedy flipper, and then you'll be able to get there a lot faster."

"Gee, that's swell," said the Sea Horse, and paid the money and put on the flipper and slithered off at twice the speed. Soon he came upon a Sponge who said,

"Psst. Hey, bud. Where ya goin'?"

"I'm going out to find my fortune," replied the Sea Horse.

"You're in luck," said the Sponge. "For a small fee I will let you have this jet propelled scooter so that you will be able to travel a lot faster."

So the Sea Horse bought the scooter with his remaining money and went zooming through the sea five times as fast. Soon he came upon a Shark, who said,

"Psst. Hey, bud. Where ya goin'?"

"I'm going out to find my fortune," replied the Sea Horse.

"You're in luck. If you'll take this short cut," said the Shark, pointing to his open mouth, "you'll save yourself a lot of time.

"Gee, thanks," said the Sea Horse, and zoomed off into the interior of the Shark, there to be devoured.

The moral of this fable is that if you're not sure where you're going, you're liable to end up someplace else--and not even know it.

From <u>Preparing Instructional Objectives</u>,
by Ralph Mager, 1962,
Palo Alto, CA: Fearon Publishers

This fable has as much importance for the health care professions today as it did for teaching nearly 30 years ago. We are being challenged to declare where we are going and what will happen as a result of our trip before we begin our journey. Specifically, we are being challenged to demonstrate that what we deliver as health care services will (most likely) result in improved health status for the consumer of those services, commonly knows as OUTCOMES! Demonstrable, measurable <u>outcomes</u>.

If someone were to ask you, "Does what you do (in your profession) make a difference," I suspect your response would be a quick and somewhat indignant retort such as "of course it does!" The very foundations of professions like ours are based upon the premises that:

1. What we do for people makes them more productive, happier, healthier, and generally better than they would have been without our intervention.

2. Our <u>methods</u> of intervention or "practices" have been carefully developed so that our services have the maximum positive <u>effect</u> on those who receive them.

3. We are professionals whose services merit the recognition and respect of those who manage the care of patients such that we will be called in to deliver those services.

4. We expect to be paid for the services we deliver.

Well, times are changing. These time-honored premises are being challenged. Our own declarations about the efficacy of our services are no longer being accepted at face value. No longer will it be taken for granted that the services we render are beneficial to patients because we, as professionals in the field, possess a particular set of knowledge and skills and use them to <u>do</u>

something for others. We must demonstrate that what we do for others results in a predictable, desirable **outcome**. For those demonstrations of outcomes to be accepted by the entities that pay the bills, two criteria need to be met:

1. There must be a body of empirical research, validated by repetition and rigorous peer review, that supports achievement of the desired outcome in a respectable number of cases.

2. The outcomes that we intend to achieve, and demonstrate that we can achieve, must be ones that are valued by third party payers.

That is, the outcomes should be ones which our particular profession is the most qualified to deliver and which result in returning patients to their highest level of independent (and least expensive) functional status.

The concept of outcomes assessment is one which educators have been wrestling with in one way or another for decades. The use of behavioral objectives to design instruction and assess outcomes of instruction was espoused by Ralph Mager in his classic 1962 publication, <u>Preparing Instructional Objectives</u>. Since that time, the concept has been molded, shaped, increased in complexity, and renamed to include performance objectives, terminal performance objectives, competency based instruction, performance based instruction, and, now, outcomes assessment. All of these terms have as their basis the principle that the result of instruction is more important than the method used to achieve the result. Now this concept is being applied to the delivery of health care!

Those of us in health professions, even medicine, face a long and difficult process of getting our proverbial acts together to produce health services research which documents the effectiveness of our interventions in patient care. Few health professions other than medicine have substantial research programs addressing clinical effectiveness. By not having this research base, we leave ourselves vulnerable to being eliminated from patient care plans. If we do not produce this research base for our own professions, others will determine when and how we practice and will control whether we are compensated for the services we deliver.

In today's health care system, with governmental sources paying as much of the health care bill as they are, justifying the need for services is becoming more and more difficult. This difficulty has arisen because the needs for service have been determined more by historical tradition than by clear evidence of the results of professional interventions. Dr. Timothy Johnson, medical editor for ABC News, stated in his recent presentation to the American Physical Therapy Association:

We have a system (of health care) where everything and anything is tried and, until recently, paid for without question. We know very little about true effectiveness--what really works in the long run. We will have to reluctantly and sometimes very painfully address what really is effective.

Just this month, the American Medical NEWS, the newsletter of the American Medical Association, had a front page headline reading, **"More doctors studying data to improve quality of care."** Stating in that article that Medicare peer review organizations have commissioned researchers to start the process (of outcomes assessment), the newsletter calls on physicians to take the lead in "translating practice pattern data analysis into care that is more scientifically based."

There is an adage that says something like, "If there is a void and we don't fill it, the government will." In response to the great variability in health care delivery, the rising cost of health care, and, most likely, in response to the fact until recently, health care professionals showed little inclination to institute standards of quality and cost effectiveness across the health care system for themselves, in 1989, the Agency for Health Care Policy and Research was established as part of the Public Health Service.

The planners of this conference asked me to tell you something about this federal Agency, because of its potential implications for Therapeutic Recreation, so please bear with me. Some of the information you may wish to recover for later use. I understand that my remarks will become a part of the conference proceedings, so you will have them in their entirety.

The purpose of the Agency for Health Care Policy and Research is to enhance the quality and appropriateness of health care services and access to such services. Why is this agency important to professionals in Therapeutic Recreation? Very simple. Because the Agency for Health Care Policy and Research will have the capability of recommending to other federal agencies whether a profession's services have been empirically demonstrated that they contribute significantly to the prevention, diagnosis, treatment, or management of health care conditions. Furthermore, their recommendation may well determine whether professional services are compensated. In other words, if you consider Therapeutic Recreation to be a health profession, the AHCPR and its research programs may, in time, become critical to the continuation of practice in the field.

The AHCPR has the primary responsibility for implementation of the Medical Treatment Effectiveness Program (MEDTEP) within the Department of Health and Human Services.

MEDTEP's major goal is to improve the effectiveness and appropriateness of medical practice by developing and disseminating scientific information regarding the effects of presently used health care services and procedures on patients' survival, health status, functional capacity, and quality of life" (AHCPR Program Note, March, 1990).

In short, MEDTEP emphasizes evaluation of outcomes (results) rather than processes (what was done) and is funding projects to "facilitate the development, review, and updating of clinically relevant guidelines for the practice of health care." A guideline in this context can be loosely defined as a series of statements for use in decision-making by practitioners and patients that describe appropriate and inappropriate health care for specific clinical conditions. Guidelines are tools to change patient and provider behavior. Guidelines will also identify areas where additional research is needed.

Research over the last 2 decades has revealed that there are wide variations in the type and amount of health care provided to apparently similar patients. While some variations can be due to differences in the needs and preferences of patients, it is apparent that some variations are the result of inadequate information about treatment effectiveness or variations in the practice styles of physicians and other providers. When practice variations are related to differences in patient outcomes or resource use, they raise serious questions about the quality, appropriateness, and cost effectiveness of health care (AHCPR Program Note, March, 1990).

For example, the treatment for a particular health condition, such as clinical depression, may differ widely among physicians, medical specialties, regions of the country, and economic levels of patients. Some treatments may be very costly and effective; others less expensive and just as effective. Some treatment protocols require the intervention of only a physician and pharmacist; while others include the services of additional health professions such as Therapeutic Recreation. Whether the patient outcomes differ significantly related to the differences in cost and location is important when determining efficacy of practice and subsequent reimbursement for services. If the intervention of Therapeutic Recreation increases the patient's social and coping skills such that she is discharged for an inpatient facility sooner than she would have otherwise been discharged, then the cost effectiveness of the intervention is validated if the cost of institutionalization exceeds the cost of the intervention. Even if a monetary benefit is not realized, if it can be demonstrated empirically that the quality of life for the patient is significantly improved, the outcome of therapeutic intervention may be validated and the intervention justified.

Do these "guidelines" sound suspiciously like they might be interpreted as standards of practice to you? They do to me. While it is not explicitly stated in any of the literature of the AHCPR, I believe that we are moving closer to standards of practice against which our practices will be measured and our services reimbursed. RESULTS will be the name of the game and we will have to show that our services can achieve results, or we may not be in the game at all!

Reimbursement for health care services is currently established by third party payers and adjusted for the professional delivering the service, the region of the country, and the type of site where the service was rendered. For example, an obstetrician providing services in a hospital in New York is reimbursed at a much higher rate than a nurse midwife providing those same services in the same location. But both may be reimbursed at different rates if they were delivering services in a hospital in West Virginia.

The Agency has established and funded Patient Outcomes Research Teams (PORTs) to study 11 health care conditions and make recommendations regarding the most effective and efficient methods of treatment. These PORTs will manage large-scale, multifaceted, multidisciplinary projects that will identify and analyze the outcomes and costs of current alternative practice patterns in order to determine the best treatment strategy. Further the PORTs will develop and test methods for reducing inappropriate variations. As I read the list of currently funded PORTs, think about whether Therapeutic Recreation has a contribution to make in the prevention, diagnosis, treatment, or management (rehabilitation) of any of these health care conditions. Current PORT projects include:

1. Benign Prostatic Hyperplasia--Dartmouth Medical School

2. Cataracts--Johns Hopkins Medical School

3. Low Back Pain--University of Washington, Seattle

4. Myocardial Infarction--Harvard Medical School

5. Total Knee Replacement--Indiana University School of Medicine

6. Ischemic Heart Disease--Duke University

7. Biliary Tract Disease--University of Pennsylvania

8. Hip Fracture--University of Maryland

9. Diabetes--New England Medical Center

10. Obstetrical Decision-Making--RAND Corporation

Also within the Agency, the Office of the Forum for Quality and Effectiveness has been mandated to manage the development of clinically relevant guidelines for patient care and facilitate the development of standards of quality, performance measures, and medial review criteria.

Criteria for the selection of health care conditions for which "clinically relevant guidelines" will be developed include: (a) the number of individuals affected, (b) the extent of uncertainty or controversy with respect to the use of a procedure or its effectiveness, (c) the level of related expenditure, and (d) the availability of data. The Agency wants to support research projects that affect large numbers of people, that address conditions where not everyone agrees on the "right" treatment methods, those in which differing methods of treatment have large variations in cost, and for which there is sufficient research already reported to make an assessment of a "best" treatment method based upon outcomes assessment.

You might not be surprised to learn that all but one of the first group of conditions chosen were those that affected the very young and the very old. Why? Because those are the conditions for which our government pays the most through Medicaid and Medicare. Again, as I read the list of conditions for which panels have been or soon will be formed, consider in which conditions Therapeutic Recreation might have a significant contribution to make in the prevention, diagnosis, treatment, or management of patient care. The list of existing panels includes:

1. Prediction, Prevention, and Early Treatment of Pressure Sores in Adults

2. Acute Pain Management: Operative or Medical Procedures or Trauma

3. Diagnosis and Treatment of Depressed Outpatients in Primary Care Settings

4. Urinary Incontinence in Adults

5. Visual Impairment Due to Cataracts in the Aging Eye

6. Provision of Comprehensive Care in Sickle Cell Disease

7. Guidelines for the Diagnosis and Treatment of Benign Prostatic Hyperplasia

8. Provision of Comprehensive Care in Sickle Cell Disease

New panels are being structured for the development of the following guidelines:

1. Management of Cancer-Related Pain

2. Treatment of Pressure Ulcers

3. HIV + Asymptomatic Patient

4. Low Back Disorders

5. Development of Quality Determinants of Mammography

6. Otitis Media in Children

7. Diagnosis and Treatment of Heart Failure Secondary to Coronary Vascular Disease

8. Post Stroke Rehabilitation

All but one of the existing panels are chaired by physicians; the one on pressure sores is chaired by a nurse. Allied health professionals were considered having expertise to contribute only after the initial panels were structured. Those health professions that do not include themselves in the rubric of the allied health professions have still not, to my knowledge, been identified for the purposes of the PORTs as having a significant role to play in the treatment of individuals with these conditions. Included are such disciplines as clinical psychology, dietetics, pharmacy, and, of course, therapeutic recreation.

Again, what does any of this have to do with Therapeutic Recreation, you might ask. The time is coming rapidly when federal grants will be channeled into those fields which have demonstrated that their treatments work!

It is my understanding that the agency which is supporting this conference, the National Institute on Disability and Rehabilitation Research, has charged Therapeutic Recreation to speak to outcomes in its research programs. Even more pragmatically, you can assume that to maximize the potential for federal funding, the conditions for which PORTs have been funded and for which guidelines are being developed are the areas for which research on outcomes in

Therapeutic Recreation should be focused!! I would suggest that you take a hard look at these conditions and determine what, if any, contributions Therapeutic Recreation can make to the quality of life. Then it will be up to the researchers in the field to empirically demonstrate those contributions as patient outcomes.

In my cursory review of the recommendations in the five papers prepared for this conference, I noted that your profession finds itself in the same unenviable position as the traditional allied health professions. You have little empirical research which documents outcomes of the intervention of Therapeutic Recreation in health care delivery. That does not mean that research is not being conducted. It means that the research that is being conducted is **not** appropriately structured or targeted to the measurement of specific outcomes of treatment interventions.

For example, for the past 18 months or so a colleague of mine, Dr. Judith Barr of Northeastern University, has been working under contract with the Agency for Health Care Policy and Research to lead the development of a bibliography of clinical effectiveness research within selected allied health fields. She and her small research team have combed the literature in the Medlars and Index Medicus data bases for all publications relating to efficacy studies done within health related professions. Just out of curiosity I asked if she had seen any publications relating to Therapeutic Recreation. She had not. While the absence of publications on Therapeutic Recreation can be explained by noting that these two data bases are not ones where literature in your discipline would be found, should that be the case? These data bases are where anyone looking for efficacy studies would look. So, my point is if you wish to be considered among the health related professions when money is awarded for research, I suggest that you have your research identified with health care practice. If your journals are not routinely abstracted for Medlars or Index Medicus, you might look into having them included in those data bases.

As I have indicated, the allied health professions are finding themselves in this same position with a paucity of clinical outcomes research. Even a profession, such as physical therapy, which is generally well accepted as producing positive results with patients in a variety of settings and with a variety of clinical conditions, does not have a substantial foundation of empirical research to document that what physical therapists do makes a difference in patient health status. In large part, outcomes have been projected on the basis of anecdotal evidence, descriptive surveys, and case studies. Professions that in the past were accepted at face value as having value are now being challenged to document their value or they risk being denied reimbursement for services by third party payers.

Appropriately designed research programs targeted at validating our practices as medically effective as well as cost effective interventions are essential if we are going to remain viable as health professions. Recognition by the Agency for Health Care Policy and Research will lead to recognition by NIDRR; HCFA (Health Care Financing Administration), which houses Medicare; and state agencies which administer Medicaid. While such recognition is not now essential for funding, future government funding will likely follow paths where clear and effective outcomes have been demonstrated.

So, what can we do to make things happen in a hurry? Where should we put our emphasis? Where should our resources be spent? These are questions currently being addressed by leaders in allied health research in colleges and universities.

First, what can we do in a hurry? As a result of the participation of allied health representatives in two workshops sponsored by the AHCPR in 1990, the Agency sponsored a separate workshop for health services researchers to inform them of the types of research and research methods that would be most valuable in determining outcomes of practice. Hopefully, experienced researchers could be convinced to revise their research strategies to perform studies that would demonstrate outcomes, producing at least some results in a relatively short period of time.

Next, where should we put our emphasis? You are well on your way to answering this question in Therapeutic Recreation. The five papers prepared for this consensus conference identify several priorities for outcomes research. As I stated earlier, focusing on the conditions for which the AHCPR is developing guidelines and for which your profession has a contribution to make would seem prudent. Emphasis in the profession should be placed on achieving consensus on the benefits of your intervention. The areas you have identified with this project (i.e., pediatrics, geriatrics, mental health, substance abuse and dependency, and developmental disabilities) also provide rich ground for research. Identifying and documenting what you **do** know about the efficacy of intervention of Therapeutic Recreation, identifying what you **don't** know, and deciding what you **need** to know will set the research agenda for the profession for the foreseeable future.

And finally, where should our resources be spent? The answer to that is short, sweet, and expensive--doctoral programs; doctoral programs which produce researchers who will use the appropriate methods and who will have the motivation to conduct the empirical research necessary to verify patient outcomes; researchers who will thrive on the competition in the very tough market for grants and who will publish and present their results in multidisciplinary forums to be recognized and scrutinized by members of other professions. The time has passed for doctoral students to be permitted to conduct just enough research to get by, doing a descriptive study using a standardized questionnaire. The faculty in doctoral programs should set the tone by establishing a clinical research program for themselves that doctoral students can work within. That will mean that current faculty who have not focused their research on clinical outcomes will need to redirect their own thinking. They may even need additional "training" themselves. The only consolation I can offer you in this regard is that you are NOT ALONE! Professions such as occupational therapy, medical technology, respiratory therapy, physical therapy, dental hygiene, and many others are in the same predicament or worse. At least you have doctoral programs in place with which to start the changes. Some of the fields I just mentioned have no discipline specific doctoral programs.

I suggest to you that the place to <u>start</u> while you are here for this conference is to <u>reach consensus</u> on the benefits of Therapeutic Recreation in improving the quality of life. Where those quality-of-life benefits impact individuals needing or receiving interventions by health care professionals, plan a research agenda to document those benefits as clinical outcomes. If appropriate, consider strongly focusing your efforts on the health care conditions for which guidelines are being developed by the AHCPR. Assume that each of you has a role to play in moving the research agenda forward. Identify that role. You may be a researcher yourself. You may be a mentor to younger professionals whom you can influence to become researchers. You may be a leader who can influence agencies like AHCPR or NIDRR to fund some of the needed research. Make an agreement with someone here that each of you will accomplish one task in that role by the first of the year and make the commitment now to check in with that person in January for a mutual report. Then, once you get home, set out within whatever sphere you work to move that research agenda forward. Do what you do with your patients, or clients, or students. Start with small steps so that you can keep focused and experience success, but maintain the momentum.

I believe that if you start with these considerations, your outcomes for the future of the profession in the arena of health care will be more attainable. The future will surely be brighter and more long lasting than that of our errant Sea Horse.

CHAPTER 3

THE BENEFITS OF THERAPEUTIC RECREATION IN CHEMICAL DEPENDENCY

Ann Rancourt

Drug abuse/dependence* is not just an individual problem, it is also a social problem. While interest in researching this problem continues to increase, there still remains a dearth of research addressing the relationship between recreation/leisure and drug use and abuse. Several leisure researchers have documented a need for investigations of this subject (Berg & Neulinger, 1976; Hitzhusen, 1977; McLaughlin, 1980; Rainwater, 1983; Sessoms & Oakley, 1969; Sheridan, 1976). Berg and Neulinger indicate that the relationship between those individuals dependent on drugs and their leisure involvement has not been systematically explored and that further research is needed. As McLaughlin observes, "only a few studies on leisure have been done with alcoholics and even fewer with persons dependent on drugs" (p. 9).

According to the National Institute on Drug Abuse (NIDA) (1987), "Substance abuse is a multifaceted syndrome that cannot be treated as a straightforward medical problem that will respond to medical treatment only" (p. 5). Duncan and Gold (1982) noted that when professionals (including therapeutic recreation specialists [TRSs]) are working with individuals recovering from substance abuse, they are involved in a web of complex behaviors and physiological problems. A multiplicity of theories exist that attempt to explain reasons for abuse and approaches to treatment. There does seem, however, to be consensus that the effects of abuse are a result of the specific <u>drug</u>, the <u>dose</u>, the <u>setting</u> (interpersonal and environmental factors), and the <u>set</u> (internal physiological and psychological states of the drug taker). Several authors (Ashery, 1985; Jacobs, Harvill, & Mason, 1988) have cautioned that persons who abuse drugs are among the most difficult client populations to work with and treat. Often clients experience several relapses and remissions before achieving success. Therefore, therapists should not expect rapid or large scale behavioral change during the early stages of treatment.

*   Throughout this paper drug abuse/chemical dependency refers to abuse of or dependence on any drug(s) including alcohol.

A review of the literature reveals a potential contribution of therapeutic recreation services in the treatment of substance abuse. George and Dustin (1988) indicated that persons who have been chemically dependent typically need to develop positive ways to structure their free time and to learn to cope with feelings and situations that were previously addressed by abusing drugs (including alcohol). Jacobs et al. (1988) suggested topics and themes to have in mind for therapeutic sessions, including how to structure time, how to communicate feelings, ways to cope with stress and how to socialize without drinking.

Within the scope of the substance abuse/chemical dependency and methods of treatment, the primary purpose of this paper is to identify and describe the role of therapeutic recreation services as part of the treatment process. More specifically, this paper will offer the following: (a) an overview of the diagnostic groups and the continuum of service settings; (b) discussion of theoretical, etiological, and treatment paradigms most relevant to the provision of therapeutic recreation services; (c) discussion of expected and documented outcomes of therapeutic recreation intervention; and (d) recommendations for further research regarding therapeutic recreation intervention for those individuals recovering from substance abuse and dependency.

Diagnostic Groups and Settings

Demographic Variables

Individuals who are drug dependent can be categorized by demographic groupings or according to drug(s) abused. Demographically these categories include age, gender, race, economic status, and education. It is important to be aware of these demographic characteristics because treatment interventions and outcomes will vary depending on these categories. For example, in a simple comparison to adult treatment, in adolescent treatment the goal is habilitation rather than rehabilitation (Henry, 1989). The adult who begins abusing drugs post adolescent development may have established identity and interpersonal relationships. The teen, adolescent, or preadolescent who begins abusing drugs during these developmental stages has not had the opportunity to develop an identity or interpersonal relationships. These relationships must be established rather than reestablished in treatment.

With respect to gender research, some authors have suggested the pattern of drug abuse by men and women is becoming more similar (Clayton, Voss, Robbins, & Skinner, 1986). Other research has concluded that the problems of female abusers are gender specific (Glynn, Pearson, & Sayers, 1983). Duckert

(1987) found that "treatment [of women] appears to focus primarily on such issues as sex-role conflicts, the improvement of family or social relationships, self-esteem, and other areas of psychosocial functioning" (p. 141).

Frances and Franklin (1989) indicate a paucity of research in the area of substance abuse by minority individuals even though abuse is a major problem in this subset of the population. The authors cautioned that "we cannot assume that research and program design applicable to middle-class white Americans will be equally applicable to minority communities" (p. 160). As a result, the authors called for cultural sensitivity in treatment programs.

One particular group that is of increasing interest to both researchers and practitioners is the group identified as "dually diagnosed individuals." Several researchers (Barchas, 1985; Cohen, 1985; Conroy, 1985; Dougherty & Lesswing, 1989; Frances & Franklin, 1989; Kaufman, 1989; Kosten, Kosten, & Rounsaville, 1989; Kosten & Kleber, 1988; Levy & Mann, 1988; Mann, 1989; O'Connell, 1989; Regier et al., 1990; Wallace, 1987; Zweben, 1986) have addressed treatment implications for dually diagnosed patients/clients. Patients/clients identified as dually diagnosed have problems related to substance abuse and mental illness. This population consists of individuals who abuse substances and who also have psychiatric disorders, or individuals with psychiatric problems who also have significant substance abuse problems. Zweben summarized that:

> The current gap between mental health and substance abuse has
> created a situation in which drug and alcohol problems are grossly
> underdiagnosed in the mental health system, and psychiatric
> disorders are often missed in the substance abuse treatment setting.
> (p. 257)

Addressing Zweben's (1986) contention that this problem is "grossly underdiagnosed," Kosten and Kleber (1988) estimated that "dual diagnosis patients constitute 30% to 50% of psychiatric populations and as much as 80% of substance abusers" (p. 201). Regier et al. (1990) found:

> Of persons with any drug (other than alcohol) disorder diagnosis,
> more than 50% have at least one other mental disorder diagnosis,
> including 26% with affective, 28% with anxiety, 18% with antisocial
> personality (ASP) disorder, and 7% with schizophrenia. Among
> other drug users who seek specialty mental health treatment during
> a six-month period, fully 64% have a current coexisting mental
> disorder. Among those with alcohol disorders, another mental
> disorder appears in 37% of cases. Because the prevalence rate of
> alcohol disorders is about twice that of other drug disorders, there
> are more people with both alcohol and mental disorders than other

drug and mental disorders. For alcohol disorders, the highest specific disorder comorbidity rates are for affective, anxiety, and ASP disorders. Almost 20% of individuals with mental disorders who come to specialty treatment settings will have a current diagnosis of substance abuse disorder, and 29% of all persons with mental disorders have a lifetime diagnosis of substance abuse disorder. For schizophrenia, the lifetime rate of substance dependence-abuse is 47%; for bipolar disorder, the rate increases to 56%. (p. 2517)

A growing subset of the dual diagnosed population are those who are homeless. Frances and Franklin (1989) indicated that 20 to 60% of the homeless may be alcohol dependent and as many as 90% have a primary psychiatric diagnosis.

Specific etiologic reasons for dual diagnoses are not known. Current findings suggest certain mental disorders may precede substance abuse behaviors, and perhaps substances are used in an attempt to self-medicate (Kosten & Kleber, 1988; Mann, 1989; McLellan & Druley, 1977; O'Connell, 1989; Regier et al., 1990). On the other hand, Regier et al. suggested that certain mental disorders may be the result of substance abuse. Other researchers suggested that symptomatic behaviors of substance abuse can mimic many mental disorders (Cliffside, 1989; Kosten & Kleber, 1988; Levy & Mann, 1988). Several authors agreed that in order to make an accurate diagnosis and establish an effective treatment plan, an essential first step is for the person to be drug free and remain abstinent for a sufficient amount of time so that accurate data can be gathered (Kaufman, 1989; Kosten & Kleber; Levy & Mann).

It is important to note that within the dual diagnosis category there are individuals who have other accompanying disabilities. Little has been written about individuals with physical disabilities, mental retardation, and visual and hearing impairments with related substance use behaviors. Frances and Franklin (1989) suggested that individuals with a primary disability might have feelings of frustration and anger. Being socially isolated and discriminated against may lead to depression, low motivation, low self-esteem, and inability to effectively cope. This may lead to subsequent drug use/abuse. For these individuals drugs are often used as a means to socialize and be accepted. Additionally, individuals with physical disabilities may have access to prescription drugs that are often too readily prescribed. The category of individuals with dual diagnoses presents unique challenges for both leisure researchers and practitioners. Persons within the dual diagnosis category present unique intervention/treatment challenges. Issues related to dual diagnosis must be addressed "because relapse in one area usually results in relapse in the other" (Zweben, 1986, p. 257). Because this category is receiving increasing attention, it is likely that our ability to more effectively address these unique treatment challenges will continue to develop.

Types of Drugs Abused

The United States Department of Health and Human Services estimated "that 20 to 40 percent of all U.S. hospital beds are occupied by persons whose health conditions are complications of alcohol abuse and alcoholism" (National Institute on Alcohol Abuse and Alcoholism [NIAAA], 1990, p. vii). Cohen (1985) stated that "addictive diseases are related to 25% of all deaths in the country" (p. xvii).

An estimated 10.5 million U.S. adults exhibit some symptoms of alcoholism or alcohol dependence and an additional 7.2 million abuse alcohol, but do not yet show symptoms of dependence. Projections for 1995 suggest that 11.2 million will exhibit symptoms of alcohol dependence and the size of the group of alcohol abusers will not change (NIAAA, 1990, p. ix).

Frances and Franklin (1989) indicated a fivefold increase in the past decade of the number of Americans who have tried cocaine (estimated between 25 and 40 million). Dougherty and Lesswing (1989) reported that as many as 8 million Americans use cocaine regularly and that anywhere from 5 to 20% may be seriously dependent. Frances and Franklin estimated that there are as many as 500,000 opioid addicts in the United States. The United States Department of Health and Human Services estimated the total annual cost of substance abuse (other than alcohol) at nearly $100 billion (NIDA, 1987). The estimated cost of alcohol abuse was $128 billion (NIAAA, 1990).

Common drugs of abuse are: (a) marijuana (hashish), (b) cocaine, (c) stimulants, (d) depressants, (e) narcotics, (f) hallucinogens, (g) alcohol, and (h) inhalants. It is rare, however, that an individual abuses a single drug. Multihabituation (polydrug use) is a relatively newly described phenomenon (Cohen, 1985; Frances & Franklin, 1989). "The only drug for which a genetic predisposition has substantial scientific support is alcohol, although psychological predispositions may exist [for other drugs]" (Cohen, pp. 208-209). Researchers support the premise that the underlying causes of abuse and dependence are multifactorial (Cohen; Ellis, McInerney, DiGiuseppe, & Yeager, 1988; Vaillant, 1983), and that treatment programs must be multimodal (Brower, Blow, & Beresford, 1989; Craig, Olson, & Shalton, 1990; Rioux & Van Meter, 1990).

The reasons why someone chooses one or more drugs over others and the affects of those drugs are critical data to be assessed and evaluated prior to treatment planning. As the data are assessed and evaluated, the therapist needs to pay specific attention to the effects of the drug, the dose, the set, and the setting. All of these variables will influence the diagnosis and concomitant treatment interventions. Differences in demographic variables and type(s) of drug(s) abused or dependent on present challenges to the therapeutic recreation specialist.

Settings

Treatment for those recovering from substance abuse and dependence occurs in various settings. Often, treatment or intervention outcomes are dependent on the type of treatment setting in which the therapeutic recreation specialist will be practicing. Typically treatment occurs in hospital, outpatient, and residential settings. Lewis, Dana, and Blevins (1988) identified the following treatment settings:

1. *Detoxification Centers*--short-term treatment settings which oversee safe withdrawal from the addicted substance(s). Two types of detox centers include medical (usually in a hospital under medically trained personnel) and nonmedical or social (usually in nonhospital settings with counseling and support services, with medical personnel on call). Persons who are physically dependent on a drug need supervised detoxification.

2. *Inpatient Rehabilitation*--programs housed in medical or nonmedical facilities. The focus is typically on psychological factors and education. Generally goals are to:

Allow clients the opportunity to develop personal recovery goals, to learn the skills needed to prevent a relapse, to prepare for resocialization into the community, and to plan and rehearse an abstinent life-style. (p. 31)

3. *Therapeutic Communities (TC)*--residential, mutual-help environments where a patient/client, isolated from the outside world, learns to lead a drug-free life.

The principle aim of the TC is a global change in lifestyle and abstinence from illicit substances, elimination of antisocial activity, employability, and prosocial attitudes and values. A critical assumption of the TC is that stable recovery depends upon a successful integration of both social and psychological goals. (DeLeon, 1988, p. 75)

4. *Methadone Maintenance Programs*--use of methadone to treat heroin addiction. This program tries to free clients from obtaining illegal drugs. Clients come to a clinic regularly to receive methadone. At first treatment involved only methadone; now there is recognition that methadone treatment should be part of a more comprehensive treatment program.

5. *Outpatient Counseling Agencies*--programs that allow clients the opportunity to establish short- and long-term goals and to practice behaviors in familiar or everyday environments. Outpatient settings include:

> Comprehensive community mental health centers to the offices of private practitioners, from highly intensive nightly group meetings to biweekly individual sessions, from brief interventions to long-term therapy. (Lewis et al., 1988, p. 35)

6. *Occupational Substance Abuse Programs*--known as "employee assistance programs" (EAP). Clients are usually linked with outside resources and assisted in identifying and solving problems.

Though Lewis et al. (1988) do not specifically mention halfway houses, it is worth noting that this approach is now a growing part of treatment environments. Kunstler (1991) viewed houses as "communal living situations providing a transition between a 24-hour-a-day treatment environment and independent living" (p. 124).

Each of the identified settings provides varying intervention approaches. Though therapeutic recreation specialists might be employed in any one of these settings, it is most likely that they will practice in hospital, residential, or outpatient settings. The specific agency of employment will dictate the philosophy of treatment and intervention and treatment strategies.

Theoretical Foundations

Proposed Reasons for Substance Use, Abuse, and/or Dependence

Drug dependence is a complex and multifaceted problem. Several explanations have been proposed to address the effect, impact, and motivation toward abusive behavior. Some researchers suggested that the degree of access to drugs or *drug availability* is one of the most precipitating factors in drug dependence (Ausubel, 1980; Hill, 1980; Robins, 1980; Smart, 1980; Smith, 1980; Steffenhagen, 1980; Winick, 1980). Another causal factor appears to be *normative expectations* or the extent to which a drug culture is accepted with the subpopulation (Jessor & Jessor, 1980; Johnson, 1980; Lukoff, 1980). The more likely drug use is accepted as part of one's reference group, the more likely one is to use drugs. A contrasting view regarding normative expectations is Kaplan's (1980) who suggested that some people begin taking drugs to deviate from norms which reject various drug taking behaviors (e.g., rebellious adolescent behavior).

In studying causes of drug initiation by adolescents, researchers have determined that (a) *beliefs and values* (Kandel, 1980); (b) *curiosity* (Bejerot, 1980; Dole & Nyswander, 1980); and (c) *conformity* (Gorsuch, 1980) effect or contribute to drug use. Some researchers suggested that people take drugs as a means of *sensation and stimulation seeking*, or as *relief from boredom* (Gorsuch; Prescott, 1980; Smith, 1980). Two reasons often cited in the literature regarding adolescents and drug abuse are (a) *peer influence* (Ausubel, 1980; Bejerot; Chein, 1980; Gorsuch; Hendin, 1980; Johnson, 1980; Kandel; Loney, 1980; Lukoff, 1980; Milkman & Frosch, 1980; Robins, 1980); and (b) *parental/family influence* (Bejerot; Chein; Coleman, 1980; Gorsuch; Hendin; Kandel; Loney; Lukoff; Robins; Spotts & Shontz, 1980; Stanton, 1980). Gold (1980) and Lindesmith (1980) suggested *cognitive style*, or one's situational response patterns, contributes to drug initiation. Several researchers have seemed to support or expand on this proposition by suggesting drug taking behavior is *learned behavior* (Bejerot; Frederick, 1980; Hill, 1980; Huba, Wingard, & Bentler, 1980; Lindesmith, 1980; McAuliffe & Gordon, 1980; Wikler, 1980; Zinberg, 1980).

Certain *personality traits*, particularly those associated with self-esteem, motivation, goal directedness, and locus of control have been identified as contributing to substance abuse (Ausubel, 1980; Chein, 1980; Jessor & Jessor, 1980; Robins, 1980). Some researchers believe people use drugs in an attempt at achieving *ego-enhancement*, to overcome and cope with ego and self-identity problems (Khantzian, 1980; Milkman & Frosch, 1980; Spotts & Shontz, 1980; Wurmser, 1980). *Low self-esteem* is often cited as effecting or correlating with drug abuse. Researchers have suggested that people use drugs in an attempt to maximize positive self-attitudes and minimize negative ones (Chein; Hendin, 1980; Jessor & Jessor; Kaplan, 1980; Loney, 1980; Smith, 1980; Steffanhagen, 1980; Wurmser). Hill (1980) and Steffenhagen purported that drug taking is an attempt at *immediate gratification*. Failure and fear of failure, and an attempt to experience a sense of *achievement* are also suggested as possible reasons contributing to substance abuse (Hendin; Jessor & Jessor; Misra, 1980; Smith).

Genetic predispositions have been suggested by some researchers as a possible cause of dependency (Bejerot, 1980; Goodwin, 1980; Hochhauser, 1980; Schuckit, 1980). Several researchers have suggested dependency occurs as a result of trying to *self-medicate* or to avoid withdrawal symptoms (Dole & Nyswander, 1980; Goodwin; Greaves, 1980; Hill, 1980; Hochhauser; Lindesmith, 1980; McAuliffe & Gordon, 1980; Smith, 1980). Martin (1980) hypothesized that drug abuse may result because of an affective disorder (*hypophoria*) which produces feelings opposite of well-being; the person then seeks a more *euphoric* state initiated by drug(s). Other researchers have also attributed the euphoric effects of drugs to leading to dependence (Ausubel, 1980; Hill; Jonas & Jonas, 1980; Martin, 1980; McAuliffe & Gordon; Simon, 1980; Wikler, 1980).

Several researchers (Ausubel, 1980; Khantzian, 1980; Milkman & Frosch, 1980; Peele, 1980; Steffenhagen, 1980) have suggested that drugs are used as *coping mechanisms* in addressing various psychosocial problems and issues. *Isolation, emptiness, and alienation* (including lack of relationships and spiritual alienation) have been cited as reasons why someone initiates and continues drug use (Chein, 1980; Coleman, 1980; Lukoff, 1980; Prescott, 1980). Other researchers have associated drug abuse with attempts to *reduce anxiety, stress, and conflict* (Ausubel; Frederick, 1980; Gold, 1980; Gorsuch, 1980; Hill, 1980; Milkman & Frosch; Misra, 1980; Peele; Wurmser, 1980).

Social and environmental influences including family, socioeconomic status, lack of acceptance, discrimination, and social entrapment have been cited by some researchers as important contributors to abuse and dependence (Becker, 1980; Chein, 1980; Coleman, 1980; Gorsuch, 1980; Hendin, 1980; Hill, 1980; Huba et al., 1980; Jessor & Jessor, 1980; Jonas & Jonas, 1980; Loney, 1980; Lukoff, 1980; Schuckit, 1980; Smith, 1980; Steffenhagen, 1980; Wikler, 1980; Zinberg, 1980). In an attempt to overcome feelings of *helplessness, hopelessness, and powerlessness* some people take drugs (Coleman; Gold, 1980; Hochhauser, 1980). Coleman suggested some people take drugs in *search for meaning*. Drugs provide a vehicle that allows one an opportunity to not only escape (Misra, 1980; Smart, 1980) one's self and environment, but an opportunity to seek a life of excitement or one with purpose that brings a sense of belonging. Some researchers suggest, then, that drug taking is an attempt at *lifestyle changes and enhancement* (McAuliffe & Gordon, 1980; Smart; Spotts & Shontz, 1980; Steffenhagen).

Regardless of the specific causes, it seems obvious that as long as the *perceived positive effects* (Becker, 1980; Peele, 1980; Smith, 1980) of drug taking outweigh the perceived negative effects, people will continue to take drugs. Some will continue to abuse and become dependent on them. Having presented some proposed reasons for substance abuse, the next step is to more specifically identify theories on substance abuse/dependency.

Theories Regarding Substance
Abuse and Dependency

There are several methods of examining theories on substance abuse and dependency including examining a person's self-concept, and one's relationship to others, to society, and to his or her environment. When examining and formulating theories, it is important to be aware that the effects of abuse and dependence are a result of the specific <u>drug</u>, the <u>dose</u>, the <u>setting</u> (interpersonal and environmental factors), and the <u>set</u> (internal physiological and psychological states of the drug taker). Also, in an attempt to fully comprehend how one moves along a continuum of use to abuse, theories must explain several components including: (a) initiation (why people begin taking drugs); (b) continuation (why people maintain drug-taking behavior); (c) transition (how or why drug-taking behavior escalates to abuse); (d) cessation (why or how people stop taking drugs); and (e) relapse (what accounts for restarting the drug dependence behavior or cycle once stopped (Lettieri, Sayers, & Pearson, 1980).

Theories on substance abuse have ranged from those focusing on the bio-neuro-genetic causes to those that address abuse and dependency from a developmental, psychosocial perspective. Before beginning a discussion of developmental and psychosocial theories regarding substance abuse, it is important to address the disease model as it is the foundation for many substance abuse treatment programs. Many researchers (Jellinek, 1960; Keller, 1976; Kurtz, 1979; Peters, 1984; Talbott, 1983; Wallace, 1986) have supported the disease model as a viable treatment model. Others refute it based upon the model's failure to address addiction within the larger context of an individual's life, and its contention that individuals cannot control their behaviors (Douglas, 1986; Ellis et al., 1988; Peele, 1989; Shaffer, 1987).

Levine (1978) wrote that alcoholism has been considered a disease for approximately 175 to 200 years, and is a concept born out of the Temperance Movement. He indicated physicians (particularly Dr. Benjamin Rush) were responsible for the modern conception of addiction. Levine concluded it was their medical orientation that led physicians to examine behavior from a medical rather than a psychosocial perspective. During the prohibition era the focus shifted from the person to the environment de-emphasizing alcoholism as a disease. Levine reported that the "rediscovery" of alcoholism as an addiction and disease occurred in the 1930s and 1940s.

Shaffer (1985) identified the disease model as having three cornerstones: (a) loss of control, (b) progression, and (c) predisposition. However, Peele (1989) refuted that a distinctive genetic indicator exists, and Ellis et al. (1988) cautioned against viewing those dependent on drugs as helpless victims of a disease. Shaffer (1987) stated that:

Just because many social scientists and drug treatment specialists are encouraging the application of the disease label to various forms of substance abuse and dependency, that does not make it so. (p. 103)

Douglas (1986) believed we cannot rely on the disease concept alone to describe the essential nature of the addictive process.

For therapeutic recreation specialists, it seems most advantageous, while being aware of the bio-neuro-genetic theories of substance abuse and dependency, to focus on those theories that address abuse from a developmental, psychosocial perspective. It is the writer's contention that therapeutic recreation interventions are most likely to positively impact psychosocial outcomes in treating substance abuse and dependence. Therefore, those theories which the writer believes are most applicable to therapeutic recreation intervention are presented and discussed. The exclusion of certain theories does not imply that they lack value; it is just that the constraints of this paper do not allow for full examination and discussion of all theories that may apply to substance abuse treatment. Thus, this theoretical overview focuses on those theories that attempt to explain substance abuse from a developmental, psychosocial perspective.

The writer is in consensus with researchers who propose that underlying causes of abuse and dependence are multifactorial (Cohen, 1985; Ellis et al., 1988; Vaillant, 1983) and that treatment programs must be multimodal (Brower et al., 1989; Craig et al., 1990; Rioux & Van Meter, 1990). However, there are theories that address specific factors that therapeutic recreation specialists would very likely incorporate in a multimodal intervention plan.

Given a recognized continuum of therapeutic recreation services (therapy, leisure education, recreation participation) it is reasonable to assume that researchers and practitioners would be interested in those theories that discuss factors typically addressed within the continuum. Theories addressing: (a) *social influences* (Hendin, 1980); (b) *adaptational* and *coping mechanisms* (Gold, 1980; Milkman & Frosch, 1980); (c) *existentialism* (Greaves, 1980); (d) *ego/self-enhancement* (Khantzian, 1980) and *self-esteem* (Gold, 1980; Kaplan, 1980; Milkman & Frosch; Steffenhagen, 1980); (e) *family* (Coleman, 1980; Stanton, 1980); (f) *problem behavior* (Jessor & Jessor, 1980); (g) *learned behavior* (Frederick, 1980); and (h) *social learning theory* (Bandura, 1977a) are theories of potential interest to both researchers and therapeutic recreation practitioners.

Hendin (1980) in presenting a psychosocial theory of drug abuse suggested that we:

> View drug use as part of the individual's attempt to deal with needs
> and conflicts, relations with others, and the social environment in
> which he or she lives. Since all these vary with age and stage of life,
> one would expect drugs to be used and abused for different
> purposes at different points in the life cycle. (p. 196)

Theories addressing adaptational and coping mechanisms as they relate to drug abuse are tied closely with theories addressing self-esteem and learning. Gold (1980) purports that how we label and evaluate a situation will determine our emotional/behavioral response to it. He believes the abuse process begins with conflict as a predisposing factor. Personal or societal demands or expectations are in conflict resulting in stress and anxiety. Crucial to this theory is the person's perception of anxiety. Underlying the anxiety of drug abusers is the belief that they are powerless to cope with stress, and this sense of powerlessness lowers self-esteem.

> Drugs do for abusers what they believe they cannot do for
> themselves: get rid of anxiety, lead to a good feeling about
> themselves, and make them believe they are competent, in control,
> and able to master their environment. (p. 9)

Accompanying this sense of powerlessness comes an increase in drug use and abuse, and the person is less capable of coping without the drug(s).

> Effective and lasting change is based on learning that behavior has
> consequences and that one can have an effect on his or her own life.
> To replace a sense of powerlessness with a sense of mastery, the
> abuser has to be taught alternative ways of responding to external
> and internal stress, and more adaptive coping mechanisms. (p. 9)

Khantzian (1980) indicated that drug dependence is tied ultimately to an individual's attempt to "use drugs adaptively to overcome and cope with ego and self problems" (p. 32). These ego and self problems include internal emotional and external social and physical environment, drive, and need satisfaction problems.

Kaplan (1980) indicated that we behave so as to maximize positive self attitudes and minimize negative ones. When a person is:

> Unable to defend against, adapt to, or cope with circumstances
> having self-devaluing implications, [he/she] will begin to seek
> alternative (deviant) response patterns which offer hope of reducing
> negative self-attitude experiences and increasing positive
> self-attitude experiences. (p. 129)

Steffenhagen's (1980) self-esteem theory of substance abuse postulated that "all behavior is mediated by the individuals's attempt to protect the 'self' within the social milieu" (p. 157). He wrote that self-esteem develops as a result of how we cope with feelings of inferiority and/or superiority, social interest or other directedness, goal orientation and lifestyle. He believed that "feelings of inferiority reflect the extent to which the individual perceives him/herself as able or unable to obtain goals" (p. 158). Individuals feeling inadequate or inferior may feel a need to protect their self-image. Often, the compensatory mechanisms chosen are drugs.

In examining the role of the family as it relates to drug abuse both Coleman (1980) and Stanton (1980) purported that drug taking plays an important role in maintaining family homeostasis. Both have also found that a high percentage of drug abusers' families have experienced a premature separation or loss. Because of the loss the family may experience a sense of hopelessness and a lack of meaning. By using drugs and remaining in that role the person becomes helpless and dependent and re-establishes family equilibrium.

One theory which seems directly related to leisure research and therapeutic recreation intervention is Greaves' (1980) existential theory of drug dependence. As the reader may be aware, existential psychology deals "with a person's experience of the quality and meaning of his or her life" (p. 24). Greaves submitted that, as a group, those dependent on drugs do not know how to play without the influence of drugs. Without the drug induced state, very little seems interesting or exciting. "They have lost contact with their natural child within them, and with it their spontaneity, creativity, and joy" (p. 27). Persons dependent on drugs seem not to respond to pleasurable somatic feedback, and Greaves purported that this may be one reason they do not enjoy play. He believed that those dependent on drugs have difficulty attaining pleasure in conventional ways. Regarding treatment for those dependent on drugs, Greaves (1974) wrote:

> Our major unreasonable demand is that we want a person to give
> up something that gives him pleasure and/or relieves distress, while
> offering little in return except vague, distant promises of a better life
> and improved self-esteem. We need to teach drug-dependent
> persons to turn themselves on as a substitute for the
> euphoria-producing properties of drugs, and to relax in order to
> replace the anxiety-reducing effects of drugs. We need to help
> persons to become the agents of their pleasure, not the passive
> recipients. We need to turn our clients on to music, dancing,
> fishing, camping, boating, photography . . . . We need to help
> clients to realize that not only is it all right to pursue actively a wide
> range of pleasurable experiences, but how to.
> (pp. 270-271)

A theory which seems particularly suited to changing behavior (an implicit if not explicit purpose of therapeutic recreation services) is Frederick's (1980) learned behavior theory. He believed that "the sine qua non for drug abuse/addiction is to be found in learning theory" (p. 191). Frederick thought that a number of variables (environment, availability, exposure to drug use patterns, and needs) contribute to drug abuse and dependency as learned behavior resulting in a cycle consisting of stimulation situation (stress, shame, guilt) --> tension (anxiety) --> addictive acts (drug seeking/receiving/ingesting) --> tension reduction --> stimulus situation, and so forth.

Several researchers have addressed learning as contributing to drug abuse/dependence (Bennett, 1989; Botvin, 1983; Crowley, 1972; Ellis et al., 1988; Jaffe, 1970; Marlatt, 1985; Miller & Pechacek, 1987; Nathan, 1985; Rohsenow, Corbett, & Devine, 1988; Wikler, 1973; Zweben, 1986). Nathan, in a discussion of cognitive social learning approaches to alcoholism, stated that, "much importance to an understanding of substance abuse has to do with learning" (p. 169), and he suggested that if inappropriate behaviors can be learned they can be unlearned. Social learning researchers (Marlatt & Gordon, 1985; Miller, 1985; Vogler & Bartz, 1982) have cautioned that to think of substance abuse and dependency as only a disease or a behavioral disorder may affect the continuum of treatment services needed in recovery. Botvin offered Bandura's (1977a) social learning theory and Jessor and Jessor's (1977) problem behavior theory as useful for their "conceptual framework for understanding the etiology of substance use" (p. 121). From the perspective of these two theories, "substance use is conceptualized as a socially learned, positive, and functional behavior which is the result of the interplay of social (environmental) and personal factors" (Botvin, p. 133).

Conceptually, problem behavior theory postulates that: (a) *personality* (values, expectations, beliefs, attitudes, orientation toward self and others); (b) *environment* (supports, influences, controls, models, expectations of others); and (c) *behavior* (socially learned purposes, functions or significances) interrelate resulting in problem-behavior proneness. In addition to the aforementioned variables, behavior is also influenced by: (a) the value placed on goals and expectation of attaining goals, (b) self-esteem, (c) locus of control, (d) positive and negative feedback, (e) alienation and inclusiveness, (f) attitudinal tolerance of deviance, and (g) perceived positive and negative effects of drug use. Contributing to problem behavior are the issues of: (a) low self-esteem, (b) external locus of control, (c) criticism, (d) alienation, and (e) an attitudinal tolerance of deviance. Also, when a person places little value on goals or has little expectation of attaining them, or when the perceived positive effects of drug use outweigh the perceived negative effects, problem behavior is likely to occur.

Similar to the conceptual framework of the problem behavior theory, the social learning theory of psychological functioning is viewed as an interaction among personal, environmental, and behavioral determinants. A distinguishing feature of social learning theory application is helping people "exercise some measure of control over their own behavior" (Bandura, 1977a, p. 13). People are encouraged to take responsibility for the social consequences of their behavior, and function as "active agents in their own self-motivation" (p. 165). Self-reinforcement and self-evaluation play key roles in:

> Successful self-directed change. Findings related to several lines of research on self-regulatory processes indicate that social learning approaches hold considerable promise for increasing a person's capacity to regulate his/her own feelings, thoughts and actions. (pp. 144- 145)

In a subsequent work, Bandura (1982) explained that self-efficacy is an important variable because it involves a general ability to deal with one's environment and to mobilize cognitive and behavioral skills needed to manage challenging situations, consequently enhancing one's perceived ability to cope with one's environment.

One premise of the social learning theory is that if a person is resorting to socially unacceptable means to attain personal needs, then as part of treatment one needs to cultivate more functional alternatives. Bandura (1977a) indicated that "in order to change, people need corrective learning experiences" (p. 78). He also wrote that providing better alternatives is more effective in modifying behavior than is imposing prohibitions.

> Within the social learning framework, freedom is defined in terms of the number of options available to people and the right to exercise them. The more behavioral alternatives and prerogatives people have, the greater is their freedom of action. Freedom can be fostered by cultivating competencies, and is enhanced by eliminating dysfunctional self-restraints. Given the same environmental constraints, individuals who have many behavioral options and are adept at regulating their own behavior will experience greater freedom than will individuals whose personal resources are limited. (pp. 201-203)

Tober (1989) concluded that social learning theory has not been given adequate consideration in the design of treatment and service delivery for substance abuse and dependency. He stated that adopting a social learning approach:

Not only provides an understanding of addiction behavior which accounts for the observed phenomena, it also informs and directs responses to produce a wide variety of interventions which are able to meet the demands of the whole spectrum of drug problems rather than the very select few currently catered for. (p. 24)

Given that therapeutic recreation services attempt to impact behavioral change, it seems that the problem behavior theory and social learning theory provide conceptual frameworks from which leisure researchers and therapeutic recreation practitioners can draw inferences. For example, having identified problems associated with substance abuse and dependency, the therapeutic recreation specialist designs specific intervention/treatment plans to address specific problems. In leisure education, the therapeutic recreation specialist attempts to facilitate new learning that will positively impact social, free time, and recreational and leisure choices. By providing general recreation opportunities, the therapeutic recreation specialist facilitates the client's ability in a natural environment to address problems associated with substance abuse and dependence, to practice new learning, and to pursue positive, alternative ways of behaving.

Treatment Models and Matching

A variety of treatment models for substance abuse have been discussed in the literature (Brickman et al., 1982; Brower et al., 1989; Donovan, 1986; Kissin, 1977; Ludwig, 1988; Marlatt, 1985). Brower et al. suggested that because people go through different stages of recovery, the use of different models during different phases of treatment may be beneficial. The authors concluded that effective intervention requires an eclectic approach to maximize individual treatment plans. Several researchers have addressed the need for a multifaceted approach to treatment, and the importance of matching clients and treatment interventions (Brower et al.; Cohen, 1986; Kaufman, 1990-1991; Laskowitz, 1990; Maisto & Caddy, 1981; Marlatt, 1988; Pattison, Sobell, & Sobell, 1977; Shaffer & Neuhaus, 1984; Smart et al., 1990-91; Stimmel, 1983). Marlatt (1988) reported that the emphasis upon treatment should address matching phases of recovery to various models in order to maximize treatment outcome. He indicated:

. . . Data on recovery and relapse do not support the effectiveness of the uniformity approach to treatment. One alternative is the notion that treatment for addiction problems should be graded in intensity, relevant to the magnitude of the presenting problems. (p. 480).

Marlatt's (1988) graded intensity approach may serve as a model for leisure researchers and therapeutic recreation specialists to determine which clients need therapy, leisure education, and/or general recreation participation and to what degree of intensity.

Brickman et al. (1982) identify four models for treating those with addictive behaviors: (a) moral, (b) compensatory, (c) medical, and (d) enlightenment models. The premise of the moral model is that individuals are responsible for their problems and solutions, and only need proper motivation to remain abstinent. The premise of the compensatory model is that individuals are not responsible for their problems but are responsible for solutions, and only need a sense of power to overcome dependency. The premise of the medical model is that individuals are neither responsible for their problems or solutions, and need treatment. The premise of the enlightenment model is that individuals are responsible for problems but are unable or unwilling to provide solutions, and need discipline in overcoming their problems. The authors thought that matching a client to one of these models is dependent upon an assessment of the client's attribution and perceived efficacy toward the behaviors illustrated within each of the four models.

Brower et al. (1989) distinguish between basic (moral, learning, disease, self-medication, social) treatment models which they suggest are singularly focused, and integrative (bio-psychosocial, AA, dual diagnosis) models which they suggest are multi-focused. The authors provide an interesting discussion of the etiology, treatment goals, advantages, and disadvantages of each model.

The basis of the moral model is that chemical dependency results from a lack of willpower or moral weakness. The treatment goal of this model is to increase willpower against evil temptations. The advantages of this model are that the person must do a moral inventory, and it holds the person responsible for the consequences of his/her actions. The disadvantages are that it is blaming and punitive, and according to Brower et al. (1989) that "a treatment strategy that depends solely on willpower, sets the stage for failure and decreases the substance abuser's sense of self-esteem" (p. 169).

The basis of the learning model is that chemical dependency results from learning maladaptive behaviors. The treatment goal is self-control via new learning. The advantages are: (a) it is not blaming or punitive; (b) it emphasizes new learning (coping skills, cognitive restructuring); and (c) it holds the person responsible for the consequences of his or her actions. The primary disadvantage is its emphasis on control. Brown (1985) contended that the concept of control is paradoxical in that one may have to admit loss of control in order to gain control.

"Therapists who can appreciate this paradox of control are in the best position to integrate, as needed, the models that emphasize loss of control with models that emphasize self-control" (Brower et al., 1989, p. 150).

The basis of the disease model, which is most likely the dominant model utilized in treatment, is that though the etiology of chemical dependency is unknown, biological or genetic factors are important. The person is thought to be "ill" because of the "disease" of chemical dependency. The treatment goal is complete abstinence. The advantages are that it is not punitive or blaming, and that disease implies treatment as an appropriate response. The focus is on self-care. The disadvantages are the inability to explain a return to asymptomatic drinking, and underestimating coexisting mental disorders.

The basis of the self-medication model is that chemical dependency is a symptom of a primary mental disorder. The treatment goal is improved mental functioning. The advantages are it is not punitive or blaming, and its emphasis upon identifying and treating coexisting mental disorders. The primary disadvantage is the implication that treatment of the primary mental disorder is sufficient. "Problems are more likely to improve if the chemical dependency is treated first and a period of abstinence is required in order to assess better the other problems" (Brower et al., 1989, p. 152).

The basis of the social model is that chemical dependency is a result of environmental influences. The treatment goal is improved social functioning. The advantages are that it emphasizes the need for social supports and skills, and is easily integrated into other models. The disadvantages are that it projects blame, and implies treatment of social problems is sufficient.

Brower et al. (1989) reported that integrative models combine elements of the basic models, are multi-focused in addressing the multiple problems of those recovering from chemical dependency, and they facilitate optimal client-treatment matching. The authors encouraged researchers to investigate integrative models to determine their effectiveness in optimizing treatment outcomes. The decision to adopt and implement a basic or integrative treatment model impacts directly on the goals of treatment.

Treatment Goals

Several researchers (Akerlind, Hornquist, & Bjurulf, 1988; Cohen, 1986; Kaplan, 1990; Kaufman, 1990-1991; Laskowitz, 1990; Martin, 1990; O'Dea-Evans, 1990; Wallace, McNeil, Gilfillan, MacLean, & Fanella, 1988; Wolber, Carne, & Alexander, 1990) have discussed goals related to treatment of those recovering from chemical dependency that support the provision of recreation and leisure services. O'Dea-Evans identified a comprehensive list of therapeutic recreation goals that she posits assist the individual during the recovery process including goals related to "problem solving, acceptance, self-disclosure, esteem building, and behavioral changes" (p. 32). Among the goals cited by Rancourt (1991a) that should be part of a comprehensive leisure education program are: (a) goal setting, (b) identifying low-cost activities to participate in, (c) increasing a sense of playfulness--getting in touch with the child within, (d) increasing self-esteem, (e) increasing internal locus of control-empowering, (f) increasing opportunities to trust, (g) developing a pro-active decision-making style, (h) increasing opportunities for family socialization/recreation, (i) helping the individual to identify how recreational activities and leisure experiences can fulfill needs, (j) enhancing opportunities to develop competencies, (k) stress reduction, (l) providing opportunities for socialization without drugs, (m) providing opportunities for self-enhancement, (n) developing positive relations with children, and (o) developing support networks.

Both practitioners and researchers have stressed the importance of quality sobriety and improved overall life functioning as important criteria in treatment (Akerlind et al., 1988; Kanfer, 1986; Kaplan, 1990; Laskowitz, 1990; O'Dea-Evans, 1990; Wolber et al., 1990). These writers indicate the goal of quality sobriety is not only to remain abstinent, but to improve one's ability for effective living. Using psychosocial interventions, the therapist assists the individual in changing his or her lifestyle. O'Dea-Evans remarked that an active leisure lifestyle is critical to effective rehabilitation.

In assisting the individual in changing his or her lifestyle it is important to help the individual explore nonchemical alternatives for meeting needs and achieving goals (Brown, 1985; Conroy, 1985; Kaplan, 1990; Kaufman, 1990-1991; Laskowitz, 1990; McAuliffe & Ch'ien, 1986; Miller & Pechacek, 1987; O'Dea-Evans, 1990; Wallace et al., 1988). Laskowitz indicated a need to "effectively counter the need to get high" (p. 855). Kaufman noted the importance for the individual to learn "newer and more adaptive ways to get needs met" (p. 102). O'Dea-Evans viewed recreational alternatives as important to recovery, also indicating that individuals "who are exposed to leisure alternatives in the community are more likely to use them after discharge" (p. 96). She believed that well-rounded holistic care treatment programs must include therapeutic recreation, but indicated that therapeutic recreation as a modality "is underutilized within chemical dependency treatment programs" (p. 1). Wallace et al. and McAuliffe and Ch'ien suggest that alternatives must be presented to help the individual deal with phases of boredom and loneliness.

Problem solving (Laskowitz, 1990; O'Dea-Evans, 1990; Rancourt, 1991b) and social interaction skills and adjustment (Hawkins & Fraser, 1987; Kaplan, 1990; Laskowitz; Martin, 1990; McAuliffe & Ch'ien, 1986; O'Dea-Evans; Rancourt) are also seen as important goals for treatment. Laskowitz stated that it is important to help the individual assess the congruency between personal abilities and interests, and available community resources. O'Dea-Evans felt that it is important for the individual to "identify and solve problematic issues related to their use of leisure" (p. 14). Hawkins and Fraser indicated that it is important to assist individuals in altering the composition of their social networks to include members who are supportive of their recovery. McAuliffe and Ch'ien remarked that one of the greatest threats to recovery are friends who are using drugs. In response to which criteria should be used in selecting treatment goals, Martin stated "The sole criterion is the improvement of social adjustment by the user" (p. 585).

Another important goal that has been identified is helping the individual master stressors and to effectively cope with them without resorting to chemicals (Kaufman, 1990-1991; Laskowitz, 1990; O'Dea-Evans, 1990; Rancourt, 1991b). O'Dea-Evans added that recreation activities "can assist the addicted person in developing stress management skills" (p. 18). Laskowitz urged that the person in recovery must be assisted in adaptively mastering stressors without recourse to self-medication or chemical escape.

As previously mentioned the achievement of treatment goals often relies on new learning (Brower et al., 1989; Kaufman, 1990-1991; McAuliffe & Ch'ien, 1986). The individual recovering from chemical dependency needs to learn newer and more adaptive ways to meet his/her needs. However, McAuliffe and Ch'ien noted that a systematic educational component has been missing from drug treatment programs. Certainly, leisure education is one such systematic educational component which can contribute to the acquisition of knowledge and skills related to a balanced lifestyle and quality sobriety.

Many researchers support family therapy and improving family relations as an important modality in contributing to treatment goals and recovery (Bennun, 1985; Corder, Corder, & Laidlaw, 1972; Hawkins & Catalano, 1985; Kaufman, 1990-1991; Kaufman & Kaufman, 1979; Laskowitz, 1990; Miller & Hester, 1986; O'Farrell, 1989; Rancourt, 1991b; Weidman, 1985; Yoder, 1990; Zweben, Pearlman, & Li, 1983). Bennun reported that ignoring the effect of substance abuse on the family system may be detrimental to treatment effectiveness. The role of the family is a crucial factor in recovery. A family leisure education program (Rancourt, 1989) might assist family members in identifying repetitive, maladaptive recreation and leisure patterns, and might facilitate greater participation in more positive recreation activities which enhance interaction and communication between and among family members.

As the therapist interacts with the client in choosing treatment models, interventions and programs, and goals, it is important that not only age, but gender and cultural profiles be identified. Addressing the issue of gender, several researchers (MacDonald, 1987; Mondanaro, 1988; Naegle, 1981; Vourakis, 1983) have made suggestions regarding treatment of women recovering from chemical dependency. Mondanaro suggested that the unique problems of women who are chemically dependent have been under- recognized and undertreated. Likewise, Smith-Peterson (1983) and Trimble (1990) indicated cultural diversity must be addressed in research and in practice. "Failure to acknowledge cultural and ethnic differences in prevention and treatment programs have perpetuated program ineffectiveness" (Smith-Peterson, p. 370).

Treatment Effectiveness

Martin (1990) stated that if problems are not amenable to medical treatment, other skills and conceptual bases have to be incorporated into treatment. He suggested, however, that we do not know enough about the pathology of drug abuse to know what therapist skills are needed to most effectively treat it. We cannot prove the effectiveness of treatment until we comprehend the pathology and prove which interventions effect which changes. Kaplan (1990) recommended improving the effectiveness of treatment by understanding the meaning of substance abuse to the individual, why abuse was adopted to begin with, what purpose substance abuse serves, and what the results of abstinence would mean.

Miller and Hester (1986) investigated the effectiveness of alcoholism treatment programs and found a significant body of knowledge on the subject. However, they found treatment approaches discussed in the literature:

> Are rarely used in American treatment programs. The list of elements that are typically included in alcoholism treatment in the United States likewise evidenced a commonality: virtually all of them lacked adequate scientific evidence of effectiveness. (p. 122)

These researchers found that practitioners were not applying interventions identified by researchers as being effective.

In a comparison of research supported methods versus standard alcoholism treatment methods (see Table 1) Miller and Hester (1986) found that there was a lack of congruency between the two lists, and that the standard practice list contained few modalities supported by efficacy research. They posited that:

American treatment of alcoholism follows a standard formula that appears to be impervious to emerging research evidence, and has not changed significantly for at least two decades. Current empirical evidence suggests that a combination of these ingredients would not be expected to yield therapeutic gains substantially greater than the spontaneous remission rate, and indeed this appears to have been the overall result of American alcoholism treatment over the past few decades. (pp. 162-163)

Table 1. Supported Versus Standard Alcoholism Treatment Methods

Treatment Methods Currently Supported by Controlled Outcome Research	Treatment Methods Currently Employed Standard Practice in Alcoholism Programs
Aversion Therapies	AA
Behavioral Self-Control Training	Alcoholism Education
Community Reinforcement Approach	Confrontation
Marital and Family Therapy	Disulfiram
Social Skills Training	Group Therapy
Stress Management	Individual Counseling

Miller, W. R., & Hester, R. K. (1986). The effectiveness of alcoholism treatment: What research reveals. In W. R. Miller & N. Heather (Eds.), Treating addictive behaviors: Processes of change (pp. 121-174). New York: Plenum.

Miller and Hester (1986) offered three guidelines for designing future treatment programs:

1. Intervention should be supported by research as being effective.

2. Initial interventions should be the least intensive and intrusive with more extensive interventions occurring after first attempts have failed.

3. Clients should be matched to optimal interventions.
The authors believed that most treatment programs pay lip service to individual treatment programs. Yoder (1990) indicated "only about ten percent of recovery

occurs in treatment" (p. 18). Yoder and Annis (1986) posited that treatment programs must teach relapse prevention skills, and must be designed to not only initiate but to maintain behavioral change.

Relapse

Several researchers support Yoder (1990) and Annis' (1986) call for the necessity, during treatment, to teach individuals skills, and enhance their ability to identify and confront aversive problems that may cause relapse (Laskowitz, 1990; Litman, 1986; Marlatt, 1985; Marlatt & Gordon, 1985; McCrady, Dean, Dubreuil, & Swanson, 1985; Miller & Pechacek, 1987). Miller and Pechacek contended that if individuals do not possess skills to deal with aversive problems, it should be no surprise that they relapse to some maladaptive behavioral pattern. Marlatt wrote that "relapse is the most common outcome of alcoholism treatment" (p. 8), and estimated over 90% of individuals relapse within 2 years following treatment.

Some authors cautioned that relapse cannot be viewed as a full blown catastrophe or failure. Rather it should be viewed from a social learning perspective as a "misstep" (Laskowitz, 1990); a "breakdown or setback in a person's attempt to change or modify any target behavior" (Marlatt, 1985, p. 3), or a lapse, a moment of crisis presenting both dangers and opportunities (Marlatt). Douglas (1986) stated:

> To define 'relapse' as a result of 'disease' is to remove humanity and decision and so cast the individual into the very helplessness from which the disease concept was supposed to rescue him. An excuse to remove 'guilt' is brought at the expense of volition and selfhood, of humanity itself. (p. 117)

Marlatt in questioning steps 5 and 8 of the 12 step program of AA asked:

> Why should someone with an uncontrollable disease feel guilty and responsible for their past misdeeds? Why is there such an insistence on admitting that one is an alcoholic instead of accepting the fact that one has experienced problems as a result of excessive drinking. (p. 14)?

Laskowitz believed that if we view a mistake as a total relapse we are increasing the likelihood the person will perceive him/herself as a failure, and relapse vulnerability is heightened. He cautioned that individuals should be made aware that a slip does not equate with a full-blown relapse.

Though Donovan and Chaney (1985) claimed that there are "insufficient data available to propose a comprehensive theory on relapse" (p. 407), several hypotheses have been generated as to why relapse occurs. Cohen (1986) believed the high rate of relapse may be due to the ineffective or nonexistent matching between treatment and clients' needs and motivations. Among the factors that appear to be related to relapse, Hawkins and Catalano (1985) found lack of involvement in active leisure/recreational activities, isolation, and absence of a prosocial network. Interpersonal pressures and negative emotional states (Hawkins & Catalano; Laskowitz, 1990; Marlatt, 1985) have been identified as contributing to relapse. Marlatt reported that over 50% of alcoholic relapses are attributable to interpersonal conflicts. He also cited social pressures as a high risk situations potentially leading to relapse. Zweben (1986) indicated "holidays, birthdays, anniversaries, and other celebrations are times of increased vulnerability" (p. 260). O'Dea-Evans (1990) said that stress is the most often cited reason for relapse. Marlatt believed that urges and cravings, often cited reasons for relapse, can be the result of learned conditioned response and expectancy of positive effects. However, he did not hold the person morally responsible for past learning. He believed that even if one may have learned a behavior it does not mean one has voluntary control over it. What one is capable of is changing behavior, and that is what one has control over. Marlatt also wrote that mini-decisions and choices can set a person up for relapse. Regardless of what triggers a relapse, what is important is that individuals are taught to recognize and avoid those triggers or high risk situations (Laskowitz; Marlatt; Yoder, 1990).

Social Learning/Self-Efficacy

A social learning approach appears to be a viable approach to treatment and relapse prevention. Bandura's (1977b, 1978, 1981) self-efficacy theory provides the major theoretical thrust for many researchers investigating relapse. A major tenet of the theory is that techniques and methods utilized in *initiating* behavioral change may not be the most effective for *maintaining* behavioral change. Marlatt (1985) indicated that high risk situations pose a threat to the individual's sense of control and increase the risk of relapse. Self-efficacy will be enhanced with increased ability to identify and cope with these high-risk situations. Many researchers (Annis, 1986; Bandura; Litman, 1986; Marlatt; Yoder, 1990) see a direct relationship between coping behavior and perception of self-efficacy (mastery, competence). "If the individual is able to execute an effective cognitive or behavioral coping response in the high-risk situation, the probability of relapse decreases significantly" (Marlatt, p. 40). Basically, as we cope with and experience success with one problematic situation, it leads us to expect we can cope with others and leads to greater self-efficacy (Bandura).

Self-efficacy theory would predict that avoidance of drinking (abstinence), even for a period of years, would not develop a sense of self-efficacy about coping with drinking. Given low-efficacy expectations, coping behavior would be easily extinguished in the face of difficult experiences encountered in remaining sober in the natural environment. In addition, outcome expectations emphasizing the certainty of a return to uncontrollable drinking after a single drink would tend to function as a self-fulfilling prophecy, drastically increasing the severity of any relapse episode. (Annis, pp. 408- 409)

From a social learning/self-efficacy perspective it is important for care providers to help individuals to be agents of their treatment, intervention, and behavioral change--not just recipients of it.

Relapse Prevention Strategies

"Based on the principles of social-learning theory, relapse prevention is a self-control program that combines behavioral skill training, cognitive interventions, and lifestyle change procedures" (Marlatt, 1985, p. 3). Strategies include: (a) identifying high-risk situations; (b) acquiring problem-solving and adaptive coping skills; (c) fostering new attitudes, attributions and expectancies; and (d) developing a satisfying and gratifying, rather than destructive, daily lifestyle. Goal setting and realization of goals is important (Laskowitz, 1990; Marlatt). Helping the individual develop a "balanced lifestyle" (Marlatt; O'Dea-Evans, 1990) is critical to recovery and relapse prevention.

Marlatt (1985) purported that a person needs balance between day-to-day perceived "shoulds" and "wants." The more prevalent the perceived "shoulds," the more the justification for indulgence and gratification. He cites lifestyle intervention as "one of the major global self-control strategies employed in the relapse prevention approach" (p. 63). He stated that such lifestyle intervention techniques as exercise and relaxation increase coping capacity and reduce "the frequency and intensity of urges and cravings that are often the product of an unbalanced lifestyle" (p. 53).

Lifestyle intervention approaches suggest the importance of recreation, leisure, and therapeutic recreation interventions as part of treatment and relapse prevention programs. Zackon, McAuliffe, and Ch'ien (1985) discussed the need for drug-free recreation in recovery. McAuliffe and Ch'ien (1986) offered that recreational and social activities are important components in relapse prevention programs. They believed that the emphasis should be on "the need for new forms of fun and the need to learn how to enjoy them, and on taking stock of one's social circle in preparation for improving it" (p. 13). Laskowitz (1990) recommended that treatment programs include activities with "alumni" and family which would also imply a role for recreation and leisure programming. Based on these observations, it can be hypothesized that recreation and leisure interventions are critical to new learning, self-efficacy, balance, and lifestyle changes. Recreation and leisure interventions would seem to play a significant role in treatment and relapse prevention outcomes.

Treatment Outcomes

General Treatment Outcomes

Alfano, Thurston, and Nerviano (1987) stated that "as fiscal constraints limit the amount of research and treatment dollars, better methods of showing cost-effectiveness, as well as treatment benefits, will have to be delineated" (p. 867). They suggested that the focus is on outcomes. However, Annis (1980) declared that as part of the outcome documentative process, before outcome criteria are determined, the client must be collaborated with. Miller and Hester (1986) concurred with Annis suggesting a possible reason for mediocre outcomes in alcoholism treatment is the absence of appropriate client-treatment matching. They offered that the failure stems from:

> The absence of differential diagnosis and alternative efficacious interventions, and that clinical efficacy will be significantly advanced by determining which treatments are optimal for which types of clients. (pp. 176-177)

Amaro, Beckman, and Mays (1987), and Reed (1987) have found treatment outcome studies lacking which focus on "culturally sensitive" treatment interventions. According to the authors, we don't know if more "culturally sensitive" programs produce better outcomes (i.e., for women and specific ethnic groups). Brower et al. (1989) declared that "future research on treatment matching should focus on the use of integrative models to optimize treatment outcomes" (p. 156). Their contention is that multifaceted treatment programs have the best chance of holistically meeting individual needs.

Some researchers (Donovan, 1986; Miller & Hester, 1986; Raw, 1986) have found that treatment programs addressing a broad spectrum of problems and employing multiple treatment strategies are more effective with respect to abstinence rates. However, Marlatt (1985) disagreed citing two major drawbacks to the multi-modal approach to treatment. The author stated first, the more techniques and procedures used in treatment, the more difficult it is for the client to comply with the program requirements. Secondly, techniques are typically aimed at initial behavioral change, but not long-term maintenance change.

Traditionally, outcome evaluation has focused on abstinence as the primary criterion in measuring treatment effectiveness. Wolber et al. (1990) indicated that "little has been accomplished in the area of wide-spectrum, quality sobriety outcome evaluation" (p. 496). Matuschka (1985) stated that though abstinence remains the most common criterion of treatment success, "many investigators have incorporated controlled drinking and general improvement as criteria in evaluating treatment outcome" (p. 143).

Several researchers have addressed the need to identify specific measures of treatment outcome, and to identify both treatment and extra-treatment variables that contribute to specific outcomes (Bennett & Woolf, 1983; Billings & Moos, 1983; Maisto & Connors, 1988; Martin, 1990; Miller & Hester, 1986; Nathan & Skinstead, 1987; Wallace et al., 1988; Wells, Hawkins, & Catalano, 1988). Wells, Hawkins and Catalano purported that due in part to a rudimentary comprehension of the rehabilitation/remission process, researchers have few guidelines regarding which outcome measures "produce the most valid, reliable, and meaningful estimates of treatment effects" (p. 869). The authors indicated that a lack of consensus and standardization of outcome measures can be attributed, in part, to differing evaluation needs and goals, and to varying opinion to what evaluators regard as useful information.

Several variables related to the treatment outcome process have been identified as being in need of investigation: (a) client heterogeneity (Wallace et al., 1988); (b) treatment settings (Bennett & Woolf, 1983; Wallace et al.); (c) length of treatment (Miller & Hester, 1986; Page & Mitchell, 1988); (d) drug use patterns (Wells et al., 1988); (e) variable life situations (Maisto & Connors, 1988; Wallace et al.); (f) treatment approaches (Bennett & Woolf); (g) interpersonal and social-environmental variables including, "motivation, past attempts to terminate or reduce use on one's own, past treatment experiences, personal treatment goals, and social supports" (Maisto & Connors, p. 439); and (h) the therapist-client relationship (Laskowitz, 1990; Woody, Luborsky, McLellan, & O'Brien, 1986). Researchers must attempt to determine which outcome measures will provide the most useful, valid and reliable data. Maisto and Connors provided three components relevant to evaluating whether treatment is successful: (a) the researcher's definition of success, (b) testing short- and long-term treatment effects, and (c) the client's own evaluation of the outcome. These authors indicated that client attrition is one of the most serious problems facing researchers investigating treatment outcomes.

With respect to treatment outcomes, Miller and Hester (1986) have drawn several conclusions that should be of interest to leisure researchers and therapeutic recreation specialists. In a comprehensive investigation of various controlled research studies focusing on alcohol treatment program effectiveness (impact of treatment on drinking behavior), they concluded:

1. *It is difficult to make valid interpretations of findings on the use of pharmacotherapy. The use of disulfiram (Antabuse) as a routine therapeutic agent is questionable. No reliable changes in drinking behavior occur as a result of psychotropic medication.*

2. *There is little or no evidence that individual and group counseling interventions have any specific long-range impact on drinking behavior.*

3. *No adequately controlled evaluation of confrontational counseling exists.*

4. *AA lacks experimental support regarding its efficacy. Its alleged effectiveness is scientifically unproved.*

5. *The efficacy of alcoholism education as an intervention is not supported by research.*

6. *Marital/family therapy is a worthwhile modality.*

7. *Aversive counterconditioning is a worthwhile modality.*

8. *"Controlled drinking appears to be an attainable and successful goal for problem drinkers who have not established significant degrees of dependence; it is not an effective method from chronic alcoholics who are severely dependent" (p. 148).*

9. *Research supports at least three broad-spectrum treatment approaches: (a) social skills training, (b) stress management, and (c) community reinforcement.*

10. *No research supports superior outcomes for inpatient treatment; several studies favor nonresidential settings.*

11. *More treatment is not necessarily better treatment. Studies favor shorter and less intensive treatment approaches. With no significant differences in cost effectiveness, it would appear that treatment should increasingly shift to an outpatient, community-based approach (p. 157).*

If these conclusions have merit then the provision of recreation and leisure services is of significant importance particularly as it relates to the provision of family leisure education, social skills training, stress management skills, and community reintegration. If the criteria used to determine successful treatment depend on the goals of treatment, then it appears that therapeutic recreation specialists need to begin to ask what are the goals and outcomes of recreation and leisure interventions as they relate to substance-use programs.

Treatment Outcomes Related to Recreation and Leisure

Implied and documented treatment outcomes for substance-abuse treatment can be broadly categorized to include the following domains: (a) cognitive, (b) affective, (c) psychomotor, (d) social, and (e) spiritual. In determining recreation/leisure program/intervention efficacy, three important questions must be asked:

1. What is the relationship between recreation and leisure interventions and successful outcomes in each of the above domains?

2. What is the relationship between changes in functioning (abstinence, quality sobriety) and recreation/leisure services/interventions?

3. What outcomes directly contributing to recovery, abstinence, and quality sobriety impact the provision of recreation and leisure services?

Iso-Ahola (1988) indicated that "empirical documentation about effects of recreation on the well-being of various populations remains largely untapped and unstudied" (p. 9). Though it is difficult to evaluate the efficacy of recreation/leisure interventions for any diagnostic group, let alone so diffuse a category as substance abuse, some findings have been documented.

Several researchers cite *improved social functioning* as important to successful treatment outcome (Brower et al., 1989; DeLeon, 1988; Duckert, 1987; Eriksen, Bjornstad, & Gotestam, 1986; Hawkins & Catalano, 1985; Jacobs et al.; Kaplan, 1990; Martin, 1990; McAuliffe & Ch'ien, 1986; Miller & Hester, 1986; O'Dea-Evans, 1990; Page & Badgett, 1984; Rancourt, 1991b). Eriksen et al. and Page and Badgett indicated more significant outcomes 6 to 12 months following treatment for alcoholism when treatment interventions were directed towards increasing environmental support and social skills. Martin cited the sole criterion for assessing successful treatment to be the individual's ability to assume social responsibilities. Kaplan indicated that interventions must assist the individual in performing conventional social roles. He posited that if the individual achieves effective social functioning and positive self-regard the need for drug use would be obviated. Miller and Hester confirmed that social skills training impacts positively on treatment outcomes. Wurmser (1987) said that most instances of substance abuse began during the teen years, and the stifling effects slowed or arrested emotional growth and development. Researchers might investigate if and what recreation activities and leisure experiences contribute to what Denton (1981) referred to as the development of "life" skills to facilitate maturational growth.

Changing one's lifestyle is cited by several researchers as an important treatment outcome (Akerlind et al., 1988; DeLeon, 1988; Laskowitz, 1990; Marlatt, 1985; O'Dea-Evans, 1990; Wells et al., 1988; Wolber et al., 1990). Akerlind et al., in a study of the rehabilitation of individuals in the advanced stages of alcoholism, found the variables of *perceived well-being* and *quality of life* related to a better prognosis. Marlatt and O'Dea-Evans emphasized the importance of "balance" as contributing to an improved lifestyle, and reducing the chances of relapse. Factors that appear to contribute to this outcome and to successful rehabilitation/recovery include: (a) *countering loneliness* (Akerlind et al.; Hawkins & Catalano, 1985; Laskowitz); (b) *effective problem-solving skills* (Laskowitz; Miller & Pechacek, 1987; O'Dea-Evans, 1990; Rancourt, 1991a, 1991b); (c) *the ability to choose nonchemical alternatives for achieving goals* (Kaplan, 1990; Kaufman, 1989, 1990-1991; Laskowitz; Miller & Pechacek; O'Dea-Evans); (d) *learning to structure free time and leisure planning* that does not involve using drugs or drug related activities (Cliffside, 1989; George & Dustin, 1988; Jacobs et al., 1988); (e) *involvement in more active than passive activities* (Akerlind et al.; Hawkins & Catalano; O'Dea-Evans); and (f) *self-enhancement, self-esteem, and self-actualization* (Kaplan; Laskowitz; O'Dea-Evans; Rancourt).

Another important outcome cited in the literature is the *ability to effectively cope with life stressors without resorting to chemicals* (Brower et al., 1989; George & Dustin, 1988; Jacobs et al., 1988; Kaplan, 1990; Kaufman, 1990-1991; Laskowitz, 1990; Marlatt, 1985; Miller & Hester, 1986; O'Dea-Evans, 1990; Rancourt, 1991a, 1991b). *Exercise and relaxation skills* are cited as two such effective coping techniques (Marlatt; O'Dea-Evans). O'Dea-Evans suggested that recreation activities can assist an individual in developing appropriate coping mechanisms to deal with life stressors. She stated, for example, that "participation in physical fitness activities is shown to increase sobriety rates" (p. 18).

In presenting a paradigm of treatment goals for each component of the therapeutic recreation continuum (therapy, leisure education, recreation participation), O'Dea-Evans (1990) has identified specific outcomes the therapeutic recreation specialist and client should try to achieve. In therapy, the outcomes include: (a) breaking denial, (b) increased self-disclosure, (c) the ability to identify with peers, (d) the ability to express one's self, (e) increased trust, and

(f) increased cohesiveness. The outcomes sought in leisure education include: (a) a balanced lifestyle, (b) decreased guilt, (c) increased problem-solving skills, (d) the ability to identify past defenses, (e) decreased anxiety, (f) learned leisure skills, (g) new skill development, (h) expanded awareness of leisure alternatives, and (i) the ability to identify and eliminate stress. Recreation participation outcomes include: (a) increased esteem, (b) increased sober identity, (c) increased perception of freedom in leisure, (d) decreased stress, (e) eliminate depression, (f) increased euphoria, (g) improved socialization and social skills, (h) improved physical conditioning, and (i) the ability to have fun.

In therapeutic recreation, particularly from a psychosocial behavioral approach, behavioral/learning domains provide a context for determining treatment outcomes. Researchers and practitioners want to determine, as a result of intervention, what changes have occurred in social, cognitive, affective, psychomotor, and spiritual functioning. However, it is obvious from this discussion that it is very difficult to categorize outcomes according to specific domains because there appears to be significant overlap across domains. Each of the outcomes identified can impact one or more of the domains.

The above identified outcomes imply the important contribution recreation/leisure programs/interventions can make to substance abuse treatment outcomes. Research findings have also documented explicit outcomes specifically attributed to recreation/leisure program and therapeutic recreation interventions. However, it is important to note that treatment effects were found in only non-controlled environments and other variables may have also influenced behavior (Maisto & Connors, 1988). Cronbach (1982) noted that behavioral and social interventions are not "fixed" like their medical counterparts, and are not independent of the setting in which they are presented. Indeed, "a treatment effect results from the interaction of population, treatment, and setting. Therefore, the quest for an effect 'free and clear' of other effects is unrealistic" (Cronbach, p. 32).

McAuliffe and Ch'ien (1986) reported that social and recreational activities help individuals manage stress; provide individuals the satisfaction of experiencing fun and socializing drug-free; and reduce boredom and loneliness. Smith-Peterson (1983) posited that when communities offer limited recreational opportunities, individuals seek to reduce boredom through substance use, and substance abuse becomes a major form of recreational activity. The importance of providing community recreation opportunities is supported by O'Dea-Evans (1990) who stated, "Research has shown patients who are exposed to leisure alternatives in the community are more likely to use them after discharge" (p. 96). Yoder (1990) found individuals recovering from chemical dependency indicate that in recovery they have "more time to play, to paint, to write, to plant flowers, to make music . . . ." (p. 5). Opportunities for these experiences can be increased through recreation and leisure services.

James and Townsley (1989), in a study investigating the contribution of activity therapies to comprehensive treatment programs involving chemical dependency, found that recreation therapy activities help promote a healthy leisure lifestyle; assist in developing interpersonal trust; improve specific communication skills; and promote group cohesion. Simpson, Crandall, Savage, and Pavia-Kreuser (1981) found that 6 years after substance abuse treatment, positive changes in leisure functioning were related to favorable outcomes on drug use, criminality, and productive roles/behavior.

Rancourt (1991a) has investigated the relationship between the variables of recreation/leisure programs/interventions and outcomes for women in substance abuse treatment. A number of specific outcomes, identified by women participating in a comprehensive leisure education program (CLEP), were presented by Rancourt (1991a). In general, the author found that a CLEP Program assists individuals: (a) in developing positive ways to structure free time, (b) to cope with feelings and situations previously addressed by using and abusing drugs, (c) to communicate feelings, (d) to cope with stress, and (e) to socialize without drinking. In another study determining the effects of a 6-month CLEP for women recovering from substance abuse Rancourt (1991b) found that CLEP was very successful in facilitating knowledge and skills in self-awareness, recreation and leisure awareness, recreation resource awareness, decision-making, social interaction, recreation skills, stress management, having fun drug-free, and family recreation and leisure participation. She remarked that CLEP can contribute to quality sobriety, more effective problem-solving, identifying nonchemical alternatives to meeting needs, changing one's lifestyle, and community reintegration. Respondents reported greater participation (3 months following completion of the treatment program) in recreation activities than prior to treatment. Findings indicated a relationship between participation in recreation activities and stress reduction. Respondents identified among the benefits of recreation and leisure, that such involvement assists in coping with stress, taking care of self, and helping one feel better; and they provide opportunities for challenge, excitement, and fun.

Rancourt and Howe (1991) surveyed practicing therapeutic recreation specialists to determine expected outcomes of therapeutic recreation services for persons with chemical dependencies. In the first round of this preliminary study, respondents were asked to rate the importance of investigator-expected outcomes on a Likert-type scale (5 = very important, 4 = important, 3 = somewhat important, 2 = important, 1 = not important, 0 = unsure/cannot rate). From a total of 64 potential outcomes, 12 with a mean rating of 4.5 or above, were identified. The outcomes identified as most important were:

1. Establish sober, chemical free balanced lifestyle.

2. Restructure positive, chemical free leisure lifestyle.

3. Identify support systems.

4. Improve self-esteem (feelings about self).

5. Participate in chemical free activities and leisure experiences.

6. Improve self-concept (thoughts about self).

7. Improve self-confidence.

8. Develop remotivation for participation in chemical free recreation.

9. Decrease isolative behavior.

10. Identify post-discharge recreation strategies (goals, plans).

11. Identify leisure choices (alternatives).

12. Develop coping skills.

Evidence has been presented of both implied and documented treatment outcomes essential to the knowledge base and practice of therapeutic recreation. Theories of human development and behavior provide a framework for understanding both the psychosocial aspects of chemical dependency and facilitating treatment outcomes. Outcomes identified in this discussion provide a foundation for testing recreation/leisure treatment/intervention efficacy. Findings might lead to improved treatment interventions, and to the development of some standardized guidelines for therapeutic recreation practice with persons recovering from chemical dependencies.

Future Research

Grant and Johnstone (1990-1991) indicated that though contemporary drug and alcohol studies present a plethora of research questions, very few have been satisfactorily addressed. In assessing the research priorities for drug and alcohol studies for the next 25 years, these authors proposed "inter-disciplinary" research as being crucial to the substance abuse research agenda. They stated that it is important "to test hypothesis and assumptions from different disciplines competitively within a common analytic framework" (p. 213). They cited important trends in contemporary research to include comparative studies, renewed interest in historical, longitudinal, and social context research, and the continuation of cultural studies.

Trimble (1990) reported increased interest in research concerning ethnic groups. However, he indicated that many studies are methodologically flawed and interpretations are questionable. He identified problems in validity, replication, and generalizability because researchers use broad ethnic descriptors in their studies. He encouraged researchers to "obtain detailed information on the sociocultural characteristics of their samples by obtaining measures on ethnic identification, situated identity, and acculturative status" (p. 149). Trimble called for researchers to be more sensitive to the sociocultural diversity and history that exist for different ethnic groups.

Gilbert (1990-1991) wrote that "research focused on how cultural factors shape consumption patterns will continue to be very important" (p. 134). She believed that when investigators differ significantly in ethnicity or cultural background, qualitative methodologies are especially useful. This is an important consideration given the propensity for differences to exist between leisure researchers and those individuals they study.

Grant and Johnstone (1990-1991) suggested that research on temporal variation has increasingly become a distinct area of study. They declared that:

Research on temporal processes is characterized by two principal thrusts: (1) on the individual level, the study of variations in the patterning of drug and alcohol use across the life course; and (2) on the aggregate level, the use of time series analyses to examine trends in substance use and problems. (p. 205)

While it has been remarked that the pattern of drug abuse by men and women is becoming more similar (Clayton et al., 1986), other research has pointed out that the problems of female abusers are gender specific (Glynn et al., 1983). Hennecke and Fox (1980) reported that until recently, researchers assumed few differences between male and female abusers. Hasin, Grant, and Weinflash (1988) found that little research exists which focuses on those differences. Women comprise only 19% of the clients in federally funded alcohol treatment programs, 31% in federally funded drug treatment programs (Mondanaro, 1988), and only 9% of recovery homes in the United States are for women only (Yoder, 1990). Mondanaro purported that the unique problems of women who are chemically dependent have been under-recognized and under-treated.

Maisto and Connors (1988) stated that, "although there is a long history of conducting research on outcome of treatments for the addictive behaviors, much of the empirical work is of fairly low quality" (p. 449). They also contended that little clinical research has been done by clinicians, and that greater involvement by them is warranted. Barlow, Hayes, and Nelson (1984) identified three activities practitioners must be involved in: (a) consuming research and applying it, (b) using empirical methods to evaluate intervention effectiveness, and (c) initiating research and publishing results. They noted that through these methods, practitioners become accountable for results/outcomes of treatment/intervention. Donovan and Chaney (1985) stated that the "task of clinician and researcher is to generate hypotheses and test them" (p. 407).

Methodology

Several suggestions have been made regarding the research methodology most applicable for drug-related studies. Maisto and Connors (1988) encouraged "outcome researchers in the addictions" to clearly present their "theoretical beliefs about the behavior(s) they are treating before presenting data" (p. 427). Such action would make data more interpretable. They also urged longer follow-up periods (minimally, 18 to 24 months) as essential to evaluate treatment outcomes. These researchers found:

> That fairly frequent follow-up contacts (every one, two, or three months) have the greatest likelihood of yielding sensitive, continuous data on addictive behavior processes, the recovery process, and overall life functioning in general. (p. 448)

Maisto and Connors do indicate, however, that one of the major pitfalls of outcome research in this field is client attrition.

Kaufman (1990-1991) wrote that a commitment must be made to long-term research funding for longitudinal research. He also said that because treatment occurs in stages, testing methods and theories within these stages "might be economically and temporally more feasible than testing an entire program" (p. 113). Marlatt (1985) recommended the use of single-subject designs for evaluating the efficacy of clinical interventions.

Outcome data are often collected using self-reports. Some researchers question the validity and reliability of such data collection. Maisto and Connors (1988) found that data collected from available individuals creates "a positive bias that can make a treatment look better than it may actually be" (p. 448). However, several researchers have determined that self-reports of drug and alcohol use have generally been found to be valid and reliable (Wells et al., 1988; Wolber et al., 1990). Because of the accuracy of self-report data these researchers suggest that further corroboration from outside sources may not be necessary. However, those relying on self-report data should be cautioned that a limitation of any self-report data is that they are subject to what the respondents wish to report to the researcher (Page & Mitchell, 1988). Also, Maisto and Connors cautioned that because data are collected from available clients, a positive bias may exist making treatment look better than it actually is. Kaufman (1990- 1991) observed that investigating treatment effectiveness is difficult because of existing confounding variables.

Both positivistic and phenomenological approaches are recommended for the study of addictions and treatment outcomes. Skog (1985, 1986) has tested social interaction models of drinking behavior using distributional and time series data. Maisto and Connors (1988) urged using regression analysis to test the predictive power of multiple variables. They suggested discriminant analysis as one formal statistical technique that can be used when investigating client successes and failures according to some outcome criterion(a). Grant and Johnstone (1990-1991), see the "emergence of meta-analysis as a set of statistical techniques to combine multiple studies" (p. 204) as a significant development. They see the attempt "to transform the comparative process into quantitative synthesis" as having "great potential to influence the future integration of alternative approaches in drug and alcohol studies" (p. 204). These researchers identified the most crucial contribution of this approach to be "the capacity to quantify the consistency of results across studies for particular research questions" (p. 204). Grant and Johnstone believed meta-analysis, cross-level approaches, and new techniques for longitudinal data analysis are going to positively impact drug related research.

Annis (1980) suggested that qualitative investigation is important to current drug-related research. Laskowitz (1990) supported the semistructured interview as a valuable method of gathering data, because of its flexibility in accumulating information. Gilbert (1990-1991) believed that qualitative research "can be helpful in identifying any mediating or moderating variables that may underlie the correlations, supplying new theoretical propositions for testing" (p. 128). She encouraged study of the meaning of chemical dependency as it relates to other significant behaviors, including recreational behaviors. She supported a variety of qualitative methods (observation, mapping, developing typologies of drinking settings and situations, unstructured and semi-structured interviews, case histories, focus group transcripts, and analysis of various documents) as important to gathering evidence about and contributing to a greater understanding of alcohol use and related variables.

Focusing on support for matching interventions to clients, Gilbert (1990-1991), advocated qualitative methodological approaches, positing that if these interventions are going to be appropriate and effective, detailed knowledge is required "of client characteristics as well as an understanding of the social and meaning contexts in which their alcohol use is embedded" (p. 140). She wrote that qualitative techniques and data collection are:

> Particularly useful for developing and refining theory about how environmental, social factors interact with biological and psychological factors in producing alcohol disorders within and across groups. (p. 139)

Gilbert suggested that qualitative research can produce findings that are especially valuable to policymakers and those providing direct person-to-person services.

Future Drug-Related Research

Smart et al. (1990-1991) stated that "predicting future needs in any research field is difficult to do" (p. 117). They do, however, attempt to outline what they consider to be important drug-related research issues. They identify a need for more research on why people continue to use and/or abuse drugs, and why they stop. Though there has been research on drug use progression, they indicated the steps of de-escalation have been under-investigated. They emphasized the need to study the relationship between ethnicity and drug abuse. These researchers pointed out a need to determine--what levels of drug use are associated with which adverse health and social effects? For many drugs we need to know more about the levels at which addiction occurs and at what levels physical or social problems arise. These issues are made more complex because many heavy users take several drugs, and hence the contribution of any single drug to specific problems is difficult to assess.

Smart et al. (1990-1991) indicated the focus of research and intervention has been on the responsibility of individual; research needs to focus on the responsibilities of the greater social system. They challenged researchers to examine if and what health-based models might serve as alternatives to the total prohibition of drug use.

Relating to student drug use research, Smart et al. (1990-1991) noted the context of decision making as it relates to drug use to be an area in critical need of study. They stated that researchers "need to study the school as the context of choices concerning peers, attitudes, leisure pursuits, and use of alcohol and other drugs" (p. 121). How students perceive stress, which sources of stress are of most concern to them, and how students cope with stress are areas in need of study, according to these researchers. In particular, Smart et al. suggested that researchers investigate the role of drug use in relieving stress, and the alternatives that exist. These researchers also declared that:

> We need to know more about how some people from drug abusing families or social groups are prevented from becoming users, and how such information could be used in developing intervention programs for high-risk groups.
> (p. 120).

Smart et al. (1990-1991) also listed the following questions related to treatment and outcome research:

> What is the minimal effective treatment for drug abusers? How much treatment is really necessary, and how inexpensively can it be delivered? What types of treatment are best for what type of users?
> (p. 122)

Finally, these researchers believed that outcome evaluation needs to be conducted on the effectiveness of self-help programs, particularly in regards for whom they are and are not effective.

Gilbert (1990-1991) stated, "concepts revolving around problematic, deviant, and antisocial alcohol use need to be discovered and evaluated in their sociocultural milieu" (p. 136). Kaufman (1990-1991) remarked that research should be conducted in the area of recovery and relapse, investigating the success of support groups versus self-recovery. Sobell, Sobell, and Ward (1980) indicated that little research exists on treatment effectiveness for poly drug use. Maisto and Connors (1988) offered that drinking behavior has been the primary measurement for outcome assessment. However, they cautioned that drinking behavior should not be the sole focus of research, and that other variables also require measurement.

Future Leisure Research

To date there is a paucity of information on the relationship between recreation/leisure and substance abuse, and on program efficacy (Rancourt, 1991a, 1991b). It seems plausible that the first item on a comprehensive leisure research agenda might be the need to develop a body of knowledge. Since there is so little research about the subject, one might question the role of recreation/leisure and therapeutic recreation interventions and their theoretical bases. There is a need to establish theoretical frameworks from which to conduct research and to choose effective interventions. The author has presented several theories she discerned as most applicable to therapeutic recreation intervention and to effecting psychosocial outcomes. Theories addressing social influences, adaptational and coping mechanisms, existentialism, ego/self-enhancement and self-esteem, family, problem behavior, learned behavior, and social learning theories provide interesting frameworks from which to conduct leisure research. In these early stages, because of a lack of theoretical underpinnings and methodological problems, the author concurs with Gilbert (1990-1991) that "theory building requires an inductive base" (p. 128).

There is a need for inductive, qualitative, exploratory, descriptive, and correlational research. Because of extra-treatment variables, it will be difficult to identify causal relationships. However, there is also a need for experimental designs, clear, theoretically based hypotheses, therapeutic interventions based on theory, and outcome measures to determine program efficacy.

Gilbert (1990-1991) and Martin (1990) have generated research questions which should be of interest to leisure researchers. Related to socialization, Gilbert encouraged researching the array of social contexts in which drinking takes place is an important area of research. Two questions she presented are:

> When and under what circumstances does drinking become the basis
> for inclusion or exclusion in male-only, female-only, and mixed-sex
> social cliques? To what extent is mutual involvement in drinking
> activities and getting drunk together seen as a symbolic
> reinforcement of interpersonal relations . . . ? (p. 137)

Martin, in discussing the efficacy of interventions, asked what are the obligations of the therapist?

Based on O'Dea-Evans (1990) discussion of "rationales" for the provision of leisure programs, the author raises the following research questions:

1. Are therapeutic recreation services able to change negative leisure attitudes that prevent patients from realizing positive leisure and recreational opportunities in their recovery?

2. What is the role of active and passive recreation/leisure pursuits in reducing substance use and abuse?

3. Why does participation in physical fitness activities increase sobriety rates?

4. Do increased socialization skills increase sobriety?

5. Do recreation activities provide mood-altering alternatives to substance use, and which activities are alternatives to which substances?

Several other questions have been generated as a result of preparing this paper. The author hopes that they will provide a foundation for future research on the relationship between recreation/leisure and drug abuse. More research is needed to determine the relationship between and among recreation and physical activity and rehabilitation, recovery, and relapse. It is imperative to determine if there is a relationship between abstinence and between quality sobriety and participation in recreation activities and leisure experiences. By measuring which post-discharge weeks and months tend to be drug free, and the degree and types of participation in recreation activities and leisure experiences, researchers might determine if any and what relationships exist. Regarding lifestyle changes, researchers need to conduct research to determine the impact of participation in recreation activities and leisure experiences on self-esteem, quality of life, life meaning, and perceived freedom.

Much research has been documented throughout this paper regarding the importance of stress reduction to recovery and relapse prevention. Leisure researchers need to determine whether participation in recreation activities reduces stress. Is there a way to measure which activities are most successful in reducing stress? Are some activities better at reducing stress than others? Why? For example, it is common knowledge that aerobic activities release endorphins and alleviate stress. How is stress impacted by listening to music or watching a movie? Findings will assist practitioners in providing efficacious activities and programs.

Regarding the benefits of participation in recreation activities, researchers might attempt to determine which types of recreation activities and leisure experiences meet which needs. Do recreation and leisure programs meet individual cultural and ethnic needs? Are there personal, family, and/or societal factors that contribute to or prevent individuals from participating in recreation activities? Do recreation activities facilitate positive, drug-free social interaction?

Finally, there are questions that need to be addressed regarding treatment interventions and program efficacy. Research data are needed on the impact of family leisure education programs on participation in activities with family and children. How do treatment setting, and length and intensity of treatment influence program effectiveness? Which components of the therapeutic recreation continuum (therapy, leisure education, recreation participation) are most effective in treating those with chemical dependencies? Which programs are most effective and why? What is the relationship between individual success and specific interventions? It might also be beneficial to examine the treatment model (basic or integrative) utilized by the treatment team to determine what, if any, affect it has on what and how recreation and leisure services are provided.

As has been discussed throughout this paper, substance abuse/chemical dependency is a major health and social problem. Yoder (1990) stated that one in four families is affected by substance abuse/chemical dependency. Many recreation and leisure professionals are working in the substance abuse treatment field. It is important that practitioners and researchers begin to systematically study and report the relationship between substance abuse/chemical dependency and recreation and leisure. Findings will not only make a contribution to the substance abuse and leisure fields, but will assist in determining intervention effectiveness and program efficacy. Ultimately, findings will result in more cost efficient and effective services.

References

Akerlind, I., Hornquist, J. O., & Bjurulf, P. (1988). Prognosis in alcoholic rehabilitation: The relative significance of social, psychological and medical factors. The International Journal of the Addictions, 23(11), 1171-1195.

Alfano, A. M., Thurstin, A. H., & Nerviano, V. J. (1987). Cost/benefit estimates from ongoing alcoholism outcome research: A working paper. The International Journal of the Addictions, 22(9), 861-868.

Amaro, H., Beckman, L. J., & Mays, V. M. (1987). A comparison of black and white women entering alcoholism treatment. Journal of Studies on Alcohol, 48, 220-228.

Annis, H. M. (1980). Treatment of alcoholic women. In G. Edwards & M. Grant (Eds.), Alcoholism treatment in transition (pp.), Baltimore: University Park Press.

Annis, H. M. (1986). A relapse prevention model for treatment of alcoholics. In W. R. Miller & N. Heather (Eds.), (pp. 407-421), Treating addictive behaviors: Processes of change. New York: Plenum Press.

Ashery, R. S. (1985). Issues in the brief treatment of drug abusers. In R. S. Ashery (Ed.), Progress in the development of cost-effective treatment for drug abusers (Research Monograph No. 58, pp. 1-5). Rockville, MD: National Institute on Drug Abuse.

Ausubel, D. P. (1980). An interactional approach to narcotic addiction. In D. J. Lettieri, M. Sayers, & H. W. Pearson (Eds.), Theories on drug abuse: Selected contemporary perspectives (Research Monograph No. 30, pp. 4-7). Rockville, MD: National Institute on Drug Abuse.

Bandura, A. (1977a). Social learning theory. Englewood Cliffs, NJ: Prentice Hall.

Bandura, A. (1977b). Self-efficacy: Toward a unifying theory of behavioral change. Psychological Review, 84, 191-215.

Bandura, A. (1978). Reflections on self-efficacy. Advances in Behavioral Research and Therapy, 1, 237-269.

Bandura, A. (1981). Self-referent thought: A developmental analysis of self-efficacy. In J. H. Flavell & L. Ross (Eds.), Social cognitive development: Frontiers and possible futures (pp. 200-239). New York: Cambridge University Press.

Bandura, A. (1982). Self-efficacy mechanism in human agency. American Psychologist, 37, 122-147.

Barchas, J. D. (1985, July). Research on mental illness and addictive disorders. American Journal of Psychiatry, 142(7) (Suppl.).

Barlow, D. H., Hayes, S. C., & Nelson, R. O. (1984). The scientist practitioner. New York: Pergaman Press.

Becker, H. S. (1980). The social bases of drug-induced experiences. In D. J. Lettieri, M. Sayers, & H. W. Pearson (Eds.), Theories on drug abuse: Selected contemporary perspectives (Research Monograph No. 30, pp. 180-190). Rockville, MD: National Institute on Drug Abuse.

Bejerot, N. (1980). Addiction to pleasure: A biological and social-psychological theory of addiction. In D. J. Lettieri, M. Sayers, & H. W. Pearson (Eds.), Theories on drug abuse: Selected contemporary perspectives (Research Monograph No. 30, pp. 246-255). Rockville, MD: National Institute on Drug Abuse.

Bennett, G. (1989). Treating drug abusers. London: Tavistock/Routledge.

Bennett, G., & Woolf, D. S. (1983). Current approaches to substance abuse therapy. In G. Bennett, C. Vourakis, & D. S. Woolf (Eds.), Substance abuse: Pharmacologic, developmental and clinical perspectives (pp. 341-369). New York: John Wiley & Sons.

Bennun, I. (1985). Two approaches to family therapy with alcoholics: Problem-solving and systemic therapy. Journal of Substance Abuse Treatment, 2, 19-26.

Berg, C., & Neulinger, J. (1976). Alcoholic's perception of leisure. Journal of Studies on Alcohol, 37(1), 1625-1632.

Billings, A. G., & Moos, R. H. (1983). Psychosocial processes of recovery among alcoholics and their families: Implications for clinicians and program evaluators. Addictive Behaviors, 8, 205-218.

Botvin, G. J. (1983). Prevention of adolescent substance abuse through the development of personal and social competence. In T. J. Glynn, C. G. Leukefeld, & J. P. Ludpond (Eds.), Preventing adolescent drug abuse: Intervention strategies (Research Monograph No. 47, pp. 115-134). Rockville, MD: National Institute on Drug Abuse.

Brickman, P., Rabinowitz, V., Karuza, J., Coates, D., Cohn, E., & Kidder, L. (1982). Models of helping and coping. American Psychologist, 37, 368-384.

Brower, K. J., Blow, F. C., & Beresford, T. P. (1989). Treatment implications of chemical dependency models: An integrative approach. Journal of Substance Abuse Treatment, 6, 147-157.

Brown, S. (1985). Treating the alcoholic: A developmental model of recovery. New York: Wiley.

Chein, I. (1980). Psychological, social, and epidemiological factors in juvenile drug use. In D. J. Lettieri, M. Sayers, & H. W. Pearson (Eds.), Theories on drug abuse: Selected contemporary perspectives (Research Monograph No. 30, pp. 76-82). Rockville, MD: National Institute on Drug Abuse.

Clayton, R. R., Voss, H. L., Robbins, C., & Skinner, W. F. (1986). Gender differences in drug use: An epidemiological perspective. In B. A. Ray & M. C. Braude (Eds.), Women and drugs: A new era for research (Research Monograph No. 65, pp. 80-98). Rockville, MD: National Institute on Drug Abuse.

Cliffside (staff). (1989). Cliffside: Four winds-westchester's program for psychiatric chemical dependency treatment. Journal of Substance Abuse Treatment, 6, 55-58.

Cohen, F. (1986). A psychosocial typology of drug addicts and implications for treatment. The International Journal of the Addictions, 21(2), 147-154.

Cohen, S. (1985). The substance abuse problems volume two: New issues for the 1980's. New York: The Haworth Press.

Coleman, S. B. (1980). Incomplete mourning and addict/family transactions: A theory for understanding heroin abuse. 8. In D. J. Lettieri, M. Sayers, & H. W. Pearson (Eds.), Theories on drug abuse: Selected contemporary perspectives (Research Monograph No. 30, pp. 83-89). Rockville, MD: National Institute on Drug Abuse.

Conroy, R. W. (1985). The alcohol and drug abuse recovery program of the C. F. Menninger Memorial Hospital. Journal of Substance Abuse Treatment, 2, 59-61.

Corder, B. F., Corder, R. F., & Laidlaw, N. D. (1972). An intensive treatment program for alcoholics and their wives. Quarterly Journal of Studies on Alcohol, 33, 1144-1146.

Craig, R. J., Olson, R., & Shalton, G. (1990). Improvement in psychological functioning among drug abusers: Inpatient treatment compared to outpatient methadone maintenance. Journal of Substance Abuse Treatment, 7(1), 11-19.

Cronbach, L. J. (1982). Designing evaluations of educational and social programs. San Francisco: Jossey-Bass.

Crowley, T. (1972). The reinforcers of drug abuse: Why people take drugs. Comprehensive Psychiatry, 13, 51-62.

DeLeon, G. (1988). The therapeutic community and behavioral science. In B. A. Ray (Ed.), Learning factors in substance abuse (Research Monograph No. 84, pp. 74-98). Rockville, MD: National Institute on Drug Abuse.

Denton, J. L. (1981). Maturation: The development of life skills. Unpublished manuscript, Kearney State College, Kearney.

Dole, V. P., & Nyswander, M. G. (1980). Methadone maintenance: A theoretical perspective. In D. J. Lettieri, M. Sayers, & H. W. Pearson (Eds.), Theories on drug abuse: Selected contemporary perspectives (Research Monograph No. 30, pp. 256-261). Rockville, MD: National Institute on Drug Abuse.

Donovan, J. M. (1986). An etiologic model of alcoholism. American Journal of Psychiatry, 143, 1-11.

Donovan, D. M., & Chaney, E. F. (1985). Alcoholic relapse prevention and intervention: Models and methods. In G. A. Marlatt, & J. R. Gordon (Eds.), Relapse prevention: Maintenance strategies in the treatment of addictive behaviors (pp. 351-416). New York: The Guilford Press.

Dougherty, R. J., & Lesswing, N. J. (1989). Inpatient cocaine abusers: An analysis of psychological and demographic variables. Journal of Substance Abuse Treatment, 6, 45-47.

Douglas, D. B. (1986). Alcoholism as an addiction: The disease concept reconsidered. Journal of Substance Abuse Treatment, 3, 115-120.

Duckert, F. (1987). Recruitment into treatment and effects of treatment for female problem drinkers. Addictive Behaviors, 12(2), 137-143.

Duncan, D., & Gold, R. (1982). Drugs and the whole person. New York: John Wiley & Sons.

Ellis, A., McInerney, J. F., DiGiuseppe, R., & Yeager, R. J. (1988). Rationale-emotive therapy with alcoholics and substance abusers. New York: Pergamon Press.

Eriksen, L., Bjornstad, S., & Gotestam, K. G. (1986). Social skills training in groups for alcoholics: One-year treatment outcome for groups and individuals. Addictive Behaviors, 11, 309-329.

Frances, R. J., & Franklin, J. E. (1989). Concise guide to treatment of alcoholism and addictions. Washington, DC: American Psychiatric Press.

Frederick, C. J. (1980). Drug abuse as learned behavior. In D. J. Lettieri, M. Sayers, & H. W. Pearson (Eds.), Theories on drug abuse: Selected contemporary perspectives (Research Monograph No. 30, pp. 191-194). Rockville, MD: National Institute on Drug Abuse.

George, R. L., & Dustin, D. (1988). Group counseling theory and practice. Englewood Cliffs, NJ: Prentice-Hall.

Gilbert, M. J. (1990-1991). The anthropologist as alcohologist: Qualitative perspectives and methods in alcohol research. The International Journal of the Addictions, 25(24), 127-148.

Glynn, T. J., Pearson, H. W., & Sayers, M. (Eds.) (1983). Women and drugs (Research Issues 31). Rockville, MD: National Institute on Drug Abuse.

Gold, S. R. (1980). The CAP control theory of drug abuse. In D. J. Lettieri, M. Sayers, & H. W. Pearson (Eds.), Theories on drug abuse: Selected contemporary perspectives (Research Monograph No. 30, pp. 8-11). Rockville, MD: National Institute on Drug Abuse.

Goodwin, D. W. (1980). The bad-habit theory of drug abuse. In D. J. Lettieri, M. Sayers, & H. W. Pearson (Eds.), Theories on drug abuse: Selected contemporary perspectives (Research Monograph No. 30, pp. 12-17). Rockville, MD: National Institute on Drug Abuse.

Gorsuch, R. L. (1980). Interactive models of nonmedical drug use. In D. J. Lettieri, M. Sayers, & H. W. Pearson (Eds.), Theories on drug abuse: Selected contemporary perspectives (Research Monograph No. 30, pp. 18-23). Rockville, MD: National Institute on Drug Abuse.

Grant, M., & Johnstone, B. M. (1990-1991). Research priorities for drug and alcohol studies: The next 25 years. The International Journal of the Addictions, 25(24), 201-219.

Greaves, G. (1974). Toward an existential theory of drug dependence. Journal of Nervous and Mental Disease, 159, 263-274.

Greaves, G. B. (1980). An existential theory of drug dependence. In D. J. Lettieri, M. Sayers, & H. W. Pearson (Eds.), Theories on drug abuse: Selected contemporary perspectives (Research Monograph No. 30, pp. 24-28). Rockville, MD: National Institute on Drug Abuse.

Hasin, D. S., Grant, B. F., & Weinflash, J. (1988). Male/female differences in alcohol-related problems: Alcohol rehabiliation patients. The International Journal of the Addictions, 23(5), 437-448.

Hawkins, J. D., & Catalano, R. F. (1985). Aftercare in drug abuse treatment. The International Journal of the Addictions, 20(6-7), 917-945.

Hawkins, J. D., & Fraser, M. W. (1987). The social networks of drug abusers before and after treatment. The International Journal of the Addictions, 22(4), 343-355.

Hendin, H. (1980). Psychosocial theory of drug abuse: A psychodynamic approach. In D. J. Lettieri, M. Sayers, & H. W. Pearson (Eds.), Theories on drug abuse: Selected contemporary perspectives (Research Monograph No. 30, pp. 195-200). Rockville, MD: National Institute on Drug Abuse.

Hennecke, L., & Fox, V. (1980). The woman with alcoholism. In S. E. Gillow & H. S. Peyser (Eds.), Alcoholism: A practical treatment guide. New York: Grune & Stratton.

Henry, P. B. (Ed.). (1989). Practical approaches in treating adolescent chemical dependency: A guide to chemical assessment and intervention. New York: The Haworth Press.

Hill, H. E. (1980). The social deviant and initial addiction to narcotics and alcohol. In D. J. Lettieri, M. Sayers, & H. W. Pearson (Eds.), Theories on drug abuse: Selected contemporary perspectives (Research Monograph No. 30, pp. 90-94). Rockville, MD: National Institute on Drug Abuse.

Hitzhusen, G. (1977). Recreation and leisure counseling for adult psychiatric and alcoholic patients. In A. Epperson et al. (Eds.), Leisure counseling: An aspect of leisure education.

Hochhauser, M. (1980). A chronobiological control theory. In D. J. Lettieri, M. Sayers, & H. W. Pearson (Eds.), Theories on drug abuse: Selected contemporary perspectives (Research Monograph No. 30, pp. 262-268). Rockville, MD: National Institute on Drug Abuse.

Huba, G. J., Wingard, J. A., & Bentler, P. M. (1980). Framework for an interactive theory of drug use. In D. J. Lettieri, M. Sayers, & H. W. Pearson (Eds.), Theories on drug abuse: Selected contemporary perspectives (Research Monograph No. 30, pp. 95-101). Rockville, MD: National Institute on Drug Abuse.

Iso-Ahola, S. E. (1988). Research in therapeutic recreation. Therapeutic Recreation Journal, 22(1), 7-13.

Jacobs, E. E., Harvill, R. L., & Mason, R. L. (1988). Group Counseling Strategies and Skills. Pacific Grove, CA: Brooks/Cole Publishing.

Jaffe, J. H. (1970). Drug addiction and drug abuse. In L. S. Goodman & A. Gilman (Eds.), The pharmacological basis of therapeutics (pp. 276-312). New York: Macmillan.

James, M. R., & Townsley, R. K. (1989). Activity therapy services and chemical dependency rehabilitation. Journal of Alcohol and Drug Education, 34(3), 48-53.

Jellinek, E. M. (1960). The disease concept of alcoholism. New Haven, CT: Hillhouse Press.

Jessor, R., & Jessor, S. (1977). Problem behavior in psychosocial development: Longitudinal study of youth. New York: Academic Press.

Jessor, R., & Jessor, S. (1980). A social-psychological framework for studying drug use. In D. J. Lettieri, M. Sayers, & H. W. Pearson (Eds.), Theories on drug abuse: Selected contemporary perspectives (Research Monograph No. 30, pp. 102-109). Rockville, MD: National Institute on Drug Abuse.

Johnson, B. D. (1980). Toward a theory of drug subcultures. In D. J. Lettieri, M. Sayers, & H. W. Pearson (Eds.), Theories on drug abuse: Selected contemporary perspectives (Research Monograph No. 30, pp. 110-119). Rockville, MD: National Institute on Drug Abuse.

Jonas, D. F., & Jonas, A. D. (1980). A bioanthropological overview of addiction. In D. J. Lettieri, M. Sayers, & H. W. Pearson (Eds.), Theories on drug abuse: Selected contemporary perspectives (Research Monograph No. 30, pp. 269-277). Rockville, MD: National Institute on Drug Abuse.

Kandel, D. B. (1980). Developmental stages in adolescent drug involvement. In D. J. Lettieri, M. Sayers, & H. W. Pearson (Eds.), Theories on drug abuse: Selected contemporary perspectives (Research Monograph No. 30, pp. 120-127). Rockville, MD: National Institute on Drug Abuse.

62

Kanfer, F. H. (1986). Implications of a self-regulation model of therapy for treatment of addictive behaviors. In W. R. Miller, & N. Heather (Eds.), Treating addictive behaviors: Processes of change. New York: Plenum Press.

Kaplan, H. B. (1980). Self-esteem and self-derogation theory of drug abuse. In D. J. Lettieri, M. Sayers, & H. W. Pearson (Eds.), Theories on drug abuse: Selected contemporary perspectives (Research Monograph No. 30, pp. 128-131). Rockville, MD: National Institute on Drug Abuse.

Kaplan, H. (1990). From theory to practice: The planned treatment of drug users. The International Journal of the Addictions, 25(8), 957-981.

Kaufman, E. (1989). The psychotherapy of dually diagnosed patients. Journal of Substance Abuse Treatment, 6, 9-18.

Kaufman, E. (1990-1991). Critical aspects of the psychodynamics of substance abuse and the evaluation of their application to a psychotherapeutic approach. The International Journal of the Addictions, 25(2A), 97-116.

Kaufman, E., & Kaufman, P. W. (1979). Family therapy of drug and alcohol abuse. New York: Gardner Press.

Keller, M. (1976). The disease concept of alcoholism reconsidered. Journal of Studies on Alcohol, 37, 1694-1717.

Khantzian, E. J. (1980). An ego/self theory of substance dependence: A contemporary psychoanalytic perspective. In D. J. Lettieri, M. Sayers, & H. W. Pearson (Eds.), Theories on drug abuse: Selected contemporary perspectives (Research Monograph No. 30, pp. 29-33). Rockville, MD: National Institute on Drug Abuse.

Kissin, B. (1977). Theory and practice in the treatment of alcoholism. In B. Kissin, & H. Begleiter (Eds.), The biology of alcoholism: Treatment and rehabilitation of the chronic alcoholic (Vol. 5, pp. 1-51). New York: Plenum Press.

Kosten, T. A., Kosten, T. R., & Rounsaville, B. J. (1989). Personality disorders in opiate addicts show prognostic specificity. Journal of Substance Abuse Treatment, 6, 163-168.

Kosten, T. R., & Kleber, H. D. (1988). Differential diagnosis of psychiatric comorbidity in substance abusers. Journal of Substance Abuse Treatment, 5, 201-206.

Kunstler, R. (1991). Substance abuse. In D. R. Austin & M. E. Crawford (Eds.), Therapeutic recreation: An introduction (pp. 119-137). Englewood Cliffs, NJ: Prentice-Hall.

Kurtz, E. (1979). Not-God, a history of alcoholics anonymous. Center City, MN: Hazelden Educational Services.

Laskowitz, D. (1990). From theory to practice: The planned treatment of drug users. The International Journal of the Addictions, 24(7), 819-859.

Lettieri, D. J., Sayers, M., & Pearson, H. W. (Eds.). (1980). Theories on drug abuse: Selected contemporary perspectives (Research Monograph No. 30). Rockville, MD: National Institute on Drug Abuse. (1980).

Levine, H. G. (1978). The discovery of addiction: Changing conceptions of habitual drunkenness in America. Journal of Studies on Alcohol, 39, 143-174.

Levy, M. S., & Mann, D. W. (1988). The special treatment team: An inpatient approach to the mentally ill alcoholic patient. Journal of Substance Abuse Treatment, 5, 219-227.

Lewis, J. A., Dana, R. Q., & Blevins, G. A. (1988). Substance abuse counseling: An individualized approach. Pacific Grove, CA: Brooks/Cole Publishing.

Lindesmith, A. R. (1980). A general theory of addiction to opiate-type drugs. In D. J. Lettieri, M. Sayers, & H. W. Pearson (Eds.), Theories on drug abuse: Selected contemporary perspectives (Research Monograph No. 30, pp. 34-37). Rockville, MD: National Institute on Drug Abuse.

Litman, G. (1986). Alcoholism survival: The prevention of relapse. In W.R. Miller, & N. Heather (Eds.), Treating addictive behaviors: Processes of change (pp. 398-405). New York: Plenum Press.

Loney, J. (1980). The Iowa theory of substance abuse among hyperactive adolescents. In D. J. Lettieri, M. Sayers, & H. W. Pearson (Eds.), Theories on drug abuse: Selected contemporary perspectives (Research Monograph No. 30, pp. 132-136). Rockville, MD: National Institute on Drug Abuse.

Ludwig, A. M. (1988). Understanding the alcoholic's mind. New York: Oxford University Press.

Lukoff, I. F. (1980). Toward a sociology of drug use. In D. J. Lettieri, M. Sayers, & H. W. Pearson (Eds.), Theories on drug abuse: Selected contemporary perspectives (Research Monograph No. 30, pp. 201-211). Rockville, MD: National Institute on Drug Abuse.

MacDonald, J. G. (1987). Predictors of treatment outcome for alcoholic women. The International Journal of the Addictions, 22(3), 235-248.

Maisto, S. A., & Caddy, G. R. (1981). Self-control and addictive behavior: Present status and prospects. International Journal of Addictions, 16, 109-133.

Maisto, S. A., & Connors, G. J. (1988). Assessment of treatment outcome. In D. M. Donovan, & G. A. Marlatt (Eds.), Assessment of addictive disorders (pp. 421-453). New York: The Guilford Press.

Mann, D. W. (1989). Inpatient treatment of the mentally ill substance abuser: Some medicolegal concerns. Journal of Substance Abuse Treatment, 6, 19-21.

Marlatt, G. A. (1985). Relapse prevention: Theoretical rationale and overview of the model. In G. A. Marlatt, & J. R. Gordon (Eds.), Relapse prevention (pp. 3-70). New York: Guilford Press.

Marlatt, G. A. (1988). Matching clients to treatment: Treatment models and stages of change. In D. M. Donovan, & G. A. Marlatt (Eds.), Assessment of addictive behaviors (pp. 474-483), New York: Guilford Press.

Marlatt, G. A., & Gordon, J. R. (1985). Relapse prevention: Maintenance strategies in the treatment of addictive behaviors. New York: Guilford Press.

Martin, W. (1990). From theory to practice: The planned treatment of drug users. The International Journal of the Addictions, 25(5), 579-598.

Martin, W. R. (1980). Emerging concepts concerning drug abuse. In D. J. Lettieri, M. Sayers, & H. W. Pearson (Eds.), Theories on drug abuse: Selected contemporary perspectives (Research Monograph No. 30, pp. 278-285). Rockville, MD: National Institute on Drug Abuse.

Matuschka, E. (1985). Treatment, outcomes, and clinical evaluation. In T. E. Bratter, & G. G. Forest (Eds.), Alcoholism and substance abuse (pp. 193-224). New York: The Free Press.

McAuliffe, W. E., & Ch'ien, J. M. N. (1986). Recovery training and self help: A relapse prevention program for treated opiate addicts. Journal of Substance Abuse Treatment, 3, 9-20.

McAuliffe, W. E., & Gordon, R. A. (1980). Reinforcement and the combination effects: Summary of a theory of opiate addiction. In D. J. Lettieri, M. Sayers, & H. W. Pearson (Eds.), Theories on drug abuse: Selected contemporary perspectives (Research Monograph No. 30, pp. 137-141). Rockville, MD: National Institute on Drug Abuse.

McCrady, B. S., Dean, L., Dubreuil, E., & Swanson, S. (1985). The problem drinker's project: A programmatic application of social-learning based treatment. In G. A. Marlatt & J. R. Gordon (Eds.), Relapse prevention: Maintenance strategies in the treatment of addictive behaviors (pp. 417-471). New York: The Guilford Press.

McLaughlin, L. T. (1980). Leisure counseling with drug dependent individuals and alcoholics. Leisurability, 71(1), 9-15.

McLellan, A. T., & Druley, K. A. (1977). Non-random relation between drugs of abuse and psychiatric diagnosis. Journal of Psychiatric Research, 13, 179-184.

Milkman, H., & Frosch, W. (1980). Theory of drug use. In D. J. Lettieri, M. Sayers, & H. W. Pearson (Eds.), Theories on drug abuse: Selected contemporary perspectives (Research Monograph No. 30, pp. 38-45). Rockville, MD: National Institute on Drug Abuse.

Miller, W. R. (1985). Motivation for treatment: A review with special emphasis on alcoholism. Psychological Bulletin, 98(1), 84-107.

Miller, W. R., & Heather, N. (1986). Treating addictive behaviors: Processes of change. New York: Plenum Press.

Miller, W. R., & Hester, R. K. (1986). The effectiveness of alcoholism treatment: What research reveals. In W. R. Miller & N. Heather (Eds.), Treating addictive behaviors: Processes of change (pp. 121-174). New York: Plenum Press.

Miller, W. R., & Pechacek, T. C. (1987). New roads: Assessing and treating psychological dependence. Journal of Substance Abuse Treatment, 4, 73-77.

Misra, R. R. (1980). Achievement, anxiety, and addiction. In D. J. Lettieri, M. Sayers, & H. W. Pearson (Eds.), Theories on drug abuse: Selected contemporary perspectives (Research Monograph No. 30, pp. 212-214). Rockville, MD: National Institute on Drug Abuse.

Mondanaro, J. (1988). Chemically dependent women: Assessment and treatment. Lexington, MA: Lexington Books.

Naegle, M. A. (1981, August 12-14). Conflicts for the alcoholic woman in treatment. Presented at the American Nurses Association's (ANA) Division on Psychiatric and Mental Health Nursing Practice and the ANA Council of Specialists in Psychiatric and Mental Health Nursing Conference, Portland, OR.

Nathan, P. E. (1985). Alcoholism: A cognitive social learning approach. Journal of Substance Abuse Treatment, 2, 169-173.

Nathan, P. E., & Skinstead, A. H. (1987). Outcomes of treatment for alcohol problems: Current methods, problems, and results. Journal of Consulting and Clinical Psychology, 55, 332-340.

National Institute on Alcohol Abuse and Alcoholism. (1990). Seventh special report to the U.S. Congress on alcohol and health from the secretary, department of health and human services (ADM-281-88-0002). Rockville, MD: Author.

National Institute on Drug Abuse. (1987). Drug abuse and drug abuse research: The second triennial report to Congress from the Secretary of Health and Human Services, (DHHS Publication No. ADU 87-1486). Washington, DC: U.S. Government Printing Office.

O'Connell, D. F. (1989). Treating the high risk adolescent: A survey of effective programs and interventions. In P. B. Henry (Ed.), Practical approaches in treating adolescent chemical dependency: A guide to clinical assessment and intervention. New York: The Haworth Press.

O'Dea-Evans, P. (1990). Leisure education for addicted persons. Algonquin, IL: Peapod Publications.

O'Farrell, T. J. (1989). Marital and family therapy in alcoholism treatment. Journal of Substance and Abuse Treatment, 6, 23-29.

Page, R. D., & Badgett, S. (1984). Alcoholism treatment with environmental support contracting. American Journal of Drug and Alcohol Abuse, 10, 589-605.

Page, R. C., & Mitchell, S. (1988). The effects of two therapeutic communities on illicit drug users between six months and one year after treatment. The International Journal of the Addictions, 23(6), 591-601.

Pattison, E. M., Sobell, M. B., & Sobell, L. C. (1977). Emerging concepts of alcohol dependence. New York: Springer.

Peele, S. (1980). Addiction to an experience: A social-psychological-pharmacological theory of addiction. In D. J. Lettieri, M. Sayers, & H. W. Pearson (Eds.), Theories on drug abuse: Selected contemporary perspectives (Research Monograph No. 30, pp. 142-146). Rockville, MD: National Institute on Drug Abuse.

Peele, S. (1989). Diseasing of America: Addiction treatment out of control. Lexington, MA: Lexington Books.

Peters, A. C. (1984). Disease or morality? Journal of the Massachusetts Dental Society, 33, 167-170.

Prescott, J. W. (1980). Somatosensory affectional deprivation (SAD) theory of drug and alcohol use. In D. J. Lettieri, M. Sayers, & H. W. Pearson (Eds.), Theories on drug abuse: Selected contemporary perspectives (Research Monograph No. 30, pp. 286-296). Rockville, MD: National Institute on Drug Abuse.

Rainwater, A. B. (1983). Drug abuse prevention: Leisure and recreation. In G. Ititzhusen (Ed.), Expanding horizons in therapeutic recreation, 11, 261-273.

Rancourt, A. M. (1989). Leisure education and the family. Visions in Leisure and Business. 7(4), 23-33.

Rancourt, A. M. (1991a). (in press). An exploration of the relationships among substance abuse, recreation, and leisure for women who abuse substances.

Rancourt, A. M. (1991b, April 7). Results of a past discharge survey of women who participated in a six month comprehensive leisure education program while in substance abuse treatment. Paper presented at the American Alliance of Health, Physical Education, Recreation, and Dance Symposium on Drugs and Drug Education, San Francisco, CA.

Rancourt, A. M., & Howe, C. Z. (1991). A preliminary, modified delphi study of expected outcomes of therapeutic recreation (TR) services for persons with chemical dependencies. Manuscript submitted for publication.

Raw, M. (1986). Smoking cessation strategies. In W. R. Miller & N. Heather (Eds.), Treating addictive behaviors: Processes of change (pp. 279-287). New York: Plenum Press.

Reed, B. G. (1987). Developing women-sensitive drug dependence treatment services: Why so difficult? Journal of Psychoactive Drugs, 19, 151-164.

Regier, D. A., Farmer, M. E., Rae, D. S., Locke, B. Z., Keith, S. J., Judd, L. L., & Goodwin, F. K. (1990, November 21). Comorbidity of mental disorders with alcohol and other drug abuse: Results from the epidemiologic catchment area (ECA) study. Journal of the American Medical Association, 264(19), 2511-2518.

Rioux, D., & Van Meter, W. (1990). The ABCs of awareness: A multimodal approach to relapse prevention and intervention. The College Hill medical center program. Journal of Substance Abuse Treatment, 7(1), 61-63.

Robins, L. N. (1980). The natural history of drug abuse. In D. J. Lettieri, M. Sayers, & H. W. Pearson (Eds.), Theories on drug abuse: Selected contemporary perspectives (Research Monograph No. 30, pp. 215-224). Rockville, MD: National Institute on Drug Abuse.

Rohsenow, D. J., Corbett, R., & Devine, D. (1988). Molested as children: A hidden contribution to substance abuse? Journal of Substance Abuse Treatment, 5, 13-18.

Sessoms, H. D., & Oakley, S. R. (1969). Recreation, leisure and the alcoholic. Journal of Leisure Research, 1(1), 21-30.

Schuckit, M. A. (1980). A theory of alcohol and drug abuse: A genetic approach. In D. J. Lettieri, M. Sayers, & H. W. Pearson (Eds.), Theories on drug abuse: Selected contemporary perspectives (Research Monograph No. 30, pp. 297-302). Rockville, MD: National Institute on Drug Abuse.

Shaffer, H. J. (1985). The discovery of addiction: Levine and the philosophical foundations of drug abuse treatment. Journal of Substance Abuse Treatment, 2, 41-57.

Shaffer, H. J. (1987). The epistemology of "addictive disease": The Lincoln-Douglas debate. Journal of Substance Abuse Treatment, 4, 103-113.

Shaffer, H. J., & Neuhaus, C., Jr. (1984). Testing hypothesis: An approach for the assessment of addictive behaviors. In H. B. Milkman, & H. J. Shaffer (Eds.), Addictions: Multidisciplinary perspectives and treatments (pp. 87-103). Lexington, MA: Lexington Books.

Sheridan, P. M. (1976). Therapeutic recreation and the alcoholic. Therapeutic Recreation Journal, 10(1), 14-17.

Simon, E. J. (1980). Opiate receptors and their implications for drug addiction. In D. J. Lettieri, M. Sayers, & H. W. Pearson (Eds.), Theories on drug abuse: Selected contemporary perspectives (Research Monograph No. 30, pp. 303-308). Rockville, MD: National Institute on Drug Abuse.

Simpson, D. D., Crandall, R., Savage, L. J., & Pavia-Krueser, E. (1981). Leisure of opiate addicts at posttreatment follow-up. Journal of Counseling Psychology, 28(1), 36-39.

Skog, O. J. (1985). The collectivity of drinking cultures: A theory of the distribution of alcohol consumption. British Journal of Addiction, 80, 83-99.

Skog, O. J. (1986). The long waves of alcohol consumption: A social network perspective on cultural change. Social Networks, 8, 1-32.

Smart, R. G. (1980). An availability-proneness theory of illicit drug abuse. In D. J. Lettieri, M. Sayers, & H. W. Pearson (Eds.), Theories on drug abuse: Selected contemporary perspectives (Research Monograph No. 30, pp. 46-49). Rockville, MD: National Institute on Drug Abuse.

Smart, R. G., Allison, K. R., Cheung, Y., Erickson, P. G., Shain, M., & Single, E. (1990-1991). Future research needs in policy, prevention, and treatment for drug abuse problems. The International Journal of the Addictions, 25(2A), 117-126.

Smith, G. M. (1980). Perceived effects of substance use: A general theory. In D. J. Lettieri, M. Sayers, & H. W. Pearson (Eds.), Theories on drug abuse: Selected contemporary perspectives (Research Monograph No. 30, pp. 50-58). Rockville, MD: National Institute on Drug Abuse.

Smith-Peterson, C. (1983). Substance abuse treatment and cultural diversity. In G. Bennett, C. Vourakis, & D. S., Woolf (Eds.), Substance abuse: Pharmacologic, developmental and clinical perspectives. New York: John Wiley and Sons.

Sobell, L. C., Sobell, M. B., & Ward, E. (Eds.). (1980). Evaluating alcohol and drug abuse treatment effectiveness: Recent advances. New York: Pergamon Press.

Spotts, J. V., & Shontz, F. C. (1980). A life-theme theory of chronic drug abuse. In D. J. Lettieri, M. Sayers, & H. W. Pearson (Eds.), Theories on drug abuse: Selected contemporary perspectives (Research Monograph No. 30, pp. 59-70). Rockville, MD: National Institute on Drug Abuse.

Stanton, M. D. (1980). A family theory of drug abuse. In D. J. Lettieri, M. Sayers, & H. W. Pearson (Eds.), Theories on drug abuse: Selected contemporary perspectives (Research Monograph No. 30, pp. 147-156). Rockville, MD: National Institute on Drug Abuse.

Steffenhagen, R. A. (1980). Self-esteem theory of drug abuse. In D. J. Lettieri, M. Sayers, & H. W. Pearson (Eds.), Theories on drug abuse: Selected contemporary perspectives (Research Monograph No. 30, pp. 157-163). Rockville, MD: National Institute on Drug Abuse.

Stimmel, B. (1983). Psychosocial constructs of alcoholism and substance abuse: Advances in alcohol and substance abuse. New York: The Haworth Press.

Talbott, G. D. (1983, July/August). The disease of chemical dependence: From concept to precept. Counselor, pp. 18-19.

Tober, G. (1989). Changing conceptions of the nature of drug abuse. In G. Bennett (Ed.), Treating drug abusers (pp. 9-24). London: Tavistock/Routledge.

Trimble, J. E. (1990). Ethnic specification, validation prospects, and the future of drug use research. The International Journal of the Addictions, 25(2A), 149-170.

Vaillant, G. E. (1983). The natural history of alcoholism: Causes, patterns, and paths to recovery. MA: Harvard University Press.

Vogler, R. E., & Bartz, W. R. (1982). The better way to drink: Moderation and control of problem drinking. New York: Simon & Schuster.

Vourakis, C. (1983). Women in substance abuse treatment. In G. Bennett, C. Vourakis, & D. S. Woolf (Eds.), Substance abuse: Pharmacologic developmental, and clinical perspectives (pp. 383-397). New York: John Wiley and Sons.

Wallace, B. C. (1987). Cocaine dependence treatment on an inpatient detoxification unit. Journal of Substance Abuse Treatment, 4, 85-92.

Wallace, J. (1986). The other problems of alcoholics. Journal of Substance Abuse Treatment, 3, 163-171.

Wallace, J., McNeil, D., Gilfillan, D., MacLean, K., & Fanella, F. (1988). Six-month treatment outcomes in socially stable alcoholics: Abstinence rates. Journal of Substance Abuse Treatment, 5, 247-252.

Weidman, A. (1985). Engaging the families of substance abusing adolescents in family therapy. Journal of Substance Abuse Treatment, 2, 97-105.

Wells, E. A., Hawkins, J. D., & Catalano, R. F. (1988). Choosing drug use measures for treatment outcome studies. I. The influence of measurement approach on treatment results. The International Journal of the Addictions, 23(8), 851-873.

Wikler, A. (1973). Dynamics of drug dependence: Implications of a conditioning theory for research and treatment. Archives of General Psychiatry, 28, 611-616.

Wikler, A. (1980). A theory of opioid dependence. In D. J. Lettieri, M. Sayers, & H. W. Pearson (Eds.), Theories on drug abuse: Selected contemporary perspectives (Research Monograph No. 30, pp. 174-179). Rockville, MD: National Institute on Drug Abuse.

Winick, C. (1980). A theory of drug dependence based on role, access to, and attitudes toward drugs. In D. J. Lettieri, M. Sayers, & H. W. Pearson (Eds.), Theories on drug abuse: Selected contemporary perspectives (Research Monograph No. 30, pp. 225-235). Rockville, MD: National Institute on Drug Abuse.

Wolber, G., Carne, W. F., & Alexander, R. (1990). The validity of self-reported abstinence and quality sobriety following chemical dependency treatment. The International Journal of the Addictions, 25(5), 495-513.

Woody, G. E., Luborsky, L., McLellan, A. T., & O'Brien, C. P. (1986). Psychotherapy as an adjunct to methadone treatment. In R. E. Meyer (Ed.), Psychotherapy and addictive disorders (pp.). New York: The Guilford Press.

Wurmser, L. (1980). Drug use as a protective system. In D. J. Lettieri, M. Sayers, & H. W. Pearson (Eds.), Theories on drug abuse: Selected contemporary perspectives (Research Monograph No. 30, pp. 71-75). Rockville, MD: National Institute on Drug Abuse.

Wurmser, L. (1987). Flight from conscience: Experiences with the psychoanalytic treatment of compulsive drug abusers. Journal of Substance Abuse Treatment, 4, 157-168.

Yoder, B. (1990). The recovery resource book. Forest Knolls, CA: Wink Books.

Zackon, F., McAuliffe, W. E., & Ch'ien, J. M. N. (1985). Addict aftercare: Recovery training and self help. Rockville, MD: National Institute on Drug Abuse.

Zinberg, N. E. (1980). The social setting as a control mechanism in intoxicant use. In D. J. Lettieri, M. Sayers, & H. W. Pearson (Eds.), Theories on drug abuse: Selected contemporary perspectives (Research Monograph No. 30, pp. 236-245). Rockville, MD: National Institute on Drug Abuse.

Zweben, A., Pearlman, S., & Li, S. (1983). Reducing attrition from conjoint therapy with alcoholic couples. Drugs and Alcohol Dependence, 11, 321-331.

Zweben, J. E. (1986). Recovery oriented psychotherapy. Journal of Substance Abuse Treatment, 3, 255-267.

CHAPTER 4

THE BENEFITS OF THERAPEUTIC RECREATION IN DEVELOPMENTAL DISABILITIES [1]

John Dattilo & Stuart Schleien

Introduction

The paper contains an examination of the concepts of leisure, recreation, play, and free time in relation to people with developmental disabilities. A review of the literature occurred in an attempt to identify recent efficacy based research studies relevant to the discipline of therapeutic recreation.

The initial section of the paper, "diagnosis and settings," includes definitions of developmental disabilities, mental retardation, and severe disabilities. Clarification of the classifications of mental retardation and a description of limitations associated with mental retardation are also provided in the first section. The first section concludes with a description of common settings where leisure services may be provided to persons with developmental disabilities.

Theoretical foundations associated with the application of therapeutic recreation for people with developmental disabilities are presented in the following section of the paper identified as "theoretical foundations." The first theoretical foundations are presented under the category of leisure skill development. An analysis of the theoretical foundations associated with autonomy in the leisure experience followed the discussion on leisure skills. The complex issue of community integration and the underlying concepts of least restrictive environments, normalization, and age-appropriate behaviors were addressed. Finally, a description is provided on the theoretical foundations related to social skills and friendships.

The major section of the paper was devoted to a description of the "documented and expected/implied outcomes." Review of the literature is presented in relation to each of the four theoretical foundations (recreation skills

[1] Authors are listed alphabetically. Contributions are considered to be equal. Development was partially supported by Grant Project No. H029F90067 funded by the Office of Special Education and Rehabilitative Services, the U.S. Department of Education. The opinions expressed herein do not necessarily reflect the opinions of the U.S. Department of Education, and no official endorsement should be inferred.

instruction, autonomy to experience leisure, community integration, social skills, and friendship development). The first section on recreation skills instruction identifies the need for the expansion of leisure repertoires in individuals with developmental disabilities. It also describes intervention studies that address comparisons between individuals with and without disabilities, skill deficits, assessment strategies, development of collateral skills, use of behavioral methods, community recreation skills, and generalization and maintenance. The section on autonomy in the leisure experience is organized into the three major categories of making choices, demonstrating preferences, and engaging in reciprocal communication. Empirical investigations are reviewed related to the section on community integration, as well as the section on social skills and friendship development. Interventions designed to facilitate integration into community recreation programs, development of social skills, and enhancement of friendships are reviewed. The literature devoted to each of these four categories is presented by the identification of the need to address these categories and a description of interventions designed and implemented in an attempt to respond to the identified need.

The narrative portion of the paper is concluded with a section describing "recommendations for future research" determining the efficacy of therapeutic recreation for people with developmental disabilities. This section is also organized based on the theoretical foundations. The first area, recreation skills instruction, is divided into the two primary sets of recommendations of research on recreation skill and collateral skill development. Recommendations associated with the theoretical foundation of autonomy to experience leisure is divided into the three primary areas of research on choice-making, identification of preferences, and facilitating reciprocal communication. Seven specific recommendations associated with community integration are presented in the third area. Finally, recommendations made relative to both research promoting social interactions and friendships are provided.

It is the hope of the authors that the contents of this paper will help clarify and organize the literature describing attempts to demonstrate the efficacy of therapeutic recreation for people with developmental disabilities. More importantly, this paper is intended to stimulate thought and discussion related to future systematic attempts at documenting the efficacy of therapeutic recreation for people with developmental disabilities.

Diagnosis and Settings

Definition of Developmental Disability

The "developmental period" refers to the time after conception when growth and change occur at a rapid rate. This rate of development typically begins to slow as the person enters adulthood (identified as age 18, 21, or 22). A "developmental disability," as reported in Public Law 95-602, the Rehabilitation Act Amendments, established in 1978, refers to a severe, chronic disability that: (a) is attributable to a mental and/or physical impairment, (b) is manifested before age 22, (c) is likely to continue indefinitely, and (d) results in substantial functional limitations (Grossman, 1983).

Definition of Mental Retardation

According to the American Association on Mental Deficiency (currently, American Association on Mental Retardation) "mental retardation" refers to significantly subaverage general intellectual functioning, resulting in or associated with concurrent impairments in adaptive behavior, and manifested during the developmental period (Grossman, 1983). Identification of "significantly subaverage intellectual functioning" occurs when a person receives a score on standardized measures of intelligence quotient (IQ) that is below the score of the average person taking the test to such a degree (two standard deviations) that society has determined this person requires assistance in development beyond what is typically provided by the family and community. The average IQ has been determined to be a score of approximately 100 and a score below approximately 70 results in a significantly subaverage intellectual functioning. Although IQ and intelligence are frequently used interchangeably, it is important to remember that these concepts are not synonymous. The IQ score is only an estimate of an individual's rate of intellectual development as compared with the average rate for same-age peers (Gottlieb, 1987). According to Gottlieb, the concept of intelligence is often clouded by: (a) terminology confusion, (b) highly specialized classification systems, (c) varying methods of assessment and data interpretation, (d) heterogeneity of population samples, and (e) limited practical application assessment of information to life situations.

Although various instruments have been developed that attempt to compensate for particular disabilities (i.e., Peabody Picture Vocabulary Test), a person's lack of performance on a particular standardized measure of IQ can be the result of many factors other than actual intelligence. For instance, some people may not have been exposed to the items presented on the test due to cultural and environmental differences, or perhaps people may have difficulty communicating their response due to physical or neurological impairments, other individuals could also be experiencing pain and sickness, the attitudes of the examiner and examinee can also influence test scores (Zigler & Butterfield, 1968). The aforementioned situations may reduce one's performance on an intelligence test and perhaps bring into question the reported scores.

According to Gunn (1975) "adaptive behavior" relates to the effectiveness with which individuals meet the standards of personal independence and social responsibility expected of their age and cultural group, including maturation, learning, and social adjustment. The focus of adaptive behavior is on the ability of an individual to function as others within the same age and cultural group (Deutsch, Bustow, Wish, & Wish, 1982). Therefore, impairments in adaptive behavior are defined as significant limitations in an individual's effectiveness in meeting standards of maturation, learning, personal independence, and/or social responsibility (Grossman, 1983). Adaptive Behavior Scales are used to determine individuals' independence relative to maturation, learning, and social adjustment. The extent of difficulty that a person with mental retardation experiences related to expressing adaptive behavior is primarily related to the degree of intellectual impairment. However, Baroff (1986) reminds us that adaptive behaviors are also strongly affected by both society's general attitudes toward persons with limited intelligence and the services they receive.

The definition of mental retardation established by the American Association on Mental Deficiency is based on the following assumptions that should alert the reader to some possible interpretation problems:

1. Retardation is a general phenomenon.

2. Intelligence, as defined by tests, is permanent.

3. Defined intelligence is sufficiently general to describe all functioning and imply potential.

4. Adaptive behavior includes both spontaneous and trained adaptation.

5. There is a specific developmental period for all people.

6. It is meaningful to catalogue people according to their tested intelligence and adaptive behavior.

7. Retardation is more meaningfully conceptualized as a phenomenon existing within individuals rather than the context in which they exist.

As a result of these assumptions, Gold (1978) proposed an alternative definition that refers to mental retardation as a level of functioning which requires from society significantly above average training procedures and superior assets in adaptive behavior, manifested throughout life. Therefore, the person with mental retardation is characterized by the extent of training required for the person to learn, and not by limitations to what the person can learn. The height of a person's level of functioning is determined by the availability of training technology and the amount of resources society is willing to allocate, and not by significant limitations in biological potential. Gold's proposed definition of mental retardation contains the following underlying assumptions:

1. Mental retardation is not a general phenomenon.

2. Intelligence, as defined by tests, has limited use.

3. No behavior clearly defines potential.

4. Adaptive behavior can be assumed.

5. Development is lifelong.

6. Educate people and avoid testing them.

7. Mental retardation is most meaningfully conceptualized as a phenomenon existing within the society which can only be observed through the depressed performance of some of the individuals in that society.

Therefore, although the phrase, mental retardation, is used throughout this chapter, the label alone means little. The unique profile of cognitive, adaptive, educational, and recreational ability, as well as the bio-medical status associated with each person is critical for appropriate planning and implementation of effective services (Wodrich & Joy, 1986).

Definition of Severe Disabilities

To what group of individuals does the term, severe multiple disability, refer? This question is not easily answered and requires an analysis of the factors influencing such a definition. A review of the terms currently being used by professionals reveals an inconsistency in defining a specific population (Fredericks, 1987). Perhaps the single greatest factor influencing this consistency is the process of definition. Definitions have been created based on the interests of the particular agency serving the individual with a severe multiple disability. This type of influence has resulted in an abundance of terms all somewhat workable but, limited by an unclear variation in who exactly is being included or excluded (Schleien, Light, McAvoy, & Baldwin, 1989).

Two types of descriptive terms have emerged. There are generic descriptions that attempt to describe the population in a broad sense. These terms include such descriptions as persons with dual sensory handicaps and profound handicaps. The second type of terms used are those that describe by referring to a specific disability. Examples of this kind of description include persons who are profoundly mentally retarded and cerebral palsied-deaf. The abundance of terms is created by four types of influencing agencies that all adopt their own definition. These agencies are categorized as: (a) residential/ community living, (b) vocational, (c) recreational, and (d) educational.

This problem of definition is made apparent by comparing the definition of "severely handicapped" as determined by the Rehabilitation Services Administration and the Office of Special Education Programs. Both agencies describe an individual with a disability that seriously limits functional ability but, this functional ability is assessed in regard to the intensive support needed to meet either vocational objectives or educational objectives, respectively. Defined in this way, two distinctly different definitions are created. The result is that a person with a severe handicap is categorized by the type of service the agency provides (Bellamy, 1985).

A definition problem also arises when the population is described by the individual's specific disability. This method may exclude some individuals from service by being too limited in who is included under that disability. For example, the assessment label, deaf-blind, refers to not only those individuals that are deaf and blind but, to those who are visually and auditorially impaired. This includes those individuals categorized as blind/severely hearing impaired or severely hearing impaired/severely vision impaired. Another factor entering into this characterization is that many individuals who are deaf-blind are either mentally retarded or are functioning in the range of mental retardation. Through this example it becomes evident that the term, deaf-blind, may not accurately reflect the dynamics of this population (Barrett, 1987; Fredericks & Baldwin, 1987).

This definition problem establishes the need for a definition that can include the numerous low incidence populations and all their variable characteristics. The following definition attempts to satisfy this need by being general enough to include the variance of this population yet, specific enough to be a viable definition for those servicing this population. Severe multiple disability refers to those individuals with a profound disability or with a combination of disabilities that it so limits their daily activities that they require services and programming more innovative, extensive, and intensive than common programming for individuals with disabilities provides. This population is characterized as, but not exclusive to being non-ambulatory, non-independently mobile, needing to be fed, needing assistance in toileting, and needing daily occupational or communication therapy (Covert, 1987; Fredericks, 1987).

Classification of Mental Retardation

Although the current American Association on Mental Retardation definition of mental retardation contains three major components, the classification of people once they are labelled mentally retarded is based primarily on the scores obtained from an intelligence test. The current definition identifies the following four levels of mental retardation: (a) mild, (b) moderate, (c) severe, and (d) profound. The levels are segmented according to the score that people receive on different intelligence tests. For example, those people receiving a score on the Stanford-Binet Intelligence Scale of 52 through 67 are identified as having mild mental retardation, those between 36 and 51 are considered to have moderate mental retardation, people are identified as having severe mental retardation if they score within a range of 20 to 35, and individuals scoring less than 20 are considered to have profound mental retardation. These scores vary slightly depending on the specific intelligence test that was administered.

Another form of classification of persons with mental retardation is by mental age. The practice of classifying individuals according to mental age has been drastically reduced in recent years. The Stanford-Binet Intelligence scale, developed by Terman (1916), calculated IQ scores by dividing the "mental age," derived from the test, by chronological age and multiplying by 100. It has been strongly suggested that practitioners avoid using the phrase, mental age, because the label tells the practitioner nothing about the particular pattern of the persons cognitive strengths and weaknesses (Baroff, 1986). According to Tansley and Gulliford (1960), the use of the phrase, mental age, may be misunderstood. Therefore, Wechsler (1949) derived IQ scores by comparing each subject's performance with their same age peers and rejected the concept of mental age.

Description of Limitations Associated
with Mental Retardation

Mental retardation is associated with more than 200 known medical entities, including genetic defects, chromosomal disorders, infections during pregnancy, accidental poisonings and injuries, metabolic disorders, and central nervous system infections (Gottlieb, 1987). However, Carter, Van Andel, and Robb (1985) identified research indicating that the present known number of causes, nearly 300, represents only one-third of those possible. According to the authors, there is rarely one cause or simple explanation of mental retardation.

Mental retardation occurs as a result of biological occurrences and environmental conditions, or, for the majority of cases, the cause is idiopathic (unknown). There are instances of mental retardation that are determined at conception due to hereditary disorders (e.g., Phenylketonuria) or to chromosomal abnormalities (e.g., Down syndrome). In addition to these two forms of biological causes, mental retardation may also be biologically developed after conception during the prenatal period (before birth), perinatal period (immediately preceding or during birth), or postnatal period of development (following birth). Approximately 90% of people who acquire mental retardation through biological reasons develop their disability during the prenatal period of development and manifest the condition at birth or early infancy (Grossman, 1983). The following are problems that can occur during the prenatal period of development that may result in mental retardation: (a) diseases (e.g., syphilis, rubella); (b) nutritional deficits; (c) infections (e.g., encephalitis); (d) toxemias (i.e., poisonous drugs such as alcohol or lead); and (e) radiation in large doses. Many of the conditions that can occur during the prenatal period may result in prematurity and low birth weight and possibly identify the infant at high-risk. In addition to prematurity and low birth weight, other possible perinatal conditions causing mental retardation may include: (a) trauma, (b) infection, (c) anoxia (oxygen deprivation), and (d) the development of antibodies by the mother (RH incompatibility). Following birth, mental retardation appears to primarily occur as a result of: (a) malnutrition; (b) trauma (e.g., automobile collisions, child abuse); or (c) poisoning (e.g., lead encephalopathy). A variety of conditions that can contribute to the occurrence of mental retardation have been identified, however, the majority of reasons for the development of mental retardation are yet unknown.

Persons with mental retardation are at significant risk for concomitant disabilities and the more severe the mental retardation, the greater the probability of an associated disability (Accardo & Capute, 1979). Because people with mental retardation have different biological deficits and environmental experiences resulting in differing levels of cognitive functioning, it is difficult to make generalizations about individuals with mental retardation (Browman, Nichols, Schasugnessy, & Kennedy, 1987).

Common Service Settings

Traditionally, individuals with developmental disabilities, especially those with severe multiple disabilities, were generally ignored by society and not considered worthy of membership. Prior to 1800, society did little in the way of systematic study, treatment, or care of these individuals. The real beginnings of therapeutic treatment and services took place in the early 1800s when education and political reform became widespread. The first successful public residential institutions serving persons with developmental disabilities were established, and schools throughout Germany, France, and the United States were created.

With the exception of an occasional after-school recreation program sponsored by a municipal park and recreation department, therapeutic recreation services in hospitals and state institutions, or a handicapped-only camp that offered individuals with developmental disabilities an opportunity to participate, few programs have been made accessible to this population over the years. It was not until the 1970s (i.e., the Decade of the Disabled) that monumental civil and human rights advances by people with developmental disabilities were achieved. The 1973 Rehabilitation Act (PL 93-112), one of the most significant landmarks in the struggle for equality for all individuals, made it illegal for any agency or organization that receives federal funds to discriminate against persons with developmental disabilities solely on the basis of his or her disability. Also, the Education for All Handicapped Children Act of 1975 (PL 94-142) mandated equal educational opportunity to all children who have disabilities. It also addressed the use of related services, including therapeutic recreation, in least restrictive environments.

During the past 15 years residential services for people with developmental disabilities have undergone a substantial shift in direction. Several thousand individuals each year have moved from large, public residential facilities to smaller residential programs in community settings. These smaller community facilities have experienced dramatic decreases in numbers of residents, averaging approximately 16 residents per agency as compared to a mean of 25 residents in 1978 (Hill, Lakin, & Bruininks, 1984). If these trends toward smaller numbers and movement to community settings continue, then community programs will be offering services to increasing numbers of people with developmental disabilities, including persons with severe and profound disabilities, since these people constitute the majority of those still residing in the large public and private facilities (Hauber et al., 1984).

Theoretical Foundations

Introduction

Participation in recreation activities in an important aspect of life in our society. When such activities meet individual's needs, they promote physical health and conditioning, provide opportunities to develop social relations, and lead to the development of new skills. Unfortunately, therapeutic recreation services have had relatively low priority in programs for persons with developmental disabilities, until recently when specific leisure skill training techniques and curricula incorporating behavioral training procedures, in conjunction with purposeful environmental arrangements, were developed. The neglect of relevant programming and services for this population is particularly unfortunate because participation in leisure is an important aspect in (a) successful community adjustment (Cheseldine & Jeffree, 1981; Schleien & Ray, 1988); (b) development of collateral skills (Schleien, Kiernan, & Wehman, 1981); and (c) reduction of maladaptive behaviors (Adkins & Matson, 1980; Favell, 1973; Voeltz & Wuerch, 1981).

Unfortunately, a discrepancy exists between what is known about short- and long-term benefits of leisure participation and the current status of services to persons with developmental disabilities. For these people to maximally participate in community recreation activities alongside their peers without disabilities, specific leisure skill training in home, school, and community environments, and specific provisions by communities to incorporate them into leisure services are necessary.

Before any attempts are made to design, deliver, and evaluate therapeutic recreation services, it is necessary to describe common characteristics of persons with developmental disabilities. In studies into their community adaptation and overall wellness, it is valuable to understand their ability to participate in recreation activities, occupy themselves during discretionary time, make choices, participate in community recreation, interact socially, and other primary variables that seem to influence leisure participation.

A review of typical repertoires and skill deficits in persons with developmental disabilities as they concern therapeutic recreation service delivery could include the following variables: (a) leisure skill repertoires, (b) developing autonomy to experience leisure, (c) community-based participation, and (d) social skills and friendship development. It is important to recognize that different individuals within the broad category of developmental disabilities have different programming needs. People will differ markedly in their motor, social, cognitive, and affective abilities. For example, a person with moderate mental retardation who uses a wheelchair has substantially different abilities and needs than a person labeled autistic with a visual impairment. Therefore, it is necessary to approach service delivery in an individualized manner, in an attempt to satisfy personal needs and preferences. Due to the risk of thinking stereotypically, generalizations must be avoided when designing programs for people with developmental disabilities.

Theoretical Foundation #1: Leisure Skills Instruction

To answer the question, "How can the leisure needs of people with developmental disabilities be met," an understanding of the role of leisure in the lives of people without disabilities is often useful. Recognition of the commonalities between people with and without disabilities sets the stage for personalized leisure programming of meaningful and diverse experiences that enhance the quality of life for everyone. Many benefits (e.g., social, emotional, intellectual, and physical) are derived from participation in recreation activities. Active engagement in recreation activities renews, refreshes, and provides opportunities for relaxation, spontaneity, and playfulness. Through recreation, people enjoy the company of others, learn the "give and take" of social relationships, and build friendships and a sense of community. By developing leisure repertoires, people learn new skills, strengthen physical and mental well-being, and build self-esteem (Heyne & Schleien, 1991).

For persons with developmental disabilities, participation in recreation activities offers these same vital benefits. However, unlike the general population who typically learn recreation skills through trial and error and by observing others, people with developmental disabilities often require systematic instruction to develop leisure repertoires (Wehman & Schleien, 1981). Individual needs, abilities, and preferences must be assessed; environments must be analyzed, adapted, and engineered to promote inclusive leisure participation; instruction must be provided via state-of-the-art behavioral methodologies; and ongoing evaluation must be provided.

Without a leisure repertoire, most people with developmental disabilities experience feelings of isolation and social withdrawal (Schleien & Meyer, 1988; Wuerch & Voeltz, 1982). Often, the absence of meaningful leisure lifestyles means the development and perpetuation of undesirable behaviors (Gaylord-Ross, 1980; Kissel & Whitman, 1977). Through development of leisure competencies, however, people with developmental disabilities can build friendships, learn greater self-sufficiency, develop fitness, and become active community members (Schleien & Ray, 1988).

Rago and Cleland (1978) stated that the focus of education for persons with developmental disabilities should be on fostering skills that encourage individuals to maximize their happiness. Therefore, all persons with disabilities should receive assistance and encouragement related to leisure involvement (Reiter & Levi, 1980). Professionals must prepare persons with developmental disabilities for leisure in a way that brings personal rewards and enables them to contribute to the life of their community. Therefore, federal and state support is needed for professionals and families to assist persons with developmental disabilities in experiencing happiness and satisfaction through leisure involvement in the community.

Theoretical Foundation #2: Autonomy
to Experience Leisure

The fundamental consideration for human beings is that the individual should have a full measure of freedom, autonomy, choice, and self-determination (Murphy, 1975). Within the context of Lee and Mobily's (1988) assertion that natural freedom involves the irrevocable power that humans have for self-determination in preference to being determined by external forces and Bregha's (1985) position that leisure is the most precious expression of our freedom, a convincing case can be made that leisure is an inherent right of all humans.

Perhaps the term "leisure" should be reserved for a person's perception of freedom to choose to participate in meaningful, enjoyable, and satisfying experiences. According to Mannell, Zuzanek, and Larson (1988), leisure is best understood from the subjective perspective of the participant, resulting in ideas of perceived freedom and intrinsic motivation becoming pillars upon which a much needed leisure theory has been constructed. Roadburg (1983) examined the relationships between perceived freedom and enjoyment to leisure and concluded that freedom is a necessary but not sufficient condition for leisure; enjoyment must also be present in order for people to experience satisfying leisure experiences. As individuals encounter positive emotions (e.g., control, competence, relaxation, excitement) associated with the leisure experience, they will be intrinsically motivated to participate (Dattilo, 1986). That is, people will desire to participate in leisure for the feelings inherent in the experience, rather than for some external outcome or reward.

Recent theorists such as Kelly (1972), Neulinger (1981a), and Iso-Ahola (1980) agree that an essential condition of leisure is the opportunity to perceive freedom and exert some degree of control over the experience. According to Bregha (1985), Ellis and Witt (1984), and Harper (1986), perceived freedom in leisure requires that people have control and choice. Not only are control and choice needed for individuals to perceive freedom in leisure, they are necessary components for leisure satisfaction (Ragheb & Beard, 1980). Choice in leisure can help provide opportunities for people to enjoy themselves and enhance the quality of their lives (Perlmuter & Monty, 1977; Voeltz & Wuerch, 1981). Participants are more involved and more alert in activities when they perceive they have choice than when they do not (Albarran & Benitez, 1985; Langer & Rodin, 1976). Choice is one of the most important variables in enhancing a person's sense of control and providing opportunities for personal expression (Guess, Benson, & Siegel-Causey, 1985; Langer & Rodin). Since making choices leads to control, and feelings of control are important factors in experiencing leisure (Neulinger, 1981b), then the greater the freedom of choice available to people the greater the chance that leisure will be experienced (Sylvester, 1987).

Neulinger (1981a) described leisure as containing dimensions of freedom, intrinsic motivation, and noninstrumentality. He explained that people engaged in leisure understand they are participating because their actions are the result of a deliberate choice, rather than from being coerced. Participation is chosen for reasons intrinsic to the activity, rather than as a means to an end. Based on this conceptualization, leisure is clearly a mental condition located in the consciousness of the person. Leisure as an experience or state of mind, uniquely individual, implying that quality rather than quantity is important, has become a significant theme of scholarship (Mannell, 1984).

Therapeutic recreation encourages efforts promoting community options for individuals with developmental disabilities reflecting the full range of choices available to persons without disabilities. Therapeutic recreation professionals recognize the intimate relationship between freedom of choice and leisure. The goal in providing leisure services for persons with developmental disabilities should be to provide these individuals with the skills and opportunities that allow them to perceive that they are free to participate in chosen experiences. Therefore, a critical component of the provision of leisure services for individuals with developmental disabilities is incorporation of choice. According to Ficker-Terrill and Rowitz (1991), practitioners must familiarize themselves with best practice strategies that facilitate and encourage informed choice (e.g., teaching decision making, self-advocacy procedures, communication techniques).

Witt, Ellis, and Niles (1984) emphasized the need for therapeutic recreation specialists to provide leisure services that promote individuals' perception of leisure control, leisure competence, and intrinsic motivation to facilitate the person's sense of freedom of choice. Demonstration of choice through selection encourages spontaneous initiation of activity, engagement with the environment, and the assertion of a degree of control over one's surroundings (Dattilo & Barnett, 1985).

When providing therapeutic recreation services to people with developmental disabilities it is important to develop functional skills through therapy or treatment and teach leisure skills and knowledge through leisure education. Although these actions are important, they are not sufficient when attempting to systematically enhance the leisure lifestyles of individuals with developmental disabilities (Wuerch & Voeltz, 1982). Dattilo (1986) noted that a person may not encounter the freedom of choice associated with the leisure experience when involved in therapy or structured leisure education. Therefore, opportunities for choice, often associated with recreation participation, must be systemically provided (Dattilo & Rusch, 1985).

Reid (1975) observed that professionals working with people with disabilities often choose the activity in which the person participates, rather than allowing the individual to decide. It is likely that the omission of choice in the participation process prevents people from experiencing leisure and obtaining maximum benefits. It is also likely that continuous involvement in situations failing to provide opportunities for choice will result in feelings of helplessness (Seligman, 1975). People who experience helplessness have difficulty in learning that their actions produce outcomes and tend to reduce voluntary participation and exploration. Further, it is likely that a high incidence of learned helplessness among individuals with disabilities occurs because they are not afforded opportunities to learn and exhibit self-determined behaviors. To prevent learned helplessness, DeVellis (1977) recommended that individuals obtain early exposure to controllable situations; they should be taught to initiate and terminate their leisure experiences (Nietupski & Svoboda, 1982). Therapeutic recreation services that include elements of choice may be critical in the prevention and treatment of learned helplessness and the encouragement of future recreation participation (Iso-Ahola, MacNeil, & Szymanski, 1980).

A critical component of the provision of services for individuals with developmental disabilities is the incorporation of the opportunity to choose (Dattilo, 1986; Ford et al., 1984). Unfortunately, activities are frequently offered as passive stimulation and the notion of choice-making among individuals with disabilities continues to be an area that receives little attention from practitioners and researchers (Dattilo, 1988; Shevin & Klein, 1984). If therapeutic recreation specialists are to provide opportunities for participants with disabilities to demonstrate leisure preferences, it is critical that they develop strategies to recognize the exhibition of preferences for people unable to indicate choices through conventional means (Houghton, Bronicki, & Guess, 1987). Nietupski et al. (1986) recommended that practitioners provide frequent opportunities for choice in a structured fashion, rather than assuming individuals with severe disabilities lack self-initiation skills. Given that choice-making skills are within the capabilities of people with the most severe developmental disabilities (Kishi, Teelucksingh, Zollers, Park-Lee, & Meyer, 1988), therapeutic recreation professionals must attempt to secure personal autonomy, freedom, and choice for these individuals.

Theoretical Foundation #3:
Community Integration

Therapeutic recreation supports the right of people with developmental disabilities to receive services in least restrictive environments. The concept of "least restrictive environment" involves people with developmental disabilities living as normally as possible and receiving appropriate services in the least separate or most integrated setting (Dattilo, 1991). The concept of least restrictive environment encouraged the development of the philosophy of deinstitutionalization described by Scheerenberger (1987) as seeking greater emphasis on freedom, independence, individuality, mobility, personalized life experiences, and a high degree of interaction in a free society. Although for at least a decade our rhetoric has called for deinstitutionalizing persons with disabilities and the creation of community services, the development of these services has lagged (Baroff, 1986). One particular service that has not been addressed adequately is leisure. It is clear that every attempt should be made to provide leisure services for persons with developmental disabilities in an integrated fashion within the community.

According to Dattilo (1991), when people are grouped together and then separated from others, for whatever reason, the differences between the groups appear to become the focus of attention rather than their similarities. In effect, when people are separated from other people in a society, they do not experience equal opportunities to receive services. Although integration has been described as consisting of those practices that maximize a person's participation in the mainstream of society, integration is only meaningful if it involves social integration and acceptance, and not merely physical presence (Wolfensberger, 1972).

Hutchinson and Lord (1979) described integration of persons with disabilities into recreation activities as experiencing participation and enjoyment similar to peers who do not possess disabilities, upgrading skills and confidence, participating in community activities of their choice, and encouraging self-confidence and the perception of dignity. Schleien and Ray (1988) encouraged the development of integrated recreation opportunities by developing communication linkages between persons and agencies concerned about community leisure services, conducting accessibility surveys, and providing comprehensive staff training. To facilitate successful integration, therapeutic recreation specialists must work to protect and expand leisure education programs designed to improve the quality of life for persons with developmental disabilities.

Introduction of normalization by Nirje (1969) nearly 2 decades ago has become the primary philosophical orientation guiding development and delivery of community-based services for persons with disabilities (Schleien & Ray, 1988). Normalization is defined as the process that involves making available for persons with developmental disabilities patterns and conditions of everyday life which are as close as possible to the norms and patterns of the mainstream of society (Nirje). Wolfensberger (1972) broadened Nirje's definition of normalization to include utilization of means which are as culturally normative as possible, to establish and/or maintain personal behaviors and characteristics which are as culturally normative as possible. Therefore, normalization involves placing a high value on the life, rights, and dignity of people with disabilities (Lakin & Bruininks, 1985). Integration of persons with disabilities into community recreation programs is essential if the process of normalization is to be completed (Schleien & Ray). According to Wolfensberger (1991), not only are people aware that individuals with mental retardation can live in the community, but people with mental retardation who formerly would have been institutionalized are actually living in the community.

The differences between the leisure lifestyle of individuals with developmental disabilities and those without tend to diminish as integration into recreation activities occurs (Knapczyk & Yoppi, 1975). Discrimination against individuals with disabilities is prohibited through federal legislation (i.e., Public Law 94-142, the Education for All Handicapped Children Act, and its amendments; Section 504 of the Rehabilitation Act of 1973; and other recent legislative mandates). These initiatives have facilitated the movement of large numbers of persons with developmental disabilities into community living situations, consequently placing the responsibility of recreation programming upon community agencies (Schleien & Ray, 1988). According to Schleien and Ray, this legislation has provided the opportunity for persons with developmental disabilities to live, learn, and engage in recreation activities in settings with their peers.

The value of integrated recreation has been recognized by the United States' Administration on Developmental Disabilities. The Commissioner, McFadden, and her assistant, Burke, (McFadden & Burke, 1991) reported in 1991 that service providers must:

> Assist people with developmental disabilities to move beyond mere
> physical presence in our communities and into the full array of
> social spaces in our communities as full and valued participants.
> We want to significantly increase the use of generic recreation and
> leisure opportunities, including participation in on-going sports, civic,
> and/or church groups, depending on the individual's preferences.

Theoretical Foundation #4: Social Skills and Friendship Development

The development of leisure skills in persons with developmental disabilities can enhance social skill development. Involvement in recreation activities offers some of the most effective means for children and adults to acquire and develop these skills. Social skill development is facilitated through group play. Individuals who fail to develop necessary skills to engage in play often experience problems in developing relationships. Development of cooperative play behavior and participation in recreation activities often leads to making friends; getting along with others; learning to share, compete, cooperate, and take turns; and a more satisfactory social adjustment.

In a national survey of families with children with disabilities, only a small portion of respondents, persons with hearing impairments, had used at least one recreational service (Brewer & Kakalik, 1979). Of the families that did use recreation services, parents favorably regarded leisure as an end in itself, in that the parents were most satisfied that their children learned independent living skills and made new friends. This study provides an example of the interplay between participation in recreation and socialization. The fact that social development could be increased through interaction with peers and adults during leisure education was also revealed by Schleien and Wehman (1986). A major reason for inappropriate behavior at play by children with developmental disabilities is their limited cooperative play skills and lack of social interaction among peers (Wehman & Schleien, 1981). Paloutzian, Hasazi, Streifel, and Edgard (1971) also noted an inordinate amount of isolated play among young children with severe developmental disabilities, reinforcing the association between play and social skills.

Independent or isolated play is a lower stage of social development than cooperative play. Children fail to develop higher level social behaviors, such as cooperative play, when they have little peer interaction during play (Wehman, 1979). Effective feedback cannot be obtained until social interactions between children occur. As an individual becomes more proficient at recreating with others, socialization skills will be acquired (Paloutzian et al., 1971). Sharing, taking turns, and teamwork are aspects of social interaction that constitute cooperative play (Knapczyk & Yoppi, 1975; Samaras & Ball, 1975). Collard (1981) identified the many roles that leisure education can play in assisting in the development of needed social skills. Individuals with developmental disabilities can learn valuable social skills to facilitate appropriate functioning in school, on the job, and in the community. Zigmond (1978) insisted that people with disabilities must be socially competent to attain maximum benefit from classroom instruction. Several authors have cited the importance of proficiency in socialization among individuals with developmental disabilities to perform successfully on the job (Neal, 1970; President's Committee on Mental Retardation, 1974; Wehman, 1977a) and within the community (Collard; Novak & Heal, 1980; Schleien & Ray, 1988).

The Alcohol, Drug Abuse, and Mental Health Administration of the United States Department of Health and Human Services (1979) outlined how play teaches children to relate to other people and helps them learn how to live in the way the culture expects. Social rules and morals are learned in this manner. Practicing principles of give and take, sharing similar space, and exchanging information with other playmates through play can assist in preparation for adult life. People with developmental disabilities often engage in seemingly unacceptable social behavior. Individuals who are constructively using their free time do not exhibit the behaviors (i.e., body rocking, head banging, violent actions, social withdrawal) typically characteristic of these individuals. Research has revealed that there is an inverse relationship between acquisition of play skills and self-stimulated or abusive behavior. Recreation activity of a social nature provides opportunities through which the participant can learn to adjust to the social demands of society.

Schleien, Kiernan, and Wehman (1981) conducted a leisure skills training program in a group home for people with developmental disabilities. An inverse relationship was found between high-quality (e.g., goal-directed, age-appropriate) leisure behaviors and inappropriate (e.g., stereotypic or age-inappropriate) behaviors. The training program included leisure counseling, reinforcement, and making materials available. In another study, prompting and positive physical reinforcement were provided to three children who were severely handicapped for appropriate toy play (Favell, 1973). Instructor guidance and reinforcement for toy play were correlated with an increase in appropriate play and a decrease in stereotypic behaviors. Wuerch and Voeltz (1982) also found increased frequencies of positive behaviors when individuals were systematically trained in recreation activities. They measured effects of leisure instruction on behaviors of four adolescents with severe developmental disabilities attending a special education school. Two participants exhibited increased constructive, exploratory, and attending behavior during down time as a result of the training. A third participant decreased self-stimulation when using the materials, but increased it when she had no objects to manipulate. The authors viewed the results as offering cautious support for associating play training with positive collateral effects.

Documented and Expected/Implied Outcomes

Theoretical Foundation #1: Recreation Skills Instruction

Identification of need. Recreation activities can promote physical health and conditioning, provide opportunities to develop social relations and friends, and lead to the development of new skills. Unfortunately, recreation services have had relatively low priority for persons with developmental disabilities, until recently when some specific recreation skill-training techniques (Schleien, Kiernan, & Wehman, 1981; Voeltz, Wuerch, & Wilcox, 1982) and leisure curricula (Bender & Valletutti, 1976; Wehman & Schleien, 1981; Wessel, 1976; Wuerch &

Voeltz, 1982) were developed. The neglect of relevant services for persons with developmental disabilities is particularly unfortunate because participation in recreation activities is an important aspect in successful community adjustment (Bell, Schoenrock, & Slade, 1975; Cheseldine & Jeffree, 1981; Eyman & Call, 1977; Gollay, 1981; Hill & Bruininks, 1981) and is associated with the development of collateral skills (Newcomer & Morrison, 1974; Schleien, Kiernan, & Wehman; Strain, Cooke, & Apolloni, 1976) and reduction of maladaptive behaviors (Adkins & Matson, 1980; Favell, 1973; Schleien, Kiernan, & Wehman; Voeltz & Wuerch, 1981).

In the past, recreation was equated with free time or with time that was not spent on required activities (Murphy, 1981). Reluctance by many people to support increased free time for persons with developmental disabilities may be in response to the inordinate amount of time such persons spend in passive, aimless activity. A major criticism of institutional care has been the lack of meaningful activity for residents and the excessive periods during which few or no actions are required (Braddock, 1977). At such times, residents tend to engage in inappropriate actions (Ford et al., 1984). The absence of services and the lack of quality programs are aspects of institutions that clearly are in need of reform (Braddock; Putnam, Werder, & Schleien, 1985). Researchers have observed more negative behaviors (e.g., stereotypic behaviors, nongoal-directed activities) during free time by persons with mental retardation who are institutionalized than those who were not (Baumeister & Forehand, 1973). Parents and caregivers reported that children with mental retardation living at home have an inordinate amount of free time spent in extremely passive activities (Marion, 1979). The critical factor, however, is how free time is used, not the amount that is available. Therefore, the qualitative aspects of recreation activities should be emphasized.

The ultimate aim of recreation programming is to teach persons with developmental disabilities to acquire and use skills in naturally occurring situations. Thus, awareness of an individual's current and future environments, especially integrated community environments, should guide selection of activities (Brown, Branston, Hamre-Nietupski, Pumpian, Certo, & Gruenewald, 1979; Certo, Schleien, & Hunter, 1983).

Many investigators have cited participation in recreation activities and the ability to experience leisure during unstructured periods as important indications of successful adjustment (Bell et al., 1975; Corcoran & French, 1977; Eyman & Call, 1977; Gollay, 1981; Hill & Bruininks, 1981; Intagliata, Willer, & Wicks, 1981; Scheerenberger & Felsenthal, 1976). Although adults with developmental disabilities may function successfully in vocational pursuits, they may not adequately adapt to community living because of difficulty in filling unstructured time in the work setting (e.g., coffee breaks) and in using recreation services in the community (Birenbaum & Re, 1979; Hill & Bruininks; Luckey & Shapiro, 1974).

Limited information is available on the recreation activities in which persons with developmental disabilities living in the community engage and on the major variables that seem to influence recreation participation. The available information supports the belief that living in a community does not, in itself, ensure a normal pattern of recreation participation (Intagliata et al., 1981). In an investigation concerning the recreation participation of residents in community facilities, most of whom formerly lived in institutions, Bjaanes and Butler (1974) found that only 3% of the residents' time was spent in active recreation behaviors (goal-oriented and engaging, such as playing games) as opposed to 22% of their time spent in passive recreation behaviors (nongoal-oriented, such as watching television or staring into space). Activity participation was observed to vary considerably between as well as within people in the different facilities. For example, no active recreation behaviors were observed in one facility, whereas active recreation behaviors were exhibited 5.5% of the time in another. According to Bjaanes and Butler, differences in recreation behaviors could not be accounted for simply by type of facility; variations in the unique environmental climate of each facility were responsible. The investigators concluded that planning and supervising active recreation activities influences how frequently such activities occur.

Cheseldine and Jeffree (1981) surveyed 214 families in Manchester, England, to examine the recreation activities of teenagers who were mentally retarded. Several teenagers (9.5%) were in residential care; the remainder lived at home. Five spare-time activities were most frequently mentioned by parents or guardians: (a) listening to records or tapes, (b) watching television, (c) shopping, (d) taking trips in the car with the family, and (e) helping in the house--all activities that are essentially passive or family-oriented. Youth clubs for persons with mental retardation existed in the area, but only 40% of the teenagers in the survey attended them. Transportation was one barrier to participation in the youth clubs. Several teenagers dropped out of the clubs because of the desire not to spend their spare time with other persons who were mentally retarded. "Indeed, it goes right against the principles of normalization, to provide a special facility for individuals who are mentally retarded to 'occupy' themselves" (Cheseldine & Jeffree, p. 52).

Hill and Bruininks (1981) compared the recreation activities of persons who were mentally retarded living in public residential facilities with those living in community facilities. Interviews with direct care staff revealed many similarities; watching television, attending religious services, or going on field-trips were equally likely to occur in both facilities. Differences were observed in the amount of time spent and type of participation in recreation activities. Residents of community facilities spent a greater proportion of their time in community recreation activities (e.g., shopping or eating out), whereas residents of public facilities were more likely to spend more time participating in large-group activities within the facilities (e.g., going for a walk, attending a dance). Residents in community facilities participated in an average of 4.7 categories of recreation activity per week, whereas the weekly average was 3.8 for residents of public residential facilities. The latter participated more often in certain types of activities (e.g., going for a walk outdoors, attending a party or dance, or going to a movie or concert). The most frequently cited reasons for lack of participation in active recreation activities were lack of: (a) someone to accompany them, (b) access to desired activities, and (c) transportation. Community facility staff reported that the unavailability of desired recreation activities was the largest single problem (14.9%) for residents.

Hill and Bruininks (1981) found that 77% of community facility residents and 51.3% of public facility residents were perceived as capable of spending time outside the boundaries of the facility without direct supervision. Gollay, Freedman, Wyngaarden, and Kurtz (1978) noted that recreation participation of persons deinstitutionalized differed according to type of residential setting. A greater range of activities was reported in group homes and in semi-independent settings than in natural/adoptive or foster homes. Whereas less than 66% of the persons living in natural/adoptive homes were allowed to decide how to spend their own money, about 75% of those living in group or semi-independent homes were allowed to make such decisions. People living in natural/adoptive or foster homes were much less likely to come and go at will than those living in semi-independent settings (less than 20%, compared to 77%).

Family attitudes influence the recreation participation of persons with developmental disabilities (Wehman & Schleien, 1981). Most investigations of parental behavior and attitudes toward recreation are on play behavior in infancy and preschool years; less is known about families with adolescents, teenagers, or young adults (especially for persons formerly in institutions). Results of two investigations on people formerly institutionalized illustrate the effect of family attitudes on acquisition of recreation skills and recreation participation. Katz and Yekutiel (1974) studied the problems of 128 graduates of sheltered workshops in Tel Aviv, Tushiyah, and Achikam, Israel. Findings indicated that most recreation was spent in essentially passive activities (e.g., watching television, listening to the radio). Parents perceived the most significant problems in improving their children's use of free time to be the absence of suitable friends and the lack of interest in recreation activities. In their study of people who had been deinstitutionalized, Gollay et al. (1978) found that persons with severe mental retardation participated in fewer recreation activities and had fewer friends than did persons with mild or moderate mental retardation, yet families rated the personal adjustment of their children more positively than did the families of children with less severe mental retardation. In explaining this contradiction, the investigators speculated that families with members with severe mental retardation may have lowered their expectations in regard to recreation activities and social relations. Cheseldine and Jeffree (1981) suggested that parents seem to cope with little support and thus do not perceive a problem. For example, the parents who were interviewed had very little awareness of the recreation activity options or resources in the community. Bell et al. (1975) observed that parents tend to encourage children's participation in activities that minimize the likelihood of embarrassment (e.g., going to church or synagogue) rather than promoting activities that are more difficult and involve others in public places.

Gollay et al. (1978) identified that age and level of retardation influence the degree of restrictiveness in recreation activity options. For example, a greater proportion of the adults than children they studied were allowed to participate in recreation activities and make personal decisions. It is expected that age influences recreation skill acquisition and activity participation for people with and without developmental disabilities. For example, teenagers are more likely to attend mixed dances and young children are observed more often participating in playground activities.

Persons with severe developmental disabilities tend to live in more restrictive environments than do persons with mild or moderate disabilities. One indicator of restrictiveness identified by Gollay et al. (1978) was the degree to which residents had the opportunity to enter and leave their homes by choice. Among subjects with mild disabilities, 36% were allowed to enter and leave their residences by choice, whereas only 33% of residents with moderate disabilities, and 20% of residents with severe disabilities were allowed to do so. Thus, residences for homogeneous groups of persons with severe disabilities may tend to prohibit recreation activity options.

Implications of Interventions

Comparative studies of persons with and without development disabilities.
To evaluate skill acquisition and the participation of persons who are developmentally disabled in community recreation activities, professionals must understand how persons without disabilities in the same communities occupy their free time. Activities will vary according to facilities (e.g., swimming pools, shopping malls) and available activities (e.g., organized clubs), which differ by geographical locale and type of neighborhood (McGregor, 1982). If the participation of persons who were developmentally disabled in recreation activities were normalized, each person would have the same activity options that persons without disabilities have, taking into account individual preferences and skills. It

is not known, at this time, if participation in activities actually departs substantially from the norm. For example, Birenbaum and Re (1979) noted that participation in recreation activities was similar for people with mental retardation and people who were not retarded, but were marginally employed or unemployed. Nevertheless, at least two empirical studies reached different conclusions on this issue.

In comparing recreation activities of 108 students with and without mild mental retardation, aged 7 to 12 years, Matthews (1982) examined the type and frequency of participation for three student groups: (a) low socioeconomic status (SES) with mental retardation, (b) low SES without mental retardation, and (c) middle SES persons without mental retardation. Students with mental retardation were found to participate significantly more often than other students in informal as opposed to formal, inexpensive to expensive, and accessible to inaccessible activities. There were many similarities in the recreational activities of the three groups, with all students having similar activity patterns in the same settings. The only difference linked to mental retardation was that persons with mental retardation engaged in fewer social activities. Matthews, contending that differences in participation between persons with and without mental retardation have been overemphasized, recommended that future research focus on how persons with and without mental retardation are alike rather than different. Matthew's results are consistent with Edgerton's (1967) finding that recreation activities of former residents of Pacific State Hospital were much like those of peers in their neighborhoods.

The finding that persons with mental retardation participate in the same types of recreation activities with similar frequencies as do other members of communities is not an assurance that their recreation activity needs are being met or that the manner of participation is typical or desirable. For example, if residents of a group home always went to movies in large, homogeneous groups, the activity would be contrary to the normalization principle. If teenagers attended a puppet show designed for young children, the activity would be considered age-inappropriate.

Skill deficits. A major factor for the limited attention given to teaching recreation skills for home and community settings to persons with developmental disabilities is their serious skill deficits (Schleien, 1991). Skill deficits could include two general skill areas of interaction--with objects and with people. Current habilitative and educational technology have not yet advanced to the point where professionals could determine reliably how many skills could be acquired or environments accessed. Professionals engaged in recreation skill instruction with persons with developmental disabilities face a variety of challenges in expanding their repertoires. Barriers center around three basic concerns: (a) specific skill deficits, (b) limited instructional materials, and (c) environmental barriers/resistance (Wehman, 1979; Wehman & Schleien, 1981). Although a totally independent leisure lifestyle, including independent functioning in community recreation environments, may be unrealistic for some people, these individuals are capable of considerably more complex skills than they typically have performed (Schleien).

To develop an appropriate recreation skills repertoire for individuals with developmental disabilities, specific skill-training techniques are often used (Adkins & Matson, 1980; Wehman & Marchant, 1977). Methods of task analysis, data-based instruction, and contingent reinforcement have been employed successfully to teach specific skills like swimming, bowling, and skiing (Bundschuh, Williams, Hollingworth, Gooch, & Shirer, 1972; Seaman, 1973; Sinclair, 1975). Specific skills trained are usually based upon task analyses of recreation activities practiced by the majority of people, as in the I CAN program (Wessel, 1976).

Application of assessments. A needs assessment is vitally important when working with individuals who are developmentally disabled. The assessment provides information which helps the therapeutic recreation specialist identify activities and materials that will best meet the participant's life-long recreation needs. Many authors (Orelove & Sobsey, 1987; Schleien & Ray, 1988; Voeltz & Wuerch, 1981a; Wehman & Schleien, 1980; Wehman & Schleien, 1981; Wuerch & Voeltz, 1982) have identified three key areas to address within a needs assessment: (a) general background information (e.g., age, abilities, physical characteristics); (b) appropriateness and functionality of targeted activities; and (c) environmental analysis which helps identify component tasks required to complete an activity and the individual's current level of proficiency relative to those tasks. Specific needs assessment inventories available include the "Client Home Environment Checklist" (Wehman & Schleien, 1981), "Home Leisure Activities Survey" (Wuerch & Voeltz), and the "Student Interest Survey" (Wuerch & Voeltz).

A second area of assessment should address the appropriateness of functionality of activities relative to the needs of the client with regard to the principle of normalization. Functional skills are those that an individual is frequently asked to demonstrate in daily life whether it be in the home, job site, or community environment. A skill that is not functional is one that has a low probability of being required by daily activities (Brown, Branston, Hamre-Nietupski, Pumpian, Certo, & Gruenwald, 1979). The age-appropriateness of an activity is assessed by determining whether peers of the same age typically engage in that activity.

Voeltz and Wuerch (1981) developed a checklist for systematic evaluation of activities in relation to the individual's characteristics and needs. Three elements make up the "Leisure Activity Selection Checklist." The first element, normalization, addresses concerns for socially appropriate or socially valid activities. Questions in this area focus on whether peers would be interested in and engage in the activity, how many people could use this activity, and whether the activity is potentially life-long in nature. The second element, individualization, addresses the adaptability of the activity as it relates to the participant's specific needs and preferences. The third and final component of the checklist addresses environmental aspects of the activity including availability, durability, safety, noxiousness, and expense (Voeltz & Wuerch).

A third area to be addressed in a needs assessment inventory concerns an individual's level of proficiency when engaged in a particular activity. An ecological assessment or an environmental analysis inventory (Belmore & Brown, 1976; Certo et al., 1983; Schleien & Ray, 1988) can be conducted to determine the specific components of the activity that the individual has already mastered and those requiring additional training. Certo et al. stated that this inventory is "a systematic method of conducting an observation of an event as it occurs in a natural setting under typical conditions" (p. 33). The environmental analysis inventory is helpful in developing instructional sequences and identifying the person's proficiency relative to a task. The inventory could be instrumental in identifying appropriate teaching strategies as well as activity adaptations that enhance participation.

Collateral skill development. One principal outcome of leisure skill instruction may be collateral skill development. In addition to providing pleasurable activity and entertainment, participation in recreation activities can enhance development in social, emotional, psychological, communication, problem solving, motor, and other collateral skills, since it allows for continued practice of newly acquired skills in positive and naturally occurring contexts. Vandercook (1987) reported that as persons with severe disabilities became more proficient in two recreation activities (i.e., pinball, bowling), their social repertoires became more sophisticated. Perhaps, increasing recreation skills allows individuals more freedom to expend greater efforts monitoring their social behavior. If social competencies can be improved "incidentally" within the context of age-appropriate recreation, valuable intervention time could be saved and social competencies could accrue within the context of activities in which they are expected to be expressed.

Although few empirical investigations supporting the development of skills in other curriculum areas through play by persons with developmental disabilities exist (Voeltz, Wuerch, & Wilcox, 1982), these potential outcomes are compelling.

For example, play experiences can enable children to perceive a more positive body-image and self-image (Verhoven, Schleien, & Bender, 1982). As self-image is cultivated and grows, social and personal security increases. This type of environment could provide a setting for accomplishment to balance the feelings of learned helplessness or inferiority, which many persons with developmental disabilities experience through repeated failure (Dattilo & Rusch, 1985; Seligman, 1975).

Other collateral skills that could be acquired within the context of a recreation program include increased communication and language skills (Rogow, 1981; Bates & Renzaglia, 1982), various social skills (e.g., cooperation, relationship building, taking turns, and sharing materials) (Kibler, 1986; Schleien & Wehman, 1986), and appropriate manipulation of materials and motor skills (Orelove & Sobsey, 1987; Sherrill, 1986). Other life domains could also be addressed during recreation activities. For example, if an individual with a developmental disability was to participate in a horseshoe activity, he would need to learn about appropriate clothing (i.e., activity of daily living), necessary motor skills involved in grasping and pitching horseshoes (i.e., gross and fine motor skills), and a method of scoring and measuring (i.e., functional academics/math).

Undesirable behaviors have been known to decrease following an individual's acquisition of appropriate object manipulation skills or functional recreation skills (Alajajian, 1981; Favell, 1973). Alajajian discovered that an added advantage to a jogging program focusing on physical fitness in students with severe sensory impairments and cognitive deficits was a noticeable decrease in their self-abusive and self-stimulatory behaviors. Such excess behaviors have been found to decrease, especially when the recreation activities include a system of reinforcement (Wehman & Schleien, 1981). Favell and Cannon's (1977) research on the use of toys by students with severe developmental disabilities indicated that behaviors were strongly influenced by toy play and that students exhibited strong preferences among toys. Data from the time-sampling measurements of the free play of 11 students indicated that the students were idle 65% of the time when they were given the 10 least popular toys, but only 25% of the time when the 10 most popular toys were available.

Schleien, Kiernan, and Wehman (1981) conducted a recreation skills training program in a group home for six adults with moderate mental retardation. An inverse relation was found between high-quality (e.g., goal-directed, age-appropriate) recreation behaviors and inappropriate (e.g., stereotypic or age-inappropriate) behaviors. The training program included leisure counseling, reinforcement, and making new, recreational materials available.

Adkins and Matson (1980) used several experimental conditions to teach the recreation skill of making pot holders to six women with moderate to severe mental retardation who were institutionalized. The intervention consisted of: (a) general instructions (informing them that the classroom and materials were available), (b) discussion on the purpose and benefits of recreation without specific instructions, and (c) specific instruction in pot holder making. Only the third condition increased the appropriate use of free time. Moreover, the learned skills generalized to a follow-up situation in which no training was given for 6 days.

Following the critical processes of assessment and skill selection, the therapeutic recreation specialist must decide on a systematic method of teaching the targeted recreation skills. Many recreation programs include behavior analytic approaches to develop individual's repertoires.

Task analysis. Numerous authors (Nietupski, Hamre-Nietupski, & Ayers, 1984; Wehman & Schleien, 1981; Wuerch & Voeltz, 1982) have supported the use of task analysis when teaching recreation skills to persons with developmental disabilities. Task analysis can serve as an assessment tool that provides skill proficiency information. Secondly, a task analysis individualizes a program, allowing for adaptations. Thirdly, it provides a teaching sequence that can be used consistently by multiple trainers. Two examples of research projects that successfully used a task analytic approach include Schleien, Ash, Kiernan, and Wehman's (1981) teaching of a woman who was profoundly mentally retarded three cooking skills (i.e., uses of an oven--boiling, baking, broiling) and Storey, Bates, and Hanson's (1984) teaching of coffee purchasing skills across several community environments to adults who were severely mentally retarded.

Reinforcement. Using reinforcers contingently and more frequently may be necessary to promote acquisition of recreation skills by some people with developmental disabilities (Wehman, 1977a). Commonly used and effective reinforcers are learner-specific and may include praise, attention, switch-activated buzzers, vestibular reinforcers, and access to favorite recreational materials (Sandler & McClain, 1987). Reactive recreational materials such as Simon, cameras, remote control vehicles, and vending machines that result in sensory feedback provide people with natural reinforcers (Schleien, 1991). Bambara, Spiegel-McGill, Shores, and Fox (1984) compared the effects of three commercial reactive toys and three nonreactive toys on the amount of time three children with severe mental retardation engaged in manipulative activity and visual attention to toy play. Results indicated that in comparison to the nonreactive toys, reactive toys had a substantially greater influence on the amount of time each child engaged in manipulative activity.

Adaptations. Individuals with developmental disabilities often have difficulty exploring and manipulating their environments due to physical, cognitive, or sensory limitations. Frequently, selecting materials and activities that are reactive in nature (i.e., producing sound, motion, visual, tactile sensations) facilitates manipulation of recreation materials (Bambara et al., 1984; Rogow, 1976; Wehman, Schleien, & Kiernan, 1980). Therefore, it is important to identify materials and activities that are optimal for recreation instruction. In most instances, it is possible to adapt existing materials and activities (Dixon, 1981; Garner & Campbell, 1987) to increase participation. Common recreation activities that have been adapted and made accessible for persons with developmental disabilities include bowling (using handle-grip bowling balls, bowling ramps, and bowling ball pushers) (Wehman & Schleien, 1981), basketball (using larger or softer balls and adjustable backboards), and camera operation (using extended shutter release buttons and color codings) (Wehman et al.). Individuals with developmental disabilities have been taught to play miniature golf using adapted golf clubs (Banks & Aveno, 1986), video games using head wands and alternative control devices (i.e., adaptive switches) (Hughes, 1981; Powers & Ball, 1983; Sedlak, Doyle, & Schloss, 1982), board games using exaggerated materials initially with gradual reductions to normal proportions as acquisition occurred (Kibler, 1986), and battery-operated toys (Meehan, Mineo, & Lyon, 1985).

Due to the complexity of certain activities, it is often necessary to alter the procedures or rules slightly so that an individual can participate. Schleien, Certo, and Muccino (1984) adapted several procedures when teaching a young adult with severe mental retardation to use a bowling alley. In some instances, a simple rearrangement of the skill sequence can promote participation by individuals with developmental disabilities. Skill sequences have been successfully rearranged for activities such as swimming (i.e., dressing in swim gear prior to leaving for pool or beach) (Ray, Schleien, Larson, Rutten, & Slick, 1986) and cooking (i.e., placing eggs in pan of cold water before boiling) (Schleien, Ash, Kiernan, & Wehman, 1981). Lead-up activities are helpful when attempting to teach more complex skills. Wehman and Schleien (1981) found that initial training activities such as practicing phone skills using a tape recorder, playing kickball prior to instruction in softball, and catch-throw newcomb before engaging in volleyball, served as effective lead-up activities. Kibler (1986) used a game to teach necessary skills for playing commercially available games. Lagomarcino, Reid, Ivancic, and Faw (1984) taught young adults with severe and profound mental retardation specific dance maneuvers in preparation for participation in community nightclubs.

Community recreation skills. Attempts to increase participation in recreation activities by people with developmental disabilities residing in community facilities are documented in the literature. Johnson and Bailey (1977) showed that access to recreation skills instruction was a critical factor in increasing participation in weaving and rug-making by people residing in group homes. High levels of participation were maintained after instruction when participants had access to these activities. Skills already in the individuals' repertoires were more likely to be used when prizes were awarded, but prizes were not needed to maintain participation in rug-making and weaving. Although the investigators did not collect data on long-term participation in the activities, they noted that collection of such data is essential for adequately evaluating effects of instruction.

A recreation skills program was developed for six adults with moderate mental retardation in a group home setting by Schleien, Kiernan, and Wehman (1981). The training program consisted of a weekly counseling session in free time use, reinforcement training, and introduction of new materials. Results indicated that during baseline, few high-quality recreation behaviors (e.g., goal-directed recreation and age-appropriate activities) were exhibited by residents. Mostly, they watched television and smoked cigarettes. However, high quality leisure behaviors averaged 60% across the instructional sessions. When the baseline was reinstated, high quality behaviors declined to almost 0%, but with the reinstitution of the intervention, most residents' inappropriate behavior were dramatically reduced.

Lagomarcino et al. (1984) demonstrated a method of training an intermediate community living skill to teenagers with severe mental retardation who were institutionalized. By using behavioral training procedures, other attempts to remediate play problems and address recreation education needs have been successful. Procedures such as contingent reinforcement, task analysis, careful selection of activities, cooperatively structured activities, skill modifications, and pairing people in environments with peers, have been successful to teach a variety of age-appropriate leisure skills to children and adults with severe developmental disabilities. Examples include miniature golf (Banks & Aveno, 1986), pinball (Hill, Wehman, & Horst, 1982; Horst, Wehman, Hill, & Bailey, 1980), video games (Powers & Ball, 1983; Sedlak et al., 1982), darts (Schleien, Wehman, & Kiernan, 1981), photography (Wehman et al., 1980), and functional use of a community recreation center (Schleien & Larson, 1986).

Generalization. Wehman (1977b) argued that however successful instruction in the use of specific toys or materials may be, it does not necessarily generalize to other activities and settings. Investigators have proposed skills instruction that will transfer to recreation activity participation in natural community environments (Brown, Branston-McLean, Baumgart, Vincent, Falvey, & Schroeder, 1979; Voeltz et al., 1982). Schleien, Wehman, and Kiernan (1981) promoted generalization by using a task analysis of motor responses, teaching adults with developmental disabilities the necessary skills for darts. The experimental group not only acquired the dart skills, but also generalized them to other appropriate environments. Sedlak et al. (1982) examined the ability of adolescents who were severely mentally retarded to generalize video game skills to a community setting. The training sequence permitted generalization with a minimal amount of re-training. Coffee purchasing (Storey et al., 1984), bowling (Schleien et al., 1984), and cooking skills (Schleien, Ash, Kiernan, & Wehman, 1981) were instructed using task analyses and graduated prompting. Participants were offered opportunities to perform the acquired skills in multiple environments with less intrusive prompts as they acquired the skills. This set of procedures resulted in successful generalization to a variety of environments. Lagomarcino et al. 1984) manipulated the training conditions by using multiple trainers to encourage participants to learn to perform the dancing skills in the presence of several individuals.

Schleien, Cameron, Rynders, and Slick (1988) demonstrated the acquisition and generalization of recreation skills, social interactions, and appropriate and cooperative play behaviors by two children with severe developmental disabilities. The recreation skills program occurred in an elementary school. Systematic training procedures incorporating task analysis, error correction, and contingent reinforcement were implemented by the instructors in school. Parents of children with severe developmental disabilities received instruction on the systematic training procedures and then provided additional instruction to their children at home. Results indicated that chronologically age-appropriate recreation skills (i.e., Toss Across, Flash, The Electronic Arcade Game, Simon) were learned by the children. Furthermore, additional training by parents facilitated acquisition of skills, generalization to the home, and maintenance across time.

**Theoretical Foundation #2: Autonomy
to Experience Leisure
Making Choices**

Identification of need. It appears that many practitioners are aware that individual control is one of the important variables in developing successful leisure programs for persons with disabilities (Hunnicutt, 1980; Mobily, 1985a). Smith (1985) stated that individuals strive for a level of independence that allows them to feel in control of their environment. Recreation activities provide opportunities for individuals with disabilities to experience a sense of control by allowing them to believe that their responses have an effect (Howe-Murphy & Charboneau, 1987; Mobily, 1985b). Yet, some practitioners believe that persons with disabilities are not capable of making choices (Guess et al., 1985). In addition, Rowitz and Stoneman (1990) reported that service providers do not consistently allow people with developmental disabilities the right to make choices regarding a variety of aspects of their lives, including the area of leisure.

Most adults with developmental disabilities have had limited opportunities to express choice (Guess et al., 1985). Based on an evaluation of residential programs for persons with developmental disabilities, Bercovici (1983) reported that opportunities for choice-making were typically absent from daily routines and participants demonstrated a reluctance or inability to make choices or express preferences across all environments. After observing over 40 people with developmental disabilities residing in the community, Kishi et al. (1988) reported that, generally, participants did not have choices about fundamental matters of living. More specifically, Kishi et al. reported that although some everyday choices were available to a few participants, persons identified as "lowest functioning" had more limited choices than those ranked as "highest functioning."

Increased attention has been given to the issue of choice making among persons with severe developmental disabilities (Guess et al., 1985; Shevin & Klein, 1984). Houghton et al. (1987) observed that this increased awareness in part, has resulted from the acknowledgment that choice making is a valued and intricate part of life and that the ability to exercise choice increases autonomy and enhances perception of a person's worth. The authors also recognized, however, that opportunities to express preferences and make choices have received only minimal attention, especially with regard to individuals with severe developmental disabilities (Guess & Siegal-Causey, 1985).

Lanagan and Dattilo (1989) observed that most participants with developmental disabilities were not accustomed to having opportunities for control and choice, however, following an intervention promoting choice-making, they reported that participants enjoyed having choices and input into the activity. Although, when given the opportunity to make choices within a recreation activity, many participants experienced difficulty making choices. Difficulty making choices gradually subsided over the course of the investigation.

Implications of interventions. Birgham and Sherman (1973) observed that people without disabilities showed a clear preference and an increased rate of responding for marbles that could be traded for items of their choice and concluded that the opportunity to choose may have been a reinforcing event independent of the changes that choices produced. For instance, when participants were then given the opportunity to earn either immediate candy selected by others during the session or marbles that they could trade after the session for their own choice of candy, they worked for marbles almost exclusively. Interestingly, after the experiment, in response to questions about the candy that was available during the session, participants reported that it was the same as the candy they were choosing after the session. These results suggested that opportunities to choose may have been as important as the reinforcers and, therefore, the opportunity for people to choose alternatives may play an important role in affecting their satisfaction.

Dattilo and Rusch (1985) conducted a study on the effects of choice-making with children with severe developmental disabilities and demonstrated that participants showed higher rates of switch activation in a free choice situation where activating a switch resulted in a television operating for 12 seconds. The noncontingent operation of the television resulted in significantly lower rates of switch activation. Dattilo and Barnett (1985) demonstrated that when recipients of leisure services who have developmental disabilities are provided opportunities and the means to freely select activities, spontaneous initiation of activity, engagement with elements of the environment, and assertion of a degree of control over one's surroundings are often the result. Teaching individuals to make choices has several benefits, including increasing interactions with materials that can facilitate leisure (especially during times when other people are unavailable), allowing them to participate in the services they receive, and increasing quality of programming by having participants indicate their likes and dislikes (Realon, Favell, & Lowerre, 1990).

Monty, Geller, Savage, and Perlmuter (1979) observed positive effects of choice-making opportunities on participants in their investigation and concluded that the positive effects may have been attributed to the extent to which participants perceived control in the situation. Dyer (1987) showed that when children with developmental disabilities were given choices of preferred rewards, decreases were shown in problem behaviors that had been reduced previously only with contingent restraint. Results of Dyer, Dublap, and Winterling's (1990) implementation of a choice-making package in which participants were permitted to make selections of rewards as well as the tasks and materials with which they would be engaged provided further evidence that choice-making produced reductions in problem behaviors.

Results of an investigation conducted by Koegel, Dyer, and Bell (1987) showed that child-preferred activities and social avoidance behaviors were significantly negatively correlated in terms of both objectively scored behavior and subjective ratings of social responsiveness in unmanipulated settings. If children with developmental disabilities were able to engage in preferred activities and therefore experience success, positive reinforcement would be obtained. Results are consistent with those of other studies (Koegel, O'Dell, & Koegel, 1987), which suggested that if activities are modified to allow a person shared control in teaching activities, improvements in speech and other areas (e.g., leisure) can occur. Perhaps shared control results in higher motivation to approach learning situations.

Realon, Favell, and Phillips (1989) compared adapted leisure materials that facilitated choice-making with typically used leisure materials and evaluated effects on engagement, aberrant behaviors, and positive affect of persons with developmental disabilities as well as staff interactions. Although results indicated that use of adapted leisure materials did not result in higher levels of interaction, results showed consistently higher rates of smiling behavior by individuals when adapted leisure materials were available in comparison to when standard leisure materials were available which were further confirmed by social validation. In addition, Lanagan and Dattilo (1989) reported that by the end of an investigation that employed a democratic leadership style encouraging adults with developmental disabilities to make leisure choices, most participants could choose immediately and others began to demonstrate preference by asking for recreation activities. These results supported earlier findings by Wetherby and Prutting (1984) who found that children with developmental disabilities frequently initiated communication with adults in a free-play setting if the adult was non-directive, which allowed opportunities for the child to engage in child-preferred activities rather than in activities that were arbitrarily determined by an adult.

Following a review of the literature devoted to examining effects of people with disabilities' preferences and choice-making opportunities (Guess et al., 1985; Houghton et al., 1987; Kishi et al., 1988; Parsons & Reid, 1990; Shevin & Klein, 1984), Dyer et al. (1990) reported that the success of procedures using choice and preference for persons with disabilities has been documented in studies showing reductions in social avoidance behavior (Koegel, Dyer, & Bell, 1987), increases in spontaneous communication (Dyer, 1987; Peck, 1985), and improvements in task performance (Mithaug & Mar, 1980; Parsons, Reid, Reynolds, & Baumgarner, 1990).

Demonstrating Preferences

Identification of need. Fehr, Wacker, Trezie, Lennon, and Meyerson (1979) observed that unless persons with severe developmental disabilities are provided with the appropriate technology to make their preferences known to staff, they may be provided inadvertently with noncontingent aversive situations. However, preferences of individuals with severe developmental disabilities are often difficult to assess, either because of an apparent lack of motivation or due to idiosyncrasies in their preference patterns (Wacker, Wiggins, Fowler, & Berg, 1988). There is a need for systematic assessment procedures designed to identify preferences for persons with developmental disabilities (Green et al., 1988) because of the impaired motor and communication skills of persons with developmental disabilities that prevent expression of preferences in ways typically used by persons without disabilities (Mithaug & Hanawalt, 1978; Reid & Hurlbut, 1977).

Typical attempts to identify preferences for persons with severe developmental disabilities rely on subjective opinions of caregivers regarding what they think other people want because typical communication of preferences are usually difficult as a result of their mental and physical impairments (Pace, Ivancic, Edwards, Iwata, & Pace, 1985). However, data support the contention that caregiver opinion regarding likes and dislikes of persons with severe developmental disabilities is not very accurate (Favell & Cannon, 1977). There can be large discrepancies among responses of people with severe developmental disabilities that influence detection of preferences.

Houghton et al. (1987) examined the amount of interaction between practitioners and their clients and observed staff responding at very low rates to client-initiated expressions of choice. In addition, Voeltz and Wuerch (1981b) and Reid (1975) concluded that many practitioners choose activities for individuals with disabilities. Dyer (1987), Green et al. (1988), Parsons, Reid, Reynolds, and Perlmutter (1990) demonstrated that practitioners' selections are not as effective in identifying reinforcers as is a procedure of systematic assessment of preferred stimuli. Results of a staff survey conducted by Parsons and Reid (1990) indicated that staff opinion of particular preferences did not consistently coincide with the results of the systematic assessment that successfully determined participants expressed preferences. An investigation conducted by Green et al. indicated that preference rankings of caregiver opinion did not coincide consistently with results from a systematic, observation of preferences.

Implications of interventions. Pace et al. (1985) conducted an evaluation of approach behaviors of persons with severe developmental disabilities toward preferred items (e.g., light, fan). The reinforcing effects of the preferred items were then established by demonstrating that contingent presentations of these items resulted in greater frequencies of target behavior. Idiosyncratic patterns of preferences occurred for the participants, indicating that separate analyses of behavior must be performed for every individual.

Although limited response repertoires of persons with severe developmental disabilities often result in unreliable assumptions regarding participants' preferences toward various items, some investigations have employed the use of technology to determine preferences. Wacker, Berg, Wiggins, Muldoon, and Cavanaugh (1985) used microswitches to quickly determine preferences for all participants who demonstrated markedly different levels of performance between baseline and training. Dattilo and Mirenda (1987) used a computerized protocol for assessing leisure preferences in order to select and quantify motivating vocabulary prior to a communication intervention. Brown, Cavalier, Mineo, and Buckley (1988) provided individuals with severe developmental disabilities with a way to control the activation of various objects in their environment (e.g., video players). Wacker et al. (1988) incorporated microswitches to assess preferences and to provide communicative control over environmental events. The authors found that participants with severe developmental disabilities learned to activate switches to request preferred objects and initiate social interactions both within school and community settings.

In a series of investigations Dattilo (1986, 1987, 1988) demonstrated that the preferences of individuals with severe developmental disabilities could be assessed and analyzed systematically with computer technology resulting in idiosyncratic written and graphic leisure profiles of each participant. The procedure employed to assess participants' leisure preferences also provided them with enjoyable opportunities to demonstrate control over their environment. Dattilo concluded that once assessment of their preferences has occurred, persons with severe developmental disabilities can experience enjoyment and control through participation in preferred activities during a time formerly characterized by boredom and passive observation.

While research has shown that persons with severe developmental disabilities can learn to operate technology (e.g., adaptive switches) which in turn operates leisure materials (Realon, Favell, & Dayvault, 1988), little research has transpired to study how these individuals might be able to make choices (i.e., what types of recreation materials they would like to use). Realon et al. (1990) examined individuals with severe developmental disabilities to determine if they could choose what leisure items they would like to operate during their free time and the effect this had on their interaction with the selected leisure items. Results indicated that leisure materials chosen by participants resulted in increased interaction with those materials. Teaching individuals with developmental disabilities to make choices has the potential to increase interactions with leisure materials allowing them to enhance their ability to experience leisure.

Engaging in Reciprocal Communication

Identification of need. MacDonald and Gillette (1986) reported that helping persons with developmental disabilities communicate more effectively may be one of the major tasks in the field of developmental disabilities that requires interdisciplinary attention. Based on the view that communication develops within reciprocal turn-taking relationships and that such relationships are central to improving communication of persons with disabilities, MacDonald and Gillette suggested that professionals teach parents and service providers how to interact so that persons with developmental disabilities learn to socialize and communicate. These skills are essential in many situations holding the potential for leisure.

Children with severe developmental disabilities need to have their expressions of preference acknowledged and integrated across environments (Siegel-Causey & Guess, 1985). Houghton et al. (1987) observed that staff responded at extremely low rates to expressions of choice or preference initiated by individuals with developmental disabilities, regardless of age and setting. The majority of observed participant initiations appeared to be ignored by staff because, as the authors concluded, professionals have not been trained to observe and respond to subtle, but potentially valuable, behavioral nuances that reflect attempts at expression.

Kohl and Beckman (1990) noted increased concern with identifying behaviors basic to a person's ability to engage in social interactions. According to the authors and Strain and Shores (1977) one such component of social interaction is the ability to engage in reciprocal exchanges (i.e., initiate or continue interaction in which the theme of discourse is maintained over successive turns).

People with disabilities often have difficulty engaging in spontaneous reciprocal exchanges and those observed reciprocal exchanges are frequently brief and simple (Beckman, 1983; Kohl & Beckman, 1990; Odum & Strain, 1984, 1986; Strain, Odum, & McConnell, 1984). For instance, Beckman noted that children with developmental disabilities did not engage in initiations and response chains. Strain, Kerr, and Ragland (1979) suggested that people with developmental disabilities may extinguish attempts of others to interact by failing to respond to initiations.

After reviewing the literature, Peck (1985) concluded that opportunities for child initiation and control of social interactions with adults may be relatively infrequent in therapeutic environments for people with severe developmental disabilities and that changing the social opportunities available to these people may result in substantial increases in their communication. Peck's study of persons with severe disabilities added support to the observation showing few opportunities for participant-initiated interactions provided by staff.

The relative absence of self-initiated communication and exploratory patterns of many people with developmental disabilities during free time may be due more to a lack of opportunities than to an inherent deficit in intrinsic motivation (Haskett & Hollar, 1978). This lack of opportunities creates a major barrier for people with developmental disabilities to develop a satisfying life

(Wuerch & Voeltz, 1982). The lack of opportunity to exhibit self-determined behaviors by people with disabilities often occurs because an effective communication system has yet to be developed.

Many individuals with developmental disabilities, especially those with some form of communication disorder, often exert little or no conversational control during discourse with speakers (Kraat, 1987). The issue of limited conversational control is especially problematic when examining the complex communication needs of people with communication disorders who also have developmental disabilities (Romski & Sevick, 1989). For those people who lack competent communication skills, initiating a new topic of discourse is not present in their conversational skill repertoire (Downing, 1987). Instead, these individuals demonstrate dependency on verbal cues and passively follow conversations chosen for them (Bedrosian & Prutting, 1978).

People who do not speak, particularly those with developmental disabilities, are generally passive during communication. Rather than initiating messages, they frequently produce inappropriate, unintelligible vocalizations and gestures rather than using their systems, and they fail to participate unless requested (or forced) to do so (Calculator & Delaney, 1986). O'Keefe and Dattilo (1991) reported that participants with developmental disabilities acted almost exclusively as respondents to the questions of their conversational partners. Participants were not able to participate in the "give and take" of the true conversation because they lacked skills for such exchanges--the ability to initiate a response in such a way that the conversational partner was required to answer the participant's question or to modify or change the topic of conversation.

Bedrosian (1988) defined conversational control as the "ability to manage discourse in such a way that one's own interpersonal goals are accomplished" (p. 274). A speaker frequently exerts control during conversations by repeatedly asking questions chained together across turns or by responding to a question with another question (Bedrosian; Mishler, 1975). Some speaking partners resort to such questioning in order to control topic, content, and interaction or to cope with perceived differences between them and people with developmental disabilities who have communication disorders (Corsaro, 1979; Mishler; Rush, 1983). In addition to the more frequent use of questions, speakers may shorten topics and make their utterances more telegraphic (Ferguson, 1975; Van Kleek & Carpenter, 1980). Speakers often fail to pause long enough to allow the person with a communication disorder a chance to seize the conversational turn or they interrupt after one or two words (Harris, 1982). Overall, the speaking partner produces a significantly greater number of words than the person with developmental disabilities that possess a communication disorder, is dominant in the proportion of total communicative turns taken in the initiation role, recaptures the initiator role more often (Farrier, Yorkston, Marriner, & Beukelman, 1985), and has a tendency to choose and control the topics of conversation (Bedrosian; Calculator & Dollaghan, 1982; Light, 1985). As a consequence, people with developmental disabilities become merely responders to continuous yes/no, simple choice, or other questions which generally require only one word (or single gesture) responses (Kraat, 1987).

Implications of interventions. Teaching people with developmental disabilities that have communication disorders to begin a conversation or to alter the direction of a conversation will help them move toward conversational balance with speaking partners. Conversational balance is vital in the development of communication between two individuals' who wish to communicate leisure preferences. If people with developmental disabilities that have communication disorders are to begin to more equally share conversations with speakers, it is essential that they learn to initiate as well as respond (Dattilo & Camarata, 1988, 1991; Light, 1988). While they will not duplicate patterns of conversation engaged in by people without communication disorders (Kraat, 1987), an increased balance between them and their speaking partners has been demonstrated.

Results of an investigation conducted by Peck (1985) suggested that substantial increases in communicative behaviors of people with limited communication repertoires can occur in a variety of instructional situations when speakers' interaction styles are modified to afford more opportunities for participants to initiate and control social interactions. Specifically, increases in non-directed communicative behavior by all participants in the study were observed when professionals increased opportunities for choices and student-initiated interactions.

"We must believe that all people, no matter how severe their level of disability, can and frequently do attempt to communicate with others throughout their lives" (Mirenda & Iacono, 1990). A major goal in developing interventions is to enhance the power of the individual over the environment (e.g., Houghton et al., 1987). To achieve this goal, items and activities must be chosen that reflect the individual's preferences. Since people with severe disabilities often become dependent on verbal prompts, Locke and Mirenda (1988) and Mirenda and Dattilo (1987) implemented a verbal prompt-free strategy designed to be participant-directed during initial instruction with people with developmental disabilities who had severe communication disorders.

Participation with peers without disabilities in social settings provides opportunities for people to develop many communication, leisure, and other skills (Gaylord-Ross, Stremel-Campbell, & Storey, 1986). Knapczyk (1989) demonstrated that integration alone is not sufficient to improve social interaction; systematic interventions may be needed. Results corroborate findings of other studies (James & Egel, 1986; Lancioni, 1982) demonstrating that peer-mediated strategies can improve social interaction between people with developmental disabilities and peers without disabilities in natural settings. Kohl and Beckman (1990) concluded that a teacher-mediated strategy designed to promote reciprocal interactions increased the number and mean length of initiation and response chains with children with developmental disabilities. These findings are particularly important in situations where people with and without disabilities are present.

Based on the belief that systematic training in conversational skills is necessary to ensure that people with developmental disabilities acquire skills needed to improve conversational competence, Downing (1987) demonstrated the effectiveness of an intervention package on increasing initiating behaviors of three adolescents with developmental disabilities. Results supported earlier findings by Halle, Baer, and Spradlin (1981) that pronounced delays by staff members (i.e., making eye contact with participants without initiation of any interaction for up to 10 seconds) appeared helpful in facilitating initiations by persons with developmental disabilities. Delays of 10 seconds well exceeded the 3-second pause considered uncomfortable in a conversation with adults of average intelligence and communication skills (McLaughlin & Cody, 1982).

Dattilo and Camarata (1991) demonstrated the value of incorporating self-initiated conversation training for persons with developmental disabilities that have a communication disorder. Simply providing participants with an alternative form of communication was not sufficient to shift them away from the conversational role of respondent; rather, specific conversation initiations training was required before shifts in conversational behavior were observed at home and in a speech clinic. In a related study, O'Keefe and Dattilo (1991) examined the implications of an intervention designed to promote reciprocal communication for persons with developmental disabilities who had communication problems. At the conclusion of training, and as long as 3 weeks after training, all participants were routinely sharing conversations with speaking partners. Results of these studies indicated that professionals may wish to consider teaching reciprocal communication strategies to people who exert little, if any, control over their conversations with speaking partners. Engaging in reciprocal communication enhances a person's ability to communicate preferences, make meaningful choices, and subsequently, experience leisure.

Theoretical Foundation #3:
Community Integration

Identification of need. Researchers have examined the leisure patterns of individuals with developmental disabilities and reported a clear absence of integration into community recreation opportunities. Luckey and Shapiro (1974) observed that a major problem of individuals with developmental disabilities is their lack of knowledge of leisure resources that frequently results in their failure to succeed in the community. Gollay et al. (1978) conducted an investigation of 440 persons who had been deinstitutionalized, many of whom possessed developmental disabilities. The investigators observed that subjects most often participated in passive and solitary recreation activities. Based on these observations, Gollay (1981) concluded that persons with developmental disabilities were less integrated in recreation activities than other individuals with disabilities.

Many individuals with developmental disabilities spend their free time inside their homes rather than participating in community recreation activities (Salzberg & Langford, 1981; Wehman et al., 1980). Cheseldine and Jeffree (1981) surveyed 214 families having at least one member who possessed a mental disability. The subject pool contained adolescents with developmental disabilities. Based on their findings, Cheseldine and Jeffree concluded that the adolescents were experiencing problems developing a satisfying leisure lifestyle because of their: (a) ignorance of existing leisure resources, (b) lack of skills necessary for participation, (c) lack of friends with whom to participate in recreation activities, and (d) parent-imposed restrictions. These barriers resulted in adolescents primarily participating in solitary, passive, family oriented activities that restricted their choice of leisure experiences.

Following an investigation of a small group of persons with developmental disabilities, Crapps, Langone, and Swaim (1985) observed that all participants, regardless of degree of disability, spent an extremely limited amount of free time participating in community recreation environments. These conclusions were supported by Kregel, Wehman, Seyfarth, and Marshall (1986) who surveyed 300 young adults with developmental disabilities and found that the majority of their recreation pursuits were passive, home-based activities.

It is apparent after reviewing the literature describing services for persons with developmental disabilities that there is a strong need for the development of effective leisure service delivery systems in the community. Quilitch and Gray (1974) conducted an investigation intended to demonstrate a teaching program to normalize and reintegrate persons with developmental disabilities into society. Participants' failure to participate in recreation activities after the instructional program was terminated underscored the need to provide leisure instruction within the community while systematically programming for generalization and maintenance.

Schleien, Porter, and Wehman (1979) administered an assessment of leisure skill needs of persons with disabilities, including those with developmental disabilities. Of 128 agencies providing services to individuals with developmental disabilities, 68% indicated they offered less than adequate or no leisure skill training for their clients. The majority of the agencies surveyed reported they could improve programs if appropriate instructional materials and professional expertise were made available to them.

Orelove, Wehman, and Wood (1982) observed that, when recreation programs do exist for people with disabilities, the majority of these programs are still segregated, especially those programs serving persons with developmental disabilities. In an attempt to determine the quantity and quality of recreation services offered in the state of Minnesota, Schleien and Werder (1985) administered a needs assessment to 405 agencies providing recreation for persons with disabilities, many of which provided services for persons with developmental disabilities. The investigators concluded that the philosophy of least restrictive environment has not been applied adequately in leisure programs as indicated by segregated programs (e.g., Special Olympics, special camps) being the prevalent organizational format for leisure instruction and programming.

It is helpful for individuals with developmental disabilities to develop age-appropriate, community leisure skill repertoires facilitating successful integration into the community (Falvey, 1986; Martin, Burke, & Findlay, 1985; Schleien, Tuckner, & Heyne, 1985). Ford et al. (1984) suggested that leisure skills be developed on the basis of those activities performed by individuals who are not disabled in a wide variety of integrated community environments. Therefore, practitioners should encourage persons with developmental disabilities to acquire leisure skills that are age-appropriate and comparable to their peers (Wehman & Moon, 1985). Practitioners should only teach those leisure skills that have the potential of being performed in the presence of, or in interaction with, peers without disabilities (Certo et al., 1983; Silberman, 1987).

In a recent review of the literature, Bedini (1990) identified the following needs regarding integrating recreation programs for people with disabilities: (a) increased accessibility (Austin & Powell, 1981); (b) more money (Vaughn & Winslow, 1979); (c) more knowledge about people with disabilities (Schleien & Ray, 1988); (d) elimination of discriminating policies and agency attitudes (Howe-Murphy, 1980); (e) integration on an individual basis (Lord, 1983); (f) increased consumer power through advocacy (West, 1982); (g) legislation to ensure equal rights (Hutchinson, 1980); and (h) high expectations about people with disabilities (Matthews, 1977). Although Bedini identified numerous barriers to integrated recreation experiences for people with disabilities, she concluded that the most devastating barrier toward people with disabilities is negative attitudes. This conclusion was supported by West (1982) who examined employees of recreation and park departments and other related social service agencies and identified agency policies reinforcing stigma, exclusion, and segregation of people with disabilities that reflected negative attitudes of personnel and members of the community. According to West (1984) 46% of visitors to public parks who were disabled perceived a negative attitude from the general public. As a result, 25% of the people with disabilities reported reducing their participation in the parks voluntarily.

People with developmental disabilities should acquire leisure skills and knowledge of leisure resources. However, the critical issue is not simply to gain an awareness of community resources, but rather, it is to become an active participant in community life (Richler, 1984). Therefore, a comprehensive approach to therapeutic recreation encouraging community involvement must be developed to integrate persons with developmental disabilities into leisure opportunities available in the community. However, Asch (1989) warned that integrated settings may have little to offer toward dispelling the isolation experienced by individuals with developmental disabilities without opportunities to develop relationships and increase competence in social interaction.

Implications of interventions. Wehman, Renzaglia, Berry, Schultz, and Karan (1978) recognized the need for persons with developmental disabilities to develop a repertoire of community leisure skills and conducted a study employing a task analysis leisure instruction program for two people with developmental disabilities. Results of the investigation demonstrated the importance of teaching age-appropriate leisure skills to persons with developmental disabilities to expand their leisure repertoire and thus provide them with increased choice for leisure involvement within their communities.

To avoid the use of infant and preschool recreation materials for adults with developmental disabilities that inhibit community integration, Horst, Wehman, Hill, and Bailey (1981) recommended expanding the range of age-appropriate leisure skill options. Therefore, the authors conducted an investigation using a task analytic approach that taught individuals to use a variety of recreation materials (i.e., frisbee, cassette player, electronic bowling). Hill et al. (1982) demonstrated the ability of individuals with developmental disabilities to acquire and generalize skills facilitating participation in age-appropriate recreation activities underscoring the value of community leisure instruction.

Following a review of the literature, Voeltz, Wuerch, and Bockhaut (1982) noted that practitioners must assist persons with developmental disabilities in developing age-appropriate leisure activity repertoires if they are to adjust to integrated community environments (Ball, Chasey, Hawkins, & Verhoven, 1976; Birenbaum & Re, 1979; Brown et al., 1979; Voeltz, Wuerch, & Wilcox, 1982; Wehman & Schleien, 1981). However, the authors reported that documentation of performance of a recreation activity skill during training sessions is a limited evaluation of the effectiveness of leisure education programs. They recommended inclusion of documentation providing evidence that community residents value skills displayed by persons with developmental disabilities. The authors, therefore, demonstrated the feasibility of employing social validation procedures to evaluate the applied significance of a leisure intervention for youth with developmental disabilities.

Dyer, Schwartz, and Luce (1984) conducted an investigation examining the functional value of materials and tasks as well as the age-appropriateness of tasks. Following completion of the intervention based on the description of age-appropriate functional skills presented by Brown et al. (1979) to facilitate community integration, Dyer et al. observed participants with developmental disabilities engaging in functional and age-appropriate activities for increased durations.

Jeffree and Cheseldine (1984) demonstrated that 10 adolescents with developmental disabilities could acquire the skills needed to play table games. More importantly, the investigators observed that participation in table games permitted the individuals to interact with other people without disabilities while engaged in an age-appropriate recreation activity. Jeffree and Cheseldine concluded that once a repertoire of leisure skills has been acquired by persons with developmental disabilities, decisions can be made regarding better use of free time in the community.

Hamre-Nietupski, Nietupski, Sandvig, Sandvig, and Ayres (1984) recommended the following considerations when selecting age-appropriate community recreation activities for persons with developmental disabilities who are deaf/blind: (a) sensory input provided by the activity, (b) motoric movements required for participation, and (c) reaction speed needed to use materials. To illustrate these considerations, the authors conducted an investigation involving attachment of permanent tactile prompts on materials, stabilization of materials, enhancement of visual and auditory feedback by materials, and simplification of the task. The authors concluded that use of task adaptation strategy in conjunction with systematic instruction can result in acquisition of age-appropriate leisure skills for persons with developmental disabilities who are deaf/blind.

Based on the observation that the majority of investigations demonstrating the acquisition of leisure skills by persons with developmental disabilities have focused only on the acquisition of specific skills, Schleien et al. (1984) conducted an investigation to demonstrate the ability of an adolescent with developmental disabilities to acquire and maintain skills required in a community recreation activity (i.e., bowling). The authors used a task analyzed instructional sequence based on skill and setting information generated from an ecological inventory, in conjunction with systematic behavioral teaching techniques. The adolescent effectively learned the recreation activity and generalized this learning across both settings and materials.

Based on previous findings of Schleien and Werder (1985) that the principle of least restrictive environment has yet to be adequately applied to recreation programs and that "handicapped-only" recreation programs are the prevalent organizational format for recreation instruction and programming, Schleien and Larson (1986) conducted an investigation using a multiple baseline design. The authors demonstrated that two individuals with severe developmental disabilities acquired age-appropriate leisure skills to independently use a community recreation center, access the center in the absence of a professional, and interact with community recreation personnel concerning personal preferences of recreation activities.

The potential advantages of integration of persons with developmental disabilities into recreation activities in the community are not limited to the people with disabilities (Howe-Murphy & Charboneau, 1987). After participating in experiences involving systematic interaction with people who possess developmental disabilities, individuals without disabilities have demonstrated an increase in positive attitudes toward people with disabilities (Donder & Nietupski, 1981; Fenrick & Petersen, 1984; McHale & Simeonsson, 1980).

Richardson, Wilson, Weatherald, and Peters (1987) conducted a needs assessment of 6,000 people with disabilities who reported that their number one priority for the recreation department was to address the problem of a lack of mainstreamed recreation opportunities. Over 90% of the respondents reported they would prefer generic recreation services as opposed to those designated as "special." Based on these findings, Richardson et al. developed a systematic procedure for integrating people with disabilities into community recreation programs. Based on the evaluation of individuals' completion of a recreation program (N = 262), opinions of mainstreaming companions, and reported perceptions by participants, the authors concluded that their attempt at facilitating integrated recreation opportunities was successful.

In response to observations that direct contact during leisure participation and frequent interaction between people with and without disabilities stimulate the formation of positive attitudes (Hamilton & Anderson, 1983; Voeltz, 1982), Schleien, Krotee, Mustonen, Kelterborn, and Schermer (1987) implemented a program incorporating responsiveness to activity preferences, cooperative group structures, and peer training, to integrate two children with severe developmental disabilities into a children's sports camp. Results of the study suggested that the integration of the children into recreation and sports settings was feasible and beneficial for those involved. The authors reported that along with the positive increases in effective play the children decreased their inappropriate play.

Schleien, Ray, Soderman-Olson, and McMahon (1987) demonstrated that implementing several strategies, including inservice training for relevant personnel, sensitivity training for children without disabilities, site visitations, social reinforcement, and cooperative grouping arrangements, facilitated integration of children with developmental disabilities into a community creative arts program. Positive changes in participants' appropriate interactions, socially appropriate behaviors, and attitudes of peers without disabilities occurred following the intervention. The investigation provided support that children with developmental disabilities and children without such disabilities can successfully participate together in a community leisure environment. Follow-up data collected by Schleien, Rynders, and Mustonen (1988) further confirmed the successful integration of children with and without severe developmental disabilities into community museum programs.

Walker and Edinger (1988) systematically examined implications of the integration of an 11-year-old boy with severe mental retardation and cerebral palsy into a 1-week camping experience involving approximately 200 children without disabilities. In addition, Walker (1988) reported on participation of a teenage girl who had Down syndrome in an integrated after-school recreation program. Based on extensive observations and interviews, the authors made several conclusions. When people were integrated in leisure environments, it appeared that a sense of belonging was critical to the success of persons with developmental disabilities. Participants without disabilities should observe people with disabilities actively participating in recreation activities. Successful integration occurs when a few people with disabilities are introduced into a leisure environment accompanied by individualized adaptations. Scheduling of time to have people with and without disabilities socialized informally during unstructured free time appears to facilitate integration.

Schleien, Cameron, Rynders, and Slick (1988) taught three age-appropriate leisure skills to two children with severe developmental disabilities while facilitating social interactions and cooperative play behaviors within an integrated leisure skill program in a public school. Improvements in social interaction, cooperative play, and appropriate play illustrated the benefits associated with the integration of children with developmental disabilities into recreation programs including children without disabilities.

The responsibility of therapeutic recreation specialists is to provide programs with the best potential for helping participants benefit from leisure (Fain, 1986). Anderson and Allen (1985) tested the utility of a leisure education program, originally developed by Joswiak (1979), on persons with developmental disabilities. The leisure education program emphasizing the development of an awareness of leisure resources within the home and community was administered to 40 individuals with developmental disabilities. Participation in the leisure education program emphasizing knowledge of leisure resources appeared to enhance the frequency of activity involvement. Lanagan and Dattilo (1989) found similar results for a group of people with developmental disabilities when they demonstrated that a leisure education program emphasizing awareness of leisure resources produced a higher incidence of involvement than a recreation participation program and showed potential for knowledge retention. The favorable and sustained results for leisure education in these studies may mean a little leisure education goes a long way.

Schleien, Fahnestock, Green, and Rynders (1990) described a case study involving a child with severe and multiple developmental disabilities. The study demonstrated successful implementation of sociometry, circle of friends, and cooperative learning techniques as strategies to include people with severe developmental disabilities into integrated community recreation programs. In another investigation using a quasi-experimental design, Rynders, Schleien, and Mustonen (1990) implemented an intervention that included social reinforcement of occurrences of appropriate behavior on the part of three campers with developmental disabilities and contingent reinforcement of the nondisabled peers social interactions. Results indicated an increase in social interaction bids and perceptions of friendship by campers without disabilities, skill acquisition in campers with disabilities, and positive ratings of staff participating in the integrated camping experience.

Theoretical Foundation #4: Social Skills and Friendship Development

Identification of need. People with developmental disabilities generally exhibit limited social and behavioral skills essential to success in home, school, and community environments. These individuals do not usually exhibit appropriate play skills and are typically characterized as possessing delayed patterns of social interaction (Knapczyk & Yoppi, 1975). Their social withdrawal often include minimal eye contact, active avoidance of social contact, and failure to initiate or sustain interactions (Shafer, Egel, & Neef, 1984). Consequently, their socialization skills may be severely impaired and stereotypic, and inappropriate behaviors become prevalent in their repertoires. Frequently, people will identify a person as being developmentally disabled, not because they observed the person's inability to perform some cognitive or physical task, but as a result of the person's display of inappropriate social behaviors. The absence of social skills is particularly noticeable during recreation participation (Marlowe, 1979) and frequently leads to isolation and an inability to function successfully (Dattilo, 1991; O'Morrow, 1980). Therefore, the development of social skills used in recreation activities appears to be important since the acquisition of these skills facilitates integration (Keogh, Faw, Whitman, & Reid, 1984). The development of meaningful friendships and effective social interaction skills can be taught through systematic recreation programs (Green & Schleien, 1991).

Many inappropriate behaviors exhibited or desired behaviors not exhibited by individuals with developmental disabilities reflect a lack of appropriate and social play with peers (Scott & Gilliam, 1987). This limits their opportunities to access integrated environments (Schleien & Ray, 1988). Fine, Feldis, and Lehrer (1982), in summarizing the play abilities of children with autism, for example, suggested that they tend to be socially unresponsive and noncommunicative preferring self-stimulating, repetitive activities, like spinning or rhythmic movements, as opposed to games which require social interaction. Much of the recreation behavior of persons with developmental disabilities involves manipulating familiar objects (Hawkins, 1982).

Individuals with developmental disabilities can learn, through games, to interact more capably with their peers (Collard, 1981; Jansma, 1982; Schleien, 1983; Wehman & Schleien, 1981). Moreover, participants in an integrated program can benefit from positive interactions with peers who have developmental disabilities, showing improvements in self-awareness and peer acceptance (Schleien & Ray, 1988; Voeltz & Brennan, 1984). Positive experiences and development of a leisure repertoire can positively influence cooperation, social skills and social adjustment, and, ultimately, development of friendships and integration into the community (Schleien, Fahnestock, Green, & Rynders, 1990).

Most persons without disabilities participate in social interactions daily, ranging from explicit verbal statements (e.g., "I'm proud of your work,") to subtle facial expressions or body language (e.g., a smile to indicate to another pleasure or acceptance). However, many individuals with developmental disabilities demonstrate minimal social interaction (Schleien & Wehman, 1986). A more critical issue is that more often than not, social interactions are not included in the instructional programs for persons with developmental disabilities (Certo &

Schleien, 1982). Additionally, many of these individuals are not frequently provided the opportunities to interact (Certo & Kohl, 1984; Hamre-Nietupski et al., 1978).

Implications of interventions. In this section, recreation programming and its influence on social interactions and friendships are explored. Social interaction and friendship skills training should be included in comprehensive recreation programs for individuals with developmental disabilities. Social interactions can be viewed as an element in recreation activities that require more than one person. Bringing individuals together for a common goal provides a multiplicity of natural opportunities for socialization and interaction. Therefore, recreation activities can be used to facilitate friendships and cooperative play between peers as well as between individuals with disabilities (Paloutzian et al., 1971; Ragland, Kerr, & Strain, 1978; Strain, 1975).

The role of recreation as a mediator of social development was summarized by Luckey and Shapiro (1974) when they stated that:

> Games with increasingly complex rules and social demands further enhance children's social adaption as they grow older, and participation in clubs and organizations takes on increasing social importance during the school years. (p. 33)

The authors suggested that "organized sports additionally provide young adults opportunities for personal achievement, while teaching rules of competition and the controlled expression of aggression" (p.33). These social traits are mandatory for successful adjustment to the community. While the effects that participating in games and sports have on people with developmental disabilities are unclear, it is likely that successful game experiences are helpful in establishing appropriate social behavior patterns and in providing opportunities for positive learning experiences (Wehman & Schleien, 1981).

For approximately 25 years, cooperative recreation activities have been investigated (Hart, Reynolds, Baer, Brawley, & Harris, 1968; Paloutzian et al., 1971; Stokes, Baer, & Jackson, 1974; Strain, 1977; Strain, Kerr, & Ragland, 1979; Strain, Shores, & Kerr, 1976; Whitman, Mercurio, & Caponigri, 1970; Young & Kerr, 1979) as one starting place to promote social interactions. Generalization and "spill-over effects" (Strain, Shores, & Kerr) of social skills to different objects (Whitman et al.), people (Hart et al.; Stokes et al.; Strain, 1975; Strain et al., 1976; Whitman et al.) and settings (Stokes et al.; Strain, 1975) have exhibited the importance and wide-reaching effects cooperative play skills can have on increasing social skills in individuals with developmental disabilities. While the introduction of cooperative play skills is not the only way to promote social skills (Deutsch & Parks, 1978; Matson & Adkins, 1984), it is one proven method to increase social interactions in natural settings (e.g., free play or recess).

Many factors influence the success of recreation activities in promoting social interactions among participants with and without disabilities. The following list is not meant to be an exhaustive collection of factors that influence social interactions and the development of friendships, as that list could conceivably be infinite. The list includes factors cited across studies as having importance in development of interpersonal and friendship skills. These factors are not described in order, as all are potentially significant and are not prerequisite for each other. Therapeutic recreation specialists should consider as many of these factors as possible to enhance socialization. For example, professionals may not have control over the age of participants or the number of people in the group. However, practitioners should have control over what objects and games are made accessible or arrangement of the environment to promote cooperative play.

One factor effecting social interactions within the context of recreation activity is the age of the participants. According to Levitt and Cohen (1976) and Peterson and Haralick (1977), younger children are more accepting of peers with developmental disabilities than older children are of their peers with disabilities. The two major implications emerging from this research were that programs should be developed for and implemented with young children to promote social interactions. The preschool age was identified as the appropriate time to promote positive attitudes in children toward their peers with disabilities (Guralnick, 1978). Teaching preschoolers with developmental disabilities appropriate social and play skills could prepare them for training of more complex social interactions as they grow older. A second major point concerns attitudes of older individuals (at least as old as elementary school age). Negative attitudes toward older peers with disabilities demonstrated the need for targeting appropriate social interactions for instruction, in an effort to foster more positive attitudes in their peers.

To develop techniques to increase social interactions between individuals with and without developmental disabilities, observations of individuals without disabilities interacting with one another should occur (Brown, Branston, Hamre-Nietupski, Johnson, Wilcox, & Gruenewald, 1979; Brown, Branston, Hamre-Nietupski, Pumpian, Certo, & Gruenewald, 1979). As a typical social interaction between individuals in a recreation activity is observed, a second factor influencing the interaction, that is, the size of the group, is noticed. In a study by Parten (1932) of the play of preschool children, the size of the play group was considered a significant factor in the amount of social interaction that transpired. Results suggested that younger children spent a majority of their play time in groups of two. Play groups of five or more were usually observed with the older children. This information could be valuable when selecting recreation activities for preschool students with developmental disabilities versus activities appropriate for older individuals. For example, an activity to teach a preschool youngster may be play skills in a playground sandbox. Most activities in a sandbox, within a preschool classroom, are limited in the number of participants permitted at one time (Parten). An appropriate activity for older individuals could be card games such as Uno, Spades, or Hearts requiring a group of people to participate concurrently.

Schleien, Rynders, Mustonen, and Fox (1990) explored the effects of four social levels of play: (a) isolate, (b) dyadic, (c) group, and (d) team, on appropriate play behavior of children with autism in an integrated physical education program. Results indicated that not only did the type of play activity influence frequency of appropriate play behavior exhibited by the children, but that they consistently played more appropriately in more developmentally advanced (i.e., team, group, dyadic) play activities as compared with their frequency of appropriate play in isolate play activities.

A third significant factor in the development of social interactions is the selection of recreation equipment and materials that affords individuals with developmental disabilities additional opportunities to interact (Quilitch & Risely, 1973). Referencing the selection according to the recreation equipment and materials most frequently used by persons without disabilities (Parten, 1932) will ensure the equipment chosen to be chronologically age-appropriate. There is a positive correlation between the number of peers without disabilities who use a given piece of equipment, and the number of opportunities the individual with a disability has to participate in the same activity and socialize with others. However, a particular piece of recreation equipment may be popular but may not facilitate social interactions during its use (e.g., portable radio, compact disc player). While it is important to teach recreation skills of a solitary nature, an emphasis should also be made to develop social interactions through group activities (Wehman & Schleien, 1981). Therefore, practitioners should select activities and equipment that promote social interactions, especially for participants with developmental disabilities (Buell, Stoddard, Harris, & Baer, 1968).

A fourth factor influencing the development of social skills through recreation activities is the arrangement of the environment. An inventory of specific social interactions occurring in a particular activity or environment is a fundamental step in social skills training (Certo & Kohl, 1984; Certo et al., 1983; Guralnick, 1978). Activities can be chosen on the basis of promoting cooperative play, by inventorying environments where cooperative play was observed among peers without disabilities.

An additional factor that may influence social interactions is the ratio of participants with and without disabilities in an integrated program. According to Peterson and Haralick (1977), the interactions of preschoolers varied depending on the ratios between the children with and without disabilities. The integrated group of children containing a larger number of children without disabilities proved to be the most effective situation for fostering social interactions. Although children without disabilities chose to play more frequently with other children without disabilities, preschoolers participated in "nonisolated play" with their peers with disabilities for more than 50% of the sessions observed. Even under ideal conditions of an integrated setting, proximity of individuals alone is not sufficient. According to Peterson and Haralick, their results may suggest that one strategy for maximizing constructive integrated play is to assure that play areas contain an appropriate ratio of children with and without disabilities. In part, the appropriateness of a social response is determined by others included in the interaction (e.g., recipient of interaction). An appropriate response has a higher probability of being reinforced in some manner by those involved in the interaction. Therefore, interactions engaged in by participants with developmental disabilities in integrated settings should have a high probability of eliciting positive peer responses (Gable, Hendrickson, & Strain, 1978).

An advantage of developing social interactions is the concurrent reduction of inappropriate behaviors (Schleien, Kiernan, & Wehman, 1981; Strain, Shores, & Kerr, 1976). In turn, a reduction in inappropriate behaviors allows the individual greater opportunities to interact with others. According to Strain, Shores, and Kerr, not only did the frequency of the students' inappropriate behaviors decrease, but "spill-over effects" of positive social interactions affected students who were not receiving direct reinforcement for their participation in social interactions.

When targeting social interactions and friendship skills for individuals with disabilities, a systematic method should be used for determining those social interactions considered to be appropriate since there is variation in interpersonal skills between and within environments (Beveridge, 1976). Certo and Kohl (1984) suggested a 5-step method of inventorying an environment so as to systematically delineate the social interactions: (a) selecting a functional, age-appropriate activity; (b) observing the activity in the natural environment; (c) developing longitudinal task analyses/skill sequences; (d) determining the interactions that occur; and, e) identifying the interactions for instruction based on individual needs.

Using the natural environment as a reference provides information concerning the appropriateness of a response according to the participant's chronological age and facilitates identification of the situational cues the participant must discriminate in order to respond (Bordy & Stoneman, 1977). For example, the eye contact of the attendant at a skating rink, and the phrase, "You're next!" are situational cues communicating to the participant to request a pair of skates. The same environment may have many situational cues, and it may not be necessary to use them all to function in the setting. However, this is when use of the method suggested by Certo and Kohl (1984) is appropriate to outline specific social interactions occurring in a setting. With this list of interactions, a priority can be determined for a particular individual. In a skating rink, a high priority may be those social interactions necessary to rent skates (i.e., mandatory task-related interactions), whereas a low priority could be initiating a greeting or smiling at the rink guard when entering the facility (i.e., contextual social interactions).

Once the social interactions and friendship skills are identified for instruction, identification of techniques to teach these skills should occur. Several methods have been used successfully to facilitate social interactions to individuals with developmental disabilities. The following studies are cited as a sampling of the literature that address social interactions and cooperative play behavior.

Hill and Wehman (1980) examined the social interactions between teenagers and young adults who were profoundly mentally retarded and peers without disabilities across several community recreation environments (i.e., scouts, community recreation, video room within a bowling alley, fast food restaurant). A significant number of youth across these environments indicated that participants with severe disabilities can benefit from integrated community recreation activity. Also, they reported that they could benefit from being around individuals who are severely disabled and could feel comfortable in close proximity. Social interactions (i.e., greetings, instructional interactions, social interactions) developed naturally early on and rose to higher levels throughout the integrated programs.

Hart et al. (1968) presented adult social reinforcement randomly throughout a school day, to a 5-year-old girl. The participant was described as socially withdrawn, behaviorally disruptive, and uncooperative when interacting with peers. In the treatment phase, reinforcement was offered to the child when she was engaged in cooperative play. The child's degree of cooperative play increased significantly while the amount of time she was withdrawn or engaged in disruptive behavior decreased. Teachers reinforced more appropriate behaviors of the entire group after the target child became a participating member of the group. Results demonstrated the positive effects of contingent social reinforcement as opposed to random teacher's attention.

Another study using contingent reinforcement to facilitate cooperative play interactions was conducted by Whitman et al. (1970). Food and social reinforcement were presented to two children who were severely mentally retarded contingent upon mutual participation in block-passing and ball-rolling tasks. Results indicated a significant increase in social interaction between the two participants. Four additional children participated in the activities, however, in the latter phase, no direct training occurred when the original participants and the new members of the group interacted together. Social interactions were generalized by both target students toward the four newest members of the group. The socialized behavior also generalized to toys not previously used, without specific training. The authors concluded that the social interactions associated with the task became somewhat reinforcing on their own. Therefore, Gable et al. (1978) recommended reinforcement for social interactions be offered on an intermittent schedule as quickly as possible. This enables the naturally occurring reinforcement derived by social interactions with peers to take control.

Deutsch and Parks (1978) used music contingently as reinforcement to facilitate conversational speech. The participant was a 14-year-old male, who was described as speaking in a high, baby-like voice (although he could speak in a normal tone of voice), mumbling, and echolalia. Music was presented contingently upon appropriate conversational responses made by the participant during a 5-minute daily training session. The contingent use of music produced significant results by increasing the amount of appropriate conversational responses engaged in by the participant. In addition, the child's inappropriate responses (e.g., mumbling, baby-like voice, and echolalia) were reduced simultaneously with the increase of appropriate speech. Music was found to be reinforcing for up to 20 trials as compared to other reinforcers, where the student satiated after only a few trials. Also, music is appreciated by people of all ages, making music a flexible reinforcer and potential recreation activity.

Matson and Adkins (1984) used audio-tapes and rehearsal methods as a means for self-instruction of social skills by two adults who were moderately mentally retarded. Appropriate social responses were described as initiating conversation, complimenting one another, making appropriate requests, and responding appropriately to requests. The procedure required participants to review tapes presenting scenes of individuals interacting during their free time and researchers questions concerning appropriate social responses. After reviewing the scenes, the researcher discussed each interaction with the participants. Role play, verbal feedback from the instructor, and social reinforcement were used as error correction procedures during training. The participants exhibited a significant improvement in their number of appropriate social skills. The researchers discussed the benefits of training in the natural setting (i.e., recreation environment), and found the self-instruction method to be more efficient, requiring fewer numbers of training sessions than that of standard methods of training social skills.

The use of socio-dramatic activities in a program conducted by Strain (1975) increased the amount of social play engaged in by a group of preschool children who were severely mentally retarded. The socio-dramatic activities consisted of the instructor reading a story and assigning each student a role. During the reading, the teacher encouraged students to perform two of the character's verbal and/or motor behaviors. The amount of social play among children increased as a result of the socio-dramatic story telling. Children who had little or no social play behaviors prior to the socio-dramatic activities increased their degree of social play, but not to the extent of the children already possessing appropriate interpersonal skills. Perhaps this type of activity would be beneficial as a supplemental activity to promote social play following the training of primary social interactions. This activity may also facilitate generalization of interactions.

Stokes et al. (1974) taught four participants who were developmentally disabled to generalize a greeting response (i.e., hand waving). Each participant was trained to wave, "hello," when passing the trainer. If the students performed the behavior incorrectly, the trainer physically prompted the students through the correct behavior and then emitted reinforcement. Prompting was gradually faded and reinforcement was given to the students for successive approximations toward the final behavior (i.e., shaping). Several personnel (not trainers) would periodically walk up to the students at various times during the day and in several locations to observe whether the waving response generalized to other people and settings other than the original training site. Prompting and reinforcement for the waving response were only provided during instructional sessions. Results indicated that all five students acquired the skills necessary to initiate a wave to greet another person and the targeted behavior generalized to other personnel and locations.

Paloutzian et al. (1971) used prompting and reinforcement successfully with 10 children who were severely mentally retarded to imitate novel social behaviors (e.g., passing a bean bag, walking up to another student and gently stroking his face, pushing a child in a swing, pulling a peer in a wagon, rocking another peer in a rocking chair or hobby horse). The first phase involved children imitating modeled responses which were not social in nature. After the participant reached criterion on this phase, phase two was initiated to teach social behaviors with two trainers and two participants working together. The first trainer offered the cue and modeled the correct response for the first student. The first student performed the behavior with or without prompting as necessary and received food and social attention as reinforcement. The roles of the students and trainers were then reversed to train the second student. Significant increases from pre- to post-test scores in the levels of social behaviors in those participants who were trained using the prompting and reinforcement methods were obtained. Adults and peer models were used providing a method of training complex social responses to a large number of children with a small number of staff.

A series of studies in the 1970s were conducted using peers either with or without disabilities as role models. Young and Kerr (1979) trained a learner with moderate mental retardation to be a peer tutor for two children with severe mental retardation. The peer tutor was to increase the social interactions of the two students. After being trained to increase social interactions, the peer tutor was placed in a play area with one student, toys, and edibles. Results indicated that the peer tutor was successful in increasing the positive responding to "social initiations" by his two peers.

Somewhat contradictory results were found in a program involving children with moderate mental retardation (Knapczyk & Peterson, 1975). In this study, older children without disabilities were integrated into the playroom with other children and encouraged to interact with each other through cooperative play. Increased rates of cooperative play occurred with the models without disabilities. When the models were withdrawn, cooperative play levels decreased to baseline levels. Another study by the same investigators was equally revealing. Introduction of preschool children without disabilities of equivalent mental ages but younger chronological ages (3- and 4-year-olds) led to little changes in cooperative play levels of the same students with moderate mental retardation. Knapczyk and Peterson interpreted these findings as indication that competence in models, when viewed by less competent observers, influences the likelihood of behavior being imitated.

Classmates were used collectively as peer models for a preschool-level girl with behavioral disorders (Strain & Timm, 1974). Adult attention was presented contingently either to the child or to peers for displaying socially appropriate behaviors during free play. In phase one of the study, adult attention, used as a reinforcer, was given to the target child's peers whenever they initiated a social interaction or appropriately responded to a social interaction initiated by another peer. In phase two, the child received reinforcement for her initiation of a social interaction or an appropriate response to a social interaction initiated by a peer. In both phases, the number of positive behaviors increased for the child as well as her peers. Contingent use of adult attention appeared to be effective in increasing positive social behaviors of preschoolers. The researchers believed that teacher/adult proximity was a factor. Whether the teacher was rewarding a particular student, the teachers' proximity to a number of students could have reinforced the social behaviors of children not directly receiving verbal praise.

A child who was mildly mentally retarded was used by Ragland, Kerr, and Strain (1978) as a peer model for three children with autism. As in other peer modeling studies, the peer model was given individual training on how to promote social interactions and cooperative play in the three target students. During intervention, the peer model was instructed to encourage the students to play with him. Cooperative play behaviors increased for all three students when the peer model reinforced appropriate social interactions. Generalization, measured as an increase in cooperative play and social interactions prior to direct training, did not occur as increases in social behaviors were only seen after the peer model procedure was implemented. The author contended that since the children had such severe disruptive behaviors, observations of the positive social behaviors of peers in training was minimal at best. Therefore, when the students were approached on a one-to-one basis by the peer model, and subsequently reinforced by this model for positive social behaviors, increases in social behaviors were obtained.

In a program conducted by Strain (1977), a preschool child was trained to initiate and reinforce positive social interactions with three preschoolers with behavior disorders. Results showed an increase in positive social interactions engaged in by the three students during the training sessions. Two of the students exhibited generalization in social behaviors during free play following training. Strain suggested that the increase of generalized social behaviors was only half the amount that was performed by the students during training, because during free play with the remaining members of the class, social interactions initiated by trained students were not positively reinforced by their classmates who did not receive training. Therefore, initiations of social interactions decreased during free play for lack of positive reinforcement. Strain also suggested programming for interpersonal skills in integrated situations as a necessity to facilitate social interactions, even when peers are used as models.

Strain et al. (1979) investigated four children labeled autistic and one child without a disability trained as a peer model. During training sessions, the peer model initiated social interactions with one pair of students with disabilities at a time. During the first phase (i.e., prompting and reinforcement), the peer model was instructed to have the two students interact with each other. During the second phase (i.e., social initiation), the peer model was to initiate social interactions between himself and one of the students with disabilities at a time during the session. An increase in the number of social behaviors for all four students when using both techniques--prompting and reinforcement, and social initiation--was found. However, generalization data, following the training sessions, displayed no significant increases in the frequencies of appropriate social behaviors for the students, perhaps due to insufficient training across multiple settings.

One of the most comprehensive efforts at analyzing the instructional components of social interaction training was conducted by Williams, Brown, and Certo (1975) with students who were moderately mentally retarded. These workers analyzed social interactions in four components: (a) initiates interaction, (b) receives interaction, (c) sustains interaction, and (d) terminates interaction. Peer functioning level, task availability, and training across environmental settings are major points considered when arranging an appropriate environment for social interaction. What made this research unique was the explicit instructional direction given for conducting the program. Supportive data are provided for each program that was completed by the student.

Several researchers in the 1960s explored the use recreation activities as a means of integrating persons with developmental disabilities into the classroom or community. Greater participation in social activities can lead to increased social acceptance by peers. Hayes (1969) investigated the integration of children with mental retardation with other children in a day camp. Using the following indices of behavior: (a) cooperation, (b) interaction, (c) parallel play, (d) self-initiated activity, (e) nonactivity, and (f) aggression, Hayes found that children with mental retardation interacted well with their peers. Successful integration of children with mild mental retardation with their peers has been achieved through outdoor education (Hayes & Brooks, 1966, 1967).

Social clubs can promote socialization skills and self-initiated behavior in people with developmental disabilities. Brown and McBaine (1965) formed a social club for high school students with developmental disabilities involving trained leaders for guidance. Hammond (1968) developed a social club for primary grade children with disabilities. Gingeland (1968) made a suggestion which may bear close examination regarding the utility and design of social clubs for persons with developmental disabilities. He recommended that, initially, generalized exploratory clubs should be formed so participants as well as club leaders may determine which activity is most preferred. Later, the person can branch out into interest programs or develop life-long hobbies.

Several successful programs have been documented to teach older students and young adults the component skills needed to access community recreation. Schleien et al. (1984) taught the necessary combination of recreation and related skills to an adolescent who was severely disabled to enable him to use a neighborhood bowling facility. The student acquired the skills for complete use of the center in just 6 weeks. Generalization data demonstrated the student's successful transfer of acquired skills to similar environments and materials. Skill sequence adaptations and adaptive devices were acceptable substitutions for component recreation and related skills. Using response methods that appear slightly different (topographically dissimilar), yet which enable students to secure the same result (i.e., are functionally equivalent) as the component responses typically employed, provides a promising tool for therapeutic recreation specialists interested in providing maximum social integration for individuals with developmental disabilities.

Corcoran and French (1977) and Schleien and Larson (1986) also described programs designed to teach older students (high school, college age, and adults) social participation in existing community recreation programs. Corcoran and French's description of a college-based continuing education program--supported by state taxes, service organizations, and a student registration fee--represents a particularly promising approach to establishing for persons with disabilities the kinds of social experiences which adults typically have access to in most communities. Schleien, Krotee, Mustonen, Kelterborn, and Schermer (1987) and Schleien et al. (1985) provided evaluative data to support school-age children with autism and severe multiple disabilities in a range of programs. Detailed support materials and a comprehensive curriculum are available for replication of these program models (Schleien et al., 1987; Schleien & Ray, 1988).

Finally, Salzberg and Langford (1981) designed a friendship-model to foster recreation skills through instruction while providing activities. As a result of the concern of limited opportunities for age-appropriate recreation skills, the authors noted that community residences often lack the staff and funds to provide recreation opportunities. They also argued that recreation programming is often overly structured and does not foster independence. In their "companion" program, persons with mental retardation were interviewed to determine interests, past experiences in activities, and individualized recreation skill needs. Each interviewee was then matched with a volunteer on the basis of mutual recreation preferences. After an orientation session, volunteers were asked to accompany their companion weekly to a mutually agreed upon activity. Salzberg and Langford reported that friendships developed, participants enjoyed the activities, and persons with disabilities learned normative protocols from their companions. The authors recommended that in establishing such "companionships," individuals should be carefully matched through preliminary interviews and orientation and support for volunteers must be provided.

Recommendations

Theoretical Foundation #1: Recreation Skills Instruction

Research on skill development. 1. There is a presumption that similarities can be drawn between persons with and without developmental disabilities with similar mental ages. Yet this remains to be empirically validated when examining play and social behavior patterns of persons who are developmentally disabled.

This has serious implications in the recreation activity selection process as well. Can research findings involving the play and social behavior of young children (and infants) be generalized for use with individuals with developmental disabilities?

2. What are the optimal materials for the development of recreational and social skills for different individuals with developmental disabilities? Research in controlled environments with individuals at varying skill levels may lead to a more prudent choice of recreational materials.

3. Researchers have reported benefits of behavioral methods and presence of peers in promoting independent recreation behavior. Other strategies must be evaluated to identify environmental variables that promote self-initiated and independent play requiring minimal intervention.

4. Participation in a recreation activity requires that participants learn a number of behaviors that are typically taught simultaneously, often in massed trials. For example, a motor behavior, such as reach and grasp, may be taught for 10 minutes and then instruction in a language behavior, such as requesting change, may be provided for another 10 minutes. In skill clusters, various behaviors are taught as a routine. Holvoet, Guess, Mulligan, and Brown (1980) devised specific methods for arranging skills sequentially and functionally into behavior clusters. These techniques are applicable to recreation activities and to the enhancement of collateral skills development through recreation activities.

5. The responsibility for improving and expanding recreation programming rests with service providers and families in home, school, and community environments. Maximizing cooperation and coordination among families, schools, community recreation, and human service agencies is an important goal that will facilitate recreation participation across natural environments. Of particular importance are procedures that enhance the maintenance and generalization of recreation skills in current and future natural environments.

Research on collateral skill development. 1. Recreation skills interaction has yielded collateral benefits in other areas of educational programming. The areas of language, functional academics, social skills, and motor behavior were shown to benefit from the skills learned during recreation. Bates and Renzaglia (1979) designed a multiple baseline study for a student with profound mental retardation that included reinforcement contingencies for language and recreation behaviors. The student acquired new verbal labels while playing a table game. Additional research needs to be conducted to determine the most cost-effective and unobtrusive methods of designing recreation programs that facilitate skills across curricular areas.

2. To promote collateral skill development in people with developmental disabilities practitioners can cluster skills during instruction. Holvoet et al. (1980) argued that people should not be taught skills in isolation but, rather, in "behavior clusters" that are common to natural environments. This teaching strategy, which is based on the premise that naturally occurring behaviors are rarely present in isolation, supports holistic and stimulus array techniques of training. Further research should be conducted on this skill cluster approach to programming.

3. Recreation activities are a natural medium for enhancing motor behavior. Marini (1978) studied the effects of a physical and recreational program on measures of the perceptual-motor ability of children who were mentally retarded. Students attended a local park and recreation department to participate in bowling, roller skating, ice skating, swimming, and miniature golf, among other activities. Improvements in body perception, balance, locomotor agility, ball throwing, and tracking were evidenced by the students. Additional research to determine how participation in gross motor, recreational activities facilitates physical fitness and motor development would contribute greatly to persons with developmental disabilities.

4. A skill area that lends itself naturally to training through recreation participation is social interaction. The development of social skills is an important component of most recreation activities, because participation with others is inherent in many activities. Some investigators propose specific group skills training (Holvoet et al., 1980), whereas others encourage skill development while reinforcing independence and integration with age peers in recreation activities (Heyne, 1987; Schleien & Ray, 1988). Careful evaluation of different strategies to promote social skills within the context of age-appropriate recreation is necessary.

5. Favell (1973), Schleien, Kiernan, and Wehman (1981), and others have documented the significant reduction of stereotypic, inappropriate behaviors among children and adults with developmental disabilities as they acquire functional recreational skills. Further research needs to be conducted to learn how to ameliorate behavior problems, especially as we attempt to serve more severely involved individuals in least restrictive environments.

Theoretical Foundation #2: Autonomy to Experience Leisure

Research on choice-making. 1. Computer technology is an effective means for providing opportunities for people with disabilities to gain control over their environments, demonstrate choice, and experience active leisure participation. According to Iacono and Miller (1989), computer applications for people with developmental disabilities reflect a belief that computers may be well suited to their particular needs and characteristics, however, the amount and quality of existing research is inadequate. Therefore, Iacono and Miller suggested that investigations into the suitability of various types of computer applications to meet educational goals should occur.

2. Findings of a study conducted by Dyer et al. (1990) suggested that choice-making options provide a simple strategy that can be used to reduce serious problems exhibited by students with severe disabilities. According to the authors, the fact that these results contributed to a growing body of literature that stresses the importance of increasing personal autonomy for persons with severe developmental disabilities indicates that this is an important area of future investigation in therapeutic recreation.

3. Practitioners try to educate individuals to achieve optimum leisure independence, yet some may neglect teaching people with developmental disabilities how to make choices (Shevin & Klein, 1984). Although the importance of control and choice in facilitating the leisure experience has been recognized for some time, it is now the role of research to empirically demonstrate the importance of individual control in leisure (Hunnicutt, 1980).

4. Realon et al. (1988) reported the availability of limited information concerning effects of adapted leisure materials on play behaviors of people with severe developmental disabilities. Future research should empirically determine preferred leisure materials. Questions which should be addressed are how people can selectively choose materials to interact with, how much the "quality of life" has been improved for individuals making choices, how adapted materials help facilitate developmental in areas other that recreation, and whether the availability of adapted materials promotes engagement with the environment to the point of reducing or preventing problem behaviors.

5. Kishi et al. (1988) reported that although few relevant data have been reported, future research should examine the extent to which persons with developmental disabilities integrated into the community can make choices (e.g., leisure participation) and thus demonstrate control over their lives.

6. Realon et al. (1989) reported that the 1980s resulted in a dramatic increase in the use of adapted leisure materials for communication, education, and leisure purposes. Unfortunately, a limited amount of research has been conducted demonstrating intervention effectiveness. According to the authors, this trend should not continue due to the high costs to purchase, adapt, and maintain these materials and the more stringent reviews by funding agencies.

130

Future research might investigate ways in which people with developmental disabilities choose or could be taught to choose what they want to do during their free time.

7. Based on observations that participant determined leisure materials could result in increased interaction with those materials, Realon et al. (1990) suggested that future research should evaluate how to incorporate choice-making opportunities into daily routines. Benefits of increasing leisure opportunities by offering choices justifies continued research.

8. According to Watson, Roggenbuck, and Williams (1991), to predict, understand, and shape recreation choice, we need to know more about individuals, the current frame of reference for which they evaluate settings, how the frame of reference evolves with experience, and how the frame of reference shapes relevance, importance, and specificity of attributes. Therefore, participants' level of experience becomes critical to understanding choice and should be analyzed.

Research on identification of preferences. 1. Parsons and Reid (1990) recommended that research should focus on examining assessment procedures to evaluate preferences so that people with even the most severe developmental disabilities can participate actively in decisions that affect their lives. For persons with developmental disabilities who do not communicate preferences independently, choice-making opportunities may represent an alternative means of allowing them to participate actively in decisions influencing their leisure participation.

2. Via procedures developed by Dattilo (1986, 1987, 1988), Green et al. (1988), Realon et al. (1988, 1989, 1990) and Wacker et al. (1985, 1988) systematic assessment of preferences for persons with severe developmental disabilities can be identified with a reasonable degree of reliability. However, research is needed to increase the predictive validity of these assessment methods of identifying preferences, especially as these preferences related to leisure.

Research facilitating reciprocal communication. 1. Kohl and Beckman (1990) recommended that future studies should be developed to investigate the ability of strategies to facilitate social interactions that are mediated by service providers attempting to promote reciprocal interactions. Examination of the promotion of reciprocal interactions that may promote more active leisure participation for individuals with developmental disabilities should also be pursued.

2. Based on observations that few empirical studies on the use of technology have been reported in the literature on persons with developmental disabilities (e.g., Nietupski et al., 1984), Wacker et al. (1988) reported that the development of a functional communication system, the establishment of sustained responses over time, and the functional assessment of preferences (e.g., leisure) via technology all require further investigation.

3. Houghton et al. (1987) recommended that future research should systematically explore instructional procedures increasing practitioner responsiveness to expressions of preferences and choice among individuals with severe developmental disabilities as well as the effects of this approach on their adaptive behaviors. According to the authors, critical dependent variables in this research might include measures of communication and social interactions skills, changes in affect, and other measures of self-directed behavior (e.g., leisure involvement).

Theoretical Foundation #3:
Community Integration

1. Investigations should be developed to respond to recommendations made by McFadden and Burke (1991) that practitioners must assist people with developmental disabilities to move beyond mere physical presence in the community and into the array of social opportunities in communities as full and valued participants. Strategies designed to increase use of leisure opportunities, depending on the individual's preferences, should be designed and their impact documented.

2. Wolfensberger (1991) reported that there remains a widespread negative view of people with mental retardation by society as a whole. Since negative attitudes by members of society can create significant barriers to the integration of people with developmental disabilities into community recreation, systematic inquiry should be devoted to examining procedures to positively influence the attitudes of society toward people with developmental disabilities.

3. Investigations should be developed that examine implementation of the model proposed by Dattilo and St. Peter (1991) involving comprehensive leisure education services designed to overcome the barrier of limited leisure awareness, knowledge, and skills of people with mental retardation that prevents them from making successful transitions into active community living.

4. Based on the initial findings of Schleien, Fahnestock, Green, and Rynders (1990) that sociometry, circle of friends, and cooperative learning technologies offer promise for including people with developmental disabilities into integrated recreation programs, research studies should be designed to determine the efficacy of such strategies.

5. Since it appears that opportunities to develop relationships and enhance competence in social interaction are critical in reducing isolation experienced by people with developmental disabilities (Asch, 1989), investigations should be designed to test the effectiveness of interventions designed to encourage social interaction and relationships through active leisure participation.

6. Based on observations by Schleien, Rynders, and Mustonen (1988) that maximizing cooperation and coordination among families, teachers, community recreation professionals, therapeutic recreation specialists, and human service agencies is an important goal that will facilitate leisure participation across settings for people with developmental disabilities, further analysis of systems and networks designed to facilitate such cooperation and communication should occur.

7. While philosophical, theoretical, and legislative mandates exist for accessible leisure services, there continue to be numerous barriers impeding progress toward achieving the goal of integrated, accessible leisure services in the community (Schleien & Ray, 1988). Investigations should be developed that clearly delineate these barriers and examine procedures designed to remove existing barriers to integrated leisure participation by people with developmental disabilities.

Theoretical Foundation #4: Social
Social Skills and Friendship
Development

Research in promoting social interactions. 1. Different strategies of encouraging social interaction in socially isolated people with developmental disabilities must be examined. Several studies have been identified for promoting socialization between people who have a history of not recreating in a cooperative manner. These methods should be evaluated in controlled settings with the most natural strategy used initially, and if this fails, more supportive techniques can be undertaken. Procedures that are identified as being effective must be replicable across settings and be able to promote maintenance and generalization.

2. Researchers must systematically determine specific recreational materials that promote cooperative recreation participation and social interactions between peers with and without developmental disabilities.

3. Recreational materials are excellent vehicles for promoting communication between peers. Stimulating and attractive recreational materials which are associated with positively reinforcing events that facilitate communication need to be studied further.

4. Social play measurement may be subjective and anecdotal, at best, if independent observers are not used with careful attention to reliability of agreement. Socialization behaviors are not as clearly distinguishable as many simple recreation and motor actions. The lack of discrete social behaviors may cause difficulty in reliable measurement and should be taken into consideration when developing cooperative recreation programs.

5. Developmental hierarchies of social behavior such as the one developed by Paloutzian et al. (1971) have been developed with people without disabilities. Whether this continuum of social play is valid for persons with developmental disabilities remains an empirical question which may only be answered through future research.

Research in promoting friendships. 1. Research on the community adjustment of persons with developmental disabilities, many of who formerly resided in institutions, indicates that community settings do not ensure meaningful participation in recreation activities. Typically, these individuals spend the majority of their lives in passive, meaningless activities regardless of where they live. Several variables predominate in influencing the quality of recreation activity participation, including availability of transportation, caregiver involvement, and friends or escorts to accompany individuals. Empirical investigations need to be conducted to determine the relative influences of these external variables.

2. Recent developments in education emphasize cooperative task and activity structures, in which each individual is encouraged to contribute his or her best performance in cooperation with other group members. Johnson, Johnson, and Maruyama (1983) and Rynders, Johnson, Johnson, and Schmidt (1980) reviewed research on the generally positive effects of cooperative goal structures on heterogeneous group task performance and social interaction behaviors. More information is needed to determine the effectiveness of cooperative group structures on the promotion of social interactions and friendship development between individuals of varying abilities.

3. There exists a paucity of research on the correlation between recreation skill acquisition and the social behavior and friendship development between peers with and without developmental disabilities. It is believed that as individuals acquire age-appropriate recreation skills, the likelihood that they will become socially connected in their communities will be increased.

References

Accardo, P. J., & Capute, A. J. (1979). The pediatrician and the delayed child. Baltimore: University Park Press.

Adkins, J., & Matson, L. (1980). Teaching institutionalized mentally retarded adults socially appropriate leisure skills. Mental Retardation, 18, 249-252.

Alajajian, L. (1981). Jogging program for deaf-blind students improves condition and reduces self-stimulation. News . . . About Deaf-Blind Student, Programmed Services in New England, 6(1), 3-4.

Albarran, M. A., & Benitez, A. C. (1985). Perceived depth of involvement in leisure of adolescent school deserters. Abstracts From the 1985 Symposium on Leisure Research (p. 19). Alexandria, VA: National Recreation and Parks Association.

Anderson, S. C., & Allen, L. R. (1985). Effects of a leisure education program on activity involvement and social interaction of mentally retarded persons. Adapted Physical Activity Quarterly, 2(2), 107-116.

Asch, A. (1989). Has the law made a difference? In D. Kerzner & A. Gartner (Eds.), Beyond separate education: Quality education for all (pp. 181-206). Baltimore: Paul H. Brookes.

Austin, D. R., & Powell, L. G. (1981). What you need to know to serve special populations. Parks and Recreation, 16(7), 40-42.

Ball, W. L., Chasey, W. C., Hawkins, D. E., & Verhoven, P. J. (1976). The need for leisure education for handicapped children and youth. Journal of Physical Education and Recreation, 47, 53-55.

Bambara, L., Spiegel-McGill, P., Shores, R., & Fox, J. (1984). A comparison of reactive and non-reactive toys on severely handicapped children's manipulative play. Journal of the Association for Persons with Severe Handicaps, 9, 142-149.

Banks, R., & Aveno, A. (1986). Adapted miniature golf: A community leisure program for students with severe physical disabilities. Journal of the Association for Persons with Severe Handicaps, 11, 209-215.

Baroff, G. S. (1986). Mental retardation: Nature, cause, and management (2nd ed.). Washington, DC: Hemisphere.

Barrett, S. (1987). Trends and issues in developing community living programs for young adults who are deaf-blind and profoundly handicapped. In A. Covert & H. Fredericks (Eds.), Transition for persons with deaf-blindness and other profound handicaps: State of the art (pp. 39-49). Monmouth, OR: Teaching Research.

Bates, P., & Renzaglia, A. (1979). Community-based recreation programs. In P. Wehman (Ed.), Recreation programming for developmentally disabled persons (pp. 97-125). Austin, TX: PRO-ED.

Bates, P., & Renzaglia, A. (1982). Language instruction with a profoundly retarded adolescent: The use of a table game in the acquisition of verbal labeling skills. Education and Treatment of Children, 5(1), 13-22.

Baumeister, A. A., & Forehand, R. (1973). Stereotyped acts. In N. R. Ellis (Ed.), International review of research in mental retardation. New York: Academic Press.

Beckman, P. J. (1983). The relationship between behavioral characteristics of young children and social interaction in an integrated setting. Journal of the Division for Early Childhood, 1, 69-77.

Bedini, L. A. (1990). Separate but equal? Segregated programming for people with disabilities. Leisure Today, 16, 16-20.

Bedrosian, J. L. (1988). Adults who are mildly to moderately mentally retarded: Communicative performance, assessment and intervention. In S. N. Calculator & J. L. Bedrosian (Eds.), Communication assessment and intervention for adults with mental retardation (pp. 265-387). London: Taylor & Francis.

Bedrosian, J. L., & Prutting, C. (1978). Communicative performance of mentally retarded adults in four conversational settings. Journal of Speech and Hearing Research, 21, 79-95.

Bell, N. J., Schoenrock, C., & Slade, R. (1975). Leisure activities of previously institutionalized retardates: A comparison with non-retarded community residents. Paper presented at the Region V American Association on Mental Deficiency Meeting, St. Louis.

Bellamy, B. T. (1985). Severe disability in adulthood. The Association for Persons with Severe Handicaps Newsletter, 1, 6.

Belmore, K., & Brown, L. (1976). A job skill inventory strategy for use in a public school vocational training program for severely handicapped potential workers. In L. Brown, N. Certo, K. Belmore, & T. Corwner (Eds.), Papers and programs related to public school services for secondary age severely handicapped students (Vol. 6, Pt. 1). Madison, WI: Madison Metro School District.

Bender, M., & Valletutti, P. J. (1976). Teaching the moderately and severely handicapped: Curriculum, objectives, strategies, and activities (Vol. 2). Baltimore: University Park Press.

Bercovici, S. (1983). Barriers to normalization: The restrictive management of retarded persons. Baltimore: University Park Press.

Beveridge, M. (1976). Patterns of interaction in the mentally handicapped. In P. Berry (Ed.), Language and communication in the mentally handicapped (pp. 142-160). Baltimore: University Park Press.

Birenbaum, A., & Re, M. A. (1979). Resettling mentally retarded adults in the community--almost four years later. American Journal of Mental Deficiency, 83, 323-329.

Birgham, T. A., & Sherman, J. A. (1973). Effects of choice and immediacy of reinforcement on single response and switching behavior of children. Journal of Experimental Analysis of Behavior, 19, 425-435.

Bjaanes, A., & Butler, E. (1974). Environmental variation in community care facilities for mentally retarded persons. The American Journal of Mental Deficiency, 78(4), 429-434.

Bordy, G., & Stoneman, W. (1977). Social competencies in the developmentally disabled: Some suggestions for research and training. Mental Retardation, 15(4), 41-43.

Braddock, D. (1977). Opening closed doors: The deinstitutionalization of disabled individuals. Reston, VA: Council for Exceptional Children.

Bregha, F. J. (1985). Leisure and freedom re-examined. In T. A. Goodale & P. A. Witt (Eds.), Recreation and leisure: Issues in an era of change (2nd ed.) (pp. 35-43). State College, PA: Venture.

Brewer, G., & Kakalik, J. (1979). Handicapped children: Strategies for improving services. New York: McGraw-Hill.

Brown, L., Branston-McClean, M. B., Baumgart, D., Vincent, L., Falvey, M., & Schroeder, J. (1979). Using the characteristics of current and subsequent least restrictive environments in the development of curricular content for severely handicapped students. AAESPH Review, 4, 407-424.

Brown, L., Branston, M. B., Hamre-Nietupski, S., Johnson, F., Wilcox, B., & Gruenewald, L. (1979). A rationale for comprehensive longitudinal interactions between severely handicapped students and other nonhandicapped citizens. AAESPH Review, 4, 3-14.

Brown, L., Branston, M. B., Hamre-Nietupski, S., Pumpian, I., Certo, N., & Gruenewald, L. (1979). A strategy for developing chronological age-appropriate and functional curricular content for severely handicapped adolescents and young adults. Journal of Special Education, 13(1), 81-90.

Brown, C., Cavalier, A., Mineo, B., & Buckley, R. (1988). Sound-to-speech translation and environmental control for people with mental retardation. Augmentative and Alternative Communication, 4, 172.

Brown, R., & McBain, O. (1965). Social activities for educable mentally retarded high school and post high school people. Journal of Psychiatric Nursing, 3(2), 133-137.

Browman, S., Nichols, P. L., Schasugnessy, P., & Kennedy, W. (1987). Retardation in young children: A developmental study of cognitive deficit. Hillsdale, NJ: Lawrence Erlbaum Associates.

Buell, J., Stoddard, P., Harris, F., & Baer, D. (1968). Collateral social development accompanying reinforcement of outdoor play in a preschool child. Journal of Applied Analysis, 1, 167-173.

Bundschuh, E. L., Williams, S. W., Hollingworth, J., Gooch, S., & Shirer, C. (1972). Teaching the retarded to swim. Mental Retardation, 10(3), 14-17.

Calculator, S. N., & Delaney, D. (1986). Comparison of nonspeaking and speaking mentally retarded adults' clarification strategies. Journal of Speech and Hearing Disorders, 51, 252-259.

Calculator, S., & Dollaghan, C. (1982). The use of communications boards in a residential setting: An evaluation. Journal of Speech and Hearing Disorders, 47, 281-287.

Carter, M. J., Van Andel, G. E., & Robb, G. M. (1985). Therapeutic recreation: A practical approach. St. Louis: Time Mirror/Mosby.

Certo, N., & Kohl, F. (1984). A strategy for developing interpersonal interaction instructional content for severely handicapped students. In N. Certo, N. Haring, & R. York (Eds.), Public school integration of severely handicapped students: Rational issues and progressive alternatives (pp. 221-244). Baltimore: Paul H. Brookes.

Certo, N. J., & Schleien, S. J. (1982). Individualized leisure instruction. In P. Verhoven, S. Schleien, & M. Bender (Eds.), Leisure education and the handicapped individual: An ecological perspective (pp. 121-153). Washington, DC: Institute for Career and Leisure Development.

Certo, N., Schleien, S., & Hunter, D. (1983). An ecological assessment inventory to facilitate community recreation participation by severely disabled individuals. Therapeutic Recreation Journal, 17(3), 29-38.

Cheseldine, S. E., & Jeffree, D. M. (1981). Mentally handicapped adolescents: Their use of leisure. Journal of Mental Deficiency Research, 25, 49-59.

Collard, K. (1981). Leisure education in the schools: Why, who, and the need for advocacy. Therapeutic Recreation Journal, 15(4), 8-16.

Corcoran, E., & French, R. (1977). Leisure activity for the retarded adult in the community. Mental Retardation, 15(2), 21-23.

Corsaro, F. (1979). Sociolinguistic patterns in adult-child interaction. In E. Ochs & B. Schiefflin (Eds.), Developmental pragmatics (pp. 372-389). New York: Academic Press.

Covert, A. (1987). Summary, conclusion, recommendations and implications of the conference: Purpose and format. In A. Covert & H. Fredericks (Eds.), Transition for persons with deaf-blindness and other profound handicaps: State of the art (pp. 147-157). Monmouth, OR: Teaching Research.

Crapps, J. M., Langone, J., & Swaim, S. (1985). Quantity and quality of participation in community environments by mentally retarded adults. Education and Training of the Mentally Retarded, 20, 123-129.

Dattilo, J. (1986). Computerized assessment of preferences for persons with severe handicaps. Journal of Applied Behavior Analysis, 19, 445-448.

Dattilo, J. (1987). Computerized assessment of leisure preferences: A replication. Education and Training in Mental Retardation, 22(2), 128-133.

Dattilo, J. (1988). Assessing music preferences of persons with severe disabilities. Therapeutic Recreation Journal, 21(2), 12-23.

Dattilo, J. (1991). Mental retardation. In D. Austin & M. Crawford (Eds.), Therapeutic recreation: An introduction (pp. 163-188). Englewood Cliffs, NJ: Prentice Hall.

Dattilo, J., & Barnett, L. (1985). Therapeutic recreation for individuals with severe handicaps: Implications of chosen participation. Therapeutic Recreation Journal, 19, 79-91.

Dattilo, J., & Camarata, S. (1988). Combining speech pathology and therapeutic recreation to encourage self-determination for persons with disabilities. Journal of Expanding Horizons in Therapeutic Recreation, 3, 12-17.

Dattilo, J., & Camarata, S. (1991). Facilitating leisure involvement through self-initiated augmentative communication training. Journal of Applied Behavior Analysis.

Dattilo, J., & Mirenda, P. (1987). The application of a leisure preference assessment protocol for persons with severe handicaps. Journal of the Association for Persons with Severe Handicaps, 12(4), 306-311.

Dattilo, J., & Rusch, F. (1985). Effects of choice on leisure participation for persons with severe handicaps. Journal of the Association for Persons with Severe Handicaps, 10, 194-199.

Dattilo, J., & St. Peter, S. (1991). A model for including leisure education in transition services for young adults with mental retardation. Education and Training in Mental Retardation, 26.

Deutsch, H., Bustow, S., Wish, C. W., & Wish, J. (1982). Developmental disabilities: A training guide. Boston: CBI.

Deutsch, M., & Parks, A. (1978). The use of contingent music to increase appropriate conversational speech. Mental Retardation, 16(1), 33-36.

DeVellis, R. F. (1977). Learned helplessness in institutions. Mental Retardation, 15(5), 10-13.

Dixon, J. (1981). Adapting activities for therapeutic recreation services: Concepts and applications. San Diego: Campanile.

Donder, D., & Nietupski, J. (1981). Nonhandicapped adolescents teaching playground skills to their mentally handicapped peers: Toward a less restrictive middle school environment. Education and Training of the Mentally Retarded, 16, 270-276.

Downing, J. (1987). Conversational skills training: Teaching adolescents with mental retardation to be verbally assertive. Mental Retardation, 25(3), 147-155.

Dyer, K. (1987). The competition of autistic stereotyped behavior with usual and specially assessed reinforcers. Research in Developmental Disabilities, 8, 607-626.

Dyer, K., Dublap, G., & Winterling, V. (1990). Effects of choice making on the serious problem behaviors of students with severe handicaps. Journal of Applied Behavior Analysis, 23, 515-524.

Dyer, K., Schwartz, I. S., & Luce, S. C. (1984). A supervision program for increasing functional activities for severely handicapped students in a residential setting. Journal of Applied Behavior Analysis, 17, 249-259.

Edgerton, R. B. (1967). The cloak of competence: Stigma in the lives of the mentally retarded. Berkeley: University of California Press.

Eichenbaum, B., & Bednarek, N. (1964). Square dancing and social adjustment. Mental Retardation, 2, 105-109.

Ellis, G. D., & Witt, P. A. (1984). The measurement of perceived freedom in leisure. Journal of Leisure Research, 16(2), 110-123.

Eyman, R. K., & Call, J. (1977). Maladaptive behavior and community placement of mentally retarded persons. American Journal of Mental Deficiency, 82, 137-144.

Fain, G. S. (1986). Leisure: A moral imperative. Mental Retardation, 24(5), 261-263.

Farrier, L. D., Yorkston, K. M., Marriner, N. A., & Beukelman, D. R. (1985). Conversational control in nonimpaired speakers using an augmentative and alternative communication system. Augmentative and Alternative Communication, 1, 65-73.

Fehr, M., Wacker, D., Trezie, J., Lennon, R., & Meyerson, L. (1979). Visual, auditory, and vibratory stimulation as reinforcers for profoundly retarded children. Rehabilitation Psychology, 26, 201-209.

Fenrick, N., & Petersen, T. K. (1984). Developing positive changes in attitudes towards moderately/severely handicapped students through a peer tutoring program. Education and Training of the Mentally Retarded, 19, 83-90.

Ferguson, C. (1975). Toward a characterization of English foreigner talk. Anthropological Linguistics, 17, 1-14.

Ficker-Terril, C., & Rowitz, L. (1991). Choices. Mental Retardation, 29, 63-65.

Fine, A., Feldis, D., & Lehrer, B. (1982). Therapeutic recreation and programming for autistic children. Therapeutic Recreation Journal, 16(1), 6-11.

Favell, J. (1973). Reduction of stereotypies by reinforcement of toy play. Mental Retardation, 11(4), 21-23.

Favell, J. E., & Cannon, P. R. (1977). Evaluation of entertainment materials for severely retarded persons. American Journal of Mental Deficiency, 81, 357-361.

Ford, A., Brown, L., Pumpian, I., Baumgart, D., Nisbet, J., Schroeder, J., & Loomis, R. (1984). Strategies for developing individual recreation/leisure plans for adolescent and young adult severely handicapped students. In N. Certo, N. Haring, & R. York (Eds.), Public school integration of severely handicapped students: Rational issues and progressive alternatives (pp. 245-275). Baltimore: Paul H. Brookes.

Fredericks, H. (1987). Those with profound handicaps: Who are they? How can they be served? In A. Covert & H. Fredericks (Eds.), Transition for persons with deaf-blindness and other profound handicaps: State of the art (pp. 3-9). Monmouth, OR: Teaching Research.

Fredericks, H., & Baldwin, V. (1987). Individuals with sensory impairments. In L. Goetz, D. Guess, & K. Stremel-Campbell (Eds.), Innovative program design for individuals with dual sensory impairments (pp. 3-12). Baltimore: Paul H. Brookes.

Gable, R., Henrickson, J., & Strain, P. (1978). Assessment, modification, and generalization of social interaction among severely retarded, multihandicapped children. Education and Training of the Mentally Retarded, 13, 279-285.

Garner, J., & Campbell, P. (1987). Technology for persons with severe disabilities: Practical and ethical considerations. The Journal of Special Education, 21(3), 122-132.

Gaylord-Ross, R. (1980). A decision model for the treatment of aberrant behavior in applied settings. In W. Sailor, B. Wilcox, & L. Brown (Eds.), Methods of instruction for severely handicapped students. Baltimore: Paul H. Brookes.

Gaylord-Ross, R., Stremel-Campbell, K., & Storey, K. (1986). Social skills training in natural contexts. In R. Horner, L. Meyer, & H. Fredericks (Eds.), Education of learners with severe handicaps. Baltimore: Paul H. Brookes.

Gingeland, D. (1968). Recreation programming for the adult retardate. In AAHPER (Ed.), Programming for the mentally retarded. (Report of a national conference, October 31-November 2, 1966). Washington, DC.

Gold, M. W. (1978). An adaptive behavior philosophy: Who needs it? In W. Coulter & H. Morrow (Eds.), Adaptive behavior (pp. 234-235). New York: Grune & Stratton.

Gollay, E. (1981). Some conceptual and methodological issues in studying the community adjustment of deinstitutionalized mentally retarded people. In R. H. Bruininks, C. E. Meyers, B. B. Sigford, & K. C. Lakin (Eds.), Deinstitutionalization and community adjustment of mentally retarded people (pp. 86-106). Washington, DC: American Association on Mental Deficiency.

Gollay, E., Freedman, R., Wyngaarden, M., & Kurtz, N. (1978). Coming back: The community experience of deinstitutionalized mentally retarded people. Cambridge, MA: Abt Books.

Gottlieb, M. (1987). Major variations in intelligence. In M. Gottlieb & J. Williams (Eds.), Textbook of developmental pediatrics (pp. 127-150). New York: Plenum Medical.

Grossman, H. J. (1983). Classification in mental retardation. Washington, DC: American Association on Mental Deficiency.

Green, C. W., Reid, D. H., White, L. K., Halford, R. C., Brittain, D. P., & Gardner, S. M. (1988). Identifying reinforcers for persons with profound handicaps: Staff opinion versus systematic assessment of preferences. Journal of Applied Behavior Analysis, 21, 31-43.

Green, F., & Schleien, S. (1991). Understanding friendship and recreation: A theoretical sampling. Therapeutic Recreation Journal.

Guess, D., Benson, H. A., & Siegel-Causey, E. (1985). Concepts and issues related to choice-making and autonomy among persons with severe disabilities. Journal of the Association for Persons With Severe Handicaps, 10(2), 79-86.

Gunn, S. L. (1975). Basic terminology for therapeutic recreation and other action therapies. Champaign, IL: Stipes.

Guralnick, M. (1978). Integrated preschools as educational and therapeutic environments: Concepts, design, and analysis. In M. Guralnick (Ed.), Early intervention and the integration of handicapped and nonhandicapped children (pp. 115-145). Baltimore: University Park Press.

Halle, J., Baer, D., & Spradlin, J. (1981). Teachers' generalized use of delay as a stimulus control procedure to increase language use in handicapped children. Journal of Applied Behavior Analysis, 14, 389-409.

Hamilton, E. J., & Anderson, S. (1983). Effects of leisure activities on attitudes toward people with disabilities. Therapeutic Recreation Journal, 17(3), 50-57.

Hammond, G. (1968). Classroom learning in a home atmosphere. Pointer, 12(3), 54-55.

Hamre-Nietupski, S., Branston, M., Ford, A., Stoll, A., Gruenewald, L., & Brown, L. (1978). Curricular strategies for developing longitudinal interactions between severely handicapped and nonhandicapped individuals in school and nonschool environments. In L. Brown, S. Hamre-Nietupski, S. Lyon, M. Branston, M. Falvey, & L. Gruenewald (Eds.), Curricular strategies for teaching severely handicapped students to acquire and perform skills in response to naturally occurring cues and prompts (Vol. VIII, Part 1, pp. 27-177). Madison, WI: Madison Metropolitan Public School District.

Hamre-Nietupski, S., Nietupski, J., Sandvig, R., Sandvig, M. B., & Ayres, B. (1984). Leisure skills instruction in a community residential setting with young adults who are deaf/blind severely handicapped. Journal of the Association for Persons with Severe Handicaps, 9, 49-53.

Harper, W. (1986). Freedom in the experience of leisure. Leisure Sciences, 8(2), 115-130.

Harris, D. (1982). Communicative interaction processes involving nonvocal physically handicapped children. Topics in Language Disorders, 2, 21-37.

Hart, B., Reynolds, N., Baer, D., Brawley, E., & Harris, F. (1968). Effect of contingent and non-contingent social reinforcement on the cooperative play of a preschool child. Journal of Applied Behavior Analysis, 1, 73-76.

Haskett, J., & Hollar, W. D. (1978). Sensory reinforcement and contingency awareness of profoundly retarded children. American Journal of Mental Deficiency, 83, 60-68.

Hauber, F., Bruininks, R., Hill, B., Lakin, K., Scheerenberger, R., & White, C. (1984). National census of residential facilities: A 1982 profile of facilities and residents. American Journal of Mental Deficiency, 89, 236-245.

Hawkins, A. (1982). Influencing leisure choices of autisticlike children. Journal of Autism and Developmental Disorders, 12, 359-366.

Hayes, G. A. (1969a). Recreation services for the mentally retarded in the state of Kansas. Therapeutic Recreation Journal, 3(3), 13.

Hayes, G. A. (1969b). The integration of the mentally retarded and non-retarded in a day camping program: A demonstration project. Mental Retardation, 7(5), 14-16.

Hayes, G., & Brooks, M. (1966). Organization of a hospital-community integrated day camp. Project News of the Persons State Hospital and Training Center, 2(8), 1-8.

Hayes, G., & Brooks, M. (1967). Organization of a day camp for institutionalized retarded children and nonretarded community children. Paper presented at the 91st Annual Meeting of the American Association on Mental Deficiency, Denver, CO.

Heyne, L. (1987). Integrating children and youth with disabilities into community recreation agencies: One agency's experience and recommendations. St. Paul: Jewish Community Center of the Greater St. Paul Area.

Heyne, L., & Schleien, S. (1991). Leisure and recreation programming to enhance quality of life. In E. Cipani & F. Spooner (Eds.), Curricular and instructional approaches for persons with severe handicaps. Boston: Allyn and Bacon.

Hill, B., & Bruininks, R. H. (1981). Family, leisure, and social activities of mentally retarded people in residential facilities. Minneapolis, MN: Developmental Disabilities Project on Residential Services and Community Adjustment, University of Minnesota.

Hill, B., Lakin, K., & Bruininks, R. (1984). Trends in residential services for people who are mentally retarded: 1972-1982. Journal of the Association for Persons with Severe Handicaps, 9, 243-250.

Hill, J., & Wehman, P. (1980). Integration of severely and profoundly handicapped youth into community-based recreation programs: A social validation. In P. Wehman & J. Hill (Eds.), Instructional programming for severely handicapped youth: A community integration approach (pp. 62-83). Richmond: Virginia Commonwealth University.

Hill, J., Wehman, P., & Horst, G. (1982). Toward generalization of appropriate leisure and social behavior in severely handicapped youth: Pinball machine use. Journal of the Association for Persons with Severe Handicaps, 6(4), 38-44.

Holvoet, G., Guess, D., Mulligan, M., & Brown, F. (1980). The individualized curriculum sequencing model (II): A teaching strategy for severely handicapped students. Journal of the Association for the Severely Handicapped, 5, 337-351.

Horst, G., Wehman, P., Hill, J., & Bailey, C. (1980). Developing chronologically age-appropriate leisure skills in severely multihandicapped adolescents: Three case studies. In P. Wehman & J. W. Hill (Eds.), Instructional programming for severely handicapped youth: A community integration approach (pp. 84-100). Richmond: Virginia Commonwealth University.

Horst, G., Wehman, P., Hill, J., & Bailey, C. (1981). Developing age-appropriate leisure skills in severely handicapped adolescents. Teaching Exceptional Children, 4, 11-15.

Houghton, J., Bronicki, G., & Guess, D. (1987). Opportunities to express preferences and make choices among students with severe disabilities in classroom settings. Journal of the Association for Persons with Severe Handicaps, 12(1), 18-27.

Howe-Murphy, R. (1980). The identification of guidelines for mainstreaming recreation and leisure services. Journal of Leisurability, 7(3), 36-41.

Howe-Murphy, R., & Charboneau, B. (1987). Therapeutic recreation intervention: An ecological perspective. Englewood Cliffs, NJ: Prentice-Hall.

Hughes, K. (1981). Adapting audio/video games for handicapped learners: Part 2. Teaching Exceptional Children, 14, 127-129.

Hunnicutt, B. (1980). To cope in autonomy: Therapeutic recreation and the limits to professionalization and intervention. In G. Hitzhusen, J. Elliott, D. J. Szymanski, & M. G. Thompson (Eds.), Expanding Horizons in Therapeutic Recreation VIII (pp. 122-134). Columbia, MO: Curators University of Missouri.

Hutchinson, P. (1980). Perceptions of disabled persons regarding barriers to community involvement. Journal of Leisurability, 7(3), 4-15.

Hutchinson, P., & Lord, J. (1979). Recreation integration: Issues and alternatives in leisure services and community involvement. Ottawa, Ontario: Leisurability.

Iacono, T. A., & Miller, J. F. (1989). Can microcomputers be used to teach communication skills to students with mental retardation? Education and Training in Mental Retardation, 24(1), 32-44.

Intagliata, J., Willer, B., & Wicks, N. (1981). Factors related to the quality of community adjustment in family care homes. In R. H. Bruininks, C. E. Meyers, B. B. Sigford, & K. C. Lakin (Eds.), Deinstitutionalization and community adjustment of mentally retarded people (pp. 217-230). Washington, DC: American Association on Mental Deficiency.

Iso-Ahola, S. E. (1980). The social psychology of leisure and recreation. Dubuque, IA: William C. Brown.

Iso-Ahola, S., MacNeil, R. D., & Szymanski, D. J. (1980). Social psychological foundations of therapeutic recreation: An attributional analysis. In S. Iso-Ahola (Ed.), Social psychological perspectives on leisure and recreation (pp. 390-413). Springfield, IL: Charles C. Thomas.

James, S. D., & Egel, A. L. (1986). A direct prompting strategy for increasing reciprocal interactions between handicapped and nonhandicapped siblings. Journal of Applied Behavior Analysis, 19, 173-186.

Jansma, P. (1982). Physical education for the severely and profoundly handicapped. Exceptional Educational Quarterly, 15(1), 35-41.

Jeffree, D. M., & Cheseldine, S. E. (1984). Leisure intervention and the interaction patterns of severely mentally retarded adolescents: A pilot study. American Journal of Mental Deficiency, 88, 619-624.

Johnson, M. S., & Bailey, J. S. (1977). Leisure training in a half-way house. Journal of Applied Behavior Analysis, 10, 273-282.

Johnson, D., Johnson, R., & Maruyama, G. (1983). Interdependence and interpersonal attraction among heterogeneous and homogeneous individuals: A theoretical formulation and a meta-analysis of the research. Review of Educational Research, 53, 5-54.

Joswiak, K. F. (1979). Leisure counseling program materials for the developmentally disabled. Washington, DC: Hawkins & Associates.

Katz, S., & Yekutiel, E. (1974). Leisure time problems of mentally retarded graduates of training programs. Mental Retardation, 12(3), 54-57.

Kelly, J. R. (1972). Work and leisure: A simplified paradigm. Journal of Leisure Research, 4(1), 50-62.

Keogh, D., Faw, G., Whitman, T., & Reid, D. (1984). Enhancing leisure skills in severely retarded adolescents through a self-instructional treatment package. Analysis and Intervention in Developmental Disabilities, 4, 333-351.

Kibler, C. (1986). Board games for multihandicapped players. Perspective for Teachers of the Hearing Impaired, 4(4), 21-23.

Kishi, G., Teelucksingh, B., Zollers, N., Park-Lee, S., & Meyer, L. (1988). Daily decision-making in community residences: A social comparison of adults with and without mental retardation. American Journal on Mental Retardation, 92, 430-435.

Kissel, R., & Whitman, T. (1977). An examination of the direct and generalized effects of a play-training and overcorrection procedure upon the self-stimulatory behavior of a profoundly retarded boy. AAESPH Review, 2, 131-146.

Knapczyk, D. (1989). Peer-mediated training of cooperative play between special and regular class students in integrated play settings. Education and Training in Mental Retardation, 24(3), 255-264.

Knapczyk, D., & Peterson, N. (1975). Social play interaction of retarded children in an integrated classroom environment. Unpublished manuscript, Development Training Center, University of Indiana, Bloomington, IN.

Knapczyk, D., & Yoppi, J. (1975). Development of cooperative and competitive play responses in developmentally disabled children. American Journal on Mental Deficiency, 80, 245-255.

Koegel, R. L., Dyer, K., & Bell, L. K. (1987). The influence of child-preferred activities on autistic children's social behavior. Journal of Applied Behavior Analysis, 20, 243-252.

Koegel, R. L., O'Dell, M. C., & Koegel, L. K. (1987). A natural language teaching paradigm for non-verbal autistic children. Journal of Autism and Developmental Disorders, 17, 187-200.

Kohl, F. L., & Beckman, P. J. (1990). The effects of directed play on the frequency and length of reciprocal interactions with preschoolers having moderate handicaps. Education and Training in Mental Retardation, 25(3), 258-266.

142

Kraat, A. (1987). Developing intervention goals. In S. Blackstone (Ed.), <u>Augmentative and alternative communication</u> (pp. 197-266). Rockville, MD: American Speech-Language-Hearing Association.

Kregel, J., Wehman, P., Seyfarth, J., & Marshall, K. (1986). Community integration of young adults with mental retardation: Transition from school to adulthood. <u>Education and Training of the Mentally Retarded</u>, <u>21</u>, 35-42.

Lagomarcino, A., Reid, D., Ivancic, M., & Faw, G. (1984). Leisure-dance instruction for severely and profoundly retarded persons: Teaching an intermediate community-living skill. <u>Journal of Applied Behavior Analysis</u>, <u>17</u>, 71-84.

Lakin, K. C., & Bruininks, R. H. (Eds.). (1985). <u>Strategies for achieving community integration of developmentally disabled citizens</u>. Baltimore: Paul H. Brookes.

Lanagan, D., & Dattilo, J. (1989). The effects of a leisure education program on individuals with mental retardation. <u>Therapeutic Recreation Journal</u>, <u>23</u>(4), 62-72.

Lancioni, G. E. (1982). Normal children as tutors to teach social responses to withdrawn mentally retarded school- mates: Training, maintenance, and generalization. <u>Journal of Applied Behavior Analysis</u>, <u>15</u>, 17-40.

Langer, E. J., & Rodin, J. (1976). The effects of choice and enhanced personal responsibility for the aged: A field experiment in an institutional setting. <u>Journal of Personality and Social Psychology</u>, <u>34</u>(2), 191-198.

Levitt, E., & Cohen, S. (1976). Attitudes of children toward their handicapped peers. <u>Childhood Education</u>, <u>52</u>, 171-173.

Light, J. (1985). <u>The communicative interaction patterns of young nonspeaking physically disabled children and their primary caregivers</u>. Unpublished master's thesis, University of Toronto.

Light, J. (1988). Interaction involving individuals using augmentative and alternative and alternate communication systems: State of the art and future directions. <u>Augmentative and Alternative Communication</u>, <u>4</u>, 66-82.

Locke, P., & Mirenda, P. (1988). A computer-supported communication approach for a child with severe communication, visual, and cognitive impairments: A case study. <u>Augmentative and Alternative Communication</u>, <u>4</u>, 15-22.

Lord, J. (1983). Reflections on a decade of integration. <u>Journal of Leisurability</u>, <u>10</u>(4), 4-11.

Luckey, R., & Shapiro, I. (1974). Recreation: An essential aspect of habilitative programming. <u>Mental Retardation</u>, <u>12</u>, 33-36.

Mannell, R. C. (1984). A psychology for leisure research. <u>Leisure and Society</u>, <u>7</u>, 13-21.

Mannell, R. C., Zuzanek, J., & Larson, R. (1988). Leisure states and "flow" experiences: Testing perceived freedom and intrinsic motivation hypotheses. <u>Journal of Leisure Research</u>, <u>20</u>(4), 289-304.

Marini, D. G. (1978). Effects of additional physical and recreational curriculum on selected perceptual-motor abilities of educable mentally retarded children. <u>Therapeutic Recreation Journal</u>, <u>12</u>(3), 31-38.

Marion, R. L. (1979). Leisure time activities for trainable mentally retarded adolescents. <u>Teaching Exceptional Children</u>, <u>11</u>, 158-160.

Marlowe, M. (1979). The game analysis intervention: A procedure to increase the peer acceptance and social adjustment of a retarded child. <u>Education and Training of the Mentally Retarded</u>, <u>14</u>, 262-268.

Martin, M., Burke, M. E., & Findlay, S. (1985). A systematic strategy for devising functional curricula for severely handicapped adolescents. <u>Australia & New Zealand Journal of Developmental Disabilities</u>, <u>11</u>, 169-178.

Matson, J., & Adkins, J. (1984). A self-instructional social skills training program for mentally retarded persons. <u>Mental Retardation</u>, <u>18</u>, 245-248.

Matthews, P. (1977). Recreation and the normalization of the mentally retarded. <u>Therapeutic Recreation Journal</u>, <u>11</u>(3), 112-114.

Matthews, P. R. (1982). Some recreation preferences of the mentally retarded. <u>Therapeutic Recreation Journal</u>, <u>16</u>(3), 42-47.

McFadden, D. L., & Burke, E. P. (1991). Developmental disabilities and the new paradigm: Directions for the 1990s. Mental Retardation, 29(1), iii-vi.

McGregor, G. (1982). Leisure and the domains of home, school and community. In P. Verhoven, S. Schleien, & M. Bender (Eds.), Leisure education and the handicapped individual: An ecological perspective (pp. 21-41). Washington, DC: Institute for Career and Leisure Development.

McHale, S. M., & Simeonsson, R. J. (1980). Effects of interaction on nonhandicapped children's attitudes toward autistic children. American Journal of Mental Deficiency, 85, 18-24.

McLaughlin, M., & Cody, M. (1982). Awkward silences: Behavioral antecedents and consequences of the conversational lapse. Human Communication Research, 8, 299-316.

Meehan, D., Mineo, B., & Lyon, S. (1885). Use of systematic prompting and prompt withdrawal to establish and maintain switch activation in a severely handicapped student. Journal of Special Education Technology, 7(1), 5-11.

Mirenda, P., & Dattilo, J. (1987). Instructional techniques in communication for students with severe intellectual handicaps. Augmentative and Alternative Communication, 3(3), 143-152.

Mirenda, P., & Iacono, T. (1990). Communication options for persons with severe and profound disabilities: State of the art and future directions. Journal of the Association for Persons with Severe Handicaps, 15(1), 3-21.

Mishler, E. (1975). Studies in dialogue and discourse: An exponential law of successive questioning. Language in Society, 4, 31-52.

Mithaug, D. E., & Hanawalt, D. A. (1978). The validation of procedures to assess prevocational task preferences in retarded adults. Journal of Applied Behavior Analysis, 11, 153-162.

Mithaug, D. E., & Mar, D. K. (1980). The relation between choosing and working prevocational tasks in two severely retarded young adults. Journal of Applied Behavior Analysis, 13, 177-182.

Mobily, K. (1985a). A philosophical analysis of therapeutic recreation: What does it mean to say "we can be therapeutic?" Part 2. Therapeutic Recreation Journal, 19(2), 7-14.

Monty, R. A., Geller, E. S., Savage, R. E., & Perlmuter, L. C. (1979). The freedom to choose is not always so choice. Journal of Experimental Psychology, 37, 170-178.

Murphy, J. (1975). Recreation and leisure service: A humanistic perspective. Dubuque, IA: W. C. Brown.

Murphy, J. (1981). Concepts of leisure. Englewood Cliffs, NJ: Prentice-Hall.

Neal, L. (1970). Recreation's role in the rehabilitation of the mentally retarded. Eugene, OR: University of Oregon Rehabilitation and Training Center in Mental Retardation.

Neulinger, J. (1981a). The psychology of leisure (2nd ed.). Springfield, IL: Charles C. Thomas.

Neulinger, J. (1981b). To leisure: An introduction. Boston: Allyn and Bacon.

Newcomer, B., & Morrison, T. L. (1974). Play therapy with institutionalized mentally retarded children. American Journal of Mental Deficiency, 78, 727-733.

Nietupski, J., Hamre-Nietupski, S., & Ayres, B. (1984). Review of task analytic leisure skill training efforts: Practitioner implications and future research needs. Journal of the Association for Persons with Severe Handicaps, 9, 88-97.

Nietupski, J., Hamre-Nietupski, S., Green, K., Varnum-Teeter, K., Twedt, B., LePera, D., Scebold, K., & Hanrahan, M. (1986). Self-initiated and sustained leisure activity participation by students with moderate/severe handicaps. Education and Training of the Mentally Retarded, 21, 259-264.

Nietupski, J., & Svoboda, R. (1982). Teaching a cooperative leisure skill to severely handicapped adults. Education and Training of the Mentally Retarded, 17, 38-43.

144

Nirje, B. (1969). The normalization principle and its human management implications. In R. Kugel & W. Wolfensberger (Eds.), <u>Changing patterns of residential services for the mentally retarded</u>. Washington, DC: President's Committee on Mental Retardation.

Novak, A., & Heal, K. (Eds.). (1980). <u>Integration of developmentally disabled individuals into the community</u>. Baltimore: Paul H. Brookes.

Odum, S. L., & Strain, P. S. (1984). Classroom based social skills instruction for severely handicapped preschool children. <u>Topics in Early Childhood Education, 4</u>, 369-382.

O'Keefe, B., & Dattilo, J. (1991). Teaching the response-recode form to adults with multiple disabilities who use augmentative communication systems. <u>Augmentative and Alternative Communication</u>.

O'Morrow, G. (1980). <u>Therapeutic recreation: A helping profession</u> (2nd ed.). Reston, VA: Reston.

Orelove, F. P., Wehman, P., & Wood, J. (1982). An evaluative review of special olympics: Implications for community integration. <u>Education and Training of the Mentally Retarded, 17</u>, 325-329.

Orelove, R., & Sobsey, D. (1987). <u>Educating children with multiple disabilities: A transdisciplinary approach</u>. Baltimore: Paul H. Brookes.

Pace, G., Ivancic, J., Edwards, G., Iwata, B., & Page, T. (1985). Assessment of stimulus preference and reinforcer value with profoundly retarded individuals. <u>Journal of Applied Behavior Analysis, 18</u>, 249-255.

Paloutzian, R., Hasazi, J., Streifel, J., & Edgard, C. (1971). Promotion of positive social interactions in severely retarded young children. <u>American Journal of Mental Deficiency, 75</u>, 519-524.

Parsons, M. B., & Reid, D. H. (1990). Assessing food preferences among persons with profound mental retardation: Providing opportunities to make choices. <u>Journal of Applied Behavior Analysis, 23</u>, 183-195.

Parsons, M. B., Reid, D. H., Reynolds, J., & Baumgarner, M. (1990). Effects of chosen versus assigned jobs on the work performance of persons with severe handicaps. <u>Journal of Applied Behavior Analysis, 23</u>, 253-258.

Parten, M. (1932). Social play among preschool children. <u>Journal of Abnormal Psychology, 28</u>, 136-147.

Peck, C. A. (1985). Increasing opportunities for social control by children with autism and severe handicaps: Effects on student behavior and perceived classroom climate. <u>Journal of the Association for Persons with Severe Handicaps, 10</u>, 183-193.

Perlmuter, L. C., & Monty, R. A. (1977). The importance of perceived control: Fact or fantasy? <u>American Scientist, 65</u>(6), 759-765.

Peterson, N., & Haralick, J. (1977). Integration of handicapped and nonhandicapped preschoolers: An analysis of play behavior and social interaction. <u>Education and Training of the Mentally Retarded, 12</u>, 235-246.

Powers, J., & Ball, T. (1983). Video games to augment leisure programming in a state hospital residence for developmentally disabled clients. <u>Journal of Special Education Technology, 6</u>(1), 48-57.

President's Committee on Mental Retardation. (1974). <u>America's needs in habilitation and employment of the mentally retarded</u>. Washington, DC: U.S. Government Printing Office.

Putnam, J. W., Werder, J. K., & Schleien, S. J. (1985). Leisure and recreation services for handicapped persons. In K. C. Lakin & R. H. Bruininks (Eds.), <u>Strategies for achieving community integration of developmentally disabled citizens</u> (pp. 253-274). Baltimore: Paul H. Brookes.

Quilitch, H. R., & Gray, J. D. (1974). Purposeful activity for the PMR: A demonstration project. <u>Mental Retardation, 12</u>, 28-29.

Quilitch, H., & Risley, T. (1973). The effects of play materials on social play. <u>Journal of Applied Behavior Analysis, 6</u>, 573-578.

Ragheb, M. G., & Beard, J. G. (1980). Leisure satisfaction: Concept, theory and measurement. In S. E. Iso-Ahola (Ed.), Social psychological perspectives on leisure and recreation (pp. 329-353). Springfield, IL: Charles C. Thomas.

Ragland, E., Kerr, M., & Strain, P. (1978). Behavior of withdrawn autistic children: Effects of peer social initiations. Behavior Modification, 2, 565-579.

Rago, W. V., & Cleland, C. C. (1978). Future direction of the profoundly retarded. Education and Training of the Mentally Retarded, 13, 184-186.

Ray, M., Schleien, S., Larson, A., Rutten, T., & Slick, C. (1986). Integrating persons with disabilities into community leisure environments. Journal of Expanding Horizons in Therapeutic Recreation, 1(1), 49-55.

Realon, R. E., Favell, J. E., & Dayvault, K., A. (1988). Evaluating the use of adapted leisure materials on the engagement of persons who are profoundly, multiply disabled. Education and Training in Mental Retardation, 23(3), 228- 237.

Realon, R. E., Favell, J. E., & Lowerre, A. (1990). The effects of making choices on engagement levels with persons who are profoundly multiply handicapped. Education and Training in Mental Retardation, 25(3), 299-305.

Realon, R. E., Favell, J. E., & Phillips, J. F. (1989). Adapted leisure materials vs. standard leisure materials: Evaluating several aspects of programming for persons who are profoundly handicapped. Education and Training in Mental Retardation, 24(2), 168-177.

Reid, D. H. (1975). An analysis of variables affecting leisure activity behavior of multi-handicapped retarded persons. Unpublished doctoral dissertation, Florida State University, Tallahassee, FL.

Reid, D. H., & Hurlbut, B. (1977). Teaching nonvocal communication skills to multihandicapped retarded adults. Journal of Applied Behavior Analysis, 10, 591-603.

Reiter, S., & Levi, A. M. (1980). Factors affecting social integration of noninstitutionalized mentally retarded adults. American Journal of Mental Deficiency, 85, 25-30.

Richardson, D., Wilson, B., Wetherald, L., & Peters, J. (1987). Mainstreaming initiative: An innovative approach to recreation and leisure services in a community setting. Therapeutic Recreation Journal, 21(2), 9-19.

Richler, D. (1984). Access to community resources: The invisible barriers to integration. Journal of Leisurability, 11(2), 4-11.

Roadburg, A. (1983). Freedom and enjoyment: Disentangling perceived leisure. Journal of Leisure Research, 15, 15-26.

Rogow, S. (1976). Play and reality: Essentials of educational planning for blind retarded children. Education and Training of the Mentally Retarded, 11, 314-317.

Rogow, S. (1981). Developing play skills and communicative competence in multiply handicapped young people. Visual Impairment and Blindness, 5, 197-202.

Rowitz, L., & Stoneman, Z. (1990). Community first. Mental Retardation, 28(3), iii-iv.

Rush, V. (1983). A personal view. Rehabilitation World, 7, 32-39.

Rynders, J., Johnson, R., Johnson, D., & Schmidt, B. (1980). Producing positive interaction among Down syndrome and nonhandicapped teenagers through cooperative goal structuring. American Journal of Mental Deficiency, 85, 268-273.

Rynders, J. E., Schleien, S. J., & Mustonen, T. (1990). Integrating children with severe disabilities for intensified outdoor education: Focus on feasibility. Mental Retardation, 28, 7-14.

Salzberg, C. L., & Langford, C. A. (1981). Community integration of mentally retarded adults through leisure activity. Mental Retardation, 19, 127-131.

Samaras, M., & Ball, T. (1975). Reinforcement of cooperation between profoundly retarded adults. American Journal on Mental Deficiency, 80, 63-71.

Sandler, A., & McClain, S. (1987). Sensory reinforcement: Effects of response-contingent vestibular stimulation on multiply handicapped children. American Journal of Mental Deficiency, 91, 373-378.

Scheerenberger, R. C. (1987). A history of mental retardation: A quarter century of promise. Baltimore: Paul H. Brookes.

Scheerenberger, R. C., & Felsenthal, D. (1976). A study of alternative community placements. Madison, WI: Research Institute of the Wisconsin Association for Retarded Citizens.

Schleien, S. (1983). Leisure education for the learning disabled student. In M. Bender (Ed.), Learning disabilities (pp. 105-122). New York: Grune & Stratton.

Schleien, S. (1991). Severe multiple disabilities. In D. Austin & M. Crawford (Eds.), Therapeutic recreation: An introduction (pp. 189-223). Englewood Cliffs, NJ: Prentice Hall.

Schleien, S. J., Ash, T., Kiernan, J., & Wehman, P. (1981). Developing independent cooking skills in a profoundly retarded woman. Journal of the Association for the Severely Handicapped, 6, 23-29.

Schleien, S., Cameron, J., Rynders, J., & Slick, C. (1988). Acquisition and generalization of leisure skills from school to the home and community by learners with severe multihandicaps. Therapeutic Recreation Journal, 22(3), 53-71.

Schleien, S. J., Certo, N. J., & Muccino, A. (1984). Acquisition of leisure skills by a severely handicapped adolescent: A data based instructional program. Education and Training of the Mentally Retarded, 19(4), 297-305.

Schleien, S. J., Fahnestock, M., Green, R., & Rynders, J. E. (1990). Building positive social networks through environmental interventions in integrated recreation programs. Therapeutic Recreation Journal, 24(4), 42-52.

Schleien, S., Kiernan, J., & Wehman, P. (1981). Evaluation of an age-appropriate leisure skills program for moderately retarded adults. Education and Training of the Mentally Retarded, 16(1), 13-19.

Schleien, S. J., Krotee, M. L., Mustonen, T., Kelterborn, B., & Schermer, A. D. (1987). The effect of integrating children with autism into a physical activity and recreation setting. Therapeutic Recreation Journal, 21(4), 52-62.

Schleien, S. J., & Larson, A. (1986). Adult leisure education for the independent use of a community recreation center. The Journal of the Association of Persons with Severe Handicaps, 11(1), 39-44.

Schleien, S., Light, C., McAvoy, L., & Baldwin, C. (1989). Best professional practices: Serving persons with severe multiple disabilities. Therapeutic Recreation Journal, 23(3), 27-40.

Schleien, S., & Meyer, L. (1988). Community-based recreation programs for persons with severe developmental disabilities. In M. Powers (Ed.), Expanding systems of service delivery for persons with developmental disabilities (pp. 93-112). Baltimore: Paul H. Brookes.

Schleien, S., Porter, R., & Wehman, P. (1979). An assessment of the leisure skill needs of developmentally disabled individuals. Therapeutic Recreation Journal, 12(3), 16-21.

Schleien, S., & Ray, M. (1988). Community recreation and persons with disabilities: Strategies for integration. Baltimore: Paul H. Brookes.

Schleien, S. J., Ray, M. T., Soderman-Olson, M. L., & McMahon, K. T. (1987). Integrating children with moderate to severe cognitive deficits into a community museum program. Education and Training in Mental Retardation, 22(2), 112-120.

Schleien, S. J., Rynders, J. E., & Mustonen, T. (1988). Art and integration: What can we create? Therapeutic Recreation Journal, 22(4), 18-29.

Schleien, S., Rynders, J., Mustonen, J., & Fox, A. (1990). Effects of social play activities on the play behavior of children with autism. Journal of Leisure Research, 22, 317-328.

Schleien, S. J., Tuckner, B., & Heyne, L. (1985). Leisure education programs for the severely disabled student. Parks and Recreation, 20(1), 74-78.

Schleien, S., & Wehman, P. (1986). Severely handicapped children: Social skills development through leisure skills programming. In G. Cartledge & J. Milburn (Eds.), Teaching social skills to children: Innovative approaches (2nd ed.) (pp. 219-245). Elmsford, NY: Pergamon Press.

Schleien, S., & Werder, J. (1985). Perceived responsibilities of special recreation services in Minnesota. Therapeutic Recreation Journal, 19(3), 51-62.

Scott, B., & Gilliam. J. (1987). Curriculum as a behavior management tool for students with autism. Focus on Autistic Behavior, 2(1), 1-8.

Seaman, J. A. (1973). The effects of a bowling program upon bowling skill number concepts and self-esteem of mentally retarded children. Dissertation Abstracts International, 33(7-A), 3359-3360.

Sedlak, R., Doyle, M., & Schloss, P. (1982). Video games: A training and generalization demonstration with severely retarded adolescents. Education and Training of the Mentally Retarded, 17, 332-336.

Seligman, M. (1975). Helplessness: On depression, development, and death. San Francisco: W. H. Freeman.

Shafer, M., Egel, A., & Neef, N. (1984). Training mildly handicapped peers to facilitate changes in the social interaction skills of autistic children. Journal of Applied Behavior Analysis, 17, 461-476.

Sherrill, C. (1986). Adapted physical education and recreation: A multidisciplinary approach (3rd ed.). Dubuque, IA: William C. Brown.

Shevin, M., & Klein, N. (1984). The importance of choice-making skills for students with severe disabilities. Journal of the Association for Persons with Severe Handicaps, 9, 159-166.

Silberman, R. (1987). Report of the working group on recreation and leisure. In A. M. Covert & H. D. Fredricks (Eds.), Transition for persons with deaf blindness and other profound handicaps: State of the art (pp. 141-146). Monmouth, OR: Teaching Research Publications.

Sinclair, N. (1975). Cross country skiing for the mentally retarded. Challenge, 5, 33-35.

Smith, R. (1985). Barriers are more than architectural. Parks and Recreation, 20(10), 58-62.

Stokes, T., Baer, D., & Jackson, R. (1974). Programming and generalization of a greeting response in four retarded children. Journal of Applied Behavior Analysis, 7, 599-610.

Storey, K., Bates, P., & Hanson, H. (1984). Acquisition and generalization of coffee purchase skills by adults with severe disabilities. Journal of the Association for Persons with Severe Handicaps, 9, 178-185.

Strain, P. (1975). Increasing social play of severely retarded preschoolers with socio-dramatic activities. Mental Retardation, 13, 7-9.

Strain, P. (1977). An experimental analysis of peer social initiations on the behavior of withdrawn preschool children: Some training and generalization effects. Journal of Abnormal Child Psychology, 5, 445-455.

Strain, P., Cooke, T., & Apolloni, T. (1976). The role of peers in modifying classmates' social behavior: A review. Journal of Special Education, 10, 351-356.

Strain, P., Kerr, M., & Ragland, E. (1979). Effects of peer-mediated social initiations and prompting/reinforcement procedures on the social behavior of autistic children. Journal of Autism and Developmental Disorders, 9(1), 41-54.

Strain, P. S., Odum, S. L., & McConnell, S. (1984). Promoting social reciprocity of exceptional children: Identification, target behavior selection, and intervention. Remedial and Special Education, 5, 21-28.

Strain, P., & Shores, R. S. (1977). Social reciprocity: A review of research and educational implications. Exceptional Children, 43, 526-530.

Strain, P., Shores, R., & Kerr, M. (1976). An experimental analysis of spillover effects on the social interaction of behaviorally handicapped preschool children. Journal of Applied Behavior Analysis, 9, 31-40.

Strain, P., & Timm, M. (1974). An experimental analysis of social interaction between a behaviorally disordered preschool child and her classroom peers. Journal of Applied Behavior Analysis, 7, 583-590.

Sylvester, C. (1987). The politics: Leisure, freedom and poverty. Parks and Recreation, 22(1), 59-62.

Tansley, A. E., & Gulliford, R. (1960). The education of slow learning children (2nd ed.). London: Routledge and Kegan Paul.

Terman, L. (1916). The measurement of intelligence. Boston: Houghton-Mifflin.

U.S. Department of Health and Human Services. (1979). Plain talk about children with learning disabilities. Rockville, MD: Alcohol, Drug Abuse, and Mental Health Administration.

Vandercook, T. (1987). Generalized performance of community leisure skills with peers. Unpublished manuscript, University of Minnesota, Minneapolis.

Van Kleek, A., & Carpenter, R. (1980). The effects of children's language comprehension level on adults' child-directed talk. Journal of Speech and Hearing Research, 23, 546-569.

Vaughn, J. L., & Winslow, R. (Eds.). (1979). Guidelines for community based recreation programs for special populations. Arlington, VA: National Therapeutic Recreation Society.

Verhoven, P., Schleien, S., & Bender, M. (1982). Leisure education and the handicapped individual: An ecological perspective. Washington, DC: Institute for Career and Leisure Development.

Voeltz, L. M. (1982). Effects of structured interactions with severely handicapped peers on children's attitudes. American Journal of Mental Deficiency, 86, 380-390.

Voeltz, L., & Brennan, J. (1984). Analysis of interactions between nonhandicapped and severely handicapped peers using multiple measures. In J. M. Berg (Ed.), Perspectives and progress in mental retardation (Vol. 1, pp. 61-72). Baltimore: University Park Press.

Voeltz, L., & Wuerch, B. (1981a). A comprehensive approach to leisure education and leisure counseling for the severely handicapped person. Therapeutic Recreation Journal, 15(3), 24-35.

Voeltz, L., & Wuerch, B. (1981b). Monitoring multiple behavioral effects of leisure activities training on severely handicapped adolescents. In L. Voeltz, J. Apffel, & B. Wuerch (Eds.), Leisure activities training for severely handicapped students: Instructional and evaluation strategies (pp. 269-307). Honolulu: University of Hawaii, Department of Special Education.

Voeltz, L., Wuerch, B., & Bockhaut, C. (1982). Social validation of leisure activities raining with severely handicapped youth. The Journal of the Association for the Severely Handicapped, 7, 3-13.

Voeltz, L., Wuerch, B., & Wilcox, B. (1982). Leisure and recreation: Preparation for independence, integration and self-fulfillment. In B. Wilcox & G. T. Bellamy (Eds.), Design of high school programs for severely handicapped students (pp. 175-209). Baltimore: Paul H. Brookes.

Wacker, D. P., Berg, W. K., Wiggins, B., Muldoon, M., & Cavanaugh, J. (1985). Evaluation of reinforcer preferences for profoundly handicapped students. Journal of Applied Behavior Analysis, 18, 173-178.

Wacker, D. P., Wiggins, B., Fowler, M., & Berg, W. K. (1988). Training students with profound or multiple handicaps to make requests via microswitches. Journal of Applied Behavior Analysis, 21, 331-343.

Walker, P. (1988). Supporting children in integrated recreation. TASH Newsletter, 13(1), 4-5.

Walker, P., & Edinger. (1988). The kid from cabin 17. Camping Magazine, 60(5), 18-21.

Watson, A. E., Roggenbuck, J. W., & Williams, D. R. (1991). The influence of past experience on wilderness choice. Journal of Leisure Research, 23(1), 21-36.

Wechsler, D. (1949). Wechsler intelligence scale for children: Manual. New York: Psychological Corporation.

Wehman, P. (1977a). Research on leisure time and the severely developmentally disabled. Rehabilitation Literature, 38, 98-105.

Wehman, P. (1977b). Helping the mentally retarded acquire play skills: A behavioral approach. Springfield, IL: Charles C. Thomas.

Wehman, P. (1979). Toward a recreation curriculum for developmentally disabled persons. In P. Wehman (Ed.), Recreation programming for developmentally disabled persons (pp. 1-13). Austin, TX: PRO-ED.

Wehman, P., & Marchant, J. A. (1977). Developing gross motor recreational skills in children with severe behavioral handicaps. Therapeutic Recreation Journal, 11(1), 48-54.

Wehman, P., & Moon, M. S. (1985). Designing and implementing leisure programs for individuals with severe handicaps. In M. P. Brady & P. L. Gunter (Eds.), Integrating moderately and severely handicapped learners: Strategies that work (pp. 214-237). Springfield, IL: Charles C. Thomas.

Wehman, P., Renzaglia, A., Berry, A., Schultz, R., & Karan, O. (1978). Developing a leisure skill repertoire in severely and profoundly handicapped adolescents and adults. AAESPH Review, 3, 162-172.

Wehman, P., & Schleien, S. (1980). Assessment and selection of leisure skills for severely handicapped individuals. Education and Training of the Mentally Retarded, 15, 50-57.

Wehman, P., & Schleien, S. (1981). Leisure programs for handicapped persons: Adaptations, techniques, and curriculum. Austin, TX: PRO-ED.

Wehman, P., Schleien, S., & Kiernan, J. (1980). Age appropriate recreation programs for severely handicapped youth and adults. Journal of the Association for the Severely Handicapped, 5, 394-407.

Wessel, J. (1976). I CAN program. Northbrook, IL: Hubbard Scientific.

West, P. C. (1982). Organizational stigma in metropolitan park and recreation agencies. Therapeutic Recreation Journal, 16(4), 35-41.

West, P. C. (1984). Social stigma and community recreation participation by the mentally and physically handicapped. Therapeutic Recreation Journal, 18(1), 40-49.

Wetherby, A. M., & Prutting, C. A. (1984). Profiles of communicative and cognitive-social abilities in autistic children. Journal of Speech and Hearing Research, 27, 364-377.

Whitman, T., Mercurio, J., & Caponigri, V. (1970). Development of social responses in two severely retarded children. Journal of Applied Behavior Analysis, 3, 133-138.

Williams, W., Brown, L., & Certo, N. (1975). Components of instructional programs for severely handicapped students. In B. McCann (Ed.), Educating the 24-hour retarded child. Arlington, TX: National Training Meeting on Education of the Severely and Profoundly Retarded, National Association for Retarded Citizens.

Witt, P. A., Ellis, G., & Niles, S. H. (1984). Leisure counseling with special populations. In T. E. Dowd (Ed.), Leisure Counseling: Concepts and applications. Springfield, IL: Charles C. Thomas.

Wodrich, D. L., & Joy, J. E. (1986). Multi-disciplinary assessment of children with learning disabilities and mental retardation. Baltimore: Paul H. Brookes.

Wolfensberger, W. (1972). The principle of normalization in human services. Toronto: National Institute on Mental Retardation.

Wolfensberger, W. (1991). Reflections on a lifetime in human services and mental retardation. Mental Retardation, 29(1), 1-15.

Wuerch, B. B., & Voeltz, L. M. (1982). Longitudinal leisure skills for severely handicapped learners: The Ho'onanea curriculum component. Baltimore: Paul H. Brookes.

Young, C., & Kerr, M. (1979). The effects of a retarded child's social initiations on the behavior of severely retarded school-age peers. Education and Training of the Mentally Retarded, 14, 185-190.

Zigler, E., & Butterfield, E. C. (1968). Motivational aspects of changes in IQ test performance of culturally deprived nursery school children. Child Development, 39, 1-14.

Zigmond, N. (1978). A prototype of comprehensive service for secondary students with learning disabilities: A preliminary report. Learning Disabilities Quarterly, 1, 39-49.

CHAPTER 5

THE BENEFITS OF THERAPEUTIC RECREATION
IN GERONTOLOGY

Carol Riddick & Jean Keller

Procedures for Position Paper Design

The Temple University Efficacy Project staff identified broad guidelines for the position paper authors. The major theme of this paper was to identify the outcomes and benefits of therapeutic recreation services with geriatric populations in terms of rehabilitation, habilitation, and overall quality of life. Given the nature of the charge, the position paper authors felt a necessity to further delimit the paper's focus. Thus, the following steps explain the process for this paper's development: (a) identification of major health problems within the geriatric populations, (b) identification of how studies would be selected for inclusion in the paper, and (c) conceptualization and development of the paper.

Various physical and psychosocial health problems are prevalent among geriatric populations. Based on a review of morbidity and mortality trends among older adults, six major health problems, for the possible focus of this position paper, emerged: (a) cancer, (b) cardiovascular and related problems, (c) orthopedic and related problems, (d) senile dementia, (e) substance abuse, and (f) loneliness and depression (Brotman, 1982). Surprisingly, the literature review failed to identify studies in the areas of cancer and substance abuse among older adults where therapeutic recreation intervention was used. At the same time, a number of studies were found that focused on loneliness and depression. Hence, this paper ultimately focused on five health concerns among geriatric populations: (a) cardiovascular and related diseases, (b) orthopedic disabilities, (c) senile dementia, (d) depression, and (e) loneliness.

A volume of literature exists that reflects both survey research and anecdotal and testimonial information regarding the benefits of therapeutic recreation with geriatric populations. Because this paper's purpose was to identify documented outcomes the following criteria were used for identifying research that would be included in the literature review:

1. An identifiable intervention had been used.

2. The intervention was designed for individuals ages 50 years and over.

3. Empirical data were reported

4. The study was reported in a journal between 1980 and April, 1991.

5. The professional affiliation of the author(s) and/or intervention staff was not limited only to therapeutic recreation professionals.

A systematic and comprehensive review of the literature was made. For each study, the investigators, subjects (number, gender, disability, and setting), research design, intervention technique, theoretical foundation, focus, measures, and outcomes were retrieved. Thirty-eight relevant empirical studies using intervention techniques are reported.

A draft of the paper emerged after the remaining steps unfolded: (a) conceptualizing the integration of selected diagnoses in geriatric populations and settings; (b) identifying theoretical perspectives for therapeutic recreation services; (c) determining the interrelationships among selected health problems, recreation services, theoretical bases, and outcome(s) of services; and (d) conducting a literature review. Upon completion of a draft to the narrative results, recommendations were then suggested in three main areas: (a) geriatric therapeutic recreation research, (b) implications for practice, and (c) implications for policy. A number of therapeutic recreation practitioners and academicians were then asked to review the draft copy. Based on the comments received from this review process, the manuscript was revised. The copy herein represents this revision.

Introduction

Since 1900, the percentage of Americans 65 and older has tripled (4.1% in 1900 to 12.5% in 1989) and the number has increased nearly 10 times between 1900 and 1989 (from 3.1 million to 31 million). In 1989, the 85+ age group (3 million) was 24 times larger than it was in 1900. A child born in 1988 could expect to live 75 years, about 28 years longer than a child born in 1900 (Fowles, 1990).

Most older persons have at least one chronic condition and many have multiple conditions (Verbrugge, Lepkowski, & Imanaka, 1989). Geriatricians are aware that older people tend to have physical, mental-emotional, and social problems of a chronic nature (Verbrugge et al.). Additionally, the frequency which everyday activities are restricted increases with age due to illness and injury. Approximately 32 million persons (or 46% of all persons aged 65 years and over) reported limitations of activity due to chronic diseases (Rice & Feldman, 1983).

As a society grows older and frailer, there are economic and health care ramifications. Older adults accounted for 33% of all hospital stays and 44% of all days of care in hospitals in 1988 (Fowles, 1990; Matthew, 1989). In 1987, total health care expenditures for the 65+ age group were $162 billion, an average of $5,360 per year for each older person (Wood & Estes, 1990). Additionally, the number of nursing homes rose 7% in 1988 to 15,385 facilities in the United States, while home health care services have expanded at rapid rates (from $8.8 billion in 1988 to an estimated $16 billion in 1995) (Bergman, 1991; Palmore, 1990; Yulish, 1991).

Given the fact that the American population is growing older and tremendous resources are spent on the geriatric population, further explorations are needed into the role of therapeutic recreation and its benefits as a treatment modality with this population. To explore the topic, this position paper is divided into five sections: (a) selected diagnoses of geriatric populations and settings for therapeutic recreation services; (b) theoretical perspectives of aging and therapeutic recreation; (c) literature review results of therapeutic recreation efficacy; (d) interrelationships among selected health problems, therapeutic recreation services, theoretical bases, and expected outcome(s) of service; and (e) future recommendations for therapeutic recreation practice, research, and policy.

Selected Diagnoses of Geriatric Populations and Settings for Therapeutic Recreation Services

The aging process is manifested in a series of physiological and behavioral changes. It cannot be assumed, however, that aging is always characterized by impairment of function (Atchley, 1985). Indeed, aging in adults is illustrated with greater diversity than any other age group. Although the incidence of disease increases with age, aging and disease are not synonymous (Butler & Lewis, 1973).

Nevertheless, some of the major health problems confronting older adults include cardiovascular and related diseases, orthopedic problems, senile dementia, depression, and loneliness. This section of the paper has three subsections. The first and second subsections present background information on selected physical and social psychological health problems, respectively. The third subsection puts forth an integration scheme for selected diagnoses in geriatric populations and settings for therapeutic recreation services.

Physical Health Problems

Cardiovascular and related diseases. Epidemiologic studies indicate the elevations of either diastolic or systolic blood pressure are risk factors for cardiovascular and cerebrovascular morbidity and mortality (Carlson & Newman, 1987). Overall, high blood pressure in the geriatric population is estimated to be responsible for 33% of all cases of cardiac disease. Similarly, 42% and 70% of strokes experienced by elderly men and women, respectively, have been linked to high blood pressure (Multiple Risk Factor Intervention Trial Research Group, 1982).

Disease, disuse, and lifestyle, rather than age alone, account for most of the deterioration in the heart (Page & Friedlander, 1986). Regarding lifestyle risk factors, it has been noted that the following practices: (a) maintaining ideal weight, (b) sodium restriction, (c) aerobic exercise, and (d) relaxation therapy are effective in the reduction of hypertension among older adults (Applegate, 1987). Therapeutic recreation programs, in order to reduce the risk of cardiovascular and cerebrovascular diseases and illnesses in geriatric populations, should be designed to stress leisure education, exercise, and relaxation.

Orthopedic disabilities. Two orthopedic disabilities common in the geriatric population are osteoarthritis (OA) and osteoporosis. OA is an extremely common rheumatic disease that increases in frequency with age (Nickerson, 1987). OA is the second leading cause of permanent disability in the United States (Carlson, 1987). The clinical features of OA are usually pain, loss of motion, and deformity. The management of OA may involve physical activity, medications, and surgery. Quinet (1986) indicated physical exercise can decrease pain and stiffness, increase strength of the supporting joint muscles, and improve joint motion with the geriatric population.

Osteoporosis heads the list of musculoskeletal diseases that cause debility in elderly women. Osteoporosis plays a major role in 200,000 hip fractures that occur annually (Brody & Schneider, 1986). Preventative treatment of osteoporosis includes adequate calcium intake, use of estrogen (by women only), and increased weight-bearing physical activity (Licata, 1987; Riis, Thomsen, & Christiansen, 1987; Smith, 1982).

Therapeutic recreation can then play a significant role in the prevention and restoration of older adults with orthopedic disabilities. That is, therapeutic recreation specialists should be offering physical activity intervention as well as leisure education programs that maintain, or restore musculoskeletal health and functioning.

Psychological Health Problems

Senile dementia. Dementia has been labeled as "...probably the most serious psychiatric disorder of old age" (Huyck & Hoyer, 1982, p. 441). While the causes of dementia are numerous (e.g., substance abuse, nutritional intake, physical health problems), the most common form of dementing illness is senile dementia of the Alzheimer's type. Alzheimer's type dementia has been linked to pathological abnormalities in the brain (Jarvik & Kumar, 1984). Dementia is a chronic disabling disease and is characterized by dramatic changes in cognition (such as memory, attention span, intelligence), personality (changes in affect, difficulties in judgement, etc.), and behavior (Huges, 1978). Among older persons living in the community, it has been estimated that between 5 and 8% have some form of senile dementia; whereas about 70% of the individuals residing in long-term care facilities have this problem (Kay & Bergman, 1980).

It has been suggested that a variety of therapeutic recreation interventions be offered to individuals who have senile dementia. Example of interventions include those targeted at promoting cognition, reminiscence, reality, sensory stimulation, exercise, relaxation, activities of daily living, and social contact (Levy, 1986).

Depression. Depression is the most common non-organic psychological problem experienced in old age (Butler & Lewis, 1973; Pfeiffer, 1977). Among older persons living in the community, it has been estimated that somewhere between 10 and 25% have clinically diagnosed depression (Gianturco & Busse, 1978; National Institutes of Mental Health, 1977). Similarly, 39% of the people residing in long-term care facilities are said to exhibit depressive symptomatology (National Center for Health Statistics, 1977).

Depression in the elderly population is due partly to individual events and partly to the biological, psychological, social, and cultural factors that are common in old age (Stenback, 1980). In particular, the losses or stressors associated with age (such as widowhood, declining health, and decreasing social and economic resources) have been found to be strongly associated with depression (Blazer & Williams, 1980; Linn, Hunter, & Harris, 1980).

How then can therapeutic specialists work with depressed clientele? It has been noted that often time individuals suffering from depression need help with learning how to enjoy themselves in leisure pursuits as well as with assertiveness, relaxation, revamping their cognitive processes, and socialization (Edinberg, 1985; Schaie & Willis, 1986).

Loneliness. One of the risks of aging is an increased vulnerability to loneliness (Creecy, Berg, & Wright, 1985). Somewhere between 12 and 30% of non-institutionalized older persons are lonely (Shanas et al., 1968). Moreover, loneliness is more concentrated in nursing homes than in community settings (Kastenbaum, Barber, Wilson, Ryder, & Hathaway, 1981). Indeed, it has been reported that persons residing in nursing homes often complain of loneliness (Busse & Pfeiffer, 1977).

Feelings of loneliness can predispose elderly persons toward physical and mental disorders (Rathbone-McCuan & Hashimi, 1982). For example, studies have demonstrated that loneliness is often accompanied by such negative consequences as depression, anxiety, and lowered self-esteem (Hojat, 1982). Dooghe, Vanderleyden, & Van Loon (1990) concluded, after surveying 360 institutionalized elderly adults, that loneliness was the major factor contributing to failure to adjust to life in a long-term facility. One obvious ramification for addressing loneliness in the geriatric populations is to promote socialization in the selection and implementation of therapeutic recreation programs and services.

Diagnoses and Settings for Therapeutic Recreation Services

The various health problems identified above can be addressed by therapeutic recreation specialists in a variety of settings. Before 1950, practically all therapeutic recreation took place within hospitals and institutions. This is no longer true. Today, therapeutic recreation is provided to the geriatric populations in a multitude of settings such as acute care hospitals, inpatient psychiatric hospitals, physical rehabilitation facilities, extended care facilities, long-term health care facilities, adult day care centers, outpatient services, in-home services, and multipurpose senior centers (Austin & Crawford, 1991; MacNeil & Teague, 1987; O'Morrow & Reynolds, 1989).

Figure 1 presents a two dimensional grid for integrating selected diagnoses in geriatric populations and settings for therapeutic recreation services. Notations appear in this figure regarding the settings where therapeutic recreation services can typically be found for treating or managing a noted health problem.

Theoretical Perspectives of Aging and Leisure

A number of paradigms are available for providing the rationale for therapeutic recreation services with geriatric populations. In particular, the following three major conceptual areas, as they relate to aging will be reviewed: (a) biological theories, (b) psychological theories, and (c) social theories.

Biological Theories of Aging

Several theoretical approaches have evolved for explaining the biology of aging. While a detailed description of these theories is beyond the scope of this paper, suffice to say that biological explanations for aging and death are grouped into three categories, including genetic, cellular, and physiological "wear-and-tear" theories (cf. Schock, 1977). Genetic theories hypothesize an existence of specific preset biological or genetic programs that dictate the death of human body cells (in either the hypothalamus or immune system). Cellular theories suggest changes in cells are caused by non genetic factors. For example, random damage theories specify the occurrence of accumulated faults in cells, at the DNA or RNA levels, and prevent cells from producing needed proteins. Physiological wear-and-tear theories speculate that human organ systems degenerate or deteriorate over time, especially as a result of extrinsic or environmental factors (Huyck & Hoyer, 1982). An implication of physiological wear-and-tear theories is that therapeutic recreation specialists should provide comprehensive services that retard physical deterioration and promote physical well-being.

Psychological Theories

Learning and memory. Learning is the acquisition of information or skills and is usually measured by improvements in task performance (Atchley, 1985). There are a number of factors, other than learning ability, that affect performance, including motivation, performance speed, socioeconomic status, ill health, and physiological stress. There is evidence that older adults can learn, given additional time (Arenberg & Robertson-Tchabo, 1980; Schaie, 1990).

Memory is related to learning, since to remember is partial evidence of learning. There are four types of memory: (a) short-term, (b) recent, (c) remote, and (d) old. Short-term memory involves recall after very little delay. Recent memory is recall after a brief period, from 1 hour to several days. Remote memory refers to recall of events that took place in the distant past and have been recalled frequently over a person's lifetime. Old memory means recall of distant personal events (Atchley, 1985). Older people who use their memories tend to maintain both remote and recent memory (Schaie, 1990).

In addition to the different types, there are three stages of memory: (a) registration, (b) retention, and (c) recall. Registration is the recording of learning or perceptions; retention refers to the ability to sustain registration over time; and recall is the retrieval of material that has been registered and retained. In all types of memory, a failure at any of these stages results in no measurable memory (Salthouse, 1982). It is not clear, whether memory decline among older adults is from failing memory or from declining ability to learn.

In the mean time a number of therapeutic recreation intervention techniques (reality orientation, pet facilitated therapy, reminiscence, etc.) have emerged for promoting and maintaining learning and memory by older adults. More research is needed on what causes memory and learning deficits in the geriatric populations to better understand the impact of these techniques.

Activity theory. The explanation and prediction of successful or optimal aging has been addressed by the activity theory. Moreover, the activity theory discusses successful aging in terms of life satisfaction. It has become common practice by gerontological researchers to apply or interchange other concepts with life satisfaction--such as mental/psychological well-being, morale, happiness, self-concept, and self-esteem (George & Bearon, 1980).

The activity theory asserts that optimal aging is positively correlated with activity (Havighurst, Neugarten, & Tobin, 1968; Lemon, Bengston, & Peterson, 1972). Activity is defined by a variety of actions in leisure as well as interactions with family and friends, and involvements in voluntary organizations. Supposedly, successful aging occurs for those who increase their middle-age activity levels, including the ability to substitute activities for those roles they are forced to discontinue. Research findings that have supported this theory (via an examination of how activities in general influence successful aging) include Adams (1971), Kelly, Steinkamp, and Kelly (1987), and Maddox (1968). Two ways this theory could be applied by therapeutic recreation specialists are to examine how certain categories of leisure activities (e.g., formal, informal, social activities) and specific types of interventions (such as reminiscence or reality orientation) affect psychological well-being.

Depression. One behaviorist view of depression is the learned helplessness theory outlined by Seligman (1975). Essentially this theory suggests that unavoidable multiple changes in life events (e.g., failing health, loss of finances, retirement, widowhood) are "shocks" to older persons and result in individuals loosing faith in their ability to affect the environment--or a feeling of helplessness. This feeling of being helpless can prevent older persons from acting to compensate for losses and consequently influences their feelings of mastery over their environment. In short, persons learn inaction--that it is useless to try to affect the environment. This sense of
helplessness may lead to cognitive, emotional, and physical symptoms of depression. One implication of this theory is that therapeutic recreation specialists should foster participants' control over different structural and/or procedural aspects of activity programs and intervention techniques.

Leisure Experience

Witt, Ellis, and Niles (1984) have attempted to cogently put forth a conceptual foundation to leisure counseling for persons with disabilities. In this theoretical paradigm, leisure is viewed as a state of mind or a way of perceiving experiences. Five major elements are linked to influencing how leisure is experienced: (a) intrinsic motivation, (b) perceived freedom, (c) perceived competence, (d) flow, and (e) playfulness (Iso-Ahola, 1980; Neulinger, 1982).

Intrinsic motivation. Intrinsic motivation refers to self-determined behavior that results in the satisfaction of the individual's internal needs (Deci, 1968). The ideal is to have one's leisure behavior intrinsically motivated--that is, determined by the individual's preferences and interests rather than by outside influences (i.e., other persons). Individuals who engage in intrinsically motivated activity are characterized by involvement and commitment to the activity and lack anxious feelings (DeCharms, 1968). Using this principle, therapeutic recreation specialists should offer activities that respond to their clientele's preferences and interests.

Perceived freedom. One problem typically confronting institutionalized older adults is their lack of "perceived freedom" or feeling capable of determining or controlling the process and outcome of recreation experiences or situations affecting them (Purcell & Keller, 1989; Schulz & Brenner, 1977; Schulz & Decker, 1985). A number of items may affect perceived freedom including: (a) poor social skills, (b) poor health, (c) stereotypic notions of older adults and their abilities, and (d) environmental restrictions (such as lack of accessible facilities and a lack of available opportunities) (Larson, 1978; Schulz & Brenner, 1977). In order to promote perceived freedom, therapeutic recreation specialists should facilitate the development of leisure abilities, an awareness of leisure resources, and the formation and enhancement of appropriate social skills (Witt et al., 1984).

Perceived competence. All individuals, including older adults, need to feel a degree of personal competence in their lives (Purcell & Keller, 1989; Witt et al., 1984). This perception of competence provides individuals with a degree of assurance that their involvement will be rewarding and satisfying and that the probability of failure resulting in an embarrassing or frustrating experience is unlikely (Purcell & Keller; Witt et al.). Older persons who perceive themselves as competent are in a better position to experience a sense of well-being and life satisfaction (Ragheb & Griffith, 1982; Russell, 1987).

Competence is multi-faceted including physical, cognitive, social, and emotional abilities and each domain has been shown to impact the health and well-being of geriatric populations (Verbrugge et al., 1989; Witt et al., 1984). Perceived competence can be developed or enhanced through therapeutic recreation experiences. For instance, an activity may be repeated until older individuals feel they can successfully complete it (Iso-Ahola, 1980; Langer & Rodin, 1976; Tinsley, Teaff, Colbs, & Kaufman, 1985).

Flow. Flow deals with a person's feelings of intrinsic or internal satisfaction. During flow experiences, individuals may be able to transcend concerns about themselves and their personal conditions. Hence, flow provides an opportunity for self-enhancement and satisfaction (Witt et al., 1984). Typically, flow emanates from familiarity and mastery with an activity (Csikszentmihalyi, 1975; Kelly, 1990). Therapeutic recreation specialist should strive to create opportunities (via activity offerings) for the geriatric clientele to achieve a flow state.

Playfulness. Playfulness is composed of cognitive, physical, and social spontaneity as well as the manifestation of joy and humor (Lieberman, 1977). Spontaneity is the ability to make something of nothing, to take chances, and to be creative (Witt et al., 1984). Thus, one challenge facing therapeutic recreation specialists is to nurture playfulness in older adults.

Social Theories

Loneliness. One way for explaining social loneliness--or a perceived deficit in social contact--is by an interactionist approach (Perlman & Peplau, 1982). Basically this theory posits that loneliness is a product of a combined or interactive effect between personality and situational factors. The result is that a socially lonely person experiences boredom and feelings of being socially marginal.

A number of implications for practitioners evolve out of the interactionist theory of loneliness. Specifically, in an effort to address loneliness, foci for therapeutic recreation interventions could include: (a) training in social skills, (b) fostering social networks, and (c) establishing a structural environment that is conducive to promoting social interaction (Rook & Peplau, 1982).

Symbolic interaction. Symbolic interactionism provides a theory for understanding how individuals structure and experience their participation in social groups. Symbolic interaction theory advocates that individuals must have interactive experiences with other people, in order to derive meaning in their own lives. In other words, what individuals value in life is influenced by their contact with others. The interactive experience requires individuals to interpret their interaction with others (Rossman, 1989). These interpretations, in turn, influence individuals' behaviors. Thus, therapeutic recreation specialists should direct some of their efforts to promoting social interaction among their clientele.

Literature Review Results of Therapeutic Recreation Efficacy Studies

In order to identify intervention studies that have been conducted in the last decade, CD-ROM computerized data search (using Psychlit and Sociofile, 1980--April, 1991) was used as well as a several other data resources. Specifically, the following data banks (with the time period under examination parenthetically noted) were reviewed: (a) Abstracts in Social Gerontology: Current Literature on Aging (1985-1991); (b) Psychological Abstracts (1980 to 1991); (c) Sociological Abstracts (1980 to 1991); (d) Leisure & Aging Bibliography (September, 1985 to September, 1990) (Tedrick, 1991); and (e) Bibliography of Doctoral Dissertations on Aging from American Institutions of Higher Learning (from 1981 to 1986) (Moore, 1985, 1986, 1987). Additionally, the contents of (a) Educational Gerontologist; (b) Journal of Gerontology; (c) Generations; (d) The Southwestern: The Journal of Aging for the Southwest; (e) Therapeutic Recreation Journal (from 1980 to 1990); (f) Expanding Horizons in Therapeutic Recreation (from VIII to XIII); and (g) Annual in Therapeutic Recreation (from 1990 to 1991) were examined.

The literature review yielded a total of 38 quantitative intervention studies that were used for the analysis described herein. Tables 1 to 3 present a summary of the findings (including methodological and outcome information). (Note: Table 1 has been set up with three subsections: (a) cardiovascular and related diseases, (b) orthopedic disabilities, and (c) nervous system problems. Likewise, Table 2 contains the following subsections: (a) memory and learning, (b) life satisfaction, (c) depression, and (d) personality characteristics. Similarly, Table 3 contains two subsections on: (a) loneliness and (b) social interaction.) Within each of the tables, the studies are alphabetized within subsections indicated with bold lines at the end of each subsection.

Cardiovascular and Related Diseases

A total of seven studies were identified which related to cardiovascular aspects (blood pressure, pulse rate, skin temperature, general skeletal muscle tension, heart rate, cholesterol, glucose, and respiration rate) of older adults. In six studies, non-institutionalized (public housing residents, home health care recipients, senior center participants, VA outpatients clinic attenders, etc.) older adults participated and, in one study, long-term care residents comprised the sample.

Various therapeutic recreation interventions were found to have significantly influenced cardiovascular aspects in later life: (a) plush pets (Francis & Munjas, 1988); (b) water aerobics (Green, 1989; Keller, 1991); (c) exercise/fitness programs (Morey et al., 1989); and (d) watching fish in aquarium (Cutler Riddick, 1985). There have been, however, inconsistent findings regarding the efficacy of viewing fish in an aquarium and caring for fish. DeSchriver and Cutler Riddick (1990) and Gowing (1984) have reported that when these interventions were used, they were ineffective in influencing aspects of cardiovascular health.

Orthopedic Disabilities

In the literature, five studies appear focused on orthopedic disabilities (three of the five studies examining orthopedic issues were also found to address cardiovascular and related disease health problems). Two of the five studies were conducted in long-term care settings (Buettner, 1988; Yoder, Nelson, & Smith, 1989). One of these two studies was designed with older adults who had been institutionalized for over 20 years (Buettner).

Exercise/fitness programs have been found to increase flexibility and strength in older adults (Buettner, 1988; Morey et al., 1989). Using an innovative approach, Yoder et al., (1989) reported that exercise (hand and wrist motion) with added purpose (stirring cookie batter) improved range of motion better than rote exercise because there was a tendency for the exercise to be repeated more often.

Similarly, water aerobics, in most cases, has been reported as effective in improving the orthopedic health of older adults. That is, Green (1989) and Keller (1991) demonstrated that water aerobics with older adults significantly reduced body fat and weight. In contrast, Morey et al.'s. (1989) findings indicated that body fat and body weight were not significantly reduced during a supervised exercise/fitness program (which contained an optional water exercise program).

Senile Dementia

A total of nine studies were identified that affected the cognitive abilities of individuals with dementia. (Note: For purposes of this review, when investigators used a nursing home sample for their study and did not provide information on the cognitive status of these individuals, it was assumed the study involved persons with dementia. This assumption was evoked for three of the nine noted studies.) The following interventions were found to have significantly influenced the cognitive abilities of individuals who had dementia and participated in a: (a) dance (Osgood, Meyers, & Orchowsky, 1990); (b) music (Wolfe, 1983); (c) plush pet (Francis & Baly, 1986); or (d) visitation (Beck, 1982) program.

Contradictory results have, however, been noted for the efficacy of reality orientation and reminiscence therapy. Conroy, Fincham, and Agard-Evans (1988) and Riegler (1980) have reported that reality therapy enhances cognitive abilities, whereas Bumanis and Yoder (1987) have reported that this intervention is ineffective in influencing cognitive memory. Similarly, Hughston and Merriam (1982) found reminiscence therapy effective for elderly residents of a public housing complex in improving cognitive functioning whereas Schafer, Berghorn, Holmes, and Quadagno (1986) did not (albeit among "mentally alert" nursing home residents).

Likewise, it has been noted that participation in a writing group was found to be ineffective in affecting cognitive functioning of disoriented nursing home residents (Supiano, Ozminkowski, Campbell, & Lapidos, 1989). Somewhat related, though not initially set up to serve elderly adults with dementia, it has also been reported that participation in a plush animal program is not associated with a significant increase in memory (Francis & Munjas, 1988).

Interventions designed to influence some other facet of an older person's life with dementia. A number of interventions have been established to serve and affect individuals with dementia. One way to group these studies is to report on those that have been designed to impact on demented individuals': (a) physical health, (b) life satisfaction, and (c) personality characteristics.

Three studies (Buettner, 1988; Norberg, Melin, & Asplund, 1986; Yoder et al., 1989) were designed to determine the efficacy of various intervention techniques on physical aspects of older adults with dementia. Interestingly, none of these studies addressed cardiovascular or related diseases. Two studies addressed the musculoskeletal system (Buettner; Yoder et al.) and the Norberg et al. study focused on the nervous system.

A developmental exercise/fitness program was shown to be effective in improving flexibility, hand strength, and ambulation of older residents with dementia (Buettner, 1988). Music stimulation enhanced the mouth movement and reduced the eye blinking for persons in the later stages of Alzheimer's disease (Norberg et al., 1986). Range of motion improved for nursing home residents with mental deficits when purpose (stirring cookie batter) was added to an exercise program compared to rote exercise (Yoder et al., 1989).

A total of six studies were found to have been set up to influence the life satisfaction of individuals with dementia. Moreover, in all of these studies, significant results were noted. That is, individuals with dementia, who participated in: (a) dance/movement (Osgood et al., 1990); (b) pet therapy/plush animal (Banziger & Rousch, 1983; Francis & Baly, 1986); (c) reminiscence (Ferguson, 1980); and (d) video game play (McGuire, 1984) experienced substantive gains in some aspect of life satisfaction. Only one study could be located that attempted to influence the personality characteristics of demented individuals. In this work (Banziger & Rousch), it was reported that nursing home residents caring for bird feeders (located outside their bedroom window) experienced significant improvement in their sense of control in life.

Depression

A total of nine interventions appear in the literature as having been targeted for depressed older adults. Three approaches--or participation by community elderly persons in: (a) a bibliotherapy program (Scogin, Hamblin, & Beutler, 1987; Scogin, Jamison, & Davis, 1990; Scogin, Jamison, & Gochneaur, 1989); (b) a pet therapy/plush animal program by institutionalized elderly adults (Francis & Baly, 1986; Francis & Munjas, 1988); and (c) a reminiscence program for nursing home residents (Fry, 1983)--have been associated with significant declines in depression. On the other hand, participation in: (a) a reality orientation (Perotta & Meacham, 1981-1982); (b) touch (Bell, 1984); or (c) writing group (Supiano et al., 1989) has not been linked to a subsequent decline in depression.

Interventions designed to influence some other facet of an older depressed person's life. Two other studies have been conducted to influence the lives of depressed elderly adults. Scogin et al. (1987) found that bibliotherapy had no significant affect on the cognitive abilities of depressed older people living in the community. Perotta & Meacham (1981-1982), in an effort to influence the self-esteem of depressed senior center attenders, offered a reminiscence program. After five sessions, no significant improvement in self-esteem was recorded.

Loneliness

Three studies were located that specifically addressed establishing an intervention designed to influence the loneliness of geriatric populations. After receiving bi weekly visits, over a 10 week period, a group of elderly residents of a public apartment complex experienced a significant reduction in their loneliness (Culter Riddick, 1985). A dance/movement program for community older adults has also been found to be effective in reducing loneliness (Osgood et al., 1990). On the other hand, it has been reported that an outdoor day camp did not impact on the loneliness experienced by nursing home participants (Preston, 1987).

Interventions designed to influence social interaction. A related construct to loneliness is social interaction. A variety of approaches have been linked to participants experiencing increased social interaction. That is, music (Cutler Riddick & Dugan-Jendzejec, 1988), singing (Olderog Millard & Smith, 1989), reminiscence (Shafer et al., 1986), videogame play (Cutler Riddick, Spector, & Drogin, 1986), and visitation (Beck, 1982) programs have all been linked to improved social health of geriatric populations.

Turning to pet therapy/plush animal programs, the results have been contradictory. On one hand, some investigators have noted that pet therapy/plush animals (Banziger & Rousch, 1983; Francis & Baly, 1986; Robb, Boyd, & Pristash, 1980) are effective in elevating social interactions of elders. On the other hand, Francis & Munjas (1988) and Gowing (1984) have reported that exposure to plush animals or stocked aquariums does little in the way of influencing older individuals' social interactions.

Life Satisfaction

A number of recreation programs--though not specifically targeted for depressed or lonely individuals--have been offered to older individuals in long-term health care or community settings. Nevertheless, it was assumed that these programs contained individuals who were experiencing depression or loneliness [this assumption being buffeted by prevalence statistics presented in the, "Selected Diagnoses of Geriatric Populations and Settings for Therapeutic Recreation Settings" section (see above)], and consequently these investigations were included in this review. Specifically, a review of interventions dealing with: (a) life satisfaction of long-term facility residents, (b) life satisfaction of community populations, and (c) the personality characteristics of elders in long-term care institutions follows.

166

Life satisfaction of long-term care facility residents. Four interventions which included: (a) taking care of a plant (Shary & Iso-Ahola, 1989); (b) music (Cutler Riddick & Dugan-Jendzejec, 1988); (c) pet therapy/plush animal (Francis & Munjas, 1988); and (d) reminiscence (Schafer et al., 1986) have emerged as significantly influencing some facet of the life satisfaction of long-term care facility residents.

Life satisfaction of community setting residents. Four studies were also conducted in an effort to influence the life satisfaction of community older adults. As evidenced through these studies' findings, three of the interventions--or autobiography (Malde, 1983), pets (i.e., goldfish) (Gowing, 1984), and visits (Munson, 1984) did not influence the mental health of non-institutionalized older adults involved in the experiments. Berryman-Miller (1988), however, did report that senior center attenders, who participated in a dance program, experienced a significant improvement in their self-concept.

Long-term care facility settings and personality characteristics. Two approaches, namely enhanced responsibility programs (that required, among other things, caring for a plant) (Shary & Iso-Ahola, 1989) and reminiscence therapy (Schafer et al., 1986) have, respectively, been reported as significantly influencing the perceived competence and internal control of nursing home residents.

Interrelationships Among Selected Health Problems, Therapeutic Recreation Services, Theoretical Bases, and Expected Outcome(s) of Service

Adopting the World Health Organization's (1947) multifaceted approach to the conceptualization of health, there are three facets of health: (a) physical, (b) psychological, and (c) social. Each of these systems can be further broken down into subsystems (e.g., physical health is made up of various systems such as the cardiovascular, musculoskeletal, and nervous systems). Influencing one or more of these systems can, in turn, become the outcome of a therapeutic recreation intervention or activity.

Figures 2 to 4 present a framework for demonstrating the interrelationships among specific: (a) health problems, (b) therapeutic recreation services, (c) theoretical foundation(s), and (d) anticipated outcomes. These figures were developed after the completion of the literature review. Some of the noted interrelationships are based on what the authors feel are plausible, rather than on the research findings alone.

It is also important to note, in developing these figures as well as the literature review, concomitant effects or sub-problems associated with the selected health problems were addressed. The rationale for doing this was twofold. First, there are more health problems (e.g., dementia) where it is unreasonable to expect therapeutic recreation will have a direct impact (such as on mortality or morbidity). Instead, therapeutic recreation becomes an adjunctive therapy [and for the dementia example, may serve the role of influencing other facets of the person's life (such as his or her depression, feelings of helplessness, or range of motion)]. The second rationale for sometimes focusing on multiple benefits of therapeutic recreation that can be achieved with older adults' health problems, is that therapeutic recreation interventions are frequently established to address a number of older adults' health problems. For instance, pet therapy may be offered with the expectation that it will impact various aspects of participants' physiological, psychological, and/or social health.

Recommendations for Therapeutic Recreation Research, Practice, and Policy

Geriatric Therapeutic Recreation Research in General

After reviewing a decade of research, that has been conducted on therapeutic recreation intervention techniques with geriatric populations, a number of observations and related suggestions can be made. That is:

1. There is a limited body of empirical research on the effects of therapeutic recreation on the health and well-being of various geriatric populations [this finding confirms what others have noted (cf. Iso-Ahola, 1988; Mannell, 1983; Riddick, DeSchriver, & Weissinger, 1984; Schleien & Yermakoff, 1983)]. For the most part, therapeutic outcomes of recreation programs have been projected on the basis of anecdotal evidence derived from case studies or from descriptive surveys that have taken place in clinical or community settings where control procedures and scientific methods of inquiry have not been utilized. If therapeutic recreation is to be viewed as a viable treatment medium with geriatric populations, the effects of these "therapies" on the individual as well as the health care system must be subjected to scientific scrutiny.

2. A significant part of the knowledge, about the effects of "therapeutic recreation" interventions, is created by researchers outside of therapeutic recreation. Indeed, 28 of the 38 studies (74%) used for this review were written by individuals not formally affiliated with recreation (as deduced from noted

therapeutic recreation, recreation, or leisure affiliation with a university, community, or institutional setting). Therapeutic recreation professionals should be documenting and disseminating information about their efforts.

3. The existing literature on geriatric therapeutic recreation programs, by-and-large, does not note a holistic or multidisciplinary approach to client development and functioning. Ironically, the geriatric and gerontological literature stresses the interrelationships between and among the physical, mental/emotional, and social components of older adults' lives as they affect their well-being (Atchley, 1985; Butler & Lewis, 1973; Schock, 1977). Research on geriatric therapeutic recreation programs should be designed to include a multifaceted approach to the benefits of specific therapeutic recreation intervention techniques and programs. In this way, geriatric therapeutic recreation research would be more applicable to the practice of therapeutic recreation, since therapeutic recreation specialists often use one activity to address several treatment goals.

4. Therapeutic recreation services with geriatric populations are offered in a wide variety of settings. None of the studies reviewed were conducted in acute care hospitals, inpatient psychiatric hospitals, physical rehabilitation facilities, extended care facilities, or adult day care facilities. Research is needed on the benefits of therapeutic recreation services in various health care settings.

Methodological Quality of Geriatric Therapeutic Recreation Research

Methodological limitations revealed in earlier works must be addressed in future research. In particular, studies need to be conducted that have:

1. A theoretical foundation--the literature review revealed that the lack of theoretical orientation was the weakest aspect of problem formulation. Almost 70% (N = 26 or 68%) of the articles lacked an explicit statement about the theoretical basis of the study. Such practices are antithetical to guiding inquiry and greatly restrict the cumulative knowledge of the therapeutic recreation field.

2. Used comparable control group(s) in the research design--of the reviewed studies, 29% (N = 11) were devoid of a control group. Having this component in the research design allows one to determine if noted changes are due to the intervention or non-treatment factors (e.g., maturation, experimenter contact).

3. Utilized appropriate statistical tests--when a control group and pre- and post-tests have been used as part of the research design, then between/among group comparisons should be made. Nevertheless, 11 (or 41%) of the studies having pre-post-tests and control group features (N = 27) simply reported within group changes over time. Such practices do not address the fundamental question of whether the treatment group relative to the control group experienced a significant change.

4. Adopted valid and reliable measures. Almost one-fourth (N = 9 or 24%) of the reviewed articles failed to address instrumentation validity or reliability even though adoption of "good measures" increases one's confidence of noted results. The fact that unknown or weak (in terms of validity and reliable) instruments are used in geriatric research is perplexing since some excellent instrument selection guides exist (cf. George & Bearon, 1980; Kane & Kane, 1981; Mangen & Peterson, 1982).

What Can Be Done? Implications for Practice

Therapeutic recreation can be used as a primary or adjunctive therapy in addressing the myriad of problems confronting geriatric populations. While the study described herein focused on five major health problems, there is a litany of problems confronting older adults in American society. What role or impact therapeutic recreation has for geriatric populations suffering from, for example, cancer and substance abuse (including addiction to prescription drugs, alcohol, opiates, and narcotics) remains for future investigation. Indeed, it was the original intent of the authors of this paper to include these two problems in the therapeutic recreation intervention review. The review of literature, however, revealed no reported research on these two areas! The facts of the matter are that cancer is the third leading cause of death among the older population (Blake, 1984), 15% of elderly adults have serious alcohol problems (Zimberg, 1974), another 5% are addicted to illegal drug abuse of narcotics and opiates (Capel, Goldsmith, & Waddell, 1972), and a large number of older adults have become addicted to prescription drugs (Whittington, 1984). Thus, the paucity of reported intervention studies in these areas is puzzling and alarming.

Furthermore, professionals working with geriatric populations must ascertain ways to structure appropriate and successful experiences. As Weiss and Kromberg (1986) note, therapeutic recreation specialists typically serve primarily as enablers (within group settings), manipulating the environment to enhance the opportunities or experiences that will be therapeutic for individuals.

Additionally, in documenting the efficacy of recreational programs, sound research methodology must be adopted (see above section, "Methodological Quality of Geriatric Therapeutic Recreation Research," for specific points). One way to facilitate this would be to have symbiotic relationships emerge between practitioners and researchers.

Other elements of a future agenda for practitioners and researchers alike should include:

1. Determining the efficacy of a therapeutic recreation program, especially on various types of geriatric populations (e.g., mobile versus immobile, disoriented versus oriented, males versus females, young old versus old, caucasians versus Blacks, Asians, Hispanics, and other minority groups). Related, some promising therapeutic recreation intervention techniques (in terms of innovative approach and promising results) are reminiscence (see Ferguson, 1980; Fry, 1983; Hughston & Merriam, 1982), dance (see Osgood et al., 1990), bibliotherapy (see Scogin et al., 1987, 1989, 1990), and sensory stimulation via music (see Wolfe, 1983).

2. Conducting leisure education programs is viewed as an essential component of a comprehensive therapeutic recreation program. Nevertheless, no research studies were found that focused on leisure education. Therapeutic recreation practitioners and researchers must explore the benefits of leisure education as an intervention technique with older adults in a systematic manner.

3. Providing therapeutic recreation programs designed to promote the health and functioning of older adults. Interestingly, no studies in this review looked at the impact of therapeutic recreation as a preventative measure to illnesses or disabilities among the geriatric populations. The role of therapeutic recreation in the area of health promotion with adults as they develop should be encouraged.

4. Examining comparative treatments designs on specific outcome(s) and their cost effectiveness. For examples of comparative designs, see Ferguson (1980), Hughston & Merriam (1982), Malde (1983), Schafer et al. (1986), and Scogin et al. (1987, 1989, 1990).

5. Analyzing how intensity of program offerings affects outcome(s). Many of the documented therapeutic recreation programs were established with minimal client contact (estimated modal = $\leq$ 10 hours). Experimentation with frequency and/or duration of contact seems warranted. Variation in exposure may reveal differential results.

6. Investigating the long-term effects (3 months or longer) of program participation. With just a few exceptions, the impact of the reviewed interventions were examined in the context of short-term (i.e., immediately after a program ended) outcomes.

7. Conducting replication studies. Virtually all (N = 33 or 87%) of the reviewed works relied on non-probability sampling techniques and most (N = 31 or 82%) involved sample sizes of less than 50 persons. Similarly, two-thirds (N = 25 or 66%) of the inquiries did not use random assignment to a control group. While it is acknowledged that adherence to all the canons of scientific inquiry (such as using probability sampling, a control group, and random assignment to a control group) are not typically possible in the "real world" or field based research, deviation from such practices have to be acknowledged and the confidence put into reached conclusions must be tempered. In short, such practices call into question the internal validity as well as seriously jeopardize the external validity of reported outcomes. Until replication studies are executed, it is premature to conclude that any of the noted interventions are effective in working with geriatric populations.

Where To Go From Here? Implications for Policy

To determine the benefits of therapeutic recreation as a treatment modality in geriatrics, both basic and applied research questions must be addressed (Anderson & Paulsen, 1984). These research questions will only be raised and answered through a concerted effort on the parts of therapeutic recreation educators and practitioners and the public, government, and private sectors. The sweep of policy issues in therapeutic recreation and aging cover a broad spectrum of concerns and considerations. Three major policy agenda issues are highlighted from the literature review on the benefits of therapeutic recreation as a treatment modality in geriatrics: (a) the multidisciplinary approach to therapeutic recreation services, (b) the need for trained personnel, and (c) the need for on-going research financing.

1. Multidisciplinary approach to service and research--due to the multiple disabling conditions among geriatric populations, there is a need to explore the benefits of multidisciplinary approaches and rehabilitation teams to designing and implementing therapeutic services with these populations. Illness stems from the interplay between biological, psychological, social, and environmental factors (Blake, 1984). Therapeutic recreation research and practice should incorporate these factors through collaborative efforts with other disciplines.

2. Trained professionals--the literature review demonstrated that only a few people with recreation backgrounds are contributing to the development of the body of knowledge in therapeutic recreation with the geriatric population. Hawkins, MacNeil, Hamilton, and Eklund (1990) have made recommendations for professional preparation in gerontological therapeutic recreation. More emphasis is needed in therapeutic recreation professional preparation programs, both at the undergraduate and graduate levels, on the importance and knowledge about how to conduct and disseminate research (Compton, 1989). Practitioners need to be able to conduct studies independently as well as with educators.

Related, there should be an on-going commitment by therapeutic recreation specialists and their employing agencies to continuing professional development. Many individuals will find job opportunities working with geriatric populations and must either retrain or further their knowledge about the aging process and how to conduct efficacy research. The therapeutic recreation certification program should encourage certified professionals to conduct quality research by rewarding them with points for recertification.

3. Ongoing funding for research--clearly, this literature review has shown a need for additional research in the area of therapeutic recreation with geriatric clients. Unfortunately, this is not a new concept. While the need for therapeutic recreation research has been well documented over the past 5 to 10 years, there has been no consistent funding for these efforts (Anderson & Paulsen, 1984; Compton, 1989). Government (e.g., the National Institute on Aging, National Institutes of Health, National Institute on Mental Health, National Institute of Handicapped Research, Administration on Aging, Center for Studies of the Mental Health of Aging, Health Resources Administration, Health Services Administration, National Center for Health Care Technology, National Center for Health Services Research, Department of Health and Human Services, and Veterans Administration), as well as private foundations and institutional endowments should be encouraged to support innovation in therapeutic recreation treatment, education, financing, and research efforts. Possibly, by designing therapeutic recreation efficacy research that will demonstrate the benefits of therapeutic recreation services to older individuals' and then ascertaining how these personal benefits can impact on the overall health care system additional funding sources may be generated.

Table 1

Effects of Selected Therapeutic Recreation (TR) Activities on Geriatric Physical Health

Investigator(s)	Subjects	TR Activity	Theoretical Foundation	Focus	Measure(s)	Outcome(s)
Cutler Riddick (1985)	Older residents in a public subsidized housing complex with a senior center $\underline{N} = 22$ (randomly assigned to 1 of 3 groups: an aquarium group, a visitor group, or a control group)	Gold fish aquariums were placed in participants' homes; 9 bi-weekly visits from the researcher (from 25-35 min./visit) for 6 months Visitor group received 10 bi-weekly visits, from the researcher, (from 30-40 min./visit) for 6 months	None	Blood pressure	Sphygmomanometer (assumed--not stated)	Significant decrease in diastolic blood pressure in aquarium group (from the pre to posttest)
DeSchriver & Cutler Riddick (1990)	Older residents in a public subsidized housing complex $\underline{N} = 27$ (randomly assigned to 1 of 3 groups: viewed a fish aquarium, viewed a fish videotape, or viewed a placebo videotape)	Viewing of the fish aquarium, fish videotape, or placebo videotape lasted 8 minutes, once a week, over a three-week period	Relaxation theory	Pulse rate Skin temperature General skeletal muscle tension	Lumiscope Digitronic I model (beat per minute) Yellow Springs Temperature Meter Bicep electromyography (EMG)	No significant change No significant change No significant change
Gowing (1989)	Elderly home health care recipients $\underline{N} = 33$ (non-equivalent control group design)	Minimal care pets (goldfish) for 6 week period	None	Blood pressure	Sphygmomanometer (assumed--not stated)	No significant improvement when comparing pre and post test scores
Green (1989)	Elderly community residents enrolled in a community service program $\underline{N} = 24$ (one-group pretest-posttest design)	Water aerobic program (2 times a week for 16 weeks)	None	Blood pressure Resting pulse	Sphygmomanometer Pulse rate	Significant reduction in diastolic blood pressure (when comparing pre and post test scores) No significant improvement

173

Table 1

Effects of Selected Therapeutic Recreation (TR) Activities on Geriatric Physical Health

Investigator(s)	Subjects	TR Activity	Theoretical Foundation	Focus	Measure(s)	Outcome(s)
Keller (1991)	Elderly senior center participants enrolled in a senior adult fitness program N = 30 (one-group pretest-posttest design)	Water aerobic program (2 times a week, 60 min./ session, for 16 weeks)	Physiological "wear and tear"	Blood pressure	Sphygmomanometer	Significant reduction in diastolic blood pressure when comparing pre and post test scores
				Resting pulse	Pulse rate	No significant improvement
Morey, Cowper, Feussner, DiPasquale, Crowley, Kitzman, & Sullivan (1989)	Older, chronically ill patients (predominately males) at a VA outpatient clinic N = 49 (one-group pretest-posttest design)	Supervised exercise program (consisting of 10 min. warm-up routine; 10-15 min. stationary cycling; 20 min. stretching and strengthening routine; 15 min. strengthening program; 30 min. of brisk walking; and 5 min. of cool-down exercise) met 3 days/week for 4 months. Additional optional water exercise program was offered (2 time/week for 30 min.) over 4 months	None	Cardiovascular	Exercise stress test (including metabolic equivalents (Mets), treadmill time, submaximal heart rate, and resting heart rate	Significant improvement in exercise stress test scores (when comparing pre and post test score)
				Blood pressure	Sphygmomanometer	No significant change
				Total serum cholesterol and HDL cholesterol	Allain et al. method	No significant change
				Plasma glucose	Beckman Oxygen Electrode	No significant change
Norberg, Melin, & Asplund (1986)	Nursing home residents with dementia of Alzheimer type N = 2 (Single subject, observation design)	Stimulated residents with music (using earphones residents listened to 3 religious songs, 2 ballads, and 2 old folkdance melodies); touch (given in a systematic manner touching resident's forehead, cheeks, ears, neck shoulders, back, forearms, hands, feet, and lower legs); and object presentation (presenting the resident with items to stimulate their auditor, tactile, olfactory, and visual senses) for 12 consecutive days, for 90 min. per session	None	Heart rate	Not stated	No significant change
				Rate of respiration	Not stated	No significant change

Table 1

Effects of Selected Therapeutic Recreation (TR) Activities on Geriatric Physical Health

Investigator(s)	Subjects	TR Activity	Theoretical Foundation	Focus	Measure(s)	Outcome(s)
Buettner (1988)	Older residents (with clinical diagnoses of dementia and physical disabilities, and "in need of total care") residing in a long term institution for over 20 years. N = 22 (random assignment, one-group pretest-posttest group)	Developmental fitness program (consisting of geriatric exercise, sensory air flow mat therapy, vestibular donut therapy, and sensory motor stimulation); met 2 times a week for ~60 min.	Developmental therapy	Flexibility of trunk and hip-forward motion	Adapted sit-and-reach test	Significant improvement (when comparing pre and post test scores)
				Hand strength	Hand-held or strap-on weights lifted from lap to chin	Significant improvement (when comparing pre and post test scores)
				Ambulation	Walking distance	Significant improvement (when comparing pre and post test scores)
Green (1989)	See above	See above	See above	Body fat	Skin folds (bicep, tricep, subscapula, and iliac crest)	Significant reduction (when comparing pre test and post test scores)
				Body weight	Scale	Significant reduction (when comparing pre test and post test scores)
Keller (1991)	See above	See above	See above	Body fat	Skin folds (bicep, tricep, subscapula, and iliac crest)	Significant reduction (when comparing pre test and post test scores)
				Body weight	Scale	Significant reduction (when comparing pre test and post test scores)

Table 1

<u>**Effects of Selected Therapeutic Recreation (TR) Activities on Geriatric Physical Health**</u>

Investigator(s)	Subjects	TR Activity	Theoretical Foundation	Focus	Measure(s)	Outcome(s)
Morey, Cowper, Feussner, DiPasquale, Crowley, Kitzman, & Sullivan (1989)	See above	See above	See above	Flexibility	Hamstring length	Significant improvement (when comparing pre test and post test scores)
				Strength	Abdominal and right quadricep strength (Hydrafitness Omnitron hydraulic testing device-foot-pounds)	Significant improvement (when comparing pre and post test scores)
				Weight	Electronic hospital scale	No significant change
				Percent of body fat	Pollock's sum of three skin fold formula	No significant change
Yoder, Nelson, & Smith (1989)	Nursing home female residents (with "deficits in understanding simple activities") N = 30 (two-group pretest-posttest design)	Rote exercise group members were asked to exercise their arms (by making circular motions); added-purpose group members were directed to exercise (residents exercised their arms by stirring cookie batter (which was part of a cooking activity) both groups met only one time for purpose of the study	None	Range of motion	Duration of rotations (number of repetitions)	Significantly more repetitions for the added-purpose exercise group than the rote exercise group

Table 1

Effects of Selected Therapeutic Recreation (TR) Activities on Geriatric Physical Health

Investigator(s)	Subjects	TR Activity	Theoretical Foundation	Focus	Measure(s)	Outcome(s)
Norberg, Melin, & Asplund (1986)	See above	See above	See above	Eye movement	Number of eye blinkings	Significant reduction with music stimulation (relative to 2 other stimulations)
				Head movement	Number of head movements	No reaction
				Mouth movement	Number of mouth movements	Significant improvement with music stimulation (relative to 2 other groups)

Table 2. Effects of Selected Therapeutic Recreation (TR) Activities on Geriatric Psychological Health

Investigator(s)	Subjects	TR Activity	Theoretical Foundation	Focus	Measure(s)	Outcome(s)
Beck (1982)	Nursing home residents ("somewhat alert") N = 45 (random assignment to 1 of 3 groups: contingency experimental group, non-contingency experimental group, or control group)	Visits (9 times over 3 week period) with token (redeemable for gifts) reward for seeking out & remembering information between visits	Cognitive activity theory	Short term memory	Lag test	Significant improvement (relative to non-contingency experimental group and control group)
				Long term memory	Developed test with questions about historical events & aspects personal lives	Significant improvement (relative to non-contingency experimental group and control group)
Bumanis & Yoder (1987)	Nursing convalescent center ("with severe degree of confusion, disorientation & memory loss") N = 15 (subjects randomly selected from list persons eligible for study, then randomly assigned to 1 of 3 groups: reality orientation group, reality orientation and music/dance group, or control group)	One group received traditional Reality Orientation (RO) (30-min. sessions, 5 days/week, for 2 week period)], other group received RO and a music/dance program (1 hour session/once week for 2 weeks)	None	Cognitive memory	Goldfarb rating scale	No significant improvement
				Sensory memory	Face hand test	No significant improvement
Conroy, Fincham, & Agard-Evans (1988)	Hospitalized (long stay) elders ("mobile and demented") N = 10 (recommended by hospital staff)	15 sessions of activity program (that offered Reality Orientation program, music, table games, craft projects, read/write, poetry, talking)	None	Cognitive ability	Clifton cognitive ability assessment	7 of 10 improved
Francis & Baly (1986)	Intermediate skill nursing home residents N = 37 (non-equivalent control group design using two different units in the same facility)	Self-selected plush animals that experimental group members carried around, placed in room, etc;; intervention lasted 8 weeks	System model theory	Mental function	Geriatric rating scale	Significant improvement (in experimental group from pre to post test; control group underwent no significant change)

Table 2. Effects of Selected Therapeutic Recreation (TR) Activities on Geriatric Psychological Health

179

Investigator(s)	Subjects	TR Activity	Theoretical Foundation	Focus	Measure(s)	Outcome(s)
Francis & Munjas (1988)	Nursing home care unit residents of VA Medical Center (who were male and had "rationality—or ability to reason and respond to interview") N = 62 (two nursing home units divided between an experimental and control group)	After participating in an "auction," experimental group members acquired a plush animal which they carried around, placed in room, etc.; intervention lasted 16 weeks (though post-test data collected at 8 and 16 weeks)	Adaptation theory	Mental function	Geriatric rating scale	No significant improvement
Hughston & Merriam (1982)	Elderly residents of public housing complex N = 83 (randomly assigned to 1 of 3 groups: reminiscence experimental group, new materials experimental group, or control group)	Reminiscence kit (containing written reminiscent tasks) and new materials kit (requiring performing operations/exercises on "new" written material presented; both groups had 4 weeks of daily tasks (though time required each day was not stated)	None	Cognitive functioning	Raven standard progressive matrice	Significant improvement (in both experimental groups relative to control group)
Osgood, Meyers, & Orchowsky (1990)	Study participants from 4 sites: apartment complex for senior citizens, retirement home (included "cognitively impaired"), senior center, and an adult day care center (included "cognitively impaired") N = 72 (37 in experimental group and a matched 35 in control group)	Creative dance & movement program (offered once/week for 1 hour over 8 month period)	None	Cognitive mental functioning	Mini-mental state examination	Significant improvement (in the experimental group relative to matched control group)
Riegler (1980)	Nursing home residents ("exhibiting moderate to severe degree of confusion, disorientation, and memory loss") N = 8 (randomly assigned to either: music based reality orientation group or traditional reality orientation group)	Music based reality orientation program and traditional reality orientation program; both programs met 30 min. twice week for 8 weeks	None	Reality orientation/ mental status ... Behavior functioning	Philadelphia Geriatric Center mental status questionnaire ... Geriatric rating scale	Significant improvement (in music based reality orientation group relative to traditional reality orientation group) ... No significant improvement

Table 2. Effects of Selected Therapeutic Recreation (TR) Activities on Geriatric Psychological Health

Investigator(s)	Subjects	TR Activity	Theoretical Foundation	Focus	Measure(s)	Outcome(s)
Schafer, Berghorn, Holmes, & Quadagno (1986)	Nursing home residents ("mentally alert, sufficiently ambulatory, and capable of listening and speaking to others") $\underline{N}$ = 185 (8 homes chosen via stratified random sampling and then assigned to 1 of 4 groups: structured discussion reminiscence group, discussion reminiscence group, radio broadcast reminiscence group, or control group)	Structured discussion reminiscence group listened to and then discussed audio tape reminiscence selections; discussion reminiscence group discussed presented topic; radio broadcast group listened to audio tapes broadcast over a closed circuit radio, followed by an on-air discussion of the material by studio panelists, and were invited to participate in a phone-in forum; all treatments lasted 1 hr./wk. for 12 weeks	None	Memory	Short term memory scale Recall of 3 historical events	No significant improvement No significant improvement
Scogin, Hamblin, & Beutler (1987)	Community dwelling individuals aged 60+ years who were "depressed" (though not severely depressed) $\underline{N}$ = 25 (randomly assigned to either the cognitive bibliotherapy group, an attention control group, or the wait-list control group)	Cognitive bibliotherapy group given a copy of a self-help book for depression, Feeling Good; attention-control group given a copy of a book that provides general information for coping with emotional difficulties Man's Search for Meaning; over a 1-month period, weekly phone contact (10 minutes) was made with members of both these groups to assess reading process	None	Dysfunctional thinking	Cognitive error questionnaire	No significant improvement
Supiano, Ozminkowski, Campbell, & Lapidos (1989)	Nursing home residents (including "disoriented & depressed" individuals) $\underline{N}$ = 106 (divided between experimental and control groups)	Writing group (offered 1 hour/week for 8 weeks)	None	Cognitive mental functioning	Mini-mental state examination	No significant improvement

Table 2. Effects of Selected Therapeutic Recreation (TR) Activities on Geriatric Psychological Health

181

Investigator(s)	Subjects	TR Activity	Theoretical Foundation	Focus	Measure(s)	Outcome(s)
Wolfe (1983)	Nursing home and rehabilitation center residents ("all exhibited mild to severe degree of memory loss and confusion") N = 22 (randomly assigned to experimental or control group)	Sensory training program that used music (met 30 min. twice/week for 16 weeks)	None	Mental status/reality orientation	Philadelphia Geriatric Center mental status questionnaire	Significant improvement (in experimental group relative to control group)
				Sensory/ environmental awareness	30-item test (developed by author) which included identification of objects and sounds in subject's environment and imitation of simple rhythmic patterns	Significant improvement (in experimental group relative to control group)
Banziger & Rousch (1983)	Nursing home residents (intermediate care) N = 39 (random assignment to control-relevant group, dependency group, or a control group)	Individuals in both control-relevant and dependency groups were given a bird feeder that was placed outside their bedroom window; the control-relevant group was told they were responsible for filling and maintaining the feeder, whereas the dependency group was told staff would maintain the feeder; treatment lasted approximately 4 months	None	Life satisfaction	Neugarten's life satisfaction scale	Significant improvement (in experimental group and not control group)
				Happiness	Self report & R.N. ratings	Significant improvement (in experimental group and not control group)
Berryman-Miller (1988)	Senior center participants (who were "retired and healthy") N = not stated (one senior center served as experimental group, another senior center served as control)	Dance/movement classes (met biweekly for 90 min., over 8 months)	None	Self-concept	Tennessee self-concept scale questionnaire	Significant improvement (when comparing post-test scores of experimental group to post-test scores of control group)
Cutler Riddick, & Dugan-Jendzejec (1988)	Nursing home residents ("mentally competent to participate in the study") N = 24 (non-equivalent control group design using two facilities)	12 music sessions held once-a-week for 30 min./session	Activity theory	Psychological health	Affect balance scale	Significant improvement (in experimental group relative to control group)

Table 2. Effects of Selected Therapeutic Recreation (TR) Activities on Geriatric Psychological Health

Investigator(s)	Subjects	TR Activity	Theoretical Foundation	Focus	Measure(s)	Outcome(s)
Ferguson (1980)	Nursing home residents <u>N</u> = 45 [randomly chosen and assigned to 1 of 3 groups: positive reminiscence and placebo (relaxation training) group, relaxation only group, or control group]	Positive reminiscence (met one hour twice week for 4 weeks) and relaxation training (met half hour twice week for 4 weeks)	Social learning theory	Psychological well-being	Affect balance scale	Significant improvement [in experimental group (or reminiscence & placebo) relative to 2 other groups]
				Adjustment	MACC behavioral adjustment scale	No significant change
Francis & Baly (1986)	See above	See above	See above	Life satisfaction	Single-item	Significant improvement (in experimental group from pre to post test; control group underwent no significant change)
				Psychological well-being	Affect balance scale	Significant improvement (in experimental group from pre to post test; control group underwent no significant change)
Francis & Munjas (1988)	See above	See above	See above	Life satisfaction	1-item question	Significant improvement at 8 weeks but not 16 weeks (in experimental group relative to control group)
				Happiness	Affect balance scale	Significant improvement at 8 and 16 weeks (in experimental group relative to control group)

Table 2. Effects of Selected Therapeutic Recreation (TR) Activities on Geriatric Psychological Health

Investigator(s)	Subjects	TR Activity	Theoretical Foundation	Focus	Measure(s)	Outcome(s)
Gowing (1984)	Elderly home health care recipients $N = 33$ (non-equivalent control group design)	Minimal care pets (goldfish) for 6 week period	None	Mental well-being	Sense of humor (1-item)	No significant improvement
					Feel fed up (1-item)	No significant improvement
					Nerves on edge (1-item)	Significant reduction (in treatment group relative control group)
Malde (1983)	Community elders $N = 39$ (random assignment to 1 of 3 groups: small personal sharing experimental group, large discussion experimental group, or a control group)	Guided autobiography (twice/week sessions for 90 min. over 5 week period)	Developmental & personality theories	Self-concept	Tennessee self-concept scale	No significant improvement
McGuire (1984)	Residents of intermediate care long term facility $N = 28$ (non-equivalent control group design using two wings of the same facility)	8 weeks of unlimited play of 5 videogames	None	Happiness	Affect balance scale	Significant improvement (in experimental group but not control group)
Munson (1984)	Community elders $N = 43$ (non-equivalent control group design)	Visitation (phone & face-to-face) program once/week for 10 weeks	Stress theory	Life satisfaction	Life satisfaction index Z	No significant improvement
Osgood, Meyers, & Orchowsky (1990)	See above	See above	See above	Life satisfaction	1-item question	Significant improvement (in experimental group relative to control group)

Table 2. Effects of Selected Therapeutic Recreation (TR) Activities on Geriatric Psychological Health

Investigator(s)	Subjects	TR Activity	Theoretical Foundation	Focus	Measure(s)	Outcome(s)
Perotta & Meacham (1981-82)	Community residents attending senior center (many described as "depressed" by staff) $\underline{N}$ = 21 (randomly assigned to 1 of 3 groups: reminiscence group, control current events group, or no treatment control group)	Experimental group received 5 sessions (over a 5-week period) lasting 30-45 min./session of reminiscence counseling; control current events group discussed current living situation and activities (not stated how often met)	None	Self-esteem	Affect balance scale	No significant improvement
Schafer, Berghorn, Holmes, & Quadagno (1986)	See above	See above	See above	Life satisfaction	Cantril ladder	Significant improvement (control group relative to radio broadcast group)
					Version of life satisfaction index	No significant improvement
Shary & Iso-Ahola (1989)	Skilled nursing home residents ("communicative and oriented") $\underline{N}$ = 28 (randomly chosen floors with assignment to the two groups randomized)	Responsibility group members attended meeting where told they were responsible for selves, then provided an "enabling" session, given a plant to care for, and an opportunity to attend special activities (where they were encouraged to exert control over what and how they did things) twice a week (for about 1 hr. 15 min. session) for 5 weeks; control group members attended a meeting where told staff was committed to residents, then given a plant and told that staff would care for it, and then were provided opportunities to attend activity sessions twice a week for 5 weeks	None	Morale	Philadelphia Geriatric Center morale scale	Significant improvement (in experimental group relative control group)
				Self-esteem	Rosenberg self-esteem scale	Significant improvement (in experimental group relative to control group)
Bell (1984)	Intermediate skilled nursing residents $\underline{N}$ = 52 (randomly assigned to 1 of 3 groups: supportive touch & reading group, reading group only, or control group)	Supportive touch & reading group and reading group only; both groups had 4 bi-weekly sessions, lasting ~20 min./session	Interpersonal intimacy theories (or equilibrium theory & reciprocity theory)	Depression	Multiple-affect adjective checklist	No significant change

Table 2. Effects of Selected Therapeutic Recreation (TR) Activities on Geriatric Psychological Health

Investigator(s)	Subjects	TR Activity	Theoretical Foundation	Focus	Measure(s)	Outcome(s)
Francis & Baly (1986)	See above	See above	See above	Depression	Beck depression inventory	Significant improvement (in experimental group from pre to post test; control group underwent no significant change)
Francis & Munjas (1988)	See above	See above	See above	Depression	Beck depression inventory	Significant improvement (in experimental group relative to control group at 8-week point, but not maintained at 16 weeks)
Fry (1983)	Nursing home residents (described as depressed by staff) $\underline{N} = 162$ (random assignment to 1 of 3 groups: structured reminiscence training group; unstructured reminiscence training group; and control group)	Reminiscence group met weekly for 5 weeks (90 minutes per session)	None	Depression	Beck depression inventory	Significant improvement (in the structured reminiscence group) relative to the 2 other groups
Perotta & Meacham (1981-82)	Community residents attending senior center (many described as "depressed" by staff) $\underline{N} = 21$ (randomly assigned to 1 of 3 groups: reminiscence group, control current events group, or no treatment control group)	Experimental group received 5 sessions (over a 5-week period) lasting 30-45 min./session of reminiscence counseling; control current events group discussed current living situation and activities (not stated how often met)	None	Depression	Modified version of Zung depression scale	No significant improvement

186

Table 2. Effects of Selected Therapeutic Recreation (TR) Activities on Geriatric Psychological Health

Investigator(s)	Subjects	TR Activity	Theoretical Foundation	Focus	Measure(s)	Outcome(s)
Scogin, Hamblin, & Beutler (1987)	See above	See above	None	Depression	Hamilton rating scale for depression	Significant improvement in cognitive bibliotherapy group (relative to 2 other groups immediately after program ended) and no significant deterioration at 1 month post-testing
					Beck depression inventory	No significant improvement
					Geriatric depression scale	Significant improvement (in cognitive bibliotherapy group relative to 2 other groups) and no significant deterioration at 1 month post-testing
Scogin, Jamison, & Davis (1990)	Community elders with depression (though not "severe") N = 30 (originally randomly assigned to 1 of 2 treatment groups: behavioral bibliotherapy group or cognitive bibliotherapy group)	(See below two year follow-up to Scogin, Jamison & Gochneaur 1989 study)	None	Depression	Hamilton rating scale for depression	Improvement was maintained over 2-year period (for both experimental groups)
					Geriatric depression scale	Significant improvement (i.e., further reduction in depression) for experimental group members

Table 2. Effects of Selected Therapeutic Recreation (TR) Activities on Geriatric Psychological Health

Investigator(s)	Subjects	TR Activity	Theoretical Foundation	Focus	Measure(s)	Outcome(s)
Scogin, Jamison, & Gochneaur (1989)	Community elders with depression (though not "severe") N = 44 (randomly assigned to 1 of 3 groups: behavioral bibliotherapy group, cognitive bibliotherapy group, or delayed treatment control group)	Behavioral bibliotherapy group given copy of self-help book on behavioral therapy, Control your depression; cognitive bibliotherapy group given a self-help book on cognitive therapy, Feeling good; over a 1-month period, weekly phone contact was made with members of both these groups to assess reading progress and answer any questions about the reading	None	Depression (general measure)	Hamilton rating scale for depression	Significant improvement (in both experimental groups relative to control group) and improvement maintained at 6-month follow-up
				Depression (general measure)	Geriatric depression scale	Significant improvement (in both experimental groups relative to control group) and improvement maintained at 6-month follow-up
				Cognitive measures of depression	Dysfunctional attitudes scale	No significant improvement
					Automatic thoughts questionnaire	No significant improvement
				Behavioral measures of depression	Older adults pleasant events schedule	No significant improvement
					Older adults unpleasant events schedule	No significant improvement
Supiano, Ozminkowski, Campbell, & Lapidos (1989)	See above	See above	See above	Depression	Geriatric depression scale	No significant improvement

188

Table 2. Effects of Selected Therapeutic Recreation (TR) Activities on Geriatric Psychological Health

Investigator(s)	Subjects	TR Activity	Theoretical Foundation	Focus	Measure(s)	Outcome(s)
Banziger & Rousch (1983)	See above	See above	See above	Control	Self report question	Significant improvement (in experimental group and not control group)
Schafer, Berghorn, Holmes, & Quadagno (1986)	See above	See above	See above	Internal control	Control of daily life	Significant improvement (3 groups relative to radio broadcast group)
					Control of life in general	Significant improvement (structured discussion reminiscence group relative to radio broadcast group)
Shary & Iso-Ahola (1989)	See above	See above	See above	Perceived competence	10 item developed scale	Significant improvement (in experimental group relative to control group)

Table 3. Effects of Selected Therapeutic Recreation (TR) Activities on Geriatric Social Health

Investigator(s)	Subjects	TR Activity	Theoretical Foundation	Focus	Measure(s)	Outcome(s)
Cutler Riddick (1985)	Older residents in a public subsidized housing complex with a senior center N = 22 (randomly assigned to 1 of 3 groups: an aquarium group; a visitor group; or a control group)	Gold fish aquariums were placed in participants' homes for 6 months with 9 bi-weekly visits from the researcher (from 25-35 minutes per visit) Visitor group received 10 bi-weekly visits, from the researcher, for 6 months (from 30-40 minutes per visit)	None	Loneliness	20-item revised UCLA Loneliness Scale	Significant reduction (in loneliness of the visitor group relative to the other two groups)
Osgood, Meyers, & Orchowsky (1990)	See above	See above	See above	Loneliness dissatisfaction	Philadelphia Geriatric Center morale scale (has 3 factors, one being loneliness	Significant improvement (in experimental group relative to control group)
Preston (1987)	Nursing home residents N = 30 (non-equivalent control group design involving two nursing homes)	Outdoor day camp (once/week for 4 hrs. over 7-week period)	Activity theory	Loneliness	UCLA Loneliness Scale	No significant reduction
Banziger & Rousch (1983)	Nursing home residents (intermediate care) N = 39 (random assignment to control-relevant group, dependency group, or a control group)	Individuals in both control-relevant and dependency groups were given a bird feeder that was placed outside their bedroom window; the control-relevant group was told they were responsible for filling and maintaining the feeder, whereas the dependency group was told staff would maintain the feeder; treatment lasted approximately 4 months	None	Sociability	R.N. ratings	Significant improvement (in experimental group)
Beck (1982)	Nursing home residents ("somewhat alert") N = 45 (random assignment to 1 of 3 groups: contingency experimental group, non-contingency experimental group, or control group)	Visits (9 times over 3-week period) with token (redeemable for gifts) reward for seeking out & remembering information between visits	Cognitive activity theory	Social adjustment	R.N. rating	Significant improvement (in both experimental groups relative to control group)
Cutler Riddick & Dugan-Jendzejec (1988)	Nursing home residents ("mentally competent to participate in the study") N = 24 (non-equivalent control group design using two facilities))	12 music sessions held once-a-week for 30 min./session	Activity theory	Verbal interactions	Observation	Significant increase (in experimental group)

189

Table 3. Effects of Selected Therapeutic Recreation (TR) Activities on Geriatric Social Health

Investigator(s)	Subjects	TR Activity	Theoretical Foundation	Focus	Measure(s)	Outcome(s)
Cutler Riddick, Spector, & Drogin (1986)	Nursing home residents (judged as "mentally competent") N = 22 (non-equivalent control group design using two facilities)	Videogame play (i.e., PacMan) 3 times/week, up to 3 hrs./session, for 6 weeks	Three factor theory of emotions	Affiliative behavior	Approach avoidance scale (measures friendliness & talkativeness to strangers)	Significant increase (in experimental group relative to control group)
Francis & Baly (1986)	Intermediate skill nursing home residents N = 37 (non-equivalent control group design using two different units in the same facility)	Self-selected plush animals that experimental group members carried around, placed in room, etc.; intervention lasted 8 weeks	System model theory	Psychosocial function	Psychosocial function scale	Significant improvement (in experimental group from pre to post test; control group underwent no significant change)
Francis & Munjas (1988)	Nursing home care unit residents of VA Medical Center (who were male and had "rationality—or ability to reason and respond to interview") N = 62 (two nursing home units divided between an experimental and control group)	After participating in an "auction," experimental group members acquired a plush animal which they carried around, placed in room, etc.; intervention lasted 16 weeks (though post-test data collected at 8 and 16 weeks)	Adaptation theory	Psycho-social function	Psychosocial function scale (includes items on ability and knowledge of how to interact with people)	No significant improvement
Gowing (1984)	Elderly home health care recipients N = 33 (non-equivalent control group design)	Minimal care pets (i.e., goldfish) for 6-week period	None	Social interaction	Visitor contact (1-item) Phone contact (1-item) Talk with others (1-item)	No significant improvement No significant improvement No significant improvement

Table

Table 3. Effects of Selected Therapeutic Recreation (TR) Activities on Geriatric Social Health

Investigator(s)	Subjects	TR Activity	Theoretical Foundation	Focus	Measure(s)	Outcome(s)
Olderog Millard & Smith (1989)	Nursing home residents (with diagnosis of being in middle stages of Alzheimer's disease) N = 10 (reversal design used)	Group singing (30 min. twice week for 2 weeks) & discussion group (30 min. twice week for 3 weeks)	None	Sit with others	Observational checklist	Significant improvement (during and after group singing activity relative to what happened during and after group discussion activity)
				Walk with others	Observational checklist	Significant increase (during and after group singing relative to what happened during and after group discussion activity)
						Significant improvement (exhibited after singing and discussion groups rather than singing group alone)
				Vocal/verbal participation	Observational checklist	Significant improvement (exhibited in group singing sessions rather than in discussion sessions)
Robb, Boyd, & Pristash (1980)	Long term residents of nursing home care unit of VA hospital ("chronically ill") N = 14-47 (observational A-B-C-D-A design)	External stimuli presentation (i.e., wine bottle, plant, and caged dog); two 90-min. sessions	None	Social behavior	Verbalization (observational)	Dramatic increase initially noted when exposed to puppy (compared to wine bottle or plant); diminished with second exposure

Table 3. Effects of Selected Therapeutic Recreation (TR) Activities on Geriatric Social Health

Investigator(s)	Subjects	TR Activity	Theoretical Foundation	Focus	Measure(s)	Outcome(s)
Schafer, Berghorn, Holmes, & Quadagno (1986)	Nursing home residents ("mentally alert, sufficiently ambulatory, and capable of listening and speaking to others") <u>N</u> = 185 (8 homes chosen via stratified random sampling and then assigned to 1 of 4 groups: structured discussion reminiscence group, discussion reminiscence group, radio broadcast reminiscence group, or a control group)	Structured discussion reminiscence group listened to and then discussed audio tape reminiscence selections; discussion reminiscence group discussed presented topic; radio broadcast group listened to audio tapes broadcast over a closed circuit radio, followed by an on-air discussion of the material by studio panelists, and were invited to participate in a phone-in forum; all treatments lasted 1 hr./wk. for 12 weeks	None	Social relations	Ratio: # people know/list	Significant improvement (in discussion reminiscence group relative to 3 other groups)
				Interaction quality	Degree of spontaneous activities initiated by the resident	Significant improvement (in discussion reminiscence group relative to 3 other groups)

Therapeutic Settings

Geriatric Health Problems	Acute Care Hospital	Inpatient Psychiatric Hospital	Physical Rehabilitation Facility	Extended Care Facility	Long-Term Health Care Facility[a]	Adult Day Care	Outpatient Services	In-Home Services	Multipurpose Senior Center
Cardiovascular & related diseases	X		X	X	X	X	X	X	X
Orthopedic disabilities	X		X	X	X	X	X	X	X
Senile dementia	X	X		X	X	X	X	X	
Depression	X	X	X	X	X	X	X	X	X
Loneliness	X	X		X	X	X	X	X	X

Note. The "X" signifies where therapeutic recreation services are generally provided to clientele with the noted geriatric health problems.

[a] Includes intermediate care and skilled nursing facilities.

Figure 1. Provision of Therapeutic Recreation Services in a Variety of Settings for Selected Health Problems of Geriatric Populations

Health Problems	Therapeutic Recreation Program/Activity	Theoretical Base(s)	Physiological Outcomes		
			Cardiopulmonary System[a]	Musculoskeletal System[b]	Nervous System[c]
Cardiovascular & related diseases	Adaptive sport	Physiological	X	X	X
	Dance/movement	Psychological	X	X	X
	Drama	Physiological		X	X
	Exercise/fitness	Physiological; developmental	X	X	X
	Gardening/horticulture	Physiological	X	X	X
	Leisure education/counseling	Psychological	X	X	X
	Pet therapy	Relaxation	X		
	Water aerobics	Physiological	X	X	
Orthopedic Disabilities	Adaptive sports	Physiological	X	X	X
	Arts & Crafts	Physiological			X
	Board games	Physiological			X
	Dance/movement	Physiological	X	X	X
	Drama	Physiological			X
	Exercise/fitness	Physiological	X	X	X
	Gardening/horticulture	Physiological	X	X	X
	Leisure education/counseling	Physiological	X	X	X
	Water aerobics	Physiological	X	X	

[a]Includes blood pressure, respiration rate, pulse rate, skin temperature, EMG, cholesterol, and glucose. [b]Includes range of motion, flexibility, muscle strength, endurance, body composition (weight and body fat). [c]Includes reaction time, senses (vision, auditory, taste, touch, and smell), reflexes, and eye-hand coordination.

Figure 2. Interrelationships among selected health problems, therapeutic recreation programs, theoretical bases, and expected physiological outcomes.

Health Problems	Therapeutic Recreation Program/Activity	Theoretical Base(s)	Psychological Outcomes			
			Memory and Learning[a]	Life Satisfaction[b]	Depression[c]	Leisure Experience[d]
Senile dementia	Arts & crafts	Memory and learning; activity; depression; leisure experience	X	X	X	X
	Board games	Memory and learning; activity; leisure experience	X	X	X	X
	Bible study	Memory and learning; activity	X	X	X	
	Dance/movement	Memory and learning; activity; leisure experience	X	X	X	X
	Drama	Memory and learning; activity; leisure experience	X	X	X	X
	Exercise/fitness	Activity; depression; leisure experience		X	X	X
	Gardening/horticulture	Activity; leisure experience		X	X	X
	Music	Activity; leisure experience		X	X	X
	Pet therapy/plush animal	Adaptation; system model; interpersonal intimacy; leisure experience	X	X	X	X
	Reality orientation	Memory and learning	X	X	X	X
	Reminiscence	Memory and learning; activity; social learning	X	X	X	X
	Supportive touch	Interpersonal intimacy			X	
	Videogames	Memory and learning; activity; leisure experience	X	X	X	X
	Visitation	Cognitive activity; depression	X		X	X
	Water aerobics	Memory and learning; activity; leisure experience	X	X	X	X
	Writing	Memory and learning; depression	X	X	X	

[a]Includes intellectual functioning and memory. [b]Includes subjective evaluations of life satisfaction, well-being, morale, life happiness, self-concept, self-esteem, and general mental health. [c]Includes cognitive, emotional, and physical symptoms of depressive syndrome. [d]Includes perceived freedom, perceived competence, intrinsic motivation, flow and playfulness.

Figure 3. Interrelationships among selected health problems, therapeutic recreation programs, theoretical base, and expected psychological outcome.

Health Problems	Therapeutic Recreation Program/Activity	Theoretical Base(s)	Psychological Outcomes			
			Memory and Learning[a]	Life Satisfaction[b]	Depression[c]	Leisure Experience[d]
Depression	Arts & crafts	Activity; depression; leisure experience		X	X	X
	Bibliotherapy	Memory and learning; depression	X	X	X	X
	Dance/movement	Activity; depression; leisure experience	X	X	X	X
	Exercise/fitness	Activity; depression; leisure experience		X	X	X
	Induced responsibility (horticulture, etc.)	Activity; depression, leisure experience		X	X	X
	Pet therapy/plush animal	Adaptation; system model; depression; leisure experience	X	X	X	X
	Reminiscence	Social learning; activity; depression	X	X	X	X
	Supportive touch	Interpersonal intimacy			X	
	Trip outings/field trip	Activity; leisure experience		X	X	X
	Visitors	Cognitive activity; stress; activity; depression	X	X	X	X
Loneliness	Autobiography	Activity		X	X	X
	Dance/movement	Activity		X	X	X
	Leisure educational counseling	Activity; leisure experience		X	X	X

[a]Includes intellectual functioning and memory. [b]Includes subjective evaluations of life satisfaction, well-being, morale, life happiness, self-concept, self-esteem, and general mental health. [c]Includes cognitive, emotional, and physical symptoms of depressive syndrome. [d]Includes perceived freedom, perceived competence, intrinsic motivation, flow and playfulness.

Figure 3. Interrelationships among selected health problems, therapeutic recreation programs, theoretical bases, and expected psychological outcome.

Health Problems	Therapeutic Recreation Program/Activity	Theoretical Base(s)	Social Outcomes	
			Loneliness	Social Interaction
Senile dementia	Music/singing	Symbolic interaction	X	X
	Pet therapy/plush animal	Loneliness; systems model; adaptation	X	X
	Visitation	Loneliness; symbolic interaction	X	X
Depression	Arts & crafts	Loneliness, symbolic interaction	X	X
	Dance/movement	Loneliness, symbolic interaction	X	X
	Exercise/fitness	Loneliness; symbolic interaction	X	X
	Music	Loneliness; symbolic interaction	X	X
	Pet therapy	Loneliness	X	X
	Reminiscence	Symbolic interaction		X
	Trip outings/field trips	Loneliness; symbolic interaction	X	X
	Visitors	Loneliness; symbolic interaction	X	X
Loneliness	Adaptive sports	Loneliness; symbolic interaction	X	X
	Arts & crafts	Loneliness; symbolic interaction	X	X
	Autobiography	Developmental & personality; symbolic interaction		X
	Board games	Loneliness; symbolic interaction	X	X
	Dance/movement	Loneliness; symbolic interaction	X	X
	Drama	Loneliness; symbolic interaction	X	X
	Exercise/fitness	Symbolic interaction	X	X
	Outdoor day camp	Loneliness; symbolic interaction	X	X

Figure 4. Interrelationships among selected health problems, therapeutic recreation programs, theoretical bases, and expected social outcomes.

Health Problems	Therapeutic Recreation Program/Activity	Theoretical Base(s)	Social Outcomes	
			Loneliness	Social Interaction
	Pet therapy/plush animal	Loneliness; adaptation; systems; symbolic interaction	X	X
	Reminiscence	Symbolic interaction	X	X
	Stimulation (caged dog, plant, wine bottle)	Symbolic interaction		X
	Videogame play	Three factor theory of emotion	X	X
	Water aerobics	Symbolic interaction	X	X

Figure 4. Interrelationships among selected health problems, therapeutic recreation programs, theoretical bases, and expected social outcomes.

References

Adams, D. (1971). Correlates of satisfaction among the elderly. The Gerontologist, 11, 64-68.

Anderson, S., & Paulsen, R. (1984). Overcoming the dearth of therapeutic recreation research. Expanding Horizons in Therapeutic Recreation, 12, 309-321.

Applegate, W. (1987). Hypertension in the elderly. Generations, 12(1), 16-19.

Arenberg, D., & Robertson-Tchabo, E. (1980). Age differences and age changes in cognitive performance: New "old" perspectives. In R. Sprott (Ed.), Age, learning ability, and intelligence. New York: Van Nostrand Reinhold.

Atchley, R. (1985). Social forces and aging. Belmont, CA: Wadsworth Publishing.

Austin, D., & Crawford, M. (1991). Therapeutic recreation: An introduction. Englewood Cliffs, NJ: Prentice Hall.

Banziger, G., & Rousch, S. (1983). Nursing homes for the birds: A control-relevant intervention with bird feeders. The Gerontologist, 23,527-531.

Beck, P. (1982). The successful interventions in nursing homes: The therapeutic effects of cognitive activity. The Gerontologist, 22, 389-383.

Bell, P. (1984). The effects of supportive touch on depression and anxiety among female residents of a nursing home. Unpublished doctoral dissertation, University of Missouri.

Bergman, G. (1991). Why build more nursing homes? Aging Today, 12(2), 6.

Berryman-Miller, S. (1988). Dance movement: Effects on elderly self concepts. Journal of Physical Education, Recreation & Dance, 59, 42-46.

Blake, R. (1984). What disables American elderly? Generations, 8(4), 6-9.

Blazer, D., & Williams, C. (1980). Epidemiology of dysphoria and depression in an elderly population. American Journal of Psychiatry, 137, 439-444.

Brody, J., & Schneider, E. (1986). Diseases and disorder of aging: An hypothesis. Journal of Chronic Diseases, 39(11), 871-876.

Brotman, H. (1982). Every ninth American: 1982 edition. Washington, DC: Select Committee on Aging, House of Representatives, 97 Congress Committee Publication, No. 97-332, U.S. Government Printing Office.

Buettner, L. (1988). Utilizing development theory and adaptive equipment with regressed geriatric patients in therapeutic recreation. Therapeutic Recreation Journal, 22(3), 72-79.

Bumanis, A., & Yoder, J. (1987). Music and dance: Tools for reality orientation. Activities, Adaptation & Aging, 10, 23-35.

Busse, E., & Pfeiffer, E. (Eds.). (1977). Behavior and adaptation in late life. Boston: Little, Brown & Co.

Butler, R., & Lewis, M. (1973). Aging and mental health. St. Louis: C.V. Mosby.

Capel, W., Goldsmith, B., & Waddell, K. (1972). The aging narcotic addict: An increasing problem for the next decades. Journal of Gerontology, 27, 102-106.

Carlson, J. (1987). The association of nonsteroidal anti-inflammatory drugs with upper gastrointestinal tract bleeding. Archives of Internal Medicine, 147(1), 85-88.

Carlson, R., & Newman, B. (1987). Issues and trends in health. St. Louis, MO: C. V. Mosby.

Compton, D. (1989). Research initiatives in therapeutic recreation. In D. Compton (Ed.), Issues in therapeutic recreation (pp. 427-444). Champaign, IL: Sagamore Publishing.

Conroy, M., Fincham, F., & Agard-Evans, C. (1988). Can they do anything? Ten single-subject studies of the engagement level of hospitalized demented patients. British Journal of Occupational Therapy, 51, 129-132.

Creecy, R., Berg, W., & Wright, R. (1985). Loneliness among the elderly: A causal approach. Journal of Gerontology, 40, 487-493.

Cutler Riddick, C. (1985). Health, aquariums, and the non-institutionalized elderly. In M. Sussman (Ed.), Pets and the family (pp.63-173). New York: Haworth Press.

Cutler Riddick, C., & Dugan-Jendzejec, M. (1988). Health related impacts of a music program on nursing home residents. In F. Humphrey & J. Humphrey (Eds.), Recreation: Current selected research (pp. 155-166). New York: AMS Press.

Cutler Riddick, C., Spector, S., & Drogin, E. (1986). The effects of videogames play on the emotional states and affiliative behavior of nursing home residents. Activities, Adaptation & Aging, 8, 95-108.

Csikszentmihalyi, M. (1975). Beyond boredom and anxiety. San Francisco: Jossey-Bass.

DeCharms, R. (1968). Personal causation. New York: Academic Press.

Deci, E. (1968). Intrinsic motivation. New York: Academic Press.

DeSchriver, M., & Cutler Riddick, C. (1990). Effects of watching aquariums on elders' stress. Anthrozoos, 9(1), 44-48.

Dooghe, G., Vanderleyden, L., Van Loon, F. (1990). Social adjustment of the elderly residing in institutional homes: A multivariate analysis. International Journal of Aging & Human Development, 11, 163-176.

Edinberg, M. (1985). Mental health practice with the elderly. New York: Prentice-Hall.

Ferguson, J. (1980). Reminiscence counseling to increase psychological well being of elderly women in nursing home facilities. Unpublished doctoral dissertation, University of South Carolina.

Fowles, D. (1990). A profile of older Americans. Washington, DC: American Association of Retired Persons.

Francis, G., & Baly, A. (1986). Plush animals: Do they make a difference? Geriatric Nursing, 7, 140-142.

Francis, G., & Munjas, B. (1988). Plush animals and the elderly. Journal of Applied Gerontology, 7, 161-172.

Fry, P. (1983). Structured and unstructured reminiscence training and depression among the elderly. Clinical Gerontologist, 1(3), 15-37.

George, L., & Bearon, L. (1980). Quality of life in older persons. New York: Human Sciences Press.

Gianturco, D., & Busse, E. (1978). Psychiatric problems encountered during a long-term study of normal aging volunteers. In A. Issacs & F. Post (Eds.), Studies in geriatric psychiatry. New York: Wiley.

Gowing, C. (1984). The effects of minimal care pets on homebound elderly and their professional caregivers. Unpublished doctoral dissertation, University of Illinois at Urbana-Champaign.

Green, J. (1989). Effects of a water aerobics program on the blood pressure, percentage of body fat, weight, and resting pulse rate of senior citizens. Journal of Applied Gerontology, 8(1), 132-138.

Havighurst, R., Neugarten, B., & Tobin, S. (1968). Disengagement and patterns of aging. In B. Neugarten (Ed.), Middle age and aging. Chicago: University of Chicago Press.

Hawkins, B., MacNeil, R., Hamilton, E., & Eklund, S. (1990). Professional preparation and practice in gerontological therapeutic recreation: Status and recommendations. Bloomington, IN: Indiana University.

Hojat, M. (1982). Loneliness as a function of selected personality variables. Journal of Clinical Psychology, 38, 137-141.

Huges, C. (1978). The differential diagnosis of dementia in the senium. In K. Nandy (Ed.), Senile dementia: A biomedical approach. New York: Elsevier/North-Holland Biomedical Press.

Hughston, G., & Merriam, S. (1982). Reminiscence: A nonformal technique for improving cognitive functioning in the aged. International Journal of Aging & Human Development, 2, 139-140.

Huyck, M., & Hoyer, W. (1982). Adult development and aging. Belmont, CA: Wadsworth Publishing.

Iso-Ahola, S. (1988). Research in therapeutic recreation. Therapeutic Recreation Journal, 22, 7-13.

Iso-Ahola, S. (1980). Perceived control and responsibility as mediators of the effects of therapeutic recreation on the institutionalized aged. Therapeutic Recreation Journal, 14, 36-43.

Jarvik, L., & Kumar, V. (1984). Update on treatment: Most approaches still prove disappointing. Generation, 8(2), 10-11.

Kane, R., & Kane, R. (1981). Assessing the elderly: A practical guide to measurement. Lexington, MA: Lexington Books.

Kastenbaum, R., Barber, T., Wilson, S., Ryder, B., & Hathaway, L. (1981). Old, sick, and helpless: Where therapy begins. Cambridge, MA: Ballinger.

Kay, D., & Bergman, K. (1980). Epidemiology of mental disorders among the aged in the community. In J. Birren & R. Sloane (Eds.), Handbook of mental health and aging. Englewood Cliffs, NJ: Prentice-Hall.

Keller, M. (1991). The impact of a water aerobics program on older adults. Unpublished manuscript.

Kelly, J. (1990). Leisure. Englewood Cliffs, NJ: Prentice Hall.

Kelly, J., Steinkamp, M., & Kelly, J. (1987). Later life satisfaction: Does leisure contribute? Leisure Sciences, 9, 189-200.

Langer, E., & Rodin, J. (1976). The effects of choice and enhanced personal responsibility for the aged: A field experiment in an institutional setting. Journal of Personality and Social Psychology, 34, 191-198.

Larson, R. (1978). Thirty years of research on the subjective well-being of older Americans. Journal of Gerontology, 3, 109-125.

Lemon, B., Bengston, V., & Peterson, J. (1972). An exploration of the activity theory of aging: Activity types and life satisfaction among in-movers to a retirement community. Journal of Gerontology, 27, 511-517.

Levy, L. (1986). A practical guide to the care of the Alzheimer's disease victim: The cognitive disability perspective. Topics in Geriatric Rehabilitation, 1, 16-26.

Licata, A. (1987). Osteoporosis in older women. Generations, 12(1), 12-15.

Liebermann, J. (1977). Playfulness: Its relationship to imagination and creativity. Brooklyn: Academic Press.

Linn, M., Hunter, X., & Harris, R. (1980). Symptoms of depression and recent life events in the community elderly. Journal of Clinical Psychology, 36, 675-682.

MacNeil, R., & Teague, M. (1987). Aging and leisure: Vitality in later life. Englewood Cliffs, NJ: Prentice Hall.

Maddox, G. (1968). Persistence of life style among the elderly: A longitudinal study of patterns of social activity in relation to life satisfaction. In B. Neugarten (Ed.), Middle age and aging. Chicago: University of Chicago Press.

Malde, S. (1983). Guided autobiography: A counseling and educational program for older adults. Unpublished doctoral dissertation, University of California, Santa Barbara.

Mangen, D., & Peterson, W. (Eds.). (1982). Research instruments in social gerontology: Volume 1: Clinical and social psychology. Minneapolis, MN: University of Minnesota Press.

Mannell, R. (1983). Research methodology in therapeutic recreation. Therapeutic Recreation Journal, 17, 9-16.

Matthew, L. (1989). Malnutrition in hospitalization: A barrier to rehabilitation. Topics in Geriatric Rehabilitation, 5(1), 61-68.

McGuire, F. (1984). Improving the quality of life for residents of long term care facilities through video games. Activities, Adaptation & Aging, 6, 1-8.

Moore, J. (1985). A bibliography of doctoral dissertations on aging from American institutions of higher learning, 1981-1983. Journal of Gerontology, 40, 509-519.

Moore, J. (1986). A bibliography of doctoral dissertations on aging from American institutions of higher learning, 1983-1985. Journal of Gerontology, 41, 535-552.

Moore, J. (1987). A bibliography of doctoral dissertations on aging from American institutions of higher learning, 1984-1986. Journal of Gerontology, 42, 561-568.

Morey, M., Cowper, P., Feussner, J., DiPasquale, R., Crowley, G., Kitzman, D., & Sullivan, R. (1989). Evaluation of a supervised exercise program in a geriatric population. Journal of American Geriatrics Society, 37, 348-354.

Multiple Risk Factor Intervention Trial Research Group. (1982). Multiple risk factor intervention trial. Journal of the American Medical Association. 248, 1465-1472.

Munson, M. (1984). Evaluation of the effectiveness of two visitation programs for isolated and lonely elderly persons: The impact on life satisfaction. Unpublished doctoral dissertation, University of Missouri-St. Louis.

National Center for Health Statistics. (1977). Profile of illness in nursing homes. (Vital and Health Statistics Series 13, Publication No. 29). Hyattsvile, MD: U.S. Department of Health, Education, and Welfare.

National Institutes of Mental Health. (1977). 1977 report of the secretary's committee on mental health and illness of the elderly. Washington, DC: National Health Center for Health.

Neulinger, J. (1982). Leisure lack and the quality of life: The broadening scope of the leisure professional. Leisure Studies, 1, 53-63.

Nickerson, P. (1987). Common, but poorly understood: Osteoarthritis. Generations, 12(1),8-11.

Norberg, A., Melin, E., & Asplund, K. (1986). Reactions to music, touch and object presentation in the final stage of dementia: An exploratory study. International Journal of Nursing Studies, 23, 315-323

Olderog Millard, K., & Smith, J. (1989). The influence of group singing therapy on the behavior of alzheimer's disease patients. Journal of Music Therapy, 26, 58-70.

O'Morrow, G., & Reynolds, R. (1989). Therapeutic recreation: A helping profession. Englewood Cliffs, NJ: Prentice Hall.

Osgood, N., Meyers, B., & Orchowsky, S. (1990). The impact of creative dance and movement training on the life satisfaction of older adults. Journal of Applied Gerontology, 9, 255-265.

Page, L., & Friedlander, J. (1986). Blood pressure, age, and cultural change. In M. Horan et al. (Eds.), Proceedings from a National Institutes of Health (NIH) symposium, Biomedical Information Corp.

Palmore, E. (1990). Predictors of outcome in nursing homes. Journal of Applied Gerontology, 9(2), 172-184.

Perlman, P., & Peplau, L. (1982). Chapter 8: Theoretical approaches to loneliness. In L. Peplau & D. Perlman (Eds.), Loneliness: A sourcebook of current theory, research and therapy (pp. 123-134). New York: John Wiley & Sons.

Perotta, P., & Meacham, J. (1981-82). Can a reminiscence intervention alter depression and self-esteem? International Journal of Aging & Human Development, 14, 23-30.

Pfeiffer, E. (1977). Psychopathology and social pathology. In J. Birren & K. Schaie (Eds.), Handbook of the psychology of aging. New York: Van Nostrand Reinhold.

Preston, E. (1987). Factors affecting nursing home residents' loneliness, leisure satisfactions, and leisure activity. Unpublished doctoral dissertation, University of Maryland.

Purcell, R., & Keller, M. (1989). Characteristics of leisure activities which may lead to leisure satisfaction among older adults. Activities, Adaptation & Aging, 13(4), 17-29.

Quinet, R. (1986). Osteoarthritis: Increasing mobility and reducing disability. Geriatrics, 41(2), 36-50.

Ragheb, M., & Griffith, C. (1982). The contribution of leisure participation and leisure satisfaction to life satisfaction of older persons. Journal of Leisure Research, 12, 295-307.

Rathbone-McCuan, E., & Hashimi, J. (1982). Isolated elders. Rockville, MD: Aspen Publishers.

Rice, D., & Feldman, J. (1983). Living longer in the United States: Demographic changes and health needs of the elderly. Milbank Memorial Fund Quarterly/Health and Society, 61(3), 362-396.

Riddick, C., DeSchriver, M., & Weissinger, E. (1984). A methodological review of research in Journal of Leisure Research from 1978 to 1982. Journal of Leisure Research, 16, 311-321.

Riegler, J. (1980). Comparison of a reality orientation program for geriatric patients with and without music. Journal of Music Therapy, 17, 26-33.

Riis, B., Thomsen, K., & Christiansen, P. (1987). Does calcium supplementation prevent postmenopausal bone loss? A double blind, controlled clinical study. New England Journal of Medicine, 316, 173-177.

Robb, S., Boyd, M., & Pristash, C. (1980). A wine bottle, plant, and puppy. Journal of Gerontological Nursing, 6, 721-728.

Rook, K., & Peplau, L. (1982). Chapter 26: Perspectives on helping the lonely. In L. Peplau & D. Perlman (Eds.), Loneliness: A sourcebook of current theory, research and therapy (pp. 351-378). New York: John Wiley & Sons.

Rossman, R. (1989). Recreation programming: Designing leisure experiences. Champaign, IL: Sagamore Publishing.

Russell, R. (1987). The importance of recreation satisfaction and activity participation to the life satisfaction of age-segregated retirees. Journal of Leisure Research, 19, 273-283.

Salthouse, T. (1982). Adult cognition: An experimental psychology of human aging. New York: Springer-Verlag.

Schafer, D., & Berghorn, F., Holmes, D., & Quadagno, J. (1986). The effects of reminiscing on the perceived control and social relations of institutionalized elderly. Activities, Adaptation & Aging, 8, 95-110.

Schaie, K. (1990). Intellectual development in adulthood. In Birren & Schaie (Eds.), Handbook of the psychology of aging (pp. 291-309). San Diego, CA: Academic Press.

Schaie, K., & Willis, S. (1986). Adult development & aging. Boston: Little, Brown & Co.

Schleien, S., & Yermakoff, N. (1983). Data-based research in therapeutic recreation: State of the art. Therapeutic Recreation Journal, 17, 17-26.

Schock, N. (1977). Systems integration. In L. Hayflick & C. Finch (Eds.), Handbook of the biology of aging. New York: Van Nostrand Reinhold.

Schulz, R., & Brenner, G. (1977). Relocation of the aged: A review and theoretical analysis. Journal of Gerontology, 32, 323-333.

Schulz, R., & Decker, S. (1985). Long-term adjustment to physical disability: The role of social support, perceived control and self-blame. Journal of Personality and Social Psychology, 48, 1162-1172.

Scogin, F., Hamblin, D., & Beutler, L. (1987). Bibliotherapy for depressed older adults: A self-help alternative. The Gerontologist, 27, 383-387.

Scogin, F., Jamison, C., & Davis, N. (1990). Two-year follow-up of bibliotherapy for depression in older adults. Journal of Consulting and Clinical Psychology, 58, 665-667.

Scogin, F., Jamison, C., & Gochneaur, K. (1989). Comparative efficacy of cognitive and behavioral bibliotherapy for mildly and moderately depressed older adults. Journal of Consulting and Clinical Psychology, 57, 403-407.

Seligman, M. (1975). Helplessness: On depression, development, and death. San Francisco: W. H. Freeman.

Shanas, E., Townsend, P., Wedderburn, D., Friis, H., Milhej, P., & Stenhouer, J. (1968). Old people in three industrial societies. New York: Atherton.

Shary, J., & Iso-Ahola, S. (1989). Effects of a control relevant intervention program on nursing home residents' perceived competence and self-esteem. Therapeutic Recreation Journal, 23, 7-16.

Smith, E. (1982). Exercise for preventing osteoporosis: A review. Physician Sports Medicine, 10, 72-88.

Stenback, A. (1980). Depression and suicidal behavior in old age. In J. Birren & R. Sloane (Eds.), Handbook of mental health and aging. Englewood Cliffs, NJ: Prentice-Hall.

Supiano, K., Ozminkowski, R., Campbell, R., & Lapidos, C. (1989). Effectiveness of writing groups in nursing homes. Journal of Applied Gerontology, 8, 382-400.

Tedrick, T. (1991). Leisure and aging bibliography; volume 4:1 through 1:1, Summer 1990-September 1985. Unpublished manuscript, Temple University, Department of Recreation, Philadelphia.

Tinsley, H., Teaff, J., Colbs, S., & Kaufman, N. (1985). A system of classifying leisure activities in terms of the psychological benefits of participation reported by older persons. Journal of Gerontology, 40, 172-178.

Verbrugge, L., Lepkowski, J., & Imanaka, Y. (1989). Comorbidity and its impact on disability. Milbank Quarterly, 67(3/4), 450-484.

Weiss, C., & Kromberg, J. (1986). Upgrading TR service to severely disoriented elderly. Therapeutic Recreation Journal, 20, 32-42.

Whittington, F. (1984). Addicts and alcoholics. In E. Palmore (Ed.), Handbook on the aged in the United States. Westport, CN: Greendwood Press.

Witt, P., Ellis, G., & Niles, S. (1984). Leisure counseling with special populations. In T. Dowd (Ed.), Leisure counseling: Concepts and applications. Springfield, IL: Charles Thomas.

Wolfe, J. (1983). The use of music in a group sensory training program for regressed geriatric patients. Activities, Adaptation & Aging, 4(1), 49-62.

Wood, J., & Estes, C. (1990). The impact of DRGs on community-based service providers: Implications for the elderly. American Journal of Public Health, 80(7), 840-843.

World Health Organization. (1947). Constitution of the World Health Organization. Chronicle of W.H.O., 1, 1.

Yoder, R., Nelson, D., & Smith, D. (1989). Added purpose versus rote exercise in female nursing home residents. American Journal of Occupational Therapy, 43(9), 581-586.

Yulish, M. (1991). Business & aging: Inclusionary strategy key to gray market. Aging Today, 12(2), 10.

Zimberg, S. (1974). The elderly alcoholic. Gerontologist, 14, 221-224.

CHAPTER 6

THE BENEFITS OF THERAPEUTIC RECREATION IN PEDIATRICS

Viki Annand & Peggy Powers

Introduction

The area of pediatrics is somewhat different than most areas of therapeutic recreation practice. Pediatrics is different because the focus is on a limited age range of recipients of services, rather than on a specific set of diseases or disabilities. The diseases and disabilities treated in pediatric settings include all illnesses and disabilities experienced by children and adolescents. The psychosocial needs of the developing child, however, warrant additional concern.

Psychosocial support of children during health care can be theoretically, clinically, and empirically documented as a major outcome of therapeutic recreation in pediatric settings. Theoretically, it has been postulated that children are especially vulnerable to much of what occurs during health care due to their limited development of understanding and coping abilities. Play is the major mechanism used by children to assimilate life experiences and master painful and unpleasant experiences. Clinically therapeutic recreation specialists reported a variety of techniques used to provide psychosocial support to children and their families during health care. Empirically, play used in a variety of ways has been shown to reduce psychological upset of children in health care settings.

Outcomes of therapeutic recreation related directly to the treatment of diseases and their secondary conditions are also addressed in pediatric settings. The outcomes of therapeutic recreation vary significantly due to the nature of the disease or disability. Therapeutic recreation specialists have reported predictable outcomes for some diseases. Within the review of literature there was, however, only limited clinical or empirical evidence for these outcomes.

What follows is an overview of the outcomes of therapeutic recreation in pediatric settings. We begin by looking at exactly what is meant by "pediatrics" and with what populations and in what settings therapeutic recreators work. For the purpose of this review, psychiatric settings and illnesses will not be included. Next, the impact of health care on children is examined from a theoretical perspective. Included in this perspective is a discussion of the influence of play on the coping ability of children. This is followed by a review of psychosocial and physiological outcomes of therapeutic recreation in pediatric settings. Outcomes identified are both those documented and those implied based upon the literature and survey of practice.

Overview of Diagnoses and Settings

Pediatrics is defined as the "medical specialty concerned with the study and treatment of children in health and disease during development from birth through adolescence" (Stedman, 1990, p. 1152). Health care services may be provided to this population in acute care hospitals, rehabilitation settings, specialty hospitals, ambulatory care facilities, and at home. In both acute care and rehabilitative hospitals, pediatrics may be found as a unit of the hospital or the entire hospital may be a specialty hospital for children. Children have special needs when facing or undergoing health care procedures or when adjusting to or rehabilitating from illness or a disabling condition and greatly benefit from therapeutic recreation.

The primary setting for therapeutic recreation addressing pediatric patient needs is the inpatient hospital, primarily serving children with acute, chronic, or rehabilitative health care needs. In the acute care setting (defined by Timmereck [1982], as a short stay hospital where stays average less than 30 days), patients may be admitted under three major categories of diagnoses: (a) acute-medical, (b) chronic-medical, or (c) surgical. An acute-medical admission in pediatrics would include illnesses or conditions such as croup, dehydration, pneumonia, bronchopulmonary dysplasia, failure-to-thrive, or endocarditis. Within the category of a chronic-medical admission, the inclusion of such illnesses as cancer, diabetes, cystic fibrosis, and AIDS would be most prominent. The last category of pediatric patients found in an acute care hospital would be the patient with surgical needs. Tonsillectomies, biopsies, shunt revisions, tumor removal, tendon releases (cerebral palsy), or trauma incidents are a few of the many pediatric surgical admissions.

A second setting for pediatrics is the inpatient rehabilitative hospital where the length of stay for the child or adolescent usually extends more than 30 days. "Rehabilitative services are provided to restore and/or improve lost functioning following illness, injury, or disease" (Timmereck, 1982, p. 549). Diagnoses common to a rehabilitative hospital serving pediatric patients include spinal cord injuries, anoxia, burns, and traumatic brain injuries.

As the trend in health care services moves from inpatient to outpatient settings, the delivery of services is being altered to ambulatory care settings. Therapeutic recreation and activity based services can be found in outpatient clinics of acute care and rehabilitative hospitals as well as being documented in emergency room care (Alcock, Feldman, Goodman, McGrath, & Park, 1985; Ipsa, Barrett, & Kim, 1988; Powers & Annand, 1991; Rasnake & Linscheid, 1989). Given the changing field of health care delivery, therapeutic recreation for pediatric population could be included in hospice and home health care. With this change from inpatient to outpatient settings there is also an increased emphasis on preventative health care. Some health maintenance organizations are beginning to understand the importance of preparing children for health care experience as a preventative to long-term psychological trauma.

Theoretical Framework

There are a variety of theories which provide the basis for therapeutic recreation intervention in pediatric settings. There are those theories which suggest the need for intervention and others that govern the techniques used. Permeating all of this is the fact that the concept "pediatrics" denotes a vulnerable developmental age and covers a wide spectrum of services provided. Due to the age factor, developmental theory must be used interactively with other theories in both choosing and shaping appropriate interventions. In terms of services provided, there are both general factors related to hospitalization as well as factors related to specific illnesses and disabilities which must be considered. Stress and coping emerge in the literature as the primary theories supporting activity intervention in the pediatric setting.

Psychological Upset

Empirical studies documenting both immediate and short-term (up to 1 month) emotional response of children to health care have suggested that children undergoing a variety of medical experiences suffer "psychological upset" (Thompson, 1985). Freud (1952), in discussing the role of bodily illness in the life of the child, suggested that there are many factors in addition to hospitalization and concurrent separation issues which can cause potentially upsetting and harmful influences on the mental life of the child. The more obvious and frequently documented factors include painful procedures, operations, and restrictions (e.g., movement). Freud made the case, though, that other less obvious factors provide the potential for causing stress and harm. These other factors include: (a) the change in parental attitude toward the sick child, (b) the experience of being nursed and consequently the releasing of gained ego control and the reverting to more passive levels of infantile development, and (c) the interactional effect of pain and anxiety.

Psychoanalytic theory. In the "psychologically normal human being" (Nemiah, 1978, p. 161), the various psychic elements (drives, ego structures, ego affects) are in balance enabling the individual to function in an integrated, self-satisfying, and socially acceptable way. Even when faced with stress, the psychic elements of this individual are able to maintain balance or quickly restore it. Psychoanalytic theory describes the development of psychopathology in terms of a dynamic process involving the psychic structures (id, ego, superego), defense mechanisms, and internal or external stress. In the individual who develops psychopathology, the psychic elements are more vulnerable to stress due to developmental experience which has caused permanent damage to one or more of the psychic structures. Given prolonged stress, this individual resorts to rigid use of defense mechanisms or exclusive reliance on defenses eventually leading to pathological disequilibrium or psychopathology. This condition of psychopathology persists even after the precipitating stressor(s) has been removed.

Early psychic trauma from a psychoanalytical point of view suggests reason for major concern for those health care professionals dealing with the stress and coping of hospitalized children. According to Nemiah (1978), environmental stress occurring at any time in life can lead to distortion in the psychic elements, but it is those stresses which occur early in life that have the "most profound" and "long lasting" (p. 166) effects. There are several factors in psychoanalytic theory which account for the profound effect of early psychic trauma. First of all, children may not have sufficiently mature or extensive enough defense mechanisms to deal with many stressful experiences. In discussing the effect of operations on children, Freud (1952) pointed out that when the child has available defense mechanisms sufficient in strength to master anxiety, all goes well. When, however, the ego is not strong enough to cope with the anxiety released, trauma results.

A second factor in psychoanalytic theory which accounts for the profound effect of early psychic trauma relates to the role of fantasy and the theme of that fantasy during certain developmental periods. Freud (1952) pointed out that some children are less affected by pain than others. The pain differential has less to do with the pain itself than with unconscious fantasies which may be present. Where fantasies are dominant, the pain is accompanied by anxiety that "represents a major event in the child's life" (p. 76) and is apt to be remembered long after the pain subsides. This anxiety and the concurrent emotions often carry more psychic weight than the actual experience.

Finally, the theory of repression in the developing child adds weight to the importance of early psychic trauma in psychoanalytic theory. Freud (1966) cautioned that repression is the most dangerous defense mechanism. Because repression renders conflict to the subconscious, the child never gains control of parts of his/her affective life. In psychoanalytic theory, repression is a normal process in the developing child occurring between the oedipal and latency phases (Nemiah, 1978). Therefore, even the child whose stressful experiences result in psychic disequilibrium represses all this at latency. The end result is that the stress is never resolved, only repressed, lying dormant, and ready to flare up in the outbreak of psychiatric disorders given the stresses of adolescence or adulthood.

Developmental theory. The primary contribution that developmental theory makes to supporting the need for psychosocial intervention in pediatrics is to suggest differential needs based on age. In other words, the age of the child dictates what in the hospital experience will be found to be stressful or threatening to the child. In summarizing developmental fears of hospitalized children, Betz (1983) identified four developmental levels with corresponding shifts in what generates fear and anxiety. Betz suggested that the toddler (1 to 2-1/2 years) is largely unable to understand hospitalization and is primarily affected by separation from the parent. While still having difficulty with separation, the author suggested that the preschooler (2-1/2 to 6 years), fearing punishment for misdeed, must also deal with fantasies of mutilation and fear of immobility. The school age child (6 to 13 years) was represented as focused primarily on punishment for misdeed and, therefore, fear of mutilation. Betz perceived the adolescent (13 to 18) to have considerable concerns including the fear of losing control, loss of independence, and threat to physical appearance.

Betz's (1983) first three levels of development and fear correlate somewhat to Freud's developmental sequence of phases (Meissner, 1978) and to several of the early stages of Erikson's (1963) eight ages of man. A similar differentiation of children's fear during hospitalization was postulated by Timmerman (1983) after review of the literature. He conceived that children less than 5 predominantly fear the unfamiliar environment and separation from family. For the child 5 to 10, the most common fear centers around the operation itself and mutilation. In Betz's configuration, it is the loss of control which most concerns the preadolescent.

Psychosocial Support

The literature suggests a variety of theory guides psychosocial intervention in pediatric settings. Some of the theory identified speaks specifically to intervention techniques aimed at helping children cope (Bolig & Gnezda, 1984; Freud, 1966; Gaynard et al., 1990). Other literature suggests that developmental theory offers guidance to selecting and shaping interventions both in terms of age differences and in terms of normal developmental processes (Erikson, 1963; Freud; Gaynard et al.; Perry, 1986; Piaget, 1954).

Coping. Some theory suggests play as an appropriate intervention to provide psychosocial support in pediatric settings. Erikson (1963) stated that child's play is how the child is able to progress forward incorporating more and more of reality into his life in what he referred to as "mastery" (p. 222). He postulated that "child's play is the infantile form of the human ability to deal with experience by creating model situations and to master reality by experiment and planning" (p. 222). In a different vein, Freud (1966) discussed children's fantasy play in terms of how such play allows the child the ability to control the world. She further suggested that some turning "away from reality" (p. 85) might be desirable in normal growth and development rather than the child always devoting him/herself to assimilating reality.

When a child is threatened, he/she may use play to deal with the situation. Freud (1966) suggested that the child can assimilate an anxiety experience by introjecting some characteristics of the anxiety object. In what Freud calls "identification with the aggressor" (p. 113), the child imitates the role of the aggressor, thereby changing him/herself from the one who is threatened to the one who is doing the threatening. In other words, the child moves from a passive to an active role in order to assimilate the traumatic experience. In a similar way, Erikson (1963) talked about play as a cure. He pointed out that when traumatized, the adult will relieve tension by talking it out. For the child, he suggested, "'to play it out' is the most natural self healing measure childhood affords" (p. 222).

Gaynard et al. (1990) suggested that information acquisition should be the primary focus of coping strategies. They suggested that in order for the child to cope with the experience of being hospitalized "the child needs to understand what is happening" (p. 18). The authors postulated a cyclic model of information processing under stress. In this model, little or no information leads to high uncertainty about the threat and how to deal with it. This high uncertainty then leads to a feeling of little to no control over the situation. The combination of low information, high uncertainty, and low perceived control leads to high levels of distress. In this model, the high emotional distress leads to ineffective information processing. Gaynard et al. suggested that stress reduction interventions should be used to interrupt this cycle by providing adequately understood information. This information, they stated, should then increase the child's sense of perceived control by helping the child learn and use techniques that might reduce or prevent harm. The emphasis of the information giving should be on helping the child to process, not just to receive the message. For young children, the authors stated, "communication techniques that emphasize play interactions assume a central role in assisting information processing" (p. 20).

Support of normal growth and development. There are two reasons why the support of normal growth and development are cited in the literature on psychosocial support. First, just as early psychic trauma is seen to disrupt normal development, removing a child from his home environment is seen as potentially affecting a child's physical, cognitive, affective, and social development (Thompson, 1985). Research cited by Thompson supports this contention, especially for children hospitalized repeatedly or for long periods of time.

The second reason why developmental theory is important in considering appropriate interventions for psychosocial support is that a child's level of development will affect his/her response to hospitalization (Gaynard et al., 1990; Thompson, 1985) and should dictate what the intervention should be (Perry, 1986). The literature made reference to a variety of developmental theorists with the developmental levels of Piaget and Erikson frequently cited as important determinants of intervention.

Documented and Expected/Implied Outcomes

Addressing activity-related outcomes in pediatrics, it is clear that a major emphasis in the literature has been in the area of psychosocial support of children during health care. Two historical reviews (Thompson, 1985; Vernon, Foley, Sipowicz, & Schulman, 1965) reviewed related literature including controlled research studies, theoretical articles, and descriptive studies. The emphasis on research and theoretical writing related to therapeutic recreation outcomes in pediatrics continues to be primarily in the area of psychosocial support. Only isolated examples of specific interventions used for diagnosis-related outcomes have been found in the literature.

Psychosocial Support

Thompson (1985) completed a fairly extensive literature review of psychosocial research in the area of pediatric health care spanning the period from 1965 to 1983. His review included both inpatient and outpatient literature, including dental care. In Thompson's review, outcomes of intervention were covered under the topics of "play" interventions and "psychosocial preparation for hospitalization and health care procedures." In addition to these subject areas, the Thompson review included the following topics: (a) children's responses to hospitalization and health care; (b) children's conceptions of hospitalization, illness, and medical care; (c) research of specific procedures and environments; (d) separation and rooming-in; (e) parent and sibling responses to hospitalization; (f) adolescent hospitalization, health care, and illness; (g) the hospital milieu; and (h) play and the hospitalized child. It should be noted that while many of these topics are important to understanding both the need and parameters for psychosocial support of children while hospitalized, this paper will be limited to review of those factors that most specifically speak to outcomes. Furthermore, given the thoroughness of the Thompson review, this paper will be limited to a review of the period between 1983 and 1990.

In discussing the controlled research between 1965 and 1983 on psychological preparation for hospitalization and health care procedures, Thompson (1985) noted several trends. One significant finding was that overall the number of research reports in this area had increased substantially. He also noted the trend for this research to focus on primary school age children with very few studies including adolescents 13 years old or older. Another trend which he identified was the tendency for studies to examine the effect of preparation for children admitted for surgical or diagnostic procedures with very few studies considering preparation of children with medical diagnoses. Specifically, the majority of experimental studies he identified focused on minor, elective, or short-term surgical patients. Finally, the last trend he noted in the area of hospital preparation was an emphasis on studying preparations that occur inpatient, or after the children arrived.

The review of literature undertaken for this paper (1983 to 1990) did not reflect the trends noted by Thompson (1985). Controlled studies focused not only on school age children under 13, but in many cases included either or both younger children and adolescents. During the present review period, a variety of children's conditions were studied, not just minor, elective, or short-term surgery. Finally, this review of literature found a variety of settings studied, not just inpatient hospitalization.

Comprehensive programs. Probably the most extensive study conducted since 1983, however, did focus on preparation after arrival at the hospital (Wolfer, Gaynard, Goldberger, Laidley, & Thompson, 1988). The uniqueness of this study lay in the fact that it involved the development of a standardized child life program based on theory and the evaluation of the effect of the total program, rather than isolated techniques, based upon a large number of outcome variables believed to be related to children's psychosocial welfare and physical recovery. Also, the sample population included a broader spectrum of varied age groups beyond the scope of previous studies.

Wolfer et al. (1988) used a quasi-experimental, phase lag design to test the overall effectiveness of a systematically developed child life program using 11 outcome variables. The sample consisted of 160 control-group subjects and 68 experimental-group subjects between the ages of 3 and 13 who were admitted with acute conditions or newly diagnosed chronic conditions in the acute phase.

Subjects were included in the study if they had not been hospitalized during the last year, were hospitalized for 3 to 14 days, and had no invasive procedures prior to being admitted.

The outcome measures used within the study included one that measured emotional distress and another that measured coping effectiveness during threatening or painful procedures. Heart rate was used as a measure of physical arousal associated with distress and was taken at four different points: (a) immediately before the admission exam, (b) after the exam when the child appeared to be in a resting state again, (c) immediately before the first medical procedure, and (d) after the first medical procedure. The fourth measure was an overall coping adjustment rating designed for the study. It combined ratings made on a daily basis to obtain a global rating on a 5-point scale, taking into account the change in emotional, social, and verbal behavior in relation to the child's developmental level from admission to discharge. Two other measures used were also developed for the study. One was a rating of the child's understanding of the reason for their hospitalization and the other was a rating of the child's understanding of the procedures they received. To determine the ratings for these two factors, the authors used a formal interview adjusted for the child's developmental level.

Other factors that were measured related to surgical recovery. These measures included: (a) the number of analgesics used, (b) the number of days on the initial narcotics, (c) the number of days to discharge, (d) the number of days under the attending physician's predicted length of stay, (e) the number of days of fever, (f) the number of hours to first voiding, (g) the number of hours to first ambulation, (h) the number of hours to first oral intake, and (i) the number of hours to return to regular diet. This information was only obtained on surgical patients.

The final four ratings were all completed by the parents. The first one was the Vernon Post-hospital Adjustment Scale. The parents completed the 127-item questionnaire 10 days after discharge to measure the amount of adjustment of the child. The second measure was a questionnaire completed by the parents at discharge to yield a measure of their degree of involvement in their child's care. The third of these parent completed measures was a questionnaire used to obtain parents' self-report on their level of tension. This instrument had the parents rate their stress at time of discharge for 10 separate occasions. The rating yielded a overall mean rating. The final measure used was a questionnaire completed by the parents to measure the child's physical condition 10 days after discharge. In all, these 11 measures yielded 21 factors.

More comprehensive and more detailed than in previous studies, the child life intervention used by Wolfer et al. (1988) was based on the philosophy that intervention should be initiated as soon as possible, be continuous, and be based on each child's illness, treatment condition, and developmental status. The program consisted of eight components that were developed into protocols including underlying principles, purpose, and techniques for each component. The intervention for each patient included each of the following eight components: (a) admission orientation and assessment, (b) stress vulnerability assessment, (c) ongoing assessment and activity planning, (d) developmental enhancement, (e) psychological preparation, (f) post-procedural medical play, (g) family involvement, and (h) supportive relationships.

Wolfer et al. (1988) found the program had a positive impact on children's psychosocial welfare and physical recovery based on the experimental group scoring significantly better on 18 of the 21 factors outlined above. The only factors where significance was not noted were parental anxiety while their children were in the hospital, parent participation in care, and the measure of stress during the first procedure. In surgical recovery which was not completed on all patients because not all patients were hospitalized for this reason, the only non-significant variables were noted in the number of analgesics used and on the number days of fever.

In another study involving the effectiveness of a comprehensive child life program, Carson, Jenkins, and Stout (1985), looked at the effects of a child life program on the anxiety level of children 4 to 15 years of age (N = 10). The condition of the children differed somewhat from previous studies and included only those hospitalized due to trauma and requiring traction. The measure used in this study to assess anxiety level was the "state" portion of the State-trait Anxiety Inventory for Children and Adults. The authors also reported measuring self-esteem using the Coopersmith Self-Esteem Inventory. After three periods of measurement, the authors found a significant statistical difference between the groups on the anxiety measure using analysis of covariance (ANCOVA) for repeated measures with the pre-test as the covariate.

Gillis (1989) similarly found that structured play was influential in reducing the impact of immobility on hospitalized children. The subjects in this study were school-aged (7 to 12) children (N = 60). Subjects were included in the study if they were immobilized due to hospitalization. The authors utilized measures of the child's perception of time, self, and space as outcome measures, arguing that these factors are of central importance to the general well-being of the child. The measures included a time duration technique which had the child estimate a 60 second interval as a measure of sense of time; the Coopersmith Self-Esteem Inventory; and the Life Space Drawing which yielded a projective measure both of self-esteem and social space.

Within 48 hours of hospitalization, the subjects were randomly assigned to either the group receiving structural play or the control group. According to the author, the structured play included age appropriate activities that were designed to encourage interaction with the environment and occurred for four 30-to-45-minute sessions, 12 to 24 hours apart. An ANCOVA adjusting for initial differences between the groups yielded statistically significant differences on both of the self-concept measures and on the time duration measure. In terms of time, both groups perceived time as passing more slowly, but the group receiving structured play perceived this to a lesser degree than the control group. On self-concept, the group receiving structured play demonstrated an increase, from the pre-play to the post-play period, whereas the self-esteem of the control group slightly decreased over time.

Not all studies utilizing a general program as intervention took place in inpatient settings. Ipsa et al. (1988) reported on a supervised play experience in an outpatient clinic. Unlike other interventions reviewed, this intervention did not include specific strategies to provide psychosocial support to children and their parents. Rather, children were simply allowed to play with provided toys and art supplies and if they chose, to explore provided medical supplies. The sample consisted of 30 children age 5 to 10. The authors gave no indication of condition of clients, but there is every reason to believe that the reasons for the visit varied.

The subjects received a controlled application of intervention during a 4 month period. Play opportunities were offered on the days when one half of the subjects received medical treatment, and not offered on the days when the other half received services. Children were rated for two 5-minute periods during their stay in the waiting room. They were rated on 13 scaled behaviors and on overall predominant affective expression. The duration of frequency of the behavior was then rated on a 3-point scale. Seven of the behaviors were combined to equal an overall anxiety score. Two behaviors were combined to equal an anger/noncompliance score, and three of the behaviors were combined to equal a positive behavior score. Parents were also rated on five behaviors: (a) active participation with their child, (b) irritation with their child, (c) conversation with staff, (d) conversation with other parents, and (e) simply reading.

The findings suggested that even relatively simple play intervention can be of value in an outpatient setting. Children who did not receive the play opportunity were more likely to cry. Children who were in the waiting room where play opportunities were available seemed less anxious than those who where there when the opportunities were not available. For adults accompanying the children, those who were present when the play opportunities were available were statistically significantly less irritable with their child and spoke significantly more with other staff.

Specific interventions. Some studies reviewed used very specific types of interventions. Froehlich (1984) compared a music therapy session with a medical play therapy session in facilitating expression. The author based her assertion on the importance of expression on the belief that children need to talk about the hospital experience in order to cope with it. She cited theoretical support for this belief in Erikson's concept that verbalization precedes understanding and mastery of anxiety. The measure of expression was based on content analysis of children's responses to four affective-type questions posed to each subject at the close of the intervention session. The responses were taped and then individually coded based on the quality of the response, with more involved answers receiving higher numbers.

The subjects for this study were 39 children randomly assigned to receive either the music therapy session or the medical play session. While the conditions of the children were not specifically discussed, further analysis of data suggests that children with both acute illnesses and chronic illnesses were involved. Children ranged in age from 5 to 12 years.

Chi square analysis of frequency distributions yielded a statistically significant difference between the two groups at the .10 level, with the music therapy responses being more involved in expression. No significant difference was found between subjects who had acute illnesses with little hospital experience and patients who had chronic illnesses with numerous prior hospitalizations. The verbalization of patients with no prior child life involvement, however, was significantly more involved than for patients with prior child life involvement. In these dichotomizations of variables (type of illness, child life experience), music therapy elicited significantly more involved verbalizations than did play therapy. Sex was the only classification variable which showed significance independent of therapy, with females presenting more involved verbalizations.

The effect of adding a nature-based experience to the child life program was measured by Jesse, Strickland, Leeper, and Hudson (1987). Seventy children were randomly assigned to either a group receiving the nature experiences (N = 30) or those receiving only the standard child life program (N = 40). Three instruments were used to measure anxiety: (a) 13-item, 5-point Fear Thermometer Test; (b) 64-item, Behavior Observation Checklist; and (c) 4-item Anxiety Rating Scale. The experimental group received four nature-oriented activities at four different times during the regular child life program. No statistically significant differences were found in reduction of fear or anxiety levels between the group receiving the additional nature oriented activities and the group receiving only the child life program.

Preparation programs. Several studies with this review were found to address very specific preparations for given selective procedures. Demarest, Hooke, and Erickson (1984) studied two preparation procedures for surgery. The first involved the subject viewing a slide show of a child who modeled most of the procedures the children would undergo as a result of their hospitalization and surgery. The second group were encouraged to actively use the equipment and role play the procedures shown in the slides. The control group was provided with directed play opportunities of the same duration and in the same setting as the other two groups.

The subjects for this study were 24 3-to-9-year-olds. As in many earlier studies, the subjects were in the hospital for elective surgery, either tonsillectomies or adenoidectomies. Unlike medical practice at the time of earlier studies, however, the subjects were only hospitalized for one to two days.

The Anxiety Scale of the Personality Inventory for Children was used to measure the long-term effect of the hospitalization. The Hospital Fears Rating Scale was used to measure the current situational anxiety. Parents rated their child on the anxiety scale upon admission and 1 week after discharge. The children were rated three times on the Hospital Fears Scale: (a) immediately after the intervention was completed, (b) at the beginning of surgery, and (c) immediately after surgery in the recovery room. A repeated measures analysis of variance found the group practicing the procedures to have significantly lower anxiety than did either the slide show group or the control group. There was, however, no statistically significant difference between these latter groups on anxiety. There were no statistically significant differences among groups for the parent rated scale of anxiety. The authors concluded that a relatively short preparation where the child is actively involved with upcoming procedures can reduce anxiety. It was suggested that the lack of difference between the slide show group and the control might be due to the difference between the model, who was black, and the subjects, only one of whom was black. The lack of difference between the slide show group and the control group was not consistent with earlier studies using this intervention (Thompson, 1985).

A specific preparation for a very specific procedure was studied by Pfaff, Smith, and Gowan (1989) in an outpatient setting. Using a within subject design, the effect of music-assisted relaxation during bone marrow aspiration was studied in six subjects, ages 7 to 15. Subjects' distress was measured by the Faces Scale for Fear, the Faces Scale for Pain, and the Observation Scale of Behavioral Distress (OSBD). To determine the OSBD score, the bone marrow aspiration was broken down into four phases: (a) anticipatory anxiety, (b) cleansing of the aspiration site and injection of the local anesthesia, (c) the aspiration, and (d) post-procedural recovery. The summed scores for the OSBD were based on observations taken every 15 seconds, limiting each phase to a specific number of intervals to control for differences in length of procedures.

Baseline data were collected 30 minutes prior to one bone marrow aspiration. The OSBD was collected during this bone marrow aspiration and then the second set of Faces Scales was completed immediately after it. On the same day, but before the intervention bone marrow aspiration, each subject was helped to select the music he/she found most relaxing. The third set of Faces Scales was then administered and then the music therapist taught the patient a music assisted, relaxation program. During the second bone marrow aspiration, the child's choice relaxation music was played and the music therapist coached the child through the relaxation exercises when necessary. The OSBD was again scored and at the completion of the bone marrow aspiration, the fourth set of Faces Scales was completed.

While the overall OSBD was not statistically significantly different, there was a strong trend for reduction in distress scores for both anticipatory phases. Of the five behavioral categories, crying revealed a statistically significant reduction from first procedure to intervention procedure. A trend for reductions in anticipatory fear, experienced fear, and experienced pain was also noted. The authors concluded that music-assisted relaxation particularly reduced children's distress associated with bone marrow aspirations.

In a study of non-hospitalized fourth graders, Wilson (1987) failed to find a significant difference in anxiety levels, hospital-related fears, or recall knowledge of medical terms after a pre-crisis hospital preparation program. There were 40 subjects in one of four intact classrooms. The interventions were specifically designed to increase the child's learning and understanding of the hospital utilizing theoretical premises of Piaget. Two different interventions were used. There was a handbook which used verbal and pictorial means to explain the hospital experience. The second one was a program designed using slides, photographs, and medical instruments to explain and demonstrate the hospital experience.

One of four conditions was randomly assigned to each intact group. One group received the program and the handbook. A second group received just the handbook and a third group received just the program. The fourth group did not receive any hospital preparation. The students' anxiety was measured by the Parents' Questionnaire before the study began and by the State-Trait Anxiety Inventory for Children at three intervals (1 week before, immediately after, and 2 weeks after the intervention). The hospital fears variable was measured by the Hospital Fears Questionnaire at the same three intervals. Finally, recall knowledge was measured by the Matching Test of Medical Terminology--People,

Places, Things in the Hospital before intervention and 2 weeks after intervention. Three way analyses of variance found no difference among the groups on any of the variables. The authors noted a trend toward increased scores in the knowledge recall measure.

Another specific preparation study dealt with children's immediate needs in an emergency room (Alcock et al., 1985). Two hundred seventy-three children requiring suturing were randomly assigned to either the intervention group or a control group. A second control group at another hospital was also used in the analysis. The group who received intervention was taught, trained, and prompted in coping responses. Play was the primary medium through which the coping responses were prompted. Since the study group ranged in age from 4 to 14, the child life specialist chose approaches that were appropriate to the child's age as well as their anxiety level. Coping techniques other than play which were used included: (a) distracting imagery, (b) relaxation techniques, (c) cognitive restructuring, and (d) problem solving. The data were analyzed using the following variables: (a) age (4 to 6, 7 to 10, and 11 to 14 year olds); (b) site of sutures (face versus body); and (c) number of sutures (five or less versus six or more).

The outcomes were measured on the following scales: (a) the Katz, Kellerman, and Siegel Procedure Behavior Rating Scale for anxiety during the procedure; (b) the Spielberger State and Trait Anxiety Inventory for the child's self-reported anxiety; (c) the Spielberger, Gorush, and Lushene Self-Evaluation Questionnaire for the parent's self-reported anxiety; (d) the Visual Analogue Scale for the children's perception of pain; (e) Vernon, Schulman, and Foley Post-hospitalization Behavior Questionnaire for behavior changes in post-emergency visits; and (f) a consumer satisfaction questionnaire completed by the parents. On the observed anxiety scale, there was no difference among groups, but the control group from the second hospital expressed statistically significantly more fear than the intervention group. There were age and sex differences on anxiety behavior with 11 to 14 year olds expressing the least fear, 4 to 6 year olds exhibiting the highest scores on overt behaviors (crying, clinging, screaming, flailing, etc.), and females displaying more observable anxiety behavior than males. There was no statistically significant difference on children's reported anxiety, but for older children receiving six or more sutures on the face, there was a statistically significant difference between the intervention group and the control groups, with the intervention group demonstrating a continual drop in reported anxieties with increasing age. While there were age differences, there was no statistically significant difference among groups on either the post-emergency visit behavior change or on the children's anxiety concerning a return visit. There also were no statistically significant differences among groups on the parents' anxiety level.

Parents in the intervention group, however, did express statistically significantly fewer negative comments and increased positive comments concerning their emergency room visit.

This study supported the clinical impression of the authors that emergency room intervention is most effective in acute distress situation (i.e., facial injury requiring more than six sutures). It also suggested age different behaviors in terms of fears and response to anxiety. It was the conclusion of the authors that the intervention group exhibited negative behaviors for a shorter duration than the control groups, but because the data was collected based on exhibiting behaviors once, this difference was not documented.

A final study on preparation for children receiving medical procedures (Rasnake & Linscheid, 1989) provides guidance related to the shaping of interventions. The authors studied the effect of "developmentally appropriate" versus "developmentally advanced" preparation. The subjects were outpatients about to receive a proctoscopy exam. There were 48 subjects in two different age groups, 3 to 5 and 7 to 10. Age groupings were narrowed to insure that the children fell into one of two cognitive groups proposed by Piaget (pre-operational thinking, age 3 to 6; and concrete operational thinking, age 6 to 10). Three developmentally different video preparations on proctoscopy were then developed, each designed to address the cognitive learning level of one of three of Piaget's established levels: (a) pre-operational thinking, (b) concrete thinking, and (c) formal operational thinking.

In this study, subjects were selected from consecutive admissions and were randomly assigned to one of three groups: (a) developmentally correct, (b) developmentally advanced, or (c) control. The control group viewed the video that had been developed as the status-quo preparation for 4 to 5 year olds or 8 to 9 year olds, depending on their age. The other groups viewed the specially developed video depicting one of three cognitive development levels as theorized by Piaget. The developmentally correct group viewed the appropriate video for their age; the developmentally advanced group viewed the video designed for the next age group.

The anxiety of children was measured using several scales. The first was a scale developed from two other scales utilizing the categories of verbal and skeletal motor behavior thought to represent behavioral manifestations of anxiety in children. The observer rated each child for 10 behaviors using 10 second observation periods followed by 5 second recording intervals for the length of the exam. Since there were no significant differences in length of exams for the groups, the behavioral observation ratings were summarized to yield an overall score by calculating the percent of intervals in which at least one distress behavior was exhibited. Another evaluation of distress was made independently by the nurse and the physician on two separate factors, expression of fear and degree of cooperation. The heart rate was used as a physiological measure of stress. It was taken immediately after viewing the video, during the exam, and after the exam was over. Parents were also asked to complete a questionnaire concerning the child's previous response to medical visits.

A multivariate analysis of the various measures found that the group that received developmentally appropriate instruction had significantly less anxiety than the other two groups. Individual analysis of specific measures found the only significant difference between groups was on the behavioral rating scale. Neither the physician's rating, nurse's ratings, or the heart rate showed a difference between groups. An ANCOVA with the parents' ratings of children's prior experience, previous reaction to medical experience, and the amount of preparation provided by the parents as the covariate, yielded no differences in the statistical analysis. The authors concluded that these findings are consistent with adult studies which indicate that the provision of accurate information yields positive effects on the way that stress is dealt with by the individual. This finding may have even more value when it is considered that in this study the control group received a limited intervention (preparation that the nurse had previously given to the two specified age groups).

Summary of controlled studies. Controlled studies of the psychosocial support of children during health care have shown a variety of approaches to be effective in reducing psychological upset. Comprehensive approaches finding decreased upset have utilized a very structured program based on theoretical premises (Wolfer et al., 1988), structured play based on age appropriateness (Carson et al., 1985; Gillis, 1989), and unstructured, free play (Ipsa et al., 1988). One study utilizing a structured music therapy intervention as opposed to a child life program increased expression which theoretically (according to the author) would lead to increased mastery of the situation and the ability to cope (Froehlich, 1984).

In addition to the more comprehensive approach to psychosocial support of children during health care, controlled studies have found decreased anxiety when specific interventions have been used to prepare children for medical procedures. In preparing children for a proctoscopy exam, developmentally appropriate versus developmentally advanced preparation was found to help children better deal with the stress of the exam (Rasnake & Linscheid, 1989). Active involvement with the procedures ("medical play") was found to be more effective than merely providing information for inpatient surgery (Demarest et al., 1984), whereas coping responses taught through play (although situationally relaxation techniques were also utilized) were found to be effective in decreasing stress in the emergency room during acute distress situations (Alcock et al., 1985). A structured music assisted relaxation intervention was found to be partially effective in reducing stress for children undergoing bone marrow aspiration (Pfaff et al., 1989).

Collectively these studies suggest that play and other activities aimed at helping children cope during health care are effective. There is also evidence that clinically, increased coping/reduced psychological upset are outcomes for which therapeutic recreation specialists structure their interventions.

Perceived outcomes of therapeutic recreation. In a recent survey of therapeutic recreators working in pediatric settings (Powers & Annand, 1991), psychosocial support of children was the most consistent and frequent outcome identified by respondents. In particular, specific preparation for procedures was identified by all agencies except one (N = 14). The responses indicated that the preparation might be generic (e.g., preparation for surgery), or might be specifically geared to a diagnoses (e.g., bone marrow aspiration, cardiac catheterization, diabetes, skin graphs, dialysis). Interventions utilized to achieve these outcomes varied but included such activities as: (a) medical play, (b) needle play, (c) puppet play, (d) dramatic play, (e) medical coloring books, (f) syringe painting, (g) "cast parties," and (h) stories.

When asked what specific diagnosis/treatment interventions were used, the majority of expected outcomes identified by respondents were of a psychosocial nature. In fact, if maintaining normal development is included as a psychosocial support, half of all respondents listed only psychosocial outcomes as expected outcomes of their interventions. Some of these psychosocial outcomes can be viewed as related to the experience of hospitalization and/or specific procedures. Other outcomes identified are directly related to the effects of a particular illness or medical condition. Outcomes secondary to the diagnosis/treatment which were identified by therapeutic recreators working in pediatric settings included: (a) relaxation, (b) pain management, (c) expression of anxiety, (d) reduction of anxiety/fear, (e) increased self-esteem, (f) increased (sic) body image, (g) increased medical compliance, (h) increased motivation, (i) increased sense of control, (j) increased decision making, (k) increased age appropriate behavior (related to regression), (l) increased medical knowledge, (m) decreased feelings of isolation and loneliness, (n) increased confidence, and (o) decreased fear of death. In addition to specific activities and programs used to achieve these outcomes, as part of their services, therapeutic recreators identified (a) efforts to normalize the medical environment (bedside mobiles and pictures, teen room, play room, normal life activities, use of community recreation facilities, resident unit pets); (b) support of parents (resource library, family dinners, family outings, parent coffee hours); and, (c) to a lesser degree, support of siblings in relation to dealing with issues surrounding the hospitalized child (sibling parties for cancer patients, medical play, preparation for visit to hospitalized child, sibling head injury group).

While the majority of outcomes identified by survey respondents were directly related to psychosocial support, some respondents did identify interventions aimed at physiological outcomes. Additional evidence of physiological outcomes attained through play were found in literature describing clinical practice. Very limited empirical study focused on this area of outcomes.

Physiological Outcomes

Physiological outcomes of therapeutic recreation in pediatric settings can be broken down into two different types: (a) outcomes related to complications of bedrest or surgery and (b) outcomes directly related to the treatment of specific medical conditions. Specific outcomes identified by therapeutic recreators in pediatric settings (Powers & Annand, 1991) related to complications of bedrest and surgery included: (a) increased inspiration following surgery to prevent pneumonia, (b) increased muscle strength and range of motion due to physical problems associated with extended bedrest, and (c) increased food intake due to decreased appetite secondary to bedrest/hospitalization. Specific play activities identified by practitioners included: (a) blowing bubbles, candles, balloons to increase inspiration; (b) games with balls and bean bags to increase arm and/or leg usage while in bed or otherwise immobilized; and (c) cooking and food play to increase appetite. While not addressed either in clinical descriptions or empirical studies of pediatric health care, the use of recreation and activity are identified for the prevention of complication of bedrest in the Handbook of Severe Disability (Stolov & Clowers, 1981).

Developmental outcomes. Some outcomes identified by therapeutic recreators (Powers & Annand, 1991) in pediatric settings related directly to the treatment of the primary medical condition. Due to the nature of the condition, some of these outcomes were of a developmental nature. These outcomes included gross and fine motor development in developmentally delayed children and reaching developmental milestones (which could be physical, cognitive, or social) for children diagnosed failure to thrive due to non-organic reasons.

In a study of severely malnourished children where a play intervention was utilized, improvement in development of the intervention group was found despite the children's failure to catch up to the control group in nutritional status (Grantham-McGregor, Schofield, & Harris, 1983). In this study two groups of severely malnourished children, one receiving a play intervention, were compared to a control group of adequately nourished children who had been hospitalized with diseases other than malnutrition. The intervention consisted of daily structured play while the children were in the hospital and then 1 hour per week follow-up for 2 years after discharge. During the follow-up the intervention focused on showing the mothers how to more effectively play with their children in a cognitively oriented manner.

Measurement of development utilized four subscales of the Griffiths Mental Development Scales for Babies and Young Children (locomotor, hearing and speech, eye and hand coordination, and performance). Children were tested at three times during hospitalization and then at 1, 6, 12, 18, and 24 months after hospitalization. The data were analyzed utilizing repeated measures ANCOVA scores being adjusted for a difference between the groups in the covariate, age at first test.

The results showed that the children who received the intervention actually scored significantly higher than the control group which was adequately nourished on both the hearing and speech and the performance subscales. The intervention group scored similarly to the control group in eye hand coordination, whereas the malnourished group which did not receive intervention showed significant decline on the performance subscale between 1 and 24 months and remained significantly behind both other groups on all subscales. The authors concluded that it was possible that the malnourished children had suffered brain damage, but even if this were so, the children receiving the play intervention were found to have a "marked capacity to compensate at least in the short term" (Grantham-McGregor et al., 1983, p. 243).

On a follow-up to this study at 6 years after leaving the hospital, Grantham-McGregor, Schofield, and Powell (1987) found the intervention group showed a decline in three of five Griffiths subscales, but that they retained a marked advantage over the non-intervention group of malnourished children on the Stanford-Binet, showing no further decline in the last year. This study began at 24 months of the 1983 study reported above. During the third year, play intervention was continued with the intervention group, but every 2 weeks instead of weekly; then the intervention was stopped. Measurement of children's development was taken at 26, 36, 48, 60, and 72 months after the children left the hospital.

The measures utilized to assess development were altered as children began scoring off the developmental scales. The locomotor scale of the Griffiths Mental Development Scales was eliminated at 60 months and the use of practical reasoning scale was began at the 24-month test session (the scale begins at 24 months of age). Because some children would be higher than the top scale of the

Griffiths by 72 months, the Stanford-Binet test was used with the Griffiths test at 60 months and then instead of the Griffiths at 72 months. The Peabody Picture Vocabulary Test (PPVT) was added at the 36-month test session.

During the third year of reduced intervention, no further improvements occurred, in fact, the intervention group declined relative to other groups on one of the Griffiths subscales. The authors suggested that the reduction in frequency of visit may have reduced the effectiveness of the intervention. The early declines in the intervention group leveled off, however, and they remained with significantly higher IQs than the malnourished non-intervention group at 72 months. While the intervention group had scored higher on two subscales of the Griffiths test and the same on one subscale as the adequately nourished group at 24 months, by the end of the follow-up they scored below the adequately nourished group. The authors suggested that this may well have occurred because the adequately nourished group came from better home backgrounds, despite efforts to match the two groups.

Other treatment outcomes. Other outcomes identified by therapeutic recreators in pediatric settings (Powers & Annand, 1991) which related directly to the treatment of the disease included: (a) increased range of motion for children with burns; (b) increased orientation, organization, planning, and sequencing for children with head injury and sickle cell anemia; (c) increased awareness of rest time for children with asthma; and (d) increased gross motor ability for children with orthopedic conditions. Concerning burns, Clarke et al. (1990) noted that in the acute management of pediatric hand burns, exercise is necessary to enhance healing with minimal loss of function. Related to this approach, Adriaenssens, Eggermont, Pyck, Boeckx, and Gilles (1988) reported on the use of video games to motivate young burn children to exercise. They pointed out the need for exercise post-burns to "maintain mobility and to anticipate deformity" (p. 417). They suggested that exercise was often painful and frightening, and for young children, it is especially hard to understand the need for it. They stated that a well-coordinated game invites the child to participate while activating different body parts. A number of adaptations of video games that can be used to retain gripping function and/or exercise the hand muscles, the wrists, and the elbow were reported on.

While relaxation has been identified by practitioners as the issue for inpatient children with asthma, several controlled and non-controlled studies of children in outpatient programs suggest that exercise may be of value in treating asthmatic children. Rothe, Kohl, and Mansfeld (1990) reported on the effects of physical training on the cardiopulmonary system and on lung function of 36 children (age 10 to 16) with asthma. The children were assigned to either a running group, a swimming group, or a control group. The two activity groups received at least 10 units of 30 minutes of exercise over a 3 week period, while the control group did not participate in any regular training. The study found increased work tolerance for the two activity groups, but not the control group. The free running group had a statistically significant decrease in heart rate at rest (.05) and at the end of bicycle ergometer exercise (.01) while the swimming group had a statistically significant decrease of heart rate at the end of bicycle ergometer exercise (.05).

A "short, sharp course" of exercise has been found to be beneficial for children with asthma in a non-residential setting (Dean, Bell, Kershaw, Guyer, & Hide, 1988). Eleven children receiving what the authors described as physiotherapy were compared with 10 children in a control group. The authors reported an improvement (in the short-term, at least) in bronchial lability, peak flow rates, nocturnal and daytime wheeze, and activity as compared with the controls.

In a non-controlled study, Szentagothai, Gyene, Szocska, and Osvath (1987) reported that a long-term physical exercise program was effective in improving the functioning of asthmatic children on an outpatient basis over a year's time. One hundred twenty-one children, ages 5 to 14, participated in swimming on their backs and gymnasium exercises for two 1-hour sessions per week. At the conclusion of the first year of the program, the authors reported that the number of days with asthmatic symptoms decreased in a large majority of the patients while medication was also decreased. They also reported that school absenteeism and hospitalization dropped markedly. The same extent of improvement continued for the second year.

After 1 or 2 years in the swimming and gymnastics program, a complete exercise program was used which weekly included two 1-hour sessions in the pool, one exercise in the gymnasium, and one running exercise outdoors (gradually increased to 4,000 to 5,000 meters). Based on data collected, the authors concluded that, "in the majority of children with asthma, regular and long-term participation in the physical exercise program accounted for most of the decrease in asthmatic symptoms" (Szentagothai et al., 1987, p. 171).

In an institutional, non-controlled study of asthmatic pre-adolescents, Nishimuta (1990) concluded that appropriate physical training therapy was very useful in the patients' physical and mental recuperation where 56.3% of severe bronchial asthmatic patients were able to recover and lead normal lives. The author reported on a program of "institution therapy" which included several aspects, the most important of which was "training therapy." Training therapy included training of the autonomic nervous system, respiratory training, and physical training. Physical training consisted of running and swimming at activity levels dependent upon the patient's condition and ability, with levels being increased in accordance with the individual's recuperation. Running was done daily. Swimming was done weekly, except during the summer when a 120-minute daily intensive program was used. The program continued during a 1 to 2 year hospitalization. The authors concluded that the physical training was not just important for increasing stamina and restoring expiration-inspiration ability, but also for restoring self-confidence.

Cerny (1989) reported on the effects of therapeutic exercise as a substitute for bronchial hygiene treatment for patients hospitalized with cystic fibrosis. Seventeen patients with cystic fibrosis were randomly assigned to one of two groups receiving inpatient treatment for exacerbation of their pulmonary disease. Eight patients (mean age = 15.9) received three bronchial hygiene treatment sessions per day; nine patients (average age = 15.4) participated in two cycle ergometer exercise sessions and one bronchial hygiene treatment session per day. Both groups showed significant improvement in pulmonary function and exercise response with no difference between groups. The author concluded that for some persons hospitalized with cystic fibrosis, exercise may be substituted for at least part of the standard protocol of bronchial hygiene therapy.

Summary of physiological outcomes. Therapeutic recreation specialists in pediatric settings report physiological outcomes primarily associated with developmentally delayed children, and individuals with burns, head injury, sickle cell anemia, asthma, and orthopedic conditions. They also reported on the use of play activities to prevent the complications of bedrest and immobility. Limited clinical descriptions of these outcomes and their antecedent interventions were found in the literature. Few of these outcomes were tested empirically. One medical condition where play intervention was found to be effective was in improving the developmental status of malnourished children. The results of both controlled and non-controlled studies, of the effect of exercise on the severity of asthmatic symptoms, lends support to this area as a possible outcome of recreational exercise. The possible use of exercise in the place of bronchial hygiene treatment for persons with cystic fibrosis was also suggested.

Conclusions

To some degree there is consistency between documented outcomes and those outcomes expected by therapeutic recreation specialists in pediatric settings. The most frequently cited outcomes of play in pediatrics and the most consistent response from therapeutic recreation practitioners were those interventions of a psychosocial nature. The emphasis on psychosocial functioning in pediatrics was supported by play literature in theoretical articles, program descriptions, and empirical studies. Studies varied greatly in terms of outcome emphasis (coping with hospitalization; coping with a specific health care procedures) and in terms of the interventions used (unstructured play, structured play, and cognitive-oriented intervention).

There was far less emphasis on physiological outcomes of therapeutic recreation in pediatrics reported by practitioners. There was even less emphasis of this type of outcome of play in the literature. Therapeutic recreation specialists identified the conditions of developmental delay, burns, head injury, sickle cell anemia, asthma, and orthopedic conditions as those in which they expected outcomes of a physiological nature. Outcomes related to play/recreation were cited in the literature associated with burns, malnourishment, asthma, and cystic fibrosis.

Recommendations

After review of current literature related to the use of play/activity in pediatrics, several summary observations can be made. The first observation is that the primary emphasis of play/activity in pediatrics has been in its use in the psychosocial support of children during health care. The majority of theoretical articles and research studies reviewed focused on this function of play. This emphasis on the psychosocial needs of children during health care was further supported by a survey of therapeutic recreation specialists in pediatric settings. Only limited reference to the use of play/activity as a treatment or rehabilitating medium for specific illnesses or disabilities was found in the literature. There were, however, very specific examples of these types of interventions identified by therapeutic recreation specialists surveyed.

In the area of psychosocial support, though the outcome sought was often the same, the specific intervention used varied greatly from study to study. Furthermore, this variation in approach existed despite the fact that the theoretical basis for intervention was often the same. There were two major differences in the type of approaches used. The approaches either focused on psychosocial support of children during health care in general, or the focus was related to the preparation for and support during a very specific procedure (e.g., bone marrow aspiration, proctoscopy exam, emergency suturing). Approaches identified included free play, structural play, and cognitive-oriented intervention. There were no repetition studies found and limited, if any, attempts at theory building in terms of intervention.

Limited literature was found in the area of play/activity as a means to physiological outcomes in specific illnesses and disabilities. However, therapeutic recreators surveyed reported a variety of interventions used with a variety of illnesses and disabilities. Specific references in the literature were made to the use of play/recreation in the rehabilitation of hand and arm burns. A combination of controlled and non-controlled studies supported the use of recreative-exercise in the treatment and control of asthma and in the treatment of cystic fibrosis. Finally, two reports of a long-term study of malnourished children suggested the validity of enhancing cognitive development through play. Therapeutic recreation specialists, on the other hand, reported the use of play in addressing the needs of children who were impaired via developmental delay, burns, head injury, sickle cell anemia, asthma, and orthopedic conditions.

One final observation can be made concerning current literature in the use of play/activity in pediatrics. That is, not one single theoretical article, program description, or research study came from therapeutic recreation literature. Rather, the literature which was found came from the disciplines of nursing, child life, social work, psychology, music therapy, and recreation.

Areas Neglected in Present Research Orientation

The most glaring omission in the research related to play/activity in pediatrics is the lack of involvement of the therapeutic recreation discipline. Despite reference to pediatrics in modern therapeutic recreation textbooks (Austin & Crawford, 1991; Carter, Van Andel, & Robb, 1985) and identification of the practice of therapeutic recreation in pediatric settings (Powers & Annand, 1991), the current literature is void of theoretical articles, program descriptions, and research studies from a therapeutic recreation perspective. While much of what was found in the literature about play/activity and pediatrics fits well within the definition of therapeutic recreation (American Therapeutic Recreation Association, n.d.; National Therapeutic Recreation Society, 1982), there is much to be gained from studying play/activity outcomes in pediatrics from a therapeutic recreation perspective. For one thing, unlike many other disciplines working in pediatrics, play/recreation is the major emphasis of therapeutic recreation. The unique definition and philosophy of therapeutic recreation may generate unique and viable approaches to treatment in pediatrics.

An area where a paucity of literature was found warrants more study. This is the broad area of physiological outcomes in specific illnesses and disabilities as a result of play/activity. The use of play/recreation as a treatment intervention in specific illnesses and disabilities is part of the paradigm of therapeutic recreation (American Therapeutic Recreation Association, n.d.; National Therapeutic Recreation Society, 1982), yet limited reference to the use of play/recreation for physiological outcomes was found in the literature. Those illnesses and conditions noted in the literature where play/recreation was used to achieve physiological outcomes (burns, malnutrition, and asthma) each need more study under controlled and varying conditions before the validity of the intervention can be determined. In addition, other illnesses and conditions identified by therapeutic recreation specialists as ones where play/recreation is used to achieve physiological outcomes (head injury, sickle cell anemia, developmental delay, and orthopedic conditions) also warrant study.

A third area that appears to be neglected in the literature is the role of play/recreation in adjustment to disability. While the role of play/activity in psychosocial support of children during health care did receive attention in a variety of fashions, the specific role of play/recreation in adjustment to disability was not part of this consideration. Most outcome measurement in the pediatric literature was of psychological upset related to health care. The specific issue of adjustment to disability of a long-term or even short-term nature, was not addressed.

Although not totally neglected in the study of psychosocial support in pediatrics, the impact of intervention on families is an area that deserves more attention. Some studies have looked at the impact of psychosocial support through the measurement of parental anxiety and parental satisfaction. Also of importance would be the impact of psychosocial support on siblings. In family systems theory, all members of the family have a role to play in the psychosocial functioning of each family member. Another area for study is the outcome that can be achieved through helping parents to use play/recreation in a therapeutic sense with their child. This becomes increasingly important in the changing health care arena with its emphasis on decreased spending and increased reliance on outpatient services.

One final area for study relates to the changing health care arena. With the increased emphasis on meeting patient needs on an outpatient basis, the nature of interventions used and perhaps the outcomes achieved will be affected. While some studies of the use of play/activity in outpatient and emergency medical care in pediatrics were found, increased emphasis needs to be placed on studying outcomes in these settings, which may well include home health care and health maintenance organizations.

Specific Issues

While most research in pediatrics has been conducted in the area of psychosocial support of children during health care, few conclusions concerning intervention can be drawn from these efforts. In terms of reduction of psychological upset during health care in general, a variety of intervention from very structured, theoretically-based play to unstructured play have been found to be successful in reducing anxiety. These interventions need to be replicated in different settings with different subjects. One question raised by these studies--is unstructured play as effective in reducing psychological upset as is structured play, and if so, under what circumstances?

Similar questions arise in terms of specific preparations for specific procedures. Do elements of intervention for one procedure generalize to other procedures? Will these preparations for procedures be as effective in other settings with other populations? Finally, is unstructured play as effective in reducing psychological upset during procedures as specific preparations?

The results of mostly uncontrolled studies in the treatment of asthma suggest that regular recreative-exercise may enhance treatment efforts. Since this is a chronic condition usually treated on an outpatient basis, the unique location of therapeutic recreation in community leisure service settings could aid in the study of regular exercise on this disease. The question remains-- does regular cardiovascular exercise result in decreased asthmatic symptoms? If so, what is the optimal exercise regimen and is it equally effective under varying conditions with varying populations?

The issue of the lack of research in the role of play/recreation in the adjustment to disability has already been identified. In relation to this, the question arises--does leisure education enhance adjustment to disability in pediatric populations? If so, what specific populations and under what conditions can this outcome be achieved?

Finally, given the role play appears to take in cognitive development of children, the role of play in the treatment of children with head injuries warrants study. Can play be used to enhance cognitive functioning of children with deficits due to head injuries? If so, under what conditions and with what populations will it be most effective?

Conclusion

The study of outcomes of play/recreation in pediatrics deserves consideration on the research agenda of therapeutic recreation. Little has been contributed by this discipline to enhance the developing body of knowledge in this area. Each setting where therapeutic recreation specialists practice offers unique populations and conditions for study. Research to date, theory, and current practice offer direction to shape these efforts. If therapeutic recreators do not take steps to validate their practice in pediatric settings, this may well cease to be an area for therapeutic recreation service.

Addendum

Despite inherent methodological problems in studies he reviewed, Bar-Or (1990) suggested that there might be possible disease specific benefits of exercise training in children with chronic diseases worth investigating. In children with cerebral palsy, he suggested exercise may enhance ambulation and reduce spasticity. Similarly he thought it worth investigating the role of exercise in children with myopathies in terms of strengthening residual muscle, prolongation of ambulation status, and weight control. Other areas for investigation that he identified included: (a) higher respiratory muscle endurance and enhanced clearance of bronchial mucus in cystic fibrosis, (b) better diabetic control in diabetes mellitus, (c) reduction of blood pressure at rest in hypertension, and (d) improved lipoprotein profile and weight and fatness control in obesity.

References

Adriaenssens, P., Eggermont, E., Pyck, K., Boeckx, W., & Gilles, B. (1988). The video invasion of rehabilitation, Burns, 14, 417-419.

Alcock, D. S., Feldman, W., Goodman, J. T., McGrath, P. J., & Park, J. M. (1985). Evaluation of child life intervention in emergency department suturing. Pediatric Emergency Care, 1, 111-115.

American Therapeutic Recreation Association. (n.d.). ATRA: American therapeutic recreation association: Your invitation to join . . . . Hattiesburg, MS: Author.

Austin, D. R., & Crawford, M. E. (1991). Therapeutic recreation: An introduction. Englewood Cliffs, NJ: Prentice Hall.

Bar-Or, O. (1990). Disease-specific benefits of training in the child with a chronic disease: What is the evidence? Pediatric Exercise Science, 2, 384-394.

Betz, C. L. (1983). Teaching children through play therapy. AORN Journal, 3, 709-721.

Bolig, R., & Gnezda, T. (1984). A cognitive-affective approach to child life programming for young children. Children's Health Care, 12, 122-129.

Carson, D. K., Jenkins, J., & Stout, C. B. (1985). Assessing child life programs: Study model with a small number of subjects. Children's Health Care, 14, 123-125.

Carter, M. J., Van Andel, G. E., & Robb, G. M. (1985). Therapeutic recreation: A practical approach. St. Louis, MI: Times Mirror/Mosby College Publishing.

Cerny, F. J. (1989). Relative effects of bronchial drainage and exercise for in-hospital care of patients with cystic fibrosis. Physical Therapy, 69, 633-638.

Clarke, H. M., Wittpenn, G. P., McLeod, A. M., Candlish, S. E., Guernsey, C. J., Weleff, D. K. & Zuker, R. M. (1990). Acute management of pediatric hand burns. Hand Clinic, 6, 221-232. (From Medline, 1990, UD 9009)

Dean, M., Bell, E., Kershaw, C. K., Guyer, B. M., & Hide, D. W. (1988). British Journal of Diseases of the Chest, 82, 155-161. (From Medline, 1988, UD 8901)

Demarest, D. S., Hooke, J. F., & Erickson, M. T. (1984). Preoperative intervention for the reduction of anxiety in pediatric surgery patients. Children's Health Care, 12, 179-183.

Erikson, E. H. (1963). Childhood and society. New York: W.W. Warton.

Freud, A. (1952). The role of bodily illness in the mental life of children. In R. Eissler, A. Freud, H. Hartmann, & E. Kris (Eds.), The psychoanalytic study of the child, 8, (pp. 69-81). New York: International Universities Press.

Freud, A. (1966). The ego and the mechanisms of defense. New York: International Universities Press.

Froehlich, M. A. R. (1984). A comparison of the effect of music therapy and medical play therapy on the verbalization behavior of pediatric patients. Journal of Music Therapy, 21, 2-15.

Gaynard, L., Wolfer, J., Goldberger, J., Thompson, R., Redburn, L., & Laidley, L. (1990). Psychosocial care of children in hospitals: A clinical practice manual from the ACCH child life research project. Bethesda, MD: Association for the Care of Children's Health.

Gillis, A. (1989). The effect of play on immobilized children in hospital. International Journal of Nursing Studies, 26, 261-269.

Grantham-McGregor, S., Schofield, W., & Harris, L. (1983). Effect of psychosocial stimulation on mental development of severely malnourished children: An interim report. Pediatrics, 72, 239-243.

Grantham-McGregor, S., Schofield, W., & Powell, C. (1987). Development of severely malnourished children who receive psychosocial stimulation: Six-year follow-up. Pediatrics, 79, 247-254.

Ipsa, J., Barrett, B., & Kim, Y. (1988). Effects of supervised play in a hospital waiting room. Children's Health Care, 16, 195-200.

Jesse, P., Strickland, M. P., Leeper, J. D. & Hudson, C. J. (1987). The effects of nature-based experiences on children's adjustment to the hospital: A comparative study. Journal of Environmental Education, 19, 10-15.

Meissner, W. W. (1978). Theories of personality. In A. M. Nicholi, Jr. (Ed.), The Harvard guide to modern psychiatry (pp. 115-146). Cambridge, MA: The Belknap Press of Harvard University Press.

National Therapeutic Recreation Society. (1982). Philosophical position statement of the national therapeutic recreation society. Arlington, VA: The National Recreation and Park Association.

Nemiah, J. C. (1978). The dynamic bases of psychopathology. In A. M. Nicholi, Jr. (Ed.), The Harvard guide to modern psychiatry (pp. 147-172). Cambridge, MA: The Belknap Press of Harvard University Press.

Nishimuta, T. (1990). Special therapy in an institutional hospital. Acta Paediatr Japan, 32, 201-204.

Perry, S. E. (1986). Teaching tools made by peers: A novel approach to medical preparation. Children's Health Care, 15, 21-25.

Pfaff, V. K., Smith, K. E., & Gowan, D. (1989). The effects of music-assisted relaxation on the distress of pediatric cancer patients undergoing bone marrow aspirations. Children's Health Care, 18, 232-236.

Piaget, J. (1954). The construction of reality in the child. New York: Basic Books.

Powers, P., & Annand, V. S. (1991). [The role of therapeutic recreation in pediatrics]. Unpublished raw data.

Rasnake, L. K., & Linscheid, T. R. (1989). Anxiety reduction in children receiving medical care: Developmental considerations. Developmental and Behavioral Pediatrics, 10, 169-175.

Rothe, T., Kohl, C., & Mansfeld, H. J. (1990). Controlled study of the effect of sports training on cardiopulmonary functions in asthmatic children and adolescents. Pneumologie, 44, 1110-1114. (From Medline, 1991, UD 9104).

Stedman, T. L. (1990). Stedman's medical dictionary (25th ed.). Baltimore, MD: Williams and Wilkins.

Stolov, W. C., & Clowers, M. R. (1981). Handbook of severe disability. Washington, DC: U.S. Government Printing Office.

Szentagothai, K., Gyene, I., Szocska, M., & Osvath, P. (1987). Physical exercise program for children with bronchial asthma. Pediatric Pulmonology, 3, 166-172.

Thompson, R. H. (1985). Psychological research on pediatric hospitalization and health care: A review of the literature. Springfield, IL: Charles C. Thomas.

Timmerman, R. (1983). Preoperative fears of older children. AORN Journal, 38, pp. 827-834.

Timmereck, T. (Ed.). (1982). Dictionary of health services management. Owings Mills, MD: National Health Publishing.

Vernon, D., Foley, J., Sipowicz, R., & Schulman, J. (1965). The psychological responses of children to hospitalization and illness. Springfield, IL: Charles C. Thomas.

Wilson, C. J. (1987). Comparison of two methods of preparation for hospitalization. Children's Health Care, 16, 24-27.

Wolfer, J., Gaynard, L., Goldberger, J., Laidley, L. N., & Thompson, R. (1988). An experimental evaluation of a model child life program. Children's Health Care, 16, 244-254.

CHAPTER 7

THE BENEFITS OF THERAPEUTIC RECREATION IN PHYSICAL MEDICINE

Doris Berryman, Ann James, & Barb Trader

Introduction

Forty-four million Americans are permanently disabled and the disability rights movement estimates that by the year 2000, half of all Americans will be disabled, over 65, or both (Johnson, 1990). Sixty-six percent of all adults (16 to 64) with physical disabilities are unemployed. The rate of unemployment varies among diagnostic groups, but is 81% for those with spinal cord injury (DeVivo, Rutt, Stover, & Fink, 1987) and it is listed as the major handicap resulting from chronic respiratory illness (Williams & Bury, 1989). Unemployment results in financial instability (Krause & Crewe, 1990), subsistence living (Trieschmann, 1987), and social isolation for many disabled individuals (Jones, 1988).

People become physically disabled in one of three ways: (a) congenitally, (b) acquired through trauma, or (c) acquired through disease. All disabilities result in some loss of physical function, but the extent of loss can be affected dramatically by when, during the individual's development, the disability occurred. For example, children with upper extremity (UE) congenital limb deficiency generally have superior adaptive skills compared to individuals who acquire a UE amputation later in life. Conversely, children with spina bifida have more perceptual motor problems than children paralyzed through traumatic spinal cord injury, partially due to reduced experiences in motor learning (Chorost, 1988).

People with disabilities are as different from each other as are people without disabilities. Vash (1981), however, notes:

The commonality of experience among people with different types of disability is great because the processes of being devaluated as a result of having a disability and learning to accept all that disablement entails are shared by all. . . . People with disabilities consistently experience devaluation in the eyes of others, and their own. This is true regardless of the nature of the disability, whether it impairs physical, sensory or mental functioning. (p. xvi-xvii)

Diagnostic Groups and Treatment Settings

Diagnostic groups which receive treatment in physical medicine and rehabilitation settings include, but are not limited to: (a) AIDS, (b) amputation, (c) arthritis, (d) burns, (e) cancer, (f) cardiovascular disease, (g) cerebral palsy, (h) chronic pain, (i) diabetes, (j) epilepsy, (k) hearing impairment, (l) hemophilia, (m) multiple sclerosis, (n) muscular dystrophy, (o) neuromuscular diseases, (p) peripheral neuropathies, (q) post-polio syndrome, (r) pulmonary disease, (s) end stage renal disease, (t) rheumatic disease, (u) spina bifida, (v) spinal cord injury, (w) stroke, (x) traumatic brain injury, and (y) visual impairment. Individuals with these disabling conditions present a wide array of impairments including: (a) hemiplegia, (b) paraplegia, (c) quadriplegia, (d) cardiopulmonary insufficiency, (e) loss of sense of touch, (f) aphasia, (g) ataxia, (h) apraxia, (i) spastic paralysis, (j) left/right neglect, (k) speech disturbances, (l) memory and other cognitive deficits, (m) perceptual motor deficits, (n) loss of vision, and (o) loss of hearing. Many individuals have multiple impairments. In addition, these disabled persons often present a number of concomitant secondary disabilities which must be taken into consideration, such as depression, anxiety, withdrawal from social contacts, stress reactions, and loss of self-esteem.

Physical medicine and rehabilitation settings include: (a) comprehensive rehabilitation centers which serve all age and diagnostic groups; (b) specialized centers which serve only children with selected types of disabilities; and (c) specialized centers which serve specific disabilities such as visual impairments, hearing impairments, and head injury. Many large medical centers also have a comprehensive rehabilitation service. Virtually all of these settings provide medical and various allied health services on both an inpatient and outpatient basis. Therapeutic recreation programs are offered in nearly all of the inpatient but few of the outpatient services.

Generally speaking, congenitally disabled individuals are recipients of medical care, but are not exposed often to other services, especially in the psychosocial domain (Rinck et al., 1989). Many never experience rehabilitation or habilitation, but are seen in acute care hospitals or medically oriented clinics. People who are disabled through trauma or experience a sudden onset of disease usually receive intensive care during the acute and rehabilitation phases (lasting up to 6 months or so) and thereafter very little. People who have degenerative diseases and disabilities receive mostly medical care as their condition worsens, but few are holistically treated.

Community based, non-medical services are generally limited to vocational rehabilitation, sheltered employment, and access to centers for independent living (CILs), though some communities have developed recreation centers and programs for persons with disabilities. The development of CILs is the one sign that the life-long need for supportive services is finally being addressed. Frieden (1989) notes that, in the middle 1970s, six CILs could be located nationwide and now over 200 are operating.

Theoretical Foundations

Rehabilitation

The rehabilitation enterprise has, in recent years, been increasingly expanding from its traditional, rather narrow base of a medical model to a broad based, more holistic one which Alexander and Fuhrer (1984) refer to as the "psychosocial rehabilitation model" (p. 52 to 55). Hahn (1985) identified three models of disability which are currently reflected in disability policy: (a) the medical model, which defines disability in terms of physical impairment; (b) the economic model, which focuses on the individual's vocational limitations; and (c) the sociopolitical model, which defines disability as the product of interaction between the individual and the environment. Szymanski, Rubin, and Rubin (1988) argue that the three models of disability "have given rise to two competing approaches to rehabilitation--the functional limitations approach and the environmental/interactional approach" (p. 4). It is their view that the functional limitations approach locates the disability in the person, is compatible with the medical and economic models of disability, and focuses on the remediation of individual deficits.

In contrast, the environmental/interactional approach, based on the sociopolitical model of disability, uses support to the individual and/or modification of the environment to optimize the interaction between individuals and environments. "The goals of this approach are: independence, self-determination . . . political change to alleviate discrimination . . . and full participation in society" (Szymanski et al., 1988, p. 4). This view is congruent with that expressed by Frey (1984) who suggested that the current views of rehabilitation refer to a process of integrating persons with physical or mental impairments into community life with the intent to "assist these individuals in obtaining those roles, rights, and responsibilities that define life in the surrounding community" (p. 12). The contemporary philosophical base and goals of rehabilitation are moving in the direction of a holistic view of human beings which holds that human beings are more than and different from the sum of their parts and that they are in constant interaction with the environment (Dubos, 1965; Lockland, 1973; Rogers, 1970; von Bertalanffy, 1950).

Unfortunately, there is often a considerable gap between the stated philosophy and goals and the practice of rehabilitation. As Szymanski et al. (1988) state, ". . . the particular form or thrust of services for disabled persons is dependent on which model holds a position of dominance in a particular service system at a given point in time" (p. 3). One of the biggest gaps in both practice and research has been created by minimal, if any, attention given to the importance of play, recreation and leisure experiences in achieving "psychosocial" goals, a personally satisfying and fulfilling lifestyle, adjustment (adaptation) to disability, and stress reduction. Also, little attention has been given to the value of using specific recreation activities, offered in a recreational context, to assist in the process of physical restoration and achieving goals related to activities of daily living. It should be added that for children, adolescents, and youth, play, recreation, and leisure experiences are essential to their optimal growth and development.

A major reason for this gap may well be that most of the literature in rehabilitation, authored primarily by physicians, psychologists, rehabilitation counselors, social workers, and occupational and physical therapists, usually refer to recreation as avocational activities and interests. Thus, the recreation participation and leisure experience domain of the lives of persons with disabilities has been, and to a large extent continues to be, defined as a life experience that is not some other life experience, namely "vocation," rather than as a clearly separate and essential strand in the intricate web of human life.

A prime example of this view is the schematic representation of the dynamic interaction between patients and their environments presented by Stolov and Clowers (1981) in which the environment is comprised of two components, social and vocational. For the social sphere, the authors include "the patient's home, family unit, social responsibilities, and interpersonal contacts" (p. 3); for the vocational sphere, they include "the place of work, the breadth of responsibilities, and the financial and personal rewards, and also vocational and recreational pursuits" (p. 3). This connotation ignores the fact that one's "recreational pursuits" and other play and leisure experiences are also integral aspects of life in the home and family unit and interpersonal contacts.

Another major reason for the gap is the lack of research published by the field of therapeutic recreation to counteract the prevailing views held by the various disciplines involved in the rehabilitation enterprise. It should be noted, however, that because recreation and therapeutic recreation services have not traditionally been seen as particularly important, opportunities to conduct meaningful research in rehabilitation settings have been minimal. In recent years, particularly since 1985, an increasing number of research reports have appeared in therapeutic recreation and leisure research journals, but, for the most part, populations studied have been children and adults with mental retardation, persons with various psychiatric disabilities, and patients in nursing homes.

There has also been little research reported in professional journals of other professions and disciplines. Berryman (1985) reviewed 115 research abstracts and articles concerned with play recreation and leisure with disabled populations, for the period 1974 to 1984, identified through the data bases PSYCINFO, MEDLINE, ERIC, and Dissertations Abstracts. Analysis of these research reports revealed that only 16 citations were studies of persons with physical disabilities (including cerebral palsy and multiple disabilities) and nine were studies of persons with sensory impairments. The literature reviewed for this paper revealed no significant increase in research focused on either the play, recreation, and leisure aspects of the lives of physically disabled persons or the effects of therapeutic recreation services in the rehabilitation of persons with physical disabilities.

Stress and Adaptation to Disability

Mikhail (1985) has defined stress as "a state which arises from an actual or perceived demand-capability imbalance in the organism's vital adjustment actions and which is partially manifested by a nonspecific response" (p. 37). This definition combines Selye's theory of biologic stress, which is manifested in the three stages of the General Adaptation Syndrome: (a) alarm, (b) adaptation, and (c) exhaustion, and psychological stress theory. Research in psychological stress theory has identified three important aspects of stress:

> Individuals differ in their reactivity to stress. . . . Stress is determined by the perception of the stressful situation rather than the situation itself. . . . The extent of stress depends partly on the capability of the individual to cope (p. 35).

These finding are congruent with the concepts of disability and stress discussed by DeLoach and Greer (1981) who argue that:

> In assessing the stress of any one situation for any one individual we must consider those factors which affect severity of stress: (1) how long the situation lasts, (2) the individual's tolerance for stress, (3) multiplicity of stressful situations, (4) the individual's perception of the situation, and (5) whether stress is combined with threat. (p. 20)

These authors contend that the three major sources of stress for disabled persons are environmental and social frustrations, conflict situations, (e.g., having to choose between two equally desirable or two equally undesirable goals), and internal and external pressures. They further contend that disabled persons encounter more potential sources of stress and encounter more stressful situations more frequently than do non-disabled persons.

In discussing strategies of adaptation, White (1985) argues:

> ... (1) that the described phenomena of coping, mastery, and defense belong in the more general category of strategies of adaptation, as part of the whole tapestry of living; and (2) that adaptation does not mean either a total triumph over the environment or total surrender to it, but rather a striving toward acceptable compromise. (p. 126)

He defines coping as adaptation under relatively difficult conditions. White presents a cogent argument for his belief that adaptive behavior, which successfully aides the individual's transactions with the environment, "involves the simultaneous management of at least three variables: securing adequate information, maintaining satisfactory internal conditions, and keeping up some degree of autonomy" (p. 133). He further notes that strategies of adaptation typically have a considerable development over time.

Both the quantity and quality (meaning of information in terms of potential benefits and harm) must be considered:

> ... There is a certain rate of information input that is conducive to unconfused, straightforward action, and that both higher rates and lower rates will tend, though for different reasons, to make action difficult. (White, 1985, p. 136).

Hamburg and Adams (1967), in their review of studies of behavior during major life transitions, suggested that in patients with severe injuries that are bound to restrict their future activity, information seeking served the following purposes:

> Keeping distress within manageable limits; maintaining a sense of personal worth; restoring relations with significant other people; enhancing prospect for recovery of bodily functions; and increasing the likelihood of working out a personally valued and socially acceptable situation after maximum physical recovery has been attained. (p. 278)

Thus, failure to provide for and encourage optimum information seeking related to patients' present and future involvement in play, recreation, and leisure experiences as an integral aspect of health restoration and optimum functioning can have deleterious effects on their overall adaptation strategies.

In relation to the variable of maintaining, and if possible, enhancing, the system's integral organization, White (1985) states that the meaning of this variable is greatly expanded by one's awareness of the "remote, the past, and the future, and especially awareness of oneself as a person" (p. 135). He argues that:

> Clearly there is much more to be maintained than bodily integrity and control over disruptive affects. One thing that must be enhanced if possible, and desperately maintained if necessary, is the level of self-esteem. In part this shows itself as a struggle to keep intact a satisfactory self-picture, in part as attempts to preserve a sense of competence, an inner assurance that one can do the things necessary for a satisfactory life. (p. 135)

DeLoach and Greer (1981) address this issue in their discussion on self-state, stigma incorporation, and physical disability. It is their view that the self-state, comprised of five components: (a) physical, (b) independence-support, (c) interpersonal, (d) industrious, and (e) creative-relaxational is positively or negatively impacted by the various ego defense mechanisms and task-oriented strategies the disabled person employs to achieve stress reduction and a more positive self-state.

DeLoach and Greer (1981) contend that successful adaptation to disability evolves, over time, in three stages. During the early stages of disablement, when most experiences are negative, "stigma isolation and its accompanying use of ego defense mechanisms plays a critical role in easing the bleak reality of disability" (p. 219). Stigma isolation results in disabled individuals perceiving disability-related stress as the result of situations, events and the attitudes of others, that is, outside their control. Continued use of ego defense mechanisms as the strategy for coping with resulting stress can result "in the non-integration of the stigma into the self-state and its components" (p. 219).

The second stage, "stigma recognition," is the process by which individuals (a) acknowledge the fact that the various frustrations, conflicts and pressures they encounter are the direct result of the limitations placed upon them by their disability; and (b) begin to explore the implications this fact will have on their lives. The methods and strategies resulting from this process will begin to be more task-oriented.

> Since many instances of physical disability begin with convalescence in a medical setting, the process of stigma recognition usually begins with the development of strategies designed to reduce stress in the physical and independence-support components of the self-state. (DeLoach & Greer, 1981, p. 220)

Successful experiences in these components will motivate individuals to begin exploring strategy alternatives in the interpersonal, the creative-relaxation, and eventually the industrious self-state.

The transition to the third stage, "stigma incorporation," occurs, over variable periods of time, after individuals have recognized their stigmatized condition and have developed "a significant number of strategies for reducing stress associated with physical disablement" (DeLoach & Greer, 1981, p. 220). They begin to fully assess the implications of their conditions on their lifestyle and the different components of their self-states. The authors describe this stage as:

> The state in which the fact of an individual's stigmatized condition becomes an integral part of both the majority of the components of the self-state as well as the total self-state. After reaching this point, the frustrations, conflicts and pressures resulting from disability-related stress are minimized by task-oriented strategies. (p. 221)

They view this state to be similar to the state of "self-actualization." For most disabled persons it is an ultimate goal which, while never fully achieved, "can be achieved to varying degrees by the development of stress resolution strategies which are reality based" (p. 221).

The transition from one stage to the next is never easy or smooth and can only be accomplished over time. No matter how successful disabled persons may be in developing and using task-oriented strategies to reduce disability-related stress, there will always be occasions, as there are for non-disabled persons, when ego-defense mechanisms will be employed to maintain their achieved self-state. Therapeutic recreation and leisure education services can provide meaningful, challenging, and autonomy producing experiences for disabled persons as they move through these stages. In fact, failure to provide such services will negatively affect the level of adaptation achieved by the disabled person by virtue of the fact that opportunities for autonomous decision making and mutual interaction with the environment will be considerably reduced as will opportunities for establishing friendships, intimacy, and a sense of being a valued person.

Leisure Theory, Adaptation, and Rehabilitation

Therapeutic recreation is a specialized area of study and practice within the broader field of recreation and leisure studies. Recent theoretical perspectives on leisure, which have evolved from and are an amalgamation of theories and paradigms developed in the fields of sociology, psychology, social psychology, economics, and political science, provide a sound foundation or theoretical base for the specialization of therapeutic recreation.

Kelly (1987), in his excellent analysis and discussion of eight theoretical models or metaphors that have been applied to the study of leisure, argues that "Within each metaphor there is a 'dialectic' that drives the approach outside itself in an attempt to cope with questions that have been raised" (p. v). That is, though each metaphor focuses on one or more elements of leisure, none of them "is a self-contained dialectic of thesis-antithesis-synthesis; rather, each pushes us beyond itself into another metaphor" (p. v).

While Kelly (1987) does not define leisure, he identifies two dimensions that seem universal in various definitions of leisure. The first is some concept of freedom to choose activity that may have its own meaning and purpose. The second is that "Leisure is chosen with at least some central element of being done for its own sake rather than in response to some external demands" (p. 17). He states that play denotes leisure as activity or action which highlights the "elements of spontaneity and recognized boundaries that create a non-serious realm of meaning" (p. 17). He refers to recreation as "...leisure activity that is organized for the attainment of personal and social benefits" (p. 17).

Kelly (1987) contends that each of the eight theories he discusses (leisure as immediate experience, existential theory, developmental theory, identity theory, interaction theory, institutional theory, political theory, and humanist theory) "are not as mutually exclusive as might be presumed by their proponents and that each contains a negation that leads to other metaphors without invalidating its own value" (p. 15). Based on his critical analysis of the various theories and the most relevant and substantiated research which has tended to support one or the other of them, he offers a new perspective which he calls "social existentialism" which, he argues, provides the basis for a more cohesive or integrated understanding of leisure.

Because leisure is an aspect of human behavior in a social context, it is necessarily complex and changing. Kelly (1987) views leisure as a dialectic process with both:

> Existential and social dimensions--sometimes in conflict. Leisure is not either/or; decision or state of being, immediate experience or personal development, relaxed or intense, flow or creation, separate or engaged, problematic or structured. Leisure is act and an environment for action, of the culture and creating the 'not yet,' developmental and community-building. Sometimes one dimension is dominant in a particular decision or episode. (p. 235)

Since a dialectic cannot be reduced to an either/or, or a both/and model, the both/and connection is as inaccurate as the either/or.

> Leisure from a dialectic perspective, is not just an inclusive blob of elements. Rather, it is a process that may require struggle to assert the existential in the midst of social structure . . . a decisive act to extend intimacy in the midst of conflict or competition. . . . Often we seek to maintain some autonomy in a structured environment, some creativity amid rigid expectations, and some separation in a social world of overlapping roles and relationships. (Kelly, 1987, p. 236)

The central theme of Kelly's (1987) social existentialism is:

> The dialectic between action and structure, between self-determination and social forces . . . [in leisure] there is no state of freedom that is asocial and no social context that totally precludes existential decision. (pp. 237-238)

Social existentialism is a metaphor of synthesis which represents an overall interpretation of a dialectical spiral comprised of the eight previously cited theories. It provides a framework for the study of leisure and leisure behaviors incorporating various social, learning, and psychological theories and constructs and the meaning of leisure to the individual. "It is a framework for tying together elements of decision and determination, creation and form" (p. 238).

Kelly (1987) contends that:

> Leisure, as context or possibility . . . <u>is the freedom to be</u>. It is an environment for self-determining action, the possibility of situated freedom. . . . It is opportunity for creation, identity development or revision, and exploration and building of relationships <u>for their own sake</u>. As situated freedom, leisure is the <u>freedom to become</u>. It is a process, not a completed act or final product. . . . Leisure does not happen to us. We create leisure by acting in the realm of possibility. This action is directed toward the experience and what may occur in that experience. . . . As environment, leisure is the possibility of becoming. . . . As act, leisure is existential--taking action without having the outcome fixed. As learning, leisure is social--profoundly of the culture. As creation, leisure is free--when something new emerges in the process. (pp. 238-239)

Kelly's (1987) theory of social existentialism is quite congruent with White's (1985) discussion on adaptation, with the holistic view of human beings cited earlier, and with DeLoach and Greer's (1981) discussion on adaptation to disability. His concluding statement addresses the importance of incorporating therapeutic recreation and leisure education as integral aspects of rehabilitation services for disabled persons.

> In human life leisure does have a special place. However defined
> and supported by the culture, leisure is more than nonwork or
> leftover time. Leisure is more than freedom from requirement. It
> is freedom for being and becoming--for the self and society. (Kelly,
> p. 240)

Impact of Disability on the Individual

This section will briefly discuss the impact of physical disability on the individual. The form and severity of a disability affects the ways in which various impairments impact people's lives as will the individual's reaction to, ability to cope with, and adjustment to the impairment and disability. People who have experienced chronic illness, congenital or acquired impairments share some common experiences, but they may interpret them differently, based on their unique personality molded by the environment and life experiences.

Adjustment to disability may be defined as a normal reaction to an abnormal situation, and may include denial, depression, and reaction to dependence. The individual and family go through the process together (Trieschmann, 1988). With congenitally disabled children, the family's ability to adjust is especially important. According to Trieschmann:

> Overall . . . studies suggest that youth, financial security, warm
> loving backgrounds, transportation, having a high activity level,
> returning to social and vocational involvement, having a good self-
> concept derived from mastery of life, and interpersonal support are
> important variables in favor of good adjustment. (p. 249)

The resiliency of the person, however, may be adversely affected by a multiplicity of crises. Traumatically disabled individuals often face loss of friends, divorce, loss of work, and financial upheaval on the heels of the injury. People with degenerative diseases often face repeated medical crises and do not know when the next one will occur (Dew, Lynch, Ernst, & Rosenthal, 1983; Lyons, 1987; Stolov, 1981).

Stress

Throughout their lives disabled individuals encounter stress from more sources and more frequently than their non-disabled peers because they live with an able bodied world's yardstick for success regardless of the greater obstacles they encounter in their day-to-day lives (DeLoach & Greer, 1981; Trieschmann, 1987). DeLoach and Greer state that disability results in higher life stress for three major reasons: (a) frustration, (b) conflict, and (c) pressure. Lewis (1985) cites deprivation and boredom as causes of stress.

The acute stage of traumatic injury is especially stressful for the individual and family, and can result in serious medical setbacks. Stress causes exacerbations in multiple sclerosis and other degenerative conditions (Stolov, 1981). Individuals with spinal cord injury have more cardiovascular disease than the general population, according to Geisler et al. (cited in Trieschmann, 1988). Trieschmann (1987) cites the symptoms of fatigue, pain, sleep disturbances, and irritability reported by two aging disabled populations, post-polio and spinal cord injury, as indicators of life-long stress experienced by many disabled persons.

Social Isolation

Social isolation stems from three major sources: (a) stigma, (b) unemployment, and (c) illness/disability. Children learn at an early age to prefer playmates who are able bodied and disabled children and non-disabled children share this preference which lasts lifelong (Austin, 1987; Godbey, 1990; Trieschmann, 1988). Stigma attached to impairments and disability is historically grounded, society-wide, and very strong, resulting in a myriad of discriminatory acts, such as hiring practices, inaccessibility, and refusal to provide service (Austin; DeLoach & Greer, 1981; Disability Rag, 1989-1991). Public attitude (discrimination) has been recognized as the most difficult barrier to overcome (Austin).

Individuals who are congenitally disabled have fewer opportunities for play, are less socially active as they get older, and have overprotective parents; all limiting factors in socialization (Rinck et al., 1989; Zoerink, 1989). Some indicators of social isolation are: (a) 25% of spinal cord injured individuals live alone compared to the 11% national average (Dew et al., 1983); (b) 31% of spinal cord Georgians leave home less than once a week--many of them, not at all (Anson & Shepherd, 1990); and (c) disabled individuals report a lower marital rate (52% compared to 70%) and higher divorce rate than their non-disabled peers (Dew et al.). Social isolation is more pervasive for individuals with concomitant communication barriers, for example, persons with cerebral palsy, brain injury, strokes, or who are deaf. Although illness, fatigue, and other disability-related factors play a part in social isolation, the most frequently cited barriers are inaccessibility and lack of transportation (Anson & Shepherd; Coyle & Kinney, 1990; DeLoach & Greer, 1981; Krause & Crewe, 1987; Lyons, 1987).

Diminished Self-Concept

DeLoach and Greer (1981) divide the self-state into the following components, indicating that disability affects all five: (a) physical self, (b) independent support self (self-care), (c) interpersonal self, (d) industrious self, and (e) creative-relaxation self. Mayer and Eisenberg (1988) found that body esteem undergoes dramatic change with disabling conditions. Spinal cord injured men rated their most negative body parts to be fingers, legs, knees, sex organs, hands, and buttocks, while cardiac patients ranked heart, sex organs, chest, feet, and lungs as their most negative body parts.

The independent support self is diminished life-long for many congenitally disabled children by overprotective parents, resulting in learned helplessness (Rinck et al., 1989; Zoerink, 1988). For people with acquired disability, independence and self-control is compromised first by the loss of control over some or many body functions; then by the hospital and rehabilitation staff who often view efforts at self-determination as noncompliance (DeLoach & Greer, 1981; Tucker, 1980) or emphasize the negative aspects of disability rather than enabling the person to develop a constructive view of life with a disability (Wright, 1984); and finally by well-meaning families. For example, in 1974, Carpenter (DeLoach & Greer) found that wives of physically dependent males made all the important family decisions. In addition, society makes self-determination very difficult through limited opportunities and complex rules that control decisions of those receiving public assistance (Trieschmann, 1988). Living through such experiences often results in the disabled person having lowered expectations (Coyle & Kinney, 1990) and reduced quality of life (Lyons, 1987). The disability rights movement was initiated as a result of society's imposed limitations, to advocate for and assist individuals to be self-determining in a world where all the important decisions affecting disabled persons are made "for" them (Disability Rag, 1989-1991; Frieden, 1989).

The interpersonal self is affected dramatically, as was addressed under social isolation. People with visually apparent disabilities find that they often must help those around them to first cope with them as disabled people before they can relate on a more interpersonal basis (DeLoach & Greer, 1981; Frieden, 1989; Frieden & Cole, 1985; Trieschmann, 1988). Other factors affecting the interpersonal self are loss of friends and social role and changes in family dynamics (Vesluys, 1980).

The industrious self is especially affected by loss of work and somewhat by the loss of other community and family roles. Trieschmann (1988) cites the case of Jack for whom:

> . . . Not working has been a devastating experience for him. Life with a physical disability has been bad enough, but Jack's self-image as a man has been challenged by the fact that he could not earn enough to support his family. (p. 25)

Finally, the creative-relaxation self is challenged by disability. Congenitally disabled individuals rarely receive exposure to the wide variety of leisure choices available to them and rely heavily on television (Chorost, 1988; Maddy, 1988; Rinck et al., 1989). Individuals who experience disability later in life often find that their disability makes continued participation in past leisure interests impossible or too frustrating. Pain and fatigue make leisure interests less of a priority for those who may need it most (Decker & Shulz, 1985; Godin, Colantino, Davis, Shepherd, & Simard, 1986; Niemi, Laaksonen, Kotila, & Wattimo, 1988). Because of the loss of a work role, people find they have much more "leisure" time on their hands than they want and view it as a burden rather than an opportunity (Lyons, 1987).

Depression

There is disagreement in the literature concerning the incidence of depression in this population. High levels of depression seem to occur in people with degenerative diseases. This is compounded in some diagnostic groups for those who experience insults to the central nervous system, especially in multiple sclerosis (Lyons, 1987) and stroke (Stolov, 1981). In recent studies, depression, as defined in DSM-III-R, was diagnosed in 35% of the spinal cord injured population. In addition, a 5 to 7% increase in suicide rate over the general population and a 9% incidence of "passive" suicide--death by neglect--were also identified (Graitcer & Maynard, 1990).

Issues in Rehabilitation

The physical and social impacts of disability are multi-faceted, extensive, and unique to each person. Researchers have challenged the current level of professional support available to disabled persons. Some examples are cited below.

Physical versus psychosocial. The overemphasis on physical limitations is at the expense of adequate psychosocial support for persons who have congenital or acquired disabilities. Even rehabilitation centers featuring multi-disciplinary team approaches are "limited by a sickness treatment or medical model that focuses on giving units of treatment to the paralysis and loss of function" (Trieschmann, 1988, p. 297).

Institution-driven versus self-determined treatment. The services available inadequately prepare individuals for life on their own (DeLoach & Greer, 1981; Lyons, 1987; Trieschmann, 1988). Individual input, self-determination, opportunities for effective problem solving, and so forth, are frequently not part of the current service delivery system.

Short term versus lifelong service delivery. Services are available on a short term, acute basis, when in fact, problems and struggles are lifelong. Day-to-day issues such as social isolation, depression, social stigma, unemployment, and strained family relationships, are often dealt with alone, with little or no support, because community-based support does not exist (Frieden, 1989).

Physical functioning versus community reintegration. Reintegration into the community has long been a goal of rehabilitation, but there are few resources dedicated or programs designed to facilitate this process (Frieden, 1989; Graitcer & Maynard, 1990). "Unfortunately, rehabilitation centers have emphasized those tasks relating to physical functioning and have essentially ignored those tasks relating to social functioning" (Trieschmann, 1988, p. 157). Interestingly enough, both reduced medical complications and enhanced survival have been positively correlated to activity level and community life, with no connection to physical ability to function (Anson & Shepherd, 1990; Krause & Crewe, 1987).

Philosophy and outcome. The philosophy of rehabilitation must change from a short term, physically oriented process which emphasizes what a person cannot do and which views the disability as central and overriding everything else about the individual to a more holistic, lifelong process which emphasizes a person's strengths and abilities and views disability "as only one aspect of a multi-faceted life that includes gratifications as well as grievances, abilities as well as disabilities" (Wright, 1984, p. 100) (Boschen, 1981; DeLoach & Greer, 1981; Frieden, 1989; Graitcer & Maynard, 1990; Krause & Crewe, 1987, 1990).

Outcomes Sought Through Therapeutic Recreation

This section discusses the research and other documented as well as expected outcomes of therapeutic recreation, recreation participation, and leisure education in the rehabilitation of persons with physical disabilities. Various psychosocial outcomes are discussed first followed by physical and cognitive outcomes, community reintegration, quality of life, and adequate support systems.

Psychosocial Outcomes

The delivery of professional therapeutic recreation services to people with physical disabilities varies based on setting and diagnostic group. Generally speaking, the outcomes addressed in the psychosocial domain are to: (a) achieve a positive sense of self, (b) achieve community reintegration, (c) develop and maintain adequate personal and social support systems, and, (d) enhance the quality of life.

As previously cited, the self-state is seriously challenged by a physical disability. Therapeutic recreation facilitates a redefining of self by enabling individuals to: (a) develop a sense of mastery and self-discovery; (b) enhance self-efficacy and personal control; (c) achieve control over stress; (d) develop a view of self as productive, life as purposeful; (e) change attitudes toward disability; and (f) enhance body image perceptions.

Mastery, Self-Efficacy, and Self-Discovery

Bandura (1977a) emphasizes that "cognitive events are induced and altered most readily by experience of mastery arising from effective performance" (p. 191). Participation in intrinsically motivating leisure activities can be a powerful mechanism in increasing feelings of mastery, a phenomenon which has been well documented in the general population (Godbey, 1990; Ulrich, Dimberg, & Driver, 1990; Wankel & Berger, 1990).

Bandura's (1977a) self-efficacy theory stresses the need to increase the perceived difficulty of a situation so that feelings of mastery build. Part of therapeutic recreation practice is to build skills by continually challenging the individual once the level of skill is attained (Krause, 1983; Peterson & Gunn, 1984). Because leisure is self-motivating, the participant becomes invested in the process (Godbey, 1990; Sylvester, 1985).

Klein (1985) stresses the need for risk taking for overprotected disabled children and teens. Participating in "risk" recreation activities has been shown to be an effective tool for building self-confidence and self-efficacy. Stuckey and Barkus (1986) found an increase in self-efficacy and self-confidence in visually impaired Boy Scouts after a 215 mile hiking trip through rugged terrain. Several authors have reported increased self-concept and self-efficacy after camping experiences (Austin, 1987; Robb & Evert, 1987).

Sports participation is a well-documented method of increasing self-efficacy (Curtis, McClanahan, Hall, Dillon, & Brown, 1986; Greenwood, Dzewattowski, & French, 1990; Hedrick, 1985; Jackson & Davis, 1983; LeVeau, 1985; Sherrill, Pope, & Arnhold, 1986; Stewart, 1981). Mastery in martial arts has been shown to be effective in building self-efficacy in quadriplegic men, as discussed by Pandavela and associates in 1986 (Trieschmann, 1988), and in visually impaired boys (Glesser & Brown, 1986).

Jackson and Davis (1983) and Sherrill and Rainbolt (1988) both found that disabled male athletes experienced a greater increase in self-concept, self-acceptance, and self-actualization than did non-disabled athletes. Greenwood et al., (1990) and Hedrick (1985) concluded that self-efficacy in tennis skills generalizes to increased self-efficacy in wheelchair mobility and other physical skills. Hedrick, however, found that developing mastery in tennis is more effective in a segregated environment until equity with non-disabled athletes is achieved at which point integration is appropriate. Trader, Nicholson, and Anson (1991) found that participants in a camping experience during spinal cord injured rehabilitation were more likely to pursue outdoor activities after discharge than those who did not participate.

Through clinical experience, Trader, one of the authors of this paper, has found that any recreation experience carefully aimed at enhancing perceived mastery has a powerful effect on hope for the future. Over the last 10 years, the most common comment made around the campfire by acute (within the first 3 months) spinal cord injured campers is "If I can do this, I can handle most anything." Indeed, that is close to the motto of National Handicapped Sports (NHS).

Participation in various art forms can also enhance self-discovery, self-efficacy, and mastery. Kennedy, Smith, and Austin (1991) note that:

> Creativity, which is the cornerstone of arts participation, requires that an individual get in touch with his or her own feelings and perceptions. Participation in the arts, therefore, may enable a person to become more aware of his or her own individuality. (p. 208)

In 1987, Jean Kennedy Smith (cited in Kennedy et al., 1991), in testifying before a Senate sub-committee, stated that participation in the arts helped to meet the personal and developmental needs of disabled persons "because they emphasize process over productivity, divergence rather than convergence, creative choice more than conformity. . . ." (p. 210). Based on her own experience, Baer (1985), a quadriplegic, concluded that art experience "represents a valuable coping tool for human beings, particularly those living with debilitating and irreversible physical conditions" (p. 213).

Stensrude, Mishkin, Craft, and Pollock (1987) conducted a pilot program using drama techniques with traumatic head injury patients to increase self-awareness, communication skills (verbal and non-verbal), self-expression, motor skill, and cognition. Results of the program, which focused on exercises that were "real world" situations, showed that "growth in clients social-communication skills and self confidence was demonstrated as measured by behavioral observation and video assessment" (p. 69). The authors concluded that the drama techniques refined during the pilot program could serve as a model for other cognitive rehabilitation programs.

Self-Control

There are two factors concerning control: (a) to what extent has perceived control been threatened by illness or disability, and (b) is the individual's locus of control or attributional style internal or external? An internal locus of control is a key factor in successful rehabilitation (Frye, 1986) as well as in coping with stressful events (Frank et al., 1987). Krause and Crewe (1990) found that traumatically injured individuals do not believe it is possible to have control again, and it is important that professionals find alternative ways for them to achieve a sense of control. Iso-Ahola (1980) argues that "the main goal of the [recreation] therapist is to increase the patients' perceived control and mastery over the environment and to prevent them from inferring helplessness" (p. 233). Helplessness is not a result of inherited traits, it is learned through environmental encounters. If patients believe they are helpless or powerless:

Motivation to reach goals or to succeed is greatly minimalized . . .
of course, some events are uncontrollable by the individual.
Therefore, it is helpful for the patient to be able to discriminate
between events that can be controlled and those that cannot.
(Howe-Murphy & Charboneau, 1987, pp. 225-226)

Therapeutic recreation is an effective tool in facilitating a restored sense of personal control. For example, using leisure experience in services delivery enables the individual to have the freedom to choose--to exercise some control.

In a highly structured and prescriptive hospital environment, this is especially important. Ellis and Niles (1985), Mobily (1985), and Sylvester (1985) all stress the importance and therapeutic benefits of making leisure choices.

Achieving a sense of control over life despite a disabling condition, is an important outcome. Mayer and Andrews (1981) found that if a disability is viewed as a barrier to achieving past goals, the individual views life negatively. In a study involving 258 spinal cord subjects, Anson and Shepherd (1990) found that physical disability was the most often stated barrier to leisure activity participation, possibly indicating a lack of perceived personal control over the physical state.

Therapeutic recreation helps to enhance patients' sense of control and their ability to discriminate between events that can and those that cannot be controlled by facilitating effective problem solving skills; exposing individuals to the many possibilities for leisure involvement; developing activity skills; and enabling the person to make choices through effective decision making and enhanced self-awareness. These are all elements of leisure education. A sense of personal control is enhanced by first choosing to do an activity and then experiencing mastery in that activity (Austin & Crawford, 1990; Krause, 1983; Mundy & Odom, 1979; Peterson & Gunn, 1984).

Control Over Stress

The level of stress an individual experiences is often determined by the perception of the situation, rather than the situation itself, and the capability of the person to cope (Girdano & Everly, 1979; Mikhail, 1985). Helping the disabled individual to develop strategies and techniques for stress management is an important outcome of therapeutic recreation services. Control over stress can be facilitated through cognitively restructuring the interpretation of stressful events, diverting attention away from distressing events, and acquiring relaxation techniques to lessen somatic responses to stress (Girdano & Everly; Mandrel & Keller, 1986).

Cognitively restructuring the interpretation of stressful events can be managed through utilization of problem solving techniques and alternative forms of expression. Journal writing is reported to be an effective way to channel anger and frustration and ultimately to reframe the meaning of events (Baer, 1985; Lewis, 1985). Involvement in other forms of creative expression such as drama, music, drawing, and painting, enables individuals to express reactions to events in ways they find meaningful and non-threatening and facilitate restructuring once the feelings are expressed. Role playing can also be effectively used to achieve the same ends. Although anecdotal reports of the positive effects of participation in such activities on stress reduction are found in the literature, no reports of research efforts to support them were located.

Diverting attention away from distress is viewed as an effective stress management tool. Mobily (1985) believes that recreation experiences can divert attention away from disability and help to reduce stress and anxiety. This concept is supported by the results of a study of spinal cord injured veterans which included the finding that the study participants cited an increase in recreational activities for diversion as one of their top choices in improving the total rehabilitation program (Dew et al., 1983). Of the 26 techniques Lewis (1985) describes as useful in dealing with the stress of chronic illness, 21 are leisure experiences; the others are prescriptive relaxation techniques. Temporary escape through such mental activity as meditation, daydreaming about a favorite recreation area, gazing out a window at a pleasant view, or actually traveling to a recreation site or area, is seen as a viable stress coping mechanism provided during leisure (Ulrich et al., 1990).

Ulrich et al. (1990) reported that:

There has been considerable research on the perceived therapeutic benefits of leisure activities in helping people cope with various stresses through temporary escape. . . . This research consistently suggests that various stress mediation/temporary escape consequences have comparatively high importance to recreationists. (pp. 159-160)

In one study conducted by Ulrich he found that "hospital patients recovering from surgery had more favorable post-operative courses if their windows overlooked trees rather than a brick wall" (p. 161). The indicators included shorter length of stay, lower intake of strong pain relief drugs, and more favorable ratings by nurses.

Seeking relief from stress in the natural environment is a pattern that is common for children and adults. Although the effects of the natural environment on stress may not be well understood, Ulrich et al. (1990) posit that:

Leisure experiences in natural environments probably reduce stress through a combination of mechanisms including achieving control through active coping or escape, through physical exercise, and therapeutic effects of exposure to natural content which might have both learned and biological origins. (p. 159)

Relaxation techniques, such as progressive muscle relaxation training and guided imagery have been used by psychologists with chemotherapy and multiple sclerosis patients (Carey & Burish, 1987; Foley, Bedell, LaRocca, Scheinberg et al., 1987) resulting in reduced pulse rate, respiration, anxiety, and other signs of distress. Health care professionals, including therapeutic recreation specialists, utilize deep breathing, creative visualization, and other techniques to reduce somatic response to stress. The long term compliance by individuals after treatment ends has not been studied.

Productive/Purposeful Sense of Self

Given a population in which 66% of the adults are unemployed, it makes sense to facilitate a sense of productivity through alternate means. Trieschmann (1984) advocated that:

> It is appropriate to consider employment to be just one type of productive effort which may or may not be relevant in an individual case...let us expand our focus to help the person to become productive in other areas. (p. 348)

She suggested education, family role, community service, avocations, scholarly pursuits, and artistic endeavors as options.

Many authors have addressed the use of leisure activities to stimulate a productive sense of self. Godbey (1990) writes, "it is their [people with physical disabilities] ability to use leisure in satisfying and appropriate ways which determines their fate as surely as their ability to do useful work" (p. 213). Parker's (cited in Godbey) view is:

> Work may lose its present characteristic feeling of constraint and gain the creativity now associated mainly with leisure, while leisure may lose in opposition to work and gain the status--now associated mainly with the product of work--of a resource worthy of planning to provide the greatest possible human satisfaction. (p. 96)

Lewis (1985) wrote:

> My avocational loves of singing, church involvements, outdoor activities, and athletics came as equally difficult areas to give up. In some ways, these avocations had greater meaning than my primary job because they were interests I had pursued and been involved with since childhood. (p. 48)

The success of using productive leisure as a replacement for work has not been measured, though anecdotal indicators abound. Many disabled adults have become community activists or have successfully run for public office. Those who became proficient at their interest of choice often turn it into an income source, and sometimes full-time employment. Crafters, actors, artists, cartoonists, gardeners, writers, musicians, poets, and taxidermists are all examples of people with disabilities who turned a leisure interest into a career. Shutlz (1985) reported that disabled men gained purpose in life through helping others and through sports.

In order to effectively channel their clients efforts, therapeutic recreation specialists need to be made aware of the clients' need to be productive and purposeful through an appropriate assessment process. Then, leisure activities can be selected, and skills developed which provide a satisfying replacement for work (Godbey, 1990).

Attitude Toward Disability

People who have physical disabilities are products of the society as a whole, and tend to embody the same attitudes and values. Brown (1988) found that wheelchair users view differences in lifestyle along stereotypical lines twice as often as their non-disabled peers. She concluded that "these results correspond with previous findings that perception of behavioral consequences of impairment are largely negative and that people with disabilities perceive more negative differences than do able-bodied" (p. 181). Trieschmann (1988) noted that self-concept post-disability is secondary to the way an individual viewed disability prior to injury. Trader, Ruzicka, and Nicholson (1991) found that, within 1 year following spinal cord injury, the majority of subjects viewed their physical disability as a significant barrier to leisure participation.

Therapeutic recreation specialists can promote change in this attitude through many of the techniques addressed earlier, especially those related to self-efficacy and productivity. For example, McAvoy, Schatz, Stutz, Schlein, and Lais (1989) found that, following an integrated wilderness adventure trip, attitudes toward disability improved in both disabled and non-disabled groups, but the change was more dramatic in the disabled group.

Body Image

The change in body image after disability has been noted. Ameliorating body image problems is effectively accomplished through sports participation. In 1979, Ross and Zoccopotti (cited in Stewart, 1981) found that disabled athletes have a better body perception than disabled non-athletes. Hopper (1988) found that hearing impaired children who felt good about their athletic ability also liked the way they looked. Other examples of positive body image changes are anecdotal and diverse: (a) getting a new wheelchair, and (b) losing weight affect body image. Congenitally disabled children and teens report an improvement in body image when allowed to choose their own clothes and hairstyles.

Silva and Klatsky (1984) addressed positive body image changes in non-disabled individuals. Their findings indicated that it was a slow process, requiring commitment from the individual, and an attitude change as well as physical change. Mastery played a key role in changing body image as well as selection of activities with built-in rewards.

Physical Outcomes

Psychoneuroimmunologists are studying the interactions among the nervous, endocrine, and immune systems and behavior. New information is emerging on the ways emotions, experiences, and attitudes effect biological change. Of particular interest to recreation therapists are the investigations into the physiological effects of humor. Dillon, Minchoff, and Baker (1985) observed that salivary immunoglobulin A concentrations increased in subjects following their viewing humorous videos. Individuals who reported that they used humor in coping with stress exhibited the highest initial levels of immunoglobulin. Berk et al. (1988) studied stress hormones in subjects, before and after they viewed humorous videos. Post-humor subjects demonstrated an increase in immune cell proliferation and marked decrease in cortisol, an immune suppressor. Lefcourt, Davidson-Katz, and Kueneman (1990) also conducted studies that yielded findings suggesting that immune-system activity increases with humor.

The potency of these results are yet to be determined (Jemmott & McClelland, 1989), but the implications loom large for therapeutic recreation services to clients fighting infectious agents; services to burn patients, for example, as well as to other patients at risk for secondary infections. Related studies suggesting relationships between anger and stress to cancer and cardiac disease also identify behaviors that therapeutic recreation attempts to modify.

Research in this area is still embryonic in development. Studies of the physiological effects of other positive emotions such as feelings of mastery, hopefulness, and self-determination or of other states facilitated by therapeutic recreation interventions were not found in the literature, thus empirical evidence is not available.

Another link between therapeutic recreation and recovery is the application of therapeutic recreation to mobilizing the patient's will to survive and to actively participate in rehabilitation efforts. By demonstrating to patients that they will be able to continue former leisure activity participation with friends or family or master new leisure challenges, therapeutic recreation specialists contend that the patient's determination to succeed can be awakened or rekindled (James, 1991). Empirical studies are also needed in this area.

Therapeutic recreation has also been enlisted to help people cope with pain. Perry, Heindrich, and Ramos (1981) concluded from their research studies that neural pathways that transmit pain merge with nerves carrying other messages. As these pathways combine, they concluded, impulses from one source can interfere with impulses from another. One of the intended outcomes of therapeutic recreation is to provide these diversional stimuli to help patients counter pain.

Benefits of Exercise

The outcomes attributed to exercise via selected recreation activities form a large category of proposed therapeutic recreation benefits. Included in these outcomes are contributions to growth and development, muscular strength, cardiovascular fitness, vital capacity, flexibility, and balance. Activities are also employed to inhibit the development of contractures, to counter obesity, and to prevent osteoporosis. Although recognizing that activities usually relinquish the specificity of prescribed exercise, physical recreation activities often lend a source of motivation not afforded by routine calisthenics. Thus, therapeutic recreation has been offered as a valuable supplement to physical therapy. Not only have patients been engaged in physical activities on the theory that enjoyable or functional activity motivates exercise but also to create a means by which patients can experience the results of their efforts to regain function. Application of new or regained abilities gives meaning to exercise and other treatment measures (MacNeil & Pringznitz, 1982).

Persons with certain disabilities have a higher than average incidence of cardiovascular disease, obesity, and osteoporosis. Cardiovascular disorders are now the leading cause of death among persons with spinal cord injuries (Hoffman, 1986). Participation in physical activity and exercise is known to be efficacious in reducing the incidence of these secondary disabilities.

Other Physical Outcomes

In addition to the above outcomes, which are fairly general throughout therapeutic recreation practice, there are others that are specific to work with particular disability groups. When working with burn patients, for example, the recreation therapist may be enlisted to incorporate activities to encourage the patient to eat. Therapeutic recreation specialists assist persons with diabetes to develop consistent activity programs supportive of optimum management of the disorder (Pederson, 1980). The outcomes sought are determined by assessments of clients and the resources of therapeutic recreation (Carter, Van Ander, & Robb, 1985). Most of the outcomes are specific applications of the goals of a general nature discussed above.

Research Relating to Physical Outcomes

The preponderance of research on the physical effects of recreation participation for persons with disabilities has been done with athletes, primarily wheelchair athletes. Organized wheelchair sports have existed for more than 45 years and today involve more than 4,000 athletes in competitive events (Stotts, 1986). In an attempt to discern whether athletes incur fewer medical complications secondary to spinal cord injury, Stotts surveyed 42 paraplegics with traumatic injuries. Half of the subjects were athletes who had participated in regional or national competition and half were not. The study, which controlled for age, gender, education, and duration of injury, found that hospital readmissions occurred three times more frequently among the non-athletes compared to the athletes. Significant differences were found in the frequency of reported decubiti and urinary tract complications. The non-athletes had more of both and only non-athletes were readmitted for treatment of decubiti.

As wheelchair sports have become more extensive, training has become more sophisticated. Exercise physiologists and sports medicine professionals have been enlisted to focus their research tools on wheelchair athletes. In developing training programs, researchers have examined the fitness status, cardiorespiratory capacity, and response to endurance training programs in the spinal cord injured population (Dal-Monte, Faina, Maglio, Sardella, & Guide, 1982; Davis, Shephard, & Jackson, 1981; Davis, Shephard, & Ward, 1984; DePauw, 1986; Figoni, Boileau, Massey & Larsen, 1988; Hoffman, 1986; Jocheim & Strohkendle, 1973; Koch, Schlegel, Pirrwitz, Jaschke, & Schlegel, 1983; Miles, Sawka, Wilde, Durbin, & Gotshall, 1982; Van Loan, McCluer, Loftin, & Boileau, 1987; Zwiren, Huberman, & Bar-Or, 1973). Positive results have been found in relation to strength, endurance, and cardiorespiratory fitness. In addition, training guidelines, assessment techniques, and equipment have been developed to assist athletes with spinal cord injuries. To a far lesser extent, similar studies have been conducted with athletes with other disabilities (Florence, 1984; Hanna, 1986).

Other than in wheelchair sports, there is little activity-specific research. Brock (1988) studied physically disabled adults before and after participation in a horseback riding program. The results reflected increased coordination among riders at the close of the eight-week program. Berger, Friedman, and Eaton (1988) found that subjects relaxed equally well from jogging as they did from directed experiences in relaxation techniques.

The activity research appears to be strongly polarized. On one end of an active-sedentary continuum, the focus is heavily on wheelchair racers. At the opposite, sedentary pole, several physicians have given serious attention to the physical effects of laughter, Fry and Rader (1977) measured increased respiratory effects and blood oxygenation during laughter. Fry and Savin (1988) also tracked blood pressure fluctuations during laughter, which they likened to "internal jogging." As referred to earlier, several investigators have associated laughter and humor with positive changes in the immune system (Berk et al., 1988; Dillon et al., 1985; Jemmott & Magloire, 1988; Lefcourt et al., 1990; Martin & Dobbin, 1988).

A few studies have suggested ties between emotional-social well-being and physical health. Gordon (1982) noted a high correlation among clients with spinal cord injuries who developed decubiti and those demonstrating poor psychosocial adjustment. Weinberger, Tierney, Booher, & Hiner (1990) observed improved functional status among clients with arthritis who were engaged in a program of social activity. Relaxation training has been associated with pain reduction in several studies (Shaw & Ehrlich, 1987; Stuckey, Jacobs, & Goldfarb, 1986).

The Canadian government has assembled a data bank of health and leisure information on an extensive nationwide sample of citizens with disabilities. The survey found that respondents ranked physical activity fairly low among a listing of health-supporting behaviors. Only 40% of the national sample regarded a physically active lifestyle as an important health behavior (Ferris, 1990).

Cognitive Outcomes

In physical medicine and rehabilitation, therapeutic recreation targets cognitive objectives most frequently when working with patients who have brain injuries or cerebral vascular accidents. The theoretical framework for cognitive rehabilitation includes concepts from (a) behavioral (Bandura, 1977b; Skinner, 1969); (b) structural-organismic (Flavell, 1977; Piaget, 1983); and (c) information processing (Dodd & White, 1980) models.

During early stages of recovery, therapeutic recreation has the capacity to engage patients in interesting but simplified activities that place few functional demands upon them. Focusing heavily on the processes of attention and perception, therapeutic recreation may seek outcomes of increased attention span, better control and selectivity of attention, increased recognition of objects and events, and improved facility with figure-ground discrimination. As attention and perception processes improve, therapeutic recreation can focus on developing the processes of memory and learning, organizing, reasoning, and problem solving and judgement (Dodd & White, 1980). Therapeutic recreation may draw upon myriad experiential interventions to apply in cognitive retraining (MacNeil & Pringnitz, 1982; Rouse, 1983; Stumbo & Bloom, 1990). Fazio and Fralish (1988) found that therapeutic recreation services were offered in 88% of the post-acute brain injury rehabilitation agencies that responded to their survey. Cognitive skills ranked high among the goals to which recreation therapists directed their interventions.

Few empirical studies were found on therapeutic recreation and cognitive outcomes. An area of investigation that has recently emerged focuses on the cognitive effects of physical exercise. Studies of clients with extensive mobility impairments found signs of increased mental alertness and cognitive activity following exercise and subsequent increased oxygen diffusion (Krebs, Eickelberg, Krobath, & Barch, 1989).

Community Reintegration

As previously stated, there are many indicators that community reintegration is difficult to achieve for people who have physical disabilities. These include social isolation, high unemployment, existence of barriers (lack of access, transportation, financial resources, etc.), difficulty with social skills, and social stigma.

Therapeutic recreation specialists are able to facilitate community reintegration by providing services that: (a) ameliorate/prevent social isolation, (b) develop/maintain social skills, (c) develop stigma integration skills, (d) develop architectural barrier management skills, and (e) develop/maintain a community resource base.

Ameliorate/Prevent Social Isolation

Some physically disabled people will be socially isolated or will go through periods of social isolation because of their disability or disease. Hospitalization and extended bed rest in the home, hospital, or convalescent center, are examples of situations that cause isolation. Therapeutic recreation has a long history of effective work with hospitalized people. Through provision of bedside activities, social activities, and a variety of materials and experiences which enable individuals to continue doing what interests them, they are less likely to become withdrawn.

The goals of homebound therapeutic recreation intervention are either to eliminate as many as of the barriers to successful community reintegration, or to help the individual best cope with the realities of some isolation. A pilot transition program for recently discharged rehabilitation patients, utilizing therapeutic recreation specialists, in North Carolina has been effective at increasing participation in community life (Bullock & Howe, 1991). The authors report that "From the clients' personal perspective, preliminary findings corroborated social role valorization theory and the use of leisure education as a transitional TRS" (p. 16). The Multiple Sclerosis Society has funded a project aimed at one-on-one therapeutic recreation services in the home. The results of this project are unknown.

Integrated and segregated recreation experiences have the potential to enhance social interaction, and the desire for it. Weiss and Jamieson (1988) found that a therapeutic water exercise program for adults with hidden disabilities (high blood pressure, post-surgery, orthopedic injury, etc.) resulted in a 25% increase in social contacts outside the program. In a group of non-disabled, unemployed adults, Jones (1988) found a high incidence of social isolation that increased over time. He recommended involving them in the "type of programs that foster participation and maintain social contacts, [including] job banks, recreational hobbies, social action, and task-oriented groups. . . ." (p. 173).

The disabled sports movement began with community integration as a main goal according to Guttmann in 1976 (cited in Trieschmann, 1988). Stein (1985) states that although sports opportunities exist for all disability groups, they are hard to find in schools where sports for non-disabled students are a main part of the social fabric. In school systems that do sponsor athletics for disabled students, the participants are perceived by parents and teachers as having significantly enhanced social status and integration, even though sports events are segregated. Stewart (1981) claims that congenitally disabled teens benefit from sports participation by enhanced socialization and Bernhardt (1985) is of the opinion that sports can be especially important to youngsters with limited social opportunity.

Brasile (1990) and Jackson and Davis (1983) indicate that integrated sports opportunities are optimal tools for social integration because the focus is on the athlete, not the disability. Brasile also found that more severely disabled athletes place more importance on the socialization values of sports than do less disabled athletes. Datillo and Guadagnolo (1988) found that disabled and non-disabled athletes have virtually the same preferences in road race attributes, indicating that integration is certainly an option.

Sports may produce additional gains by educating the public at large. Jackson and Davis (1983) state that great sports performances change perceptions. The media have progressively shifted emphasis from a human interest angle focusing on disability to a sports emphasis, focusing on the athlete. The result could feasibly be a shift in public awareness to the similarities of disabled and non-disabled people; at least in elite athletes.

Integrated sports opportunities are increasing. The Little League has recently formed a Challenger Division so youngsters with disabilities can play on integrated teams. Elite disabled athletes may compete in full-medal sports in the 2000 Olympic Games; most likely basketball, swimming, and track and field. It will be interesting to note the impact that kind of exposure and recognition will have on the efforts toward integration for the disabled population as a whole.

Develop/Maintain Social Skills

Socialization patterns of people who have disabilities are affected by the disability, as shown earlier. Children with congenital disabilities need play and recreation experiences to enhance developmentally appropriate social skills. "The modality of recreation and leisure programming has often been the key to the symbolic birth of social skills in handicapped youth" (Chorost, 1988, p. 177). Austin (1987) and Bodzioch, Roach, & Schkade (1985) both report increases in social skills for disabled campers, several with spinal bifida. Two multi-disciplinary programs with a strong emphasis on therapeutic recreation, have both reported increases in social skills in their clients with spina bifida (Leverette, 1990; Maddy, 1988).

Acquired disability also disrupts social functioning. Romano, in 1976, (cited in Trieschmann, 1988) found that patients who participate in social skills training during rehabilitation report they are able to re-enter social situations more readily and with less anxiety than individuals who received no training. Socialization skills were increased in a group of visually impaired scouts after an integrated wilderness experience (Stuckey & Barkus, 1986). McAvoy et al. (1989) found that socialization behavior increased in disabled and non-disabled wilderness program participants in an integrated experience.

Social skills training is most important for physically disabled individuals with concomitant cognitive disabilities (traumatic brain injury, some stroke, cerebral palsy, spina bifida, multiple sclerosis). Social contact is just as important to well-being, but is made more difficult by the added disability.

Although some empirical evidence exists that social skills training works, models are varied, and so far, unproven. Savell (1986) and Sneegas (1989) both suggest models for consideration. Models also exist outside the field of therapeutic recreation. It is safe to assume that recreation participation provides an opportunity for socialization, but it is not known which kinds of social situations stimulate what kinds of social learning, especially over the long term.

Social Stigma

Learning social skills is an important task for disabled people in order to overcome existing social stigma. Trieschmann (1988), Dew et al. (1985), and DeLoach and Greer (1981) note that it is the disabled person's job to put the able-bodied world at ease. Understanding that stigma is a reality, recognizing it in all its different forms and knowing how to deal with it instead of internalizing it in the form of reduced self-concept, are all tasks that should be accomplished in a supportive environment.

Dealing with these society-wide attitudinal barriers can best be managed, initially, through community outings. Again, the experiences should be numerous to generalize learning, and increasingly more challenging to allow the individual to develop mastery in stigma management (Bandura, 1977a; Savell, 1986). Processing or debriefing each outing experience and giving individuals feedback on their developing skills are techniques used by therapeutic recreation specialists to build stigma management skills.

The highest form of stigma management is self-advocacy. This skill is carefully developed over time, and requires a healthy self-concept, good communication skills, a sense of personal control, and an awareness of social stigma and the resulting impact on individual rights. This is a realistic outcome which can be facilitated by therapeutic recreation intervention.

Architectural Barrier Management Skills

For individuals with mobility impairments, dealing with the outside world can be difficult. Despite P. L. 504 legislation, and the Americans with Disabilities Act of 1990 (1990), there continue to be many barriers to overcome. These include, but are not limited to stairs, curbs, parking, bathrooms, aisles, seating arrangements, table heights, ticketing policies, rough terrain, and public transportation. People with disabling conditions often indicate that inaccessibility is one of the major barriers to full community participation (Anson & Shepherd, 1990; Austin, 1987; Coyle & Kinney, 1990; Farbman & Ellis, 1987; Graitcer & Maynard, 1990; Yerra & Locker, 1990).

Individuals with newly acquired disabilities are taught specific techniques for managing barriers by other disciplines in the rehabilitation center. Generalizing these techniques learned in a laboratory setting is difficult because of the lack of exposure to real world barriers. The real learning takes place during community outings, most often under the leadership of therapeutic recreation. Bandura's (1977a) self-efficacy theory stresses the importance of multiple exposures with increased challenge to develop mastery. It follows, then, that barrier management skills are best taught through repeated community exposures that become more difficult over time. Community outings planned by therapeutic recreation specialists are based in leisure activity, which is intrinsically motivating, so learning is more effective. The desired outcome of a community outing program is that existing barriers no longer limit community life. Ideally, individuals acquire effective problem-solving skills, learned through experience and modeling, and develop self-advocacy skills enabling them to bring about change in barriers that exist. Of 200 spinal cord injured adults who participated in a community outing program, 98% reported that the experience gained enabled them to go out more often once they returned home (Glass, Albright, Burns, Evans, & Apple, 1984).

Community Resources

In order to live an active community-based life, individuals must have resources they can use. A number of authors indicate that given appropriate resources, many citizens with physical disabilities are as involved as non-disabled citizens (Brown, 1988; Frieden, 1989; Siosteen, Lundquist, Blomstrand, Sullivan, & Sullivan, 1990).

There is evidence that resources are not readily available to most physically disabled persons. Decker and Shulz (1985) found that 85% of their sample never used a community resource. Coyle and Kinney (1990) found that as dependency increases, awareness of leisure resources decreases. As stated before, many studies list architectural barriers as a limiting factor in community involvement, leisure satisfaction, or both.

One form of convoluted logic, often expressed by community service providers is illustrated by Oestreicher (1990). "I've been in recreation for X number of years and I have never seen disabled people using the park" (p. 53). The words recreation and park could be replaced by community facility and service.

Therapeutic recreation professionals facilitate resource use most effectively through leisure education, and actual exposure to community resources. Referrals to appropriate services is an essential step in the discharge planning process. Architectural barrier and stigma management skills, discussed earlier, are also important.

Quality of Life

As people adjust to disability, they often begin to question if they will experience an acceptable quality of life. The many barriers to achieving this outcome have been addressed. Through therapeutic recreation intervention, quality of life can be enhanced by: (a) meaningful use of discretionary time, (b) developing/maintaining a satisfying activity level, (c) enhancing psychological well-being, and (d) enhancing health and wellness.

Meaningful Use of Discretionary Time

People with physical disabilities often experience an increase in discretionary time, and a concurrent lack of physical ability to pursue what interests them. Dew et al. (1983) found a drop in participation in land based sports, aquatic sports, bar hopping, and gardening after spinal cord injury. Coyle and Kinney (1990) reported that 85% of all recreation activities pursued by their sample were in isolation from others (e.g., reading and TV). Niemi et al. (1988) found that deterioration in leisure activities was the foremost problem following stroke as reported by 80% of the study population.

In the general population, leisure satisfaction is linked to life satisfaction in many studies--sometimes rating higher than work satisfaction (Godbey, 1990). Several authors have noted a problem with leisure satisfaction among physically disabled groups they have studied (Anson & Shepherd, 1990; Coyle & Kinney, 1990; Lyons, 1987). Barriers to leisure participation include lack of physical ability, lack of money, lack of transportation, lack of accessible resources, and lack of knowledge, among others (Anson & Shepherd).

The general population has turned to television as a major leisure resource. Americans spend more than one-third of their free time watching TV-- more than radio, movies, visiting, gardening, or sleeping. As unemployment increases, TV watching jumps dramatically (Godbey, 1990). Tucker (1987) found that among non-disabled teens there were many differences between light TV watchers (less than 2 hours per day) and heavy TV watchers (more than 4 hours per day). Light watchers were more physically fit, emotionally stable, sensitive, imaginative, outgoing, physically active, self-controlled, and self-confident than heavy viewers. They were also less troubled, less frustrated, and less likely to be alcohol and drug abusers.

TV watching is a major activity among disabled individuals (Anson & Shepherd, 1990; Yerra & Locker, 1990). Along with generalizations that can be made from the Tucker (1987) study, disabled individuals who are heavy viewers report more social isolation, more medical complications, and less leisure satisfaction than light viewers (Anson & Shepherd). Without therapeutic recreation intervention, TV viewing is an easy option to fall back on because it is so accessible.

It would follow, then, that related to the quality of life of disabled people, perhaps the most pressing role for therapeutic recreation is the elimination of barriers to participation in satisfying leisure activities. This includes enabling the disabled person to develop an attitude that the physical disability is not an insurmountable barrier, as indicated earlier, and providing an extensive leisure education program aimed at reducing or eliminating transportation, access, and financial barriers. Finally, individuals need to know the array of activities available to them and, when possible, try them out in a supportive atmosphere to develop some level of mastery. The final outcome would be several satisfying leisure activities which the individual can pursue without professional support.

A short rehabilitation program usually cannot accommodate a comprehensive leisure education program because it is a lengthy process. Coyle and Kinney (1990) indicate a need for after care in this respect. The major frustration is that most people with physical disabilities have limited or no access to recreation resources in their home communities. Austin (1987) addresses the dearth of services to this population from the parks and recreation profession, citing poor attitudes on the part of recreation practitioners as the cause. The pilot program in North Carolina, cited earlier, is showing some real promise in meeting long-term leisure needs of physically disabled people (Bullock & Howe, 1991). Utilizing therapeutic recreation specialists trained in community intervention, the program is designed to systematically remove barriers to leisure functioning with the end goal being satisfying leisure participation. The program participants report an increase in quality of life because of this professional intervention. The results of the pilot program have been so valued by ILCs throughout the state that they have, to date, hired 16 transitional therapeutic recreation specialists as full time staff (Bullock, 1991).

Many specific leisure activities have been linked to increased life satisfaction in people with physical disabilities. Curtis et al. (1986) found this to be the case with athletes involved in wheelchair sports. Baer (1985) lists authors who attribute enhanced quality of life to creative acts. Most leisure theorists believe it is not the activity that is important, but the meaning the individual derives from it that matters (Godbey, 1990).

Activity Level

Krause and Crewe (1987) found that the most significant contributor to survival after spinal cord injury was activity level. They did not find a difference in life satisfaction between survivors and those who did not recover.

> Perhaps persons in the deceased group had come to accept a less active life-style with a lower quality of life. It follows, then, that activity level per se, rather than a mediating emotional state, enhances survival following spinal cord injury. (p. 212)

Anson and Shepherd (1990) found that spinal cord injured individuals who leave home less often, and watch more TV, have increased medical problems compared to those who are more active.

Lahtinen (1989) found that disabled people in Finland are less active than their non-disabled peers. The disabled respondents in the study attended entertainment and cultural events less frequently, and 90% stated that their physical disability limited sports participation. Heinemann, Goranson, Ginburg, and Schnoll (1989) found that hospitalized individuals who spent their time in quiet recreation (TV, reading, smoking, drinking) were much more likely to be substance abusers after discharge. Kennedy and Smith (1990) found that individuals involved in rehabilitation for spinal cord injury, although more active than their non-disabled peers prior to injury, expected to be much less active in their future leisure pursuits. Yerra and Locker (1990) compared time use between spinal cord injured persons and non-disabled individuals and found that the spinal cord injured group watched more TV, and several ranked it as a more satisfying activity than did the non-disabled group. Lewis (1985) stressed the need to maintain optimal physical activity even in chronic illness because activity provides a sense of mastery over the body, and strengthens the ability to cope.

The need to maintain a high level of activity may be even more important to individuals who are sensory deprived as a result of disability. The human body needs a certain level of stimulation to maintain physical and psychological well-being, and those with sensory limitations experience less stimulation. This is a consideration for visual and hearing impaired individuals, especially if they have additional disabilities. Individuals with limited sensation and movement also may need heightened stimulation. Consider, for example, high level quadriplegics who receive no sensory stimulation below the chin. Perhaps a better form of treatment for high anxiety in this group is increased activity instead of relaxation training. This idea is supported by Batavia (1988) who has challenged therapeutic recreation specialists to develop more active recreation options for high quads.

Micheli (1985) has noted the need for rehabilitation professionals to be involved in setting realistic guidelines for active recreation participation. He indicated that some individuals with muscular dystrophy, quadriplegia, and multiple sclerosis have gone beyond the limits imposed on them by overprotective medical professionals, and have reported dramatic improvement in their physical and psychological well-being. He concludes that active recreation should be encouraged, not discouraged as it was in the past.

There are numerous options for active, meaningful leisure pursuits for most individuals, regardless of physical impairment. Disabled individuals often have limited knowledge of these activities and need informed professional involvement to facilitate participation. Kegel (1985) listed 47 sports and recreation options for individuals with lower limb impairment. Paciorek and Jones (1989) identified 53 different activities, 106 associations, and 200 equipment manufacturers related to active recreation for individuals with a variety of disabilities. <u>Sports N Spokes</u> magazine provides countless anecdotal examples of individuals finding renewed excitement in life through active recreation. W. Mitchell (cited in Corbet, 1980) emphasized the reality of extensive options in the following statement:

> The way I look at it, before I was paralyzed, there were ten thousand things I could do; ten thousand things I was capable of doing. Now there are nine thousand. I can dwell on the one thousand, or concentrate on the nine thousand I have left. And of course, the joke is that none of us in our lifetime is going to do more than two or three of those things in any event. (p. 32)

Again, it is important from a theoretical position to emphasize that the specific activity is not important; it is what it does for the individual that is most important. The main challenge to professionals is to assist in changing the negative attitudes held by many disabled individuals that disability precludes activity (Ferris, 1990). Stimulating involvement is not only satisfying recreation, but active recreation participation may indeed bring about a significant reduction in medical costs throughout life, and serve as a determining factor in long-term survival.

Psychosocial Well-Being

The impact of therapeutic recreation on elements of psychosocial well-being is cited throughout this paper. One area not addressed elsewhere is depression. Compton, Eisenman, and Henderson (1989a) cite four separate studies that show a significant decrease in depression as a result of exercise. Greenwood et al. (1990) noted a decrease in depression following participation in a tennis program. Katz, Adler, Mazzarella, and Inck (1985) found a decrease in depression after exercise as well. Finally, Weiss and Jamieson's (1988) study showed a decrease in depression after water exercise for individuals with physical disability. It is not known how this depression relates to the clinical description found in DSM-III-R.

Authors have cited other changes in emotional well-being following recreation activities. These changes include improved temperament, reduced tension, improved vigor, reduced confusion, anger, fatigue and anxiety, and improved coping mechanism (Greenwood et al., 1990; Hanrahan, Grove, & Lockwood, 1990; Katz et al., 1985). In a study of 79 non-disabled persons in 1987, Stone (cited in Hull, 1990) noted that leisure events were significantly and positively associated with mood.

Health and Wellness

Therapeutic recreation specialists impact on health and wellness-seeking behavior of clients. Dr. William Elizey (cited in Shivers, 1985) predicts that:

> An integral part of future therapeutics will be a more natural and more active life style. . . . Through recreational activity, we or our descendants will continually recreate strong, healthy bodies. We will play not only because we are well, but in order to be well. (p. 39)

Through pleasurable, intrinsically motivating leisure behavior, individuals learn to substitute old, counterproductive behavior (smoking, overeating, drinking) for new, healthier habits. Non-aversive conditioning, such as found in Bandura's (1977a) self-efficacy theory (Godbey, 1990; Savell, 1986) is effective in changing to healthy patterns.

Frye (1986) suggests a model for wellness-seeking behavior which includes internal locus of control, self-efficacy, and personal responsibility. Anderson and Anberg (1979) support this in part by noting that quadriplegics who had no assistance had the fewest skin problems--indicating that personal responsibility matters. These qualities are enhanced through therapeutic recreation as preciously stated.

Wellness seeking behavior is especially important in individuals who are otherwise physically compromised. It is an important outcome of the rehabilitation process, but requires post-discharge intervention for most individuals because of the time required to change old habits and attitudes.

Develop and Maintain Adequate Support Systems

Establishing support systems is related to community reintegration, but is a more intimate process which involves significant others, family, and friendship roles and relationships. Support systems for persons with disabilities play a significant role in adjustment and in long-term quality of life. Relationships are often altered by disability. DeLoach and Greer (1981) found that disability creates a whole new set of conflicts in marriage; specifically, pace of life, temperature preference, income allocation, and social activities. Olsson, Rosenthal, Greninger, and Pituch (1990) found that wives are concerned about what activities their husbands can do following stroke. Decker and Schulz (1985) cite love relationships as a major concern following spinal cord injury.

Loss of shared leisure activity is related to change in family role. Lewis (1985) stated that many avocations which had "cemented" the family together were forfeited as a result of his illness. "We had to grieve those losses together, large portions of our old lives vanished" (p. 48). Family roles can, in part, be redefined by preservation of old leisure interests and by developing new ones. Kelly (cited in Godbey, 1990) cited relational leisure and role-determining leisure as activities that build and maintain relationships (such as taking the children to the zoo). Orthner and Mancini (1990) cited many studies which show consistently that spouses who share leisure time together in joint activities report more marital satisfaction than those who do not. Recreation therapists are often told that one benefit of a disability is having more time to spend with one's family.

Friendships are more vulnerable to change following disability (Trieschmann, 1988; Vash, 1981) and are more strongly correlated with psychological well-being than intimate ones (Fitzpatrick, Newman, Lamb, & Shipley, 1988). The effects of this form of support on long-term adjustment are well documented (Cook, 1982; Decker & Schulz, 1985; Dew et al., 1983, 1985;

272

Krause & Crewe, 1990; Trieschmann, 1988). Lyons (1987) gives an anecdotal account of 50 friends and neighbors who shaved their heads to give a friend undergoing chemotherapy much-needed support.

The effects of shared leisure experiences on relationship stability has not been documented. Many individuals show great motivation to learn adaptations to old interests so that friendships will be preserved. Others acknowledge that participating in activities with friends gives them something to talk about other than the disability--something the non-disabled friend can relate to. Participating together in activities can help to diffuse anxiety the non-disabled friend may have. With the advent of truly integrated activities such as snow-skiing, scuba diving, water-skiing, and others, disabled individuals have found that their friends view their disability in a less mystical, more realistic way.

Conclusions and Research Recommendation

Physical and Cognitive Outcomes

Although therapeutic recreation services have been established on strong underpinnings in areas that have ample bases in empirical studies such as cardiovascular fitness (Pollock, Wilmore, & Fox, 1984) or learning theory (Dodd & White, 1980), limited knowledge of the physical and cognitive outcomes of therapeutic recreation services has been developed from research. Therapeutic recreation specialists are not researching the physical and cognitive outcomes of therapeutic recreation service. Virtually all of the research in this area has been done by physicians, psychologists, physical therapists, occupational therapists, and exercise physiologists. The strength of this phenomenon lies in the credibility of "outside" examiners asserting the health restoration and maintenance outcomes of activities that are components of therapeutic recreation. The major weakness of this situation is that little research into the outcomes of direct therapeutic recreation service is being conducted and that the research which is being done is not directly related to therapeutic recreation.

Explanations can be proffered that most therapeutic recreation goals are psychosocial in nature (Carter et al., 1985), that most researchers in therapeutic recreation come from a psychosocial orientation, or that therapeutic recreation researchers lack ready access to the instrumentation and the ability to use the technology applied in the measurement of physical outcomes. These problems are surmountable, however, and the value of gaining knowledge in this area is certainly worth the effort.

Does leisure education for stress management have pain-reducing outcomes similar to those demonstrated for relaxation techniques? What are the cognitive outcomes of therapeutic recreation communication skills programs for patients with brain injuries? The answers to these and to many other questions remain confined to the documentation entries of recreation therapists across the country.

The studies of humor and immune system changes (Berk et al., 1988; Lefcourt et al., 1990) suggest an exciting area for therapeutic recreation research. Are there measurable, beneficial physiological responses associated with the affective behaviors aroused by therapeutic recreation? There are many opportunities to extend the psychosocial research in therapeutic recreation to find what, if any, physical dimensions are associated with the positive psychosocial states observed.

Research into the physiological effects of therapeutic recreation is needed for planning future interventions. For example, the cognitive benefits of exercise found by Krebs et al. (1989), and the exercise properties of laughter measured by Fry and Savin (1988) cause us to hypothesize about the possible cognitive and physical benefits of humor interventions for patients with restricted mobility. It is important that the technology now available is used to pursue this information or to develop collaborative efforts with scientists adept at using relevant instrumentation. The expansion of therapeutic recreation research into physical and cognitive outcomes should open additional sources of research funding.

The data on Canadians with disabilities underscores how little is known about the leisure and health attitudes of Americans with disabilities. How are the leisure behaviors of the citizens with disabilities contributing to or detracting from their health and quality of living? Tucker (1987) found an inverse correlation among heavy television viewing and physical fitness. What is the status of television viewing among persons with disabilities? Too little information on this and other important leisure lifestyle areas is known.

Psychosocial Outcomes

Much of the research related to therapeutic recreation with this specific population focuses on the psychosocial and physical benefits of sports participation. Even this body of literature, however, is scant and is sometimes contradictory. The following is a list of additional questions which have been identified through a rather thorough literature review.

Effect on Hospitalization

1. What is the effect of or association between therapeutic recreation intervention and length of stay?

2. What is the association between participation in specified recreation activities and treatment outcomes in other therapies?

3. What is the association between participation in recreation activities for diversion and overall adjustment to the treatment setting?

Stress Management

1. What are the effects of a leisure education program on stress reduction?

2. What is the association among leisure attitudes, level of participation in recreation activities and measure of stress?

4. How do the effects of participation in recreation/leisure pursuits compare with use of standard relaxation techniques in stress management over time?

5. Does participation in exercise and sports ameliorate the impact of long-term stress?

Self-Efficacy/Self-Control

1. What is the relationship between participation in sports and exercise and self-image after trauma?

2. What are the effects of participation in a leisure education program on perceptions of self-efficacy and self-control?

3. What are the effects of participation in challenge/adventure activities on perceptions of self-efficacy and self-control over time? Of other activities, for example, creative expression or competitive activities?

4. What is the association among recreation participation patterns, leisure satisfaction and self-efficacy?

5. What are the effects of participation in various sports on achieving ADL skills? On achieving socialization skills?

6. What is the association among personality types, recreation participation patterns and perceptions of self-efficacy and self-control?

Leisure/Recreation Participation and Rehabilitation Goals

1. What is the association among leisure attitudes, leisure satisfaction, recreation participation, and secondary disabilities, for example, alcohol abuse?

2. What are the effects of specified therapeutic recreation interventions on the development of social skills by persons with head injuries? Spinal cord injuries? Other diagnostic groups?

3. What are the effects of leisure counseling on clients' leisure attitudes, leisure satisfaction, and recreation participation? On clients' adjustment to disability?

4. What are the effects of specified therapeutic recreation interventions on achievement of specified treatment goals/objectives (e.g., range of motion, cognitive retraining, restoration of speech, ambulation, wheelchair mobility)?

Community Reintegration

1. What are the perceived and actual environmental and social constraints on leisure/recreation participation for individuals with different types of disabilities?

2. What are the comparative effects of differing therapeutic recreation interventions in managing/overcoming identified constraints?

3. Which social skills/stigma management interventions work best and with which diagnostic groups?

4. What are the benefits reported by individuals who receive in-home therapeutic recreation interventions?

5. What models of behavior are predictors for successful community reintegration? How can these behaviors best be shaped in the hospital/rehabilitation center?

6. What is the association between recreation participation patterns and leisure and the ability to live independently?

7. What are the underlying beliefs of community recreation personnel which inhibit the development of comprehensive leisure/recreation services to persons with physical disabilities? What are the effective methods for changing these beliefs?

8. What role does integrated recreation play in stigma reduction in society? What forms/patterns of integrated recreation services are most effective in stigma reduction?

9. Which therapeutic recreation interventions are most effective in assisting disabled persons to cope with discriminatory practices which exist in the community?

Quality of Life

1. What are the recreation participation patterns, leisure satisfaction, leisure attitudes, and life satisfaction of deaf persons? How do these compare to non-hearing impaired peers?

2. What is the association among recreation participation patterns, leisure satisfaction, leisure attitudes, and life satisfaction of physically disabled persons? Of sensory impaired persons?

3. What are the important quality of life measures for persons with cardiovascular disease? For other diagnostic groups?

4. What are the comparative effects of various therapeutic recreation interventions in assisting disabled persons to cope with the effects of aging?

5. What is the association among leisure attitudes, leisure satisfaction, recreation participation and return to work? On successful employment over time?

This certainly is not a complete list, but it is a start at identifying some questions related to effective therapeutic recreation intervention. The groundwork for a change in rehabilitation philosophy has been established with a call for more emphasis on social skill development, community reintegration, and acknowledgement of needed support services life long. Therapeutic recreation has the potential to provide effective services in these areas as well as to contribute to the physical restoration process. It is time to measure the how, what, why, and the effectiveness of service delivery.

References

* *Designates references cited in text.*

Aivazyan, T. A. (1988). Efficacy of relaxation techniques in hypertensive patients. Health Psychology, 7, 193-200.

*Alexander, J. L., & Fuhrer, M. J. (1984). Functional assessment of individuals with physical impairments. In A. S. Halpern & M. J. Fuhrer (Eds.), Functional assessment in rehabilitation (pp. 45-60). Baltimore: Paul H. Brookes.

Allen, L. (1990). Benefits of leisure attributes to community satisfaction. Journal of Leisure Research, 22(2), 183-196.

*Americans with Disabilities Act of 1990. (1990). The National Advocate, 1(4), 10-24.

*Anderson, T. P., & Anberg, M. M. (1979). Psychological factors associated with pressure sores. Archives of Physical Medicine and Rehabilitation, 60, 341-345.

*Anson, C., & Shepherd, C. (1990, March). A survey of post-acute spinal cord patients: Medical psychological, and social characteristics. Trends: Research News From Shepherd Spinal Center.

*Austin, D. R. (1987). Recreation and persons with physical disabilities: A literature synthesis. Therapeutic Recreation Journal, 21, 36-44.

*Baer, B. (1985). The rehabilitation influences of creative experience. The Journal of Creative Behavior, 19(3), 202-214.

*Bandura, A. (1977). Social learning theory. Englewood Cliffs, NJ: Prentice-Hall.

*Bandura, A. (1987). Self efficacy: Towards a unifying theory of behavior change. Psychological Review, 84, 191-215.

*Batavia, A. (1988). Needed: Active therapeutic recreation for high level quadriplegics. Therapeutic Recreation Journal, 22(2), 8-11.

*Berger, B., Friedman, E., & Eaton, M. (1988). Comparison of jogging, the relaxation response, and group interaction for stress. Journal of Sport and Exercise Psychology, 10, 431-437.

*Berk, L., Tan, S., Nehlsen-Cannarella, S., Napier, B., Lee, J., Lewis, J., Hubbard, R., & Eby, W. (1988). Mirth modulates adrenocorticomedullary activity: Suppression of cortisol and epinephrine. Clinical Research, 36, 121.

*Berk, L. et al. (1988). Humor associated laughter decreases cortisol and increases spontaneous lymphocyte blastogenesis. Clinical Research, 36, 435.

*Bernhardt, D. B. (1985). The competitive spirit. Physical and Occupational Therapy in Pediatrics, 4(3), 77-83.

*Berryman, D. L. (1985). Analysis of trends and needs in leisure and play research related to services for disabled populations. Paper presented at National Recreation and Parks Symposium on Leisure Research.

*Bodzioch, J., Roach, J. W., & Schkade, J. (1986). Promoting independence in adolescent paraplegics: A 2-week "camping experience." Journal of Pediatric Orthopedics, 6(2), 198-201.

*Boschen, K. A. (1981). Current methods of measuring client outcome in rehabilitation programs for the physically disabled. Paper presented, 42nd Annual Convention, Canadian Psychological Association, Toronto, Ontario, June 3-5.

Brandon, J. E. (1985). Health promotion and wellness in rehabilitation services. Journal of Rehabilitation, 54-58.

*Brasile, F. (1990). Wheelchair sports: A new perspective on integration. Adapted Physical Activity Quarterly, 7(1), 3-11.

*Brock, B. J. (1988). Effects of horseback riding on physically disabled adults. Therapeutic Recreation Journal, 22(3), 34-43.

*Brown, M. (1988). The consequences of impairments in daily life activities: Belief vs. reality. Rehabilitation Psychology, 33(3), 173-184.

279

*Bullock, C. C. (1991). Personal conversation, February 8. Rehabilitation Nursing, 10(5), 20-21.

*Bullock, C. C., & Howe, C. Z. (1991). A model therapeutic recreation program for the reintegration of persons with disabilities into the community. Therapeutic Recreation Journal, 25(1), 7-17.

Burgireno, J. (1985). Maximizing learning in the adult with SCI. Rehabilitation Psychology, 33(3), 173-184.

*Carey, M. P., & Burish, T. G. (1987). Providing relaxation training to cancer chemotherapy patients: A comparison of three delivery techniques. Journal of Consulting and Clinical Psychology, 55(5), 732-737.

*Carter, M. J., Van Ander, G., & Robb, G. (1985). Therapeutic recreation: A practical approach. St. Louis: Times Mirror/Mosby.

*Chorost, S. B. (1988). Leisure and recreation of exceptional children: Theory and practice. Child and Youth Services, 10(2), 151-181.

*Compton, D. M., Eisenman, P. A., & Henderson, H. L. (1989a). Exercise and fitness for persons with disabilities. Sports Medicine, 7, 150-162.

Compton, D. M., Eisenman, P. A., & Henderson, H. L. (1989b). Exercise and fitness for persons with disabilities. Sports Medicine, 8(1), 63-64.

*Cook, D. W. (1982). Dimensions and correlates of postservice adjustments to spinal cord injury: A longitudinal inquiry. International Journal of Rehabilitation Research, 5(3), 373-375.

Cook, E. A. (1985). Dual trauma of spinal cord injury in adolescence. Rehabilitation Nursing, 10(5), 18-19.

*Corbet, B. (1980). Options: Spinal cord injury and the future. Denver: A.B. Hirschfeld.

Cory, D., & Neustadt-Noy, N. (1988). A new approach to recreational rehabilitation. Journal of Visual Impairments and Blindness, 82(5), 195-196.

*Coyle, K., & Kinney, T. (1990). Leisure characteristics of adults with physical disabilities. Therapeutic Recreation Journal, 24(4), 64-73.

Croce, R. (1987). Exercise and physical activity in managing progressive muscular dystrophy. Palaestra, 3, 9.

*Curtis, K. A., McClanahan, S., Hall, K. M., Dillon, D., & Brown, K. F. (1986). Health, vocational, and functional status in spinal cord injured athletes and nonathletes. Archives of Physical Medicine and Rehabilitation, 67, 862-867.

*Dal-Monte, A., Faina, M., Maglio, A., Sardella, G., & Guide, G. (1982). Cardiotelemetric and blood lactate investigations in paraplegic subjects during several sports activities. Journal of Sports Medicine and Physical Fitness, 22, 172-184.

*Datillo, J., & Guadagnolo, F. B. (1988). Perceptions of road races by participants in the challenged division. Adapted Physical Activity Quarterly, 5, 193-202.

Datillo, J., & Smith, R. W. (1990). Communicating positive attitudes toward people with disabilities through sensitive terminology. Therapeutic Recreation Journal, 24(1), 8-17.

*Davis, G. M., Shephard, R. J., & Jackson, R. W. (1981). Cardiorespiratory fitness and muscular strength in the lower-limb disabled. Canadian Journal of Applied Sport Sciences, 6, 159-177.

*Davis, G. M., Shephard, R. J., & Ward, G. R. (1984). Alterations of dynamic strength following forearm crank training of disabled subjects. Medicine and Science in Sports and Exercise, 16, 147.

*Decker, S. D., & Shulz, R. (1985). Correlates of life satisfaction and depression in middle-aged and elderly spinal cord injured persons. American Journal of Occupational Therapy, 39(11), 740-745.

*DeLoach, C., & Greer, B. G. (1981). Adjustment to severe physical disability: A metamorphosis. New York: McGraw-Hill.

280

*DePauw, K. (1988). Sport for individuals with disabilities: Research opportunities. Adapted Physical Activity Quarterly, 5, 80-89.

*DePauw, K. P. (1986). Research on sports for athletes with disabilities. Adapted Physical Activity Quarterly, 3(4), 292-299.

*DeVivo, M. J., Rutt, R. D., Stover, S. L., & Fink, P. R. (1987). Employment after spinal cord injury. Archives of Physical Medicine and Rehabilitation, 68, 494-498.

*Dew, M. A., Lynch, K., Ernst, J., & Rosenthal, R. (1983). Reaction and adjustments to spinal cord injury: A descriptive study. Journal of Applied Rehabilitation Counseling, 14(1), 32-39.

*Dew, M. A. et al. (1985). A causal analysis of factors affecting adjustment to spinal cord injury. Rehabilitation Psychology, 30(1), 39-46.

*Dillon, K., Minchoff, B., & Baker, K. (1985). Positive emotional states and enhancement of the immune system. International Journal of Psychiatry in Medicine, 15, 13-18.

DiPasquale, P. A. (1986). Exhaler class: A multidisciplinary program for high quadriplegic patients. American Journal of Occupational Therapy, 40(7), 482-485.

*Disability Rag. (1989-1991). Louisville, KY: The Avocado Press.

*Dodd, D., & White, R. M. (1980). Cognition, mental structures and processes. Boston: Allyn and Bacon.

Dubert, P. M., Rappaport, N. A., & Martin, J. E. (1987). Exercise in cardiovascular disease. Behavior Modification, 11, 329-347.

*Dubos, R. (1965). Man adapting. New Haven: Yale University Press.

Durgin, R. W. (1985). The guide to recreation, leisure and travel for the handicapped. Toledo, OH: Resource Directories.

*Ellis, G. D., & Niles, S. (1985). Development, reliability and preliminary validation of a brief leisure rating scale. Therapeutic Recreation Journal, 19(1), 50-61.

*Farbman, A. H., & Ellis, W. K. (1987). Accessibility and outdoor recreation for persons with disabilities. Therapeutic Recreation Journal, 21(1), 70-76.

*Fazio, S. M., & Fralish, K. B. (1988). A survey of leisure and recreation programs offered by agencies serving traumatic head injured adults. Therapeutic Recreation Journal, 22, 46-54.

*Ferris, B. (1990). Reflections on the physical activity patterns of disabled Canadians: Challenges for practitioners. Leisurability, 14(2), 18-23.

*Figoni, S., Boileau, R., Massey, B., & Larsen, J. R. (1988). Physiological responses of quadriplegic and able-bodied men during exercise at the same VO2. Adapted Physical Activity Quarterly, 5, 130-139.

*Fitzpatrick, R., Newman, S., Lamb, R., & Shipley, M. (1988). Social relationships and psychological well-being in rheumatoid arthritis. Social Science and Medicine, 27(4), 399-403.

*Flavell, J. H. (1977). Cognitive development. Englewood Cliffs, NJ: Prentice-Hall.

*Florence, J. M. (1984). Effect of training on the exercise responses of neuromuscular disease patents. Medicine and Science in Sports and Exercise, 16, 460.

*Foley, F. W., Bedell, J. R., LaRocca, N. G., Scheinberg, L. C. et al. (1987). Efficacy of stress-inoculation training in coping with multiple sclerosis. Journal of Consulting and Clinical Psychology, 55(1), 919-922.

*Frank, R. G. et al. (1987). Differences in coping styles among persons with spinal cord injury: A cluster-analytical approach. Journal of Consulting and Clinical Psychology, 55(5), 727-731.

*Frey, W. D. (1984). Functional assessment in the '80s: A conceptual enigma, a technical challenge. In A. S. Halpern & M. J. Fuhrer (Eds.), Functional assessment in rehabilitation (pp. 11-43). Baltimore: Paul H. Brookes.

Frick, N. M. (1985). Post polio sequelae and the psychology of a second disability. Orthopedics, 8, 851-856.

*Frieden, L. (1989). Community integration and follow-up. In D. F. Apple & L. M. Hudson (Eds.), Spinal cord injury: The model. Washington, DC: National Institute on Disability Rehabilitation and Research.

*Frieden, L. & Cole, J. A. (1985). Independence: The ultimate goal of rehabilitation for spinal cord injured persons. American Journal of Occupational Therapy, 39(11), 734-739.

*Fry, W. F., & Rader, C. (1977). The respiratory components of mirthful laughter. Journal of Biological Psychology, 19, 39-50.

*Fry, W. F., & Savin, W. M. (1988). Mirthful laughter and blood pressure. International Journal of Humor Research, 1, 49-62.

*Frye, B. A. (1986). A model of wellness seeking behavior in traumatic spinal cord injury victims. Rehabilitation Nursing, 11(5), 6-8.

Gentry, M. E. (1984). Developments in activity analysis: Recreation and group work revisited. Social Work with Groups, 7(1), 35-44.

*Girdano, D., & Everly, G. (1979). Controlling stress and tension: A holistic approach. Englewood Cliffs, NJ: Prentice-Hall.

*Glass, J., Albright, C., Burns, C., Evans, J., & Apple, D. (1984). Method and Outcome Analysis, presented at American Spinal Injury Association, April.

*Glesser, J. M., & Brown, P. (1986). Modified judo for visually handicapped people. Journal of Visual Impairment & Blindness, 80(5), 749-750.

*Godbey, G. (1990). Leisure in your life: An exploration. State College, PA: Venture.

*Godin, G., Colantino, A., Davis, G. M., Shepherd, R. J., & Simard, C. (1986). Prediction of leisure time exercise behavior among a group of lower-limb disabled adults. Journal of Clinical Psychology, 42(2), 272-279.

*Gordon, W. A. (1982). The relationship between pressure sores and psychosocial adjustment in persons with spinal cord injury. Rehabilitation Psychology, 27, 185-191.

*Graitcer, P. L., & Maynard, F. M. (1990). First colloquium on preventing secondary disabilities among people with spinal cord injuries. Atlanta, GA: Centers for Disease Control.

*Greenwood, C. M., Dzewattowski, D. A., & French, R. (1990). Self efficacy and psychological well-being of wheelchair tennis participants and wheelchair nontennis participants. Adapted Physical Activity Quarterly, 7(1), 12-21.

*Hahn, H. (1985). Changing perception of disability and the future of rehabilitation. In L. G. Perlman & G. F. Austin (Eds.), Social influences in rehabilitation planning: Blueprint for the 21st century (pp. 53-64). [A report of the ninth Mary E. Switzer Memorial Seminar.] Alexandria, VA: National Rehabilitation Association.

Halpern, A. S., & Fuhrer, M. J. (1984). Functional assessment in rehabilitation. Baltimore: Paul H. Brookes.

*Hamburg, D. A., & Adams, J. E. (1967). A perspective on coping behavior: Seeking and utilizing information in major transitions. Archives of General Psychiatry, 17, 277-284.

*Hanna, R. S. (1986, May). Effect of exercise on blind persons. Journal of Visual Impairment & Blindness, 722-725.

*Hanrahan, S. J., Grove, J. R., & Lockwood, R. J. (1990). Psychological skills training for the blind athlete: A pilot program. Adapted Physical Activity Quarterly, 7, 143-155.

*Hedrick, B. N. (1985). The effect of wheelchair tennis participation and mainstreaming upon the perceptions of competence of physically disabled adolescents. Therapeutic Recreation Journal, 19(2), 34-46.

*Heinemann, A. W., Goranson, N., Ginburg, K., & Schnoll, S. (1989). Alcohol use and activity patterns following spinal cord injury. Rehabilitation Psychology, 34(3), 191-205.

Hitzhusen, G. L., & Thompson, M. G. (1980). Mainstreaming community recreation and youth programs: A needs-assessment approach. Journal of Leisurability, 7(3), 42-51.

Hjeltnes, N., & Jansen, T. (1990). Physical endurance capacity, functional status and medical complications in spinal cord injured subjects with long-standing lesions. Paraplegia, 28, 428-432.

*Hoffman, M. D. (1986). Cardiorespiratory fitness and training in quadriplegics and paraplegics. Sports Medicine, 3, 312-330.

*Hopper, C. (1988). Self-concept and motor performance of hearing impaired boys and girls. Adapted Physical Activity Quarterly, 5, 293-304.

Hough, S., & Brady, D. (1988). Avocational skill development for neurobehaviorally impaired in patients. Therapeutic Recreation Journal, 22(4), 39-48.

*Howe-Murphy, R., & Charboneau, B. G. (1987). Therapeutic recreation: An ecological perspective. Englewood Cliffs, NJ: Prentice-Hall.

*Hull, B. (1990). Mood as a product of leisure: Causes and consequences. Journal of Leisure Research, 22(2), 99-111.

Hunt, S. L., & Brooks, K. W. (1982). A projection of research and development needs: Implications for disabled persons. Journal of Leisurability, 9(3), 28-32.

Hutchinson, P. (1980). Perceptions of disabled persons regarding barriers to community involvement. Journal of Leisurability, 7(3), 4-16.

*Iso-Ahola, S. E. (1980). The social psychology of leisure and recreation. Dubuque, IA: Wm. C. Brown.

*Jackson, R. W., & Davis, G. M. (1983). The value of sports and recreation for the physically disabled. Orthopedic Clinics of North America, 14, 301-315.

*James, A. (1991). Burns. In D. Austin & M. Crawford (Eds.), Therapeutic recreation: An introduction (pp. 333-351). Englewood Cliffs, NJ: Prentice Hall.

Jeffrey, D. L. (1986). The hazards of reduced mobility for the person with a spinal cord injury. Journal of Rehabilitation, 52.

*Jemmott, J., & Magloire, K. (1988). Academic stress, social support, and secretory immunoglobulin. Journal of Personality and Social Psychology, 55, 803-810.

*Jemmott, J., & McClelland, D. (1989). Secretory IgA as a measure of resistance to infectious disease: Comments on Stone, Cox, Valdimarsodottir, and Neale (1987). Behavioral Medicine, 15, 63-71.

*Jocheim, K. A., & Strohkendle, H. (1973). Value of particular sports of the wheelchair disabled in maintaining health of the paraplegic. Paraplegia, 11, 173-178.

*Johnson, M. (1990). The disability rights movement. Presentation, Georgia Recreation and Parks Association TR Member's Forum, January 12.

Johnson, R. W., & Davis, G. M. (1983). The value of sports and recreation for the physically disabled. Orthopedic Clinics of North America, 14, 301-315.

*Jones, L. (1988). Unemployment and social integration: A review. Journal of Sociology and Social Welfare, 15(4), 161-176.

*Katz, J. F., Adler, J. C., Mazzarella, N. J., & Inck, L. P. (1985). Psychological consequences of an exercise training program for a paraplegic man: A case study. Rehabilitation Psychology, 30(1), 53-58.

*Kegel, B. (1985). Physical fitness: Sports and recreation for those with lower limb amputation or impairment. Washington, DC: Veterans Administration.

*Kelly, J. R. (1987). Freedom to be: A new sociology of leisure. New York: Macmillan.

Kennedy, D. W. (1985). Using the leisure activities blank with spinal cord-injured persons: A field study. Adapted Physical Activity Quarterly, 2, 182-188.

*Kennedy, D. W., & Smith, R. W. (1990). A comparison of past and future leisure activity participation between spinal cord injured and non-disabled persons. Paraplegia, 28, 130-136.

*Kennedy, D. W., Smith, R. W., & Austin, D. R. (1991). Special recreation: Opportunities for persons with disabilities. Dubuque, IA: Wm. C. Brown.

*Klein, M. K. (1985). The therapeutics of recreation. Physical and Occupational Therapy in Pediatrics, 4(3), 9-11.

*Koch, I., Schlegel, M., Pirrwitz, A., Jaschke, B., & Schlegel, K. (1983). On objectivizing the training effect of sport therapy in wheelchair-users (In German). International Journal of Rehabilitation Research, 6, 439-448.

*Krause, J. S., & Crewe, M. M. (1987). Prediction of long-term survival of persons with spinal cord injury. Rehabilitation Psychology, 32(4), 205-213.

*Krause, J. S., & Crewe, N. M. (1990). Long term prediction of self-reported problems following spinal cord injury. Paralegia, 28.

*Krause, R. (1983). Therapeutic recreation service: Principles and practices (3rd ed.). Philadelphia: Saunders.

*Krebs, P., Eickelberg, W., Krobath, H., & Barch, I. (1989). Effects of physical exercise on peripheral vision and learning in children with spina bifida manifesta. Perceptual and Motor Skills, 68, 167-174.

*Lahtinen, V. M. (1989). Sporting behavior of special groups in Finland. Adapted Physical Activity Quarterly, 6, 159-169.

*Lefcourt, H., Davidson-Katz, K., & Kueneman, K. (1990). Humor and immune-system functioning. International Journal of Humor Research, 3, 305-321.

LeFebvre, C., & Berryman, D. (1988). Therapeutic recreation. In J. Goodgold (Ed.), Rehabilitation medicine. St. Louis, MO: C.V. Mosby.

*LeVeau, B. F. (1985). Team sports. Physical and Occupational Therapy in Pediatrics, 4(3), 65-75.

*Leverette, A. (1990). SPARX final report. Atlanta, GA: Shepherd Spinal Center.

*Lewis, K. (1985). Successful living with chronic illness. Wayne, NJ: Avery.

*Lockland, G. T. (1973). Grow or die: The unifying principle of transformation. New York: Vell.

*Lyons, R. F. (1987). Leisure adjustment to chronic illness and disability. Journal of Leisurability, 14(2), 4-10.

*MacNeil, R. D., & Pringnitz, T. D. (1982). The role of therapeutic recreation in stroke rehabilitation. Therapeutic Recreation Journal, 16(4), 26-34.

*Maddy, B. J. (1988). Close encounters: Promoting social independence in adolescents with physical disabilities. Therapeutic Recreation Journal, 22(4), 49-55.

Malec, J., & Neimeyer, R. (1983). Psychologic prediction of duration of inpatient spinal cord injury rehabilitation and performance of self-care. Archives of Physical Medicine and Rehabilitation, 64(8), 359-363.

*Mandrel, A. R., & Keller, S. M. (1986). Stress management in rehabilitation. Archives of Physical Medicine and Rehabilitation, 67, 375-379.

*Martin, R., & Dobbin, J. (1988). Sense of humor, hassles, and immunoglobulin A: Evidence for a stress-moderating effect of humor. International Journal of Psychiatry in Medicine, 18, 93-105.

284

*Mayer, J. D., & Eisenberg, M. G. (1988). Mental representation of the body: Stability and change in response to illness and disability. Rehabilitation Psychology, 33(3), 155-177.

*Mayer, T., & Andrews, H. B. (1981). Changes in self-concept following a spinal cord injury. Journal of Applied Rehabilitation Counseling, 12(3), 135-137.

*McAvoy, L. H., Schatz, E. C., Stutz, M. E., Schlein, S. J., & Lais, G. (1989). Integrated wilderness adventure: Effects on personal and lifestyle traits of persons with and without disabilities. Therapeutic Recreation Journal, 23(3), 50-64.

McCubbin, J., & Shasby, G. (1985). The effect of isokinetic exercise on adolescents with cerebral palsy. Adapted Physical Activity Quarterly, 2, 56-64.

McDonald, J. (1985). Special adaptive recreation as intervention in vocational and transitional services for handicapped youth. Therapeutic Recreation Journal, 19(3), 17-27.

*Micheli, L. J. (1985). Rehabilitation: Expanding the definition. Physical and Occupational Therapy in Pediatrics, 4(3), 3-8.

*Mikhail, A. (1985). Stress: A psychological conception. In A. Monat & R. S. Lazarus (Eds.), Stress and coping: An anthology (pp. 30-39). New York: Columbia University Press.

*Miles, D. S., Sawka, M. N., Wilde, S. W., Durbin, R. J., & Gotshall, R. W. (1982). Pulmonary function changes in wheelchair athletes subsequent to exercise training. Ergonomics, 25, 239-246.

*Mobily, K. E. (1985). A philosophical analysis of therapeutic recreation: What does it mean to say "we can be therapeutic" part I. Therapeutic Recreation Journal, 19(1), 14-26.

*Mundy, J., & Odom, L. (1979). Leisure education: Theory and Practice. New York: John Wiley & Sons.

Murphy, W. D., & Datillo, J. (1989). Wilderness preservation and accessibility for people with disabilities: A discussion. Therapeutic Recreation Journal, 23(3), 19-26.

Nachman, M. S. (1981). A descriptive study of the status of therapeutic recreation at the seven state-operated comprehensive rehabilitation centers in the United States. 12-15.

Nadolsky, J. M. (1987, April-June). Rehabilitation and wellness: In need of integration. Journal of Rehabilitation, 5-7.

Nakajima, A., & Honda, S. (1988). Physical and social condition of rehabilitated spinal cord injury patients in Japan: A long-term review. Paraplegia, 26, 165-176.

Navar, N. (1980). A rationale for leisure skill assessments with handicapped adults. Therapeutic Recreation Journal, 14(4), 21-28.

*Niemi, M. L., Laaksonen, R., Kotila, M., & Wattimo, O. (1988). Quality of life 4 years after stroke. Stroke, 19(9), 1101-1107.

Nixon, H. L. (1989). Integration of disabled people in mainstream sports: Case study of a partially sighted child. Adapted Physical Activity Quarterly, 6, 17-31.

*Oestreicher, M. (1990). Accessible recreation: 20 years behind the times. Parks and Recreation, 25(8), 52-55.

*Olsson, R. H., Rosenthal, S. G., Greninger, L. O., Pituch, M. J., & Metress, E. S. (1990). Therapeutic recreation and family therapy: A needs analysis of perceived needs of wives of stroke patients. Annual in Therapeutic Recreation, 1, 15-20.

*Orthner, D. K., & Mancini, J. A. (1990). Leisure impacts on family interaction and cohesion. Journal of Leisure Research, 22(2), 125-137.

*Paciorek, M., & Jones, J. A. (1989). Sports and recreation for the disabled: A resource manual. Indianapolis, IN: Benchmark.

*Pederson, O. (1980). Increased insulin receptors after exercise in patients with insulin-dependent diabetes mellitus. New England Journal of Medicine, 302, 886.

Pelletier, J. R., Rogers, E. S., & Thurer, S. (1985). The mental health needs of individuals with severe physical disability: A consumer advocate perspective. Rehabilitation Literature, 46(7-8), 186-193.

*Perry, S., Heindrich, G., & Ramos, E. (1981). Assessment of pain by burn patients. Journal of Burn Care Rehabilitation, 2, 322-326.

*Peterson, C. A., & Gunn, S. L. (1984). Therapeutic recreation program design. Englewood Cliffs, NJ: Prentice-Hall.

*Piaget, J. (1983). Piaget's theory. In W. Kessen (Ed.), Handbook of child psychology (Vol. 1, pp. 103-128). New York: John Wiley & Sons.

*Pollock, M. L., Wilmore, J. H., & Fox, S. M. (1984). Exercise in health and disease: Evaluation and prescription for prevention and rehabilitation. Philadelphia: W. B. Saunders.

*Rinck, C. et al. (1989). The adolescent with myelomeningocele: A review of parent experiences and expectations. Adolescence, 24(95), 699-710.

Rintala, D. H., & Williams, E. P. (1987). Behavioral and demographic predictors of post-discharge outcomes in spinal cord injury. Archives of Physical Medicine and Rehabilitation, 68(6), 357-362.

Rintala, D. H., & Williams, E. P., & Halstead, L. S. (1986). Spinal cord injury: The relationship between time out of bed and significant events. Rehabilitation Nursing, 11(3), 15-18.

*Robb, G. M., & Evert, A. (1987). Risk recreation and persons with disabilities. Therapeutic Recreation Journal, 21(1), 58-69.

*Rogers, M. E. (1970). An introduction to the theoretical basis of nursing. Philadelphia: F. A. Davis.

Roggenbuck, J. W., Ross, J. L., & Dagostino, J. (1990). The learning benefits of leisure. Journal of Leisure Research, 22(2), 112-124.

*Rouse, P. (1983). Therapeutic recreation: The value and the need. Cognitive Rehabilitation, 2(4), 4-7.

*Savell, K. (1986). Implications for therapeutic recreation leisure-efficacy: Theory and therapy programming. Therapeutic Recreation Journal, 20(1), 43-52.

*Schultz, R. C. (1985). Purpose in life among spinal cord injured males. Journal of Applied Rehabilitation Counseling, 16(2), 45-51.

*Shaw, L., & Ehrlich, A. (1987). Relaxation training as a treatment for chronic pain caused by ulcerative colitis. Pain, 29, 287-293.

*Sherrill, C., Pope, C., & Arnhold, R. (1986). Sport socialization of blind athletes: An exploratory study. Journal of Visual Impairment and Blindness, 84(2), 740-744.

*Sherrill, C., & Rainbolt, W. (1988). Self-actualization profiles of male able-bodied and elite cerebral palsied athletes. Adapted Physical Activity Quarterly, 5, 108-119.

Sherrill, C., Silliman, L., Gench, B., & Hinson, M. (1990). Self-actualization of elite wheelchair athletes. Paraplegia, 28, 252-260.

*Shivers, J. S. (1985). Leisure and society: Future trends. Alexandria, VA: National Recreation and Park Association.

*Silva, J. M., & Klatsky, J. (1984). Body image and physical activity. Physical and Occupational Therapy in Pediatrics, 4(3), 85-92.

*Siosteen, A., Lundquist, C., Blomstrand, C., Sullivan, L., & Sullivan, M. (1990). The quality of life of three functional spinal cord injury subgroups in a Swedish community. Paralegia, 28, 476-488.

*Skinner, B. F. (1969). Contingencies of reinforcement. New York: Apple-Century-Crofts.

*Sneegas, J. J. (1989). Social skills: An integral component of leisure participation and therapeutic recreation services. Journal of Therapeutic Recreation, 23(2), 30-40.

*Stensrude, C., Mishkin, L., Craft, C., & Pollock, I. (1987). The use of drama techniques in cognitive rehabilitation. Therapeutic Recreation Journal, 21(2), 64-69.

Stevenson, E. (1984). Running for therapy. Physical and Occupational Therapy in Pediatrics, 4(3), 45-64.

*Stewart, N. (1981). The value of sport in the rehabilitation of the physically disabled. Canadian Journal of Applied Sport Science, 6(4), 166-167.

*Stotts, K. M. (1986). Health maintenance: Paraplegic athletes and nonathletes. Archives of Physical Medicine and Rehabilitation, 67, 109-114.

*Stolov, W. C. (1981). Comprehensive rehabilitation: Evaluation and treatment. In W. C. Stolov & M. S. Clowers (Eds.), Handbook for severe disability (pp. 1-9). Washington, DC: 20402: U.S. Government Printing Office.

*Stolov, W. C., & Clowers, M. R. (1981). Handbook of severe disability. Washington, DC: Rehabilitation Services Administration.

*Stuckey, K., & Barkus, C. (1986). Visually Impaired scouts meet the Philmont challenge. Journal of Visual Impairment and Blindness, 80(5), 750-751.

*Stuckey, S., Jacobs, A., & Goldfarb, J. (1986). EMG biofeedback training, relaxation training, and placebo for relief of chronic back pain. Perceptual and Motor Skills, 63, 1023-1036.

*Stumbo, N., & Bloom, C. (1990). The implications of traumatic brain injury for therapeutic recreation services in rehabilitation settings. Therapeutic Recreation Journal, 24(3), 64-79.

Swanson, B., Cronin-Stubbs, D., & Sheldon, J. A. (1989). The impact of psychological factors on adapting to physical disability: A review of the research. Rehabilitation Nursing, 14(2), 64-68.

*Sylvester, C. D. (1985). Freedom, leisure, and therapeutic recreation: A philosophical view. Therapeutic Recreation Journal, 19(1), 6-13.

*Szymanski, E. M., Rubin, S. E., & Rubin, N. M. (1988). Contemporary challenges: An Introduction. In S. E. Rubin & N. M. Rubin (Eds.), Contemporary challenges to the rehabilitation counseling profession (pp. 1-14). Baltimore: Paul H. Brookes.

Thurer, S., & Rogers, E. S. (1984). The mental health needs of physically disabled persons: Their perspective. Rehabilitation Psychology, 29(4), 239-249.

*Trader, B., Nicholson, L., & Anson, C. (1991). Effectiveness of a model leisure education program for use in SCI rehabilitation. Unpublished final report to Research Review Committee; Shepherd Spinal Center, Atlanta, GA.

*Trader, B., Ruzicka, S., & Nicholson, L. (1991). The effects of active recreation participation on psychological adjustment of spinal cord injured patients. Unpublished final report to Research Review Committee, Shepherd Spinal Center, Atlanta, GA.

*Trieschmann, R. B. (1984). Vocational rehabilitation: A psychological perspective. Rehabilitation Literature, 45(11-12), 345-348.

*Trieschmann, R. B. (1987). Aging with a disability. New York: Demos.

*Trieschmann, R. B. (1988). Spinal cord injury: Psychological, social, and vocational rehabilitation (2nd ed.). New York: Demos.

*Tucker, L. A. (1987). Television, teenagers, and health. Journal of Youth and Adolescence, 16(5), 415-425.

*Tucker, S. J. (1980). The psychology of spinal cord injury: Patient-staff interaction. Rehabilitation Literature, 41(5-6), 114-121.

*Ulrich, R. S., Dimberg, V., & Driver, B. L. (1990). Psycho- physiological indicators of leisure consequences. <u>Journal of Leisure Research</u>, <u>22</u>(2), 154-166.

*Van Loan, M. D., McCluer, S., Loftin, J. M., & Boileau, R. A. (1987). Comparison of physiological responses to maximal arm exercise among able-bodied, paraplegics and quadriplegics. <u>International Medical Society of Paraplegia</u>, <u>25</u>, 397-405.

*Vash, C. L. (1981). <u>The psychology of disability</u>. New York: Springer.

*Vesluys, H. P. (1980). Physical rehabilitation and family dynamics. <u>Rehabilitation Literature</u>, <u>41</u>(3-4), 58-66.

*von Bertalanffy, L. (1950). The theory of open systems in physics and biology. <u>Science</u>, <u>111</u>, 23-25.

*Wankel, C. M., & Berger, B. G. (1990). The psychological and social benefits of sport and physical activity. <u>Journal of Leisure Research</u>, <u>22</u>(2), 167-182.

Weinberger, M., Hiner, S. L., & Tierney, W. M. (1986). Improving functional status in arthritis: The effect of social support. <u>Social Science and Medicine</u>, <u>23</u>, 899-904.

*Weinberger, M., Tierney, W. M., Booher, P., & Hiner, S. L. (1990). Social support stress and functional status in patients with osteoarthritis. <u>Journal of Social Science and Medicine</u>, <u>30</u>(4), 503-508.

*Weiss, C., & Jamieson, N. (1988). Hidden disabilities: A new enterprise for therapeutic recreation. <u>Therapeutic Recreation Journal</u>, <u>22</u>(4), 9-17.

Weitzman, D. M. (1986). Motivation: The key to physical fitness in the blind adult. <u>Journal of Visual Impairment and Blindness</u>, <u>84</u>(2), 745-748.

Wenger, N. K., Mattson, M. E., Furberg, C. D., & Elinson, J. (1984). Assessment of quality life in clinical trials of cardiovascular therapy. <u>American Journal of Cardiology</u>, <u>54</u>, 908-913.

*White, R. W. (1985). Strategies of adaptation: An attempt at systematic description. In A. Monat & R. S. Lazarus (Eds.), <u>Stress and coping: An Anthology</u> (pp. 121-143). New York: Columbia University Press.

*Williams, S. J., & Bury, M. R. (1989). Impairments, disability and handicap in chronic respiratory illness. <u>Social Science and Medicine</u>, <u>29</u>(5), 609-616.

Wilson, W. C., & Thompson, D. D. (1982). The Virginia community cadre network: Community reintegration of the spinal cord injured. <u>SCI Digest</u>, 23-28.

*Wright, B. A. (1984). Developing constructive views of life with a disability. In D. W. Krueger (Ed.), <u>Rehabilitation psychology: A comprehensive textbook</u> (pp. 99-110). Rockville, MD: Aspen.

*Yerra, E. J., & Locker, S. B. (1990). Quality of time use by adults with spinal cord injuries. <u>American Journal of Occupational Therapy</u>, <u>44</u>(4), 318-326.

*Zoerink, D. (1988). Effects of a short-term leisure education program upon the leisure functioning of young people with spina bifida. <u>Therapeutic Recreation Journal</u>, <u>22</u>(3), 44-52.

*Zoerink, D. (1989). Activity choices: Exploring perceptions of persons with physical disabilities. <u>Therapeutic Recreation Journal</u>, <u>23</u>(1), 17-23.

*Zwiren, L., Huberman, G., & Bar-Or, O. (1973). Cardiopulmonary functions of sedentary and highly active paraplegics. <u>Medicine and Science in Sport</u>, <u>5</u>, 683-686.

CHAPTER 8

THE BENEFITS OF THERAPEUTIC RECREATION IN PSYCHIATRY

Thomas Skalko, Glen Van Andel, & Gino DeSalvatore

Introduction

Therapeutic recreation has long been recognized for its role and contribution in the treatment and rehabilitation of persons with mental illness. In the early 1800s, Dr. Benjamin Rush (1745 to 1813), first superintendent of the Pennsylvania Hospital in Philadelphia, acknowledged and endorsed the use of recreation activities in the treatment of psychiatric patients. Other institutions such as The Asylum of New York Hospital, McLean Hospital in Massachusetts, and the Brattleboro Retreat in Vermont, followed this model and incorporated crafts, reading, and walking into treatment programs (Carter, Van Andel, & Robb, 1985).

Perhaps no institution did more in these early years to substantiate the value of recreation as a therapeutic modality than the Menninger Clinic in Topeka, KS. As early as the 1930s, research at this clinic, directed by Dr. Carl Menninger and reported in the clinic's journal, did much to support the merit of using recreation activities in the treatment of psychological disturbances (Carter et al., 1985).

Since this time, such prominent physicians as Howard A. Rusk, Joseph B. Wolffe, Alexander Ried Martin, and Paul Haan, have presented similar findings following their observations in this area of research (Carter et al., 1985). These studies, however, were often case studies or anecdotal observations and, therefore, lacked the rigor of sound scientific inquiry. From this rather gradual beginning, research involving the application of therapeutic recreation to mental health rehabilitation has continued to develop over the last 3 decades. A review of the literature reveals a number of studies that have explored the impact of therapeutic recreation services with a wide variety of mental disorders in an assortment of settings. The intent of this paper is to examine these studies and determine the status quo of the evidence regarding the efficacy of therapeutic recreation services for the treatment of individuals with mental disorders. The manuscript is divided into five sections. Section 1 will address background information identified in the literature of the population served including settings and the nature of the impairment. In Section 2, the theoretical perspective and strategies related to the treatment modality will be discussed. An outline of the specific outcomes and benefits achieved through these therapeutic recreation interventions will be presented in Section 3. Section 4 will make recommendations for future research needed to further define the efficacy of therapeutic recreation services in mental health. Section 5 includes manuscript references and a bibliography of supportive literature on therapeutic recreation and mental health.

Settings and Diagnostic Groups

Settings

Therapeutic recreation services for persons with psychological impairments are provided in a variety of settings that are determined by a combination of complex factors including the severity of the illness, insurance coverage or financial considerations, employment status, family or living situation, and most significantly, the ability to function in a given environment. The settings range from inpatient care, partial hospitalization or day care, transitional living situations, outpatient treatment, and individualized services such as home health care.

The key to selecting the optimum setting for the provision of services is the amount of structure needed to maintain or develop the highest level of functioning possible with each individual. Since humane treatment requires the least restrictive environment necessary to achieve shared therapeutic objectives, the therapist seeks to serve the client in a setting that provides sufficient structure for the client without promoting dependency or further regression from normalized functioning.

Therapeutic recreation services have been employed most often in inpatient units and day or partial hospitalization settings such as community mental health centers. Most of the research reviewed within this paper focuses on these settings and service areas. The popularity and necessity of short-term care in a contemporary service delivery system will likely require significant changes in how future services are provided and thus dictate the need for additional research on the efficacy of therapeutic recreation services within these particular settings. Recommendations addressing these concerns are detailed in the fourth section of this paper.

Nature of Groups Served

The classification of psychiatric disabilities resulted primarily from the work of the German psychiatrist, Emil Kraepelin, who in 1883, hypothesized that mental impairments were a result of organic or biological dysfunction and thus could be classified and treated much the same as physical impairments. The assumption that psychological disturbances are rooted in physiological processes have contributed to the so called "medical model" of diagnosis and treatment which has been the predominant orientation in clinical settings.

Although somewhat modified, this system of diagnostic classification is used in contemporary psychiatry by classifying over 200 mental disorders through the Diagnostic and Statistical Manual of Mental Disorders III-Revised (DSM III-R). Systematic classification has enabled therapists to better understand abnormal behavior and allow for more refined strategies in the treatment of psychiatric disorders. A brief outline of the major diagnostic categories referenced with child, adolescent, and adult populations is presented in Table 1 and Table 2 at the end of the chapter. These tables provide the reader with an overview of the most commonly used diagnostic categories identified in the mental health and therapeutic recreation literature.

Like physiological illnesses, psychological disorders vary widely in their origin, client symptoms, theoretical and clinical assumptions and strategies used in treatment, and client response to treatment. In order to better understand the role and function of therapeutic recreation in the treatment of mental disorders, the most common theories and treatment approaches will be reviewed in the following section of the paper.

Theoretical Perspectives

The delivery of therapeutic recreation services within mental health settings is built on several behavioral theories noted in the psychological literature. Due to the complexity and scope of these theories, it is difficult within the context of this paper to provide a comprehensive review of this literature. However, in order to examine the dominant theoretical foundations of therapeutic recreation in mental health services, a cursory view of theoretical paradigms is presented. The basis of personality theory is founded in the recognized origins of behavior (i.e., internal conflicts, learned behaviors, social influences, bio-chemical changes, etc.). Each personality theory accepts the influences of various factors in the development of the individual. An explanation addressing the origins of personality development will follow. The variables of genetics, sociocultural determinants, learning, traits, self-awareness, unconscious mechanisms, bio-chemical changes, or a combination of these factors drive the theoretical foundations of personality theory (Hergenhahn, 1980). Although each of these elements is supported in almost every theory, the theoretical foundations for personality development are based primarily on the theory of human behavior and change. The paradigms are classified according to the primary origin of the theoretical construct. Much of the literature in therapeutic recreation, either directly or by implication, acknowledges the influences of each of the dominant theoretic postulates in explaining the development of the individual and, furthermore, supports the intervention best suited to the situation and the needs of the individual (Austin, 1982; Carter et al., 1985; Kraus, 1983; O'Morrow & Reynolds, 1989; Peterson & Gunn, 1984). According to Hergenhahn, the paradigms or "schools of thought" encompassing personality theory can be classified into five major modules: (a) Psychoanalytic, (b) Sociocultural, (c) Trait, (d) Learning, and (e) Existential-Humanistic. To this, we should add the eclectic paradigm (Thorne, 1973), since many practitioners often combine two or more of these constructs in the actual delivery of services (Austin).

In addition to providing a summary of the predominant theories of personality that have influenced the role and function of therapeutic recreation, recognition will be given to the influences of play and leisure theory in the foundations of therapeutic recreation in mental health. Furthermore, recognition of the effects of activity on bio-chemical processes and social learning is presented.

Psychodynamic Paradigm

The psychodynamic paradigm supports the influences of unconscious instincts, thoughts, or motives as the basis of human behavior. The successful resolution of conflicts through insight, self-awareness, elimination of resistances, and recognition of self as a functioning human being are paramount in the psychodynamic process (Fine, 1973).

The use of psychodynamic approaches are not readily observed in therapeutic recreation services. However, as Austin (1982) states:

> Therapeutic recreation specialists will not conduct psychoanalytically oriented psychotherapy, . . . the theoretical ideas represented by the psychoanalytic viewpoint will likely pervade the practice of TR specialists. (p. 15)

Therapeutic recreation specialists utilize aspects of the psychodynamic paradigm through the use of therapeutic activities "to assist the client in gaining new insights (associations) into psychic conflicts as well as to provide ego support or build up the inner self" (Carter et al., 1985, p. 202). Furthermore, as suggested by

Menninger (1960) and Hunnicutt (1979), the psychodynamic application of recreation activities can be used as a means to express aggressive impulses and sexual drives in a socially acceptable fashion.

Sociocultural Paradigm

The sociocultural paradigm supported by theorists Adler (1956), Erikson (1963), and Horney (1950) emphasize the importance of children's early relationship with their parents and other relevant individuals in formulating adult personality characteristics (Hergenhahn, 1980). Adler emphasized the concept of "social interest" including cooperation, social relations, and the individual's need to aid society (Lundin, 1974; Mosak & Dreikurs, 1973). Horney recognized the cause of "basic anxiety" (neuroses) as being related to disturbed human relationships and the need for meaningful relationships, affection, and security in early childhood and throughout life (Hergenhahn; Lundin). Erikson also addressed the influences of both biology and culture on the development of the personality. Erikson's eight stages of human development (i.e., Trust vs. Mistrust, Autonomy vs. Shame and Doubt, Initiative vs. Guilt, Industry vs. Inferiority, Identity vs. Role Confusion, Intimacy vs. Isolation, Generativity vs. Stagnation, Ego Integrity vs. Despair) represent a highly influential contribution to the study of human developmental theory and personality development.

Therapeutic recreation specialists recognize the role of early childhood experiences, familial relationships, and cultural environment on the development of the individual. Kraus (1983), for instance, states:

> A final approach to understanding mental health and mental illness, which is of particular relevance to the field of therapeutic recreation, may be found in the 'Eight Ages of Man' theory of human development put forth by Erik Erikson. . . . (p. 193)

The application of techniques that promote successful transition from one stage to another, enhance social relationships, and assist individuals to maximize personal assets are deemed central to human development.

Trait Paradigm

The Trait Paradigm of personality development was supported by such authors as Allport (1955) and Cattell (1965). Both recognized the existence of common and individual traits within groups and individuals. Every individual possesses unique traits that affect their behavior and interactions within their environment (Borgatta, 1968; Hergenhahn, 1980; Lundin, 1974). The basic premise according to Allport (1961) is that individuals possess certain traits or personal dispositions that serve to initiate and guide behavior. In addition to possessing certain traits, the individual remains in control of the decision making process and strives to influence his future. Unlike the psychodynamic paradigm, the actions of the individual are guided by personal disposition and are founded in the present and future (Hergenhahn).

In the delivery of therapeutic recreation services, recognition of the effects of dominant personality traits upon behavior is useful. Activities that promote self-understanding of personal attributes and their effects on behavior can be beneficial in altering ineffective responses to environmental stimuli. McKechnie (1977), for instance, empirically tested relationships between demographic correlates, psychological themes, and activity participation. Ultimately, the recognition of personal attributes in the referral and/or selection of leisure activities must be addressed within recreation service delivery (McKechnie).

Behaviorism/Learning Paradigm

The basis of behaviorism and learning theory are founded in the recognition of the cause and effect (stimulus-response) relationship. The learning paradigm postulates that behavior is the result of learned responses that have been reinforced over time (Carter et al., 1985; Goldstein, 1973; Hergenhahn, 1980). An individual's personality is the sum total of his or her learned actions. These actions are a result of both imitation and social learning (Cartwright, 1979).

Contained within the learning theory are the principles of operant conditioning and behavior modification techniques that have had a profound effect on the treatment of abnormal behavior. Therapeutic recreation specialists frequently apply behavior modification and behavioral outcome measures in the therapeutic recreation treatment planning process (Austin, 1982; Dattilo & Murphy, 1987).

Existential-Humanistic Paradigm

The Existential-Humanistic Paradigm emphasizes the elements of both existentialism and humanism. Existentialists view humans as future-oriented rather than being restricted by the past, while humanism recognizes and accepts the creative power of man. This approach de-emphasizes the role of heredity and environment in the determination of personality. In addition, such therapeutic approaches as Client-Centered Therapy, Transactional Analysis, Reality Therapy, and Rational-Emotive Therapy have their roots in the Existential-Humanistic Paradigm.

The basic proposition of Existential-Humanistic theory revolves around the belief that man is basically good and is motivated by and capable of self-improvement given the right circumstances (Kelly, 1972; Maslow, 1970; Rogers, 1972). The self-actualized individual is characterized by a sense of openness to experiences, accurate perceptions of reality, a future orientation, self-actualized motivations, social consciousness, and personal acceptance (Hergenhahn, 1980).

A review of the therapeutic recreation literature identifies a number of approaches that embody the existential-humanistic school of thought. Numerous authors such as Austin (1982), Carter et al., (1985), Connolly (1977), Dickason (1977), Edwards (1977), Gunn (1979), McDowell (1976, 1977, 1979), Montagnes (1977) among others attest to the value of approaches that utilize the existential-humanistic paradigm in the delivery of therapeutic recreation services.

Eclectic Paradigm

Thorne (1973) stated:

Eclecticism in clinical practice involves consideration of all pertinent theories, methods, and standards for evaluating and manipulating clinical data according to the most advanced knowledge of time and place. (p. 451)

The Eclectic Paradigm systematically integrates various theories and methodologies to address the individual needs of the person being served. This approach does not employ aspects of all theories and methods in a given situation but applies valid approaches indicated by the therapeutic needs of the individual. Much of the therapeutic recreation literature implies the use of an eclectic approach to the delivery of services to persons with disabilities including individuals with emotional disabilities. The holistic approach to client service delivery espoused by the field is based on an eclectic orientation (Austin, 1982). The recognition of bio-psycho-social needs and the application of approaches to address these needs embraces the philosophy of eclecticism.

Supportive Paradigms

Bio-chemical paradigm. Within the last 2 decades, there has been increased interest in understanding the biochemical correlations to personality. Most of the literature has attempted to demonstrate the existence of an association between behavior and changes in hormones, neurotransmitters, and psychoactive substances (Ismail, 1987). Lobstein (1983), for example, showed that exercise training does induce psychobiological changes that affect beta-endorphine levels and emotional stability. Although it will likely be some time before we fully understand the underlying processes, there appears to be little doubt that the study of biochemical correlates is extremely important in our comprehension of personality and behavior (Ismail). Since physical activity is a basic ingredient to many therapeutic recreation programs, the psychobiological effect of exercise is essential to understanding the role of therapeutic recreation programs in the treatment of persons with emotional impairments.

Social learning paradigm. While recognizing the contributions of traditional theories of personality development, social learning (Bandura & Walters, 1963) acknowledges the multi-dimensional aspects of personality development. Through observational learning, individuals
". . . Reproduce actions, attitudes, or emotional responses exhibited by real-life or symbolized models" (Bandura & Walters, p. 89). The social learning process includes such concepts as imitation, modeling, role playing, observation, and symbolism. The results are the development of a repertoire of behaviors that enable the individual to engage in a range of social situations and interactions. Therapeutic recreation specialists utilize social learning theory in the development of social skills and independent functioning in a natural environment.

Play and leisure theory. Play and leisure theory have been shown to be extremely complex psychological, sociological, and neurobiological constructs that influence our thinking, as well as both present and future behavior (Gerson, Ibrahim, deVires, Eisen, & Lollar, 1991), thus making them essential components of therapeutic recreation services. Many theories have been proposed to suggest why people play (Ellis, 1973; Gerson et al.; Levy, 1978; Tinsley & Tinsley, 1986) but the full nature of play and leisure and their role and function remain somewhat obscure. Nonetheless, play and leisure theory serve as a basis for therapeutic recreation which by definition is an extension of these constructs. Their importance to the therapeutic recreation profession is demonstrated by the fact that, among other things, play is an essential element of normal growth and development, assists in the adaption and assimilation of information, and serves as a coping mechanism for children and adults (Gerson et al.). Because play is a natural and universal phenomenon, it is also useful as a diagnostic tool in therapeutic settings and provides an effective medium for the treatment of a variety of disabling conditions. In addition, the activity itself, as in the case of aerobic exercise (Morgan & Goldston, 1987) or in play therapy (Barnett & Storm, 1981), has been shown to contribute directly to the rehabilitation process. Thus, the value of understanding play and leisure and its implications for therapeutic recreation is obvious. Almost all therapeutic recreation services are affected, to some degree, by this critical element of human behavior.

Therapeutic Recreation Interventions

The literature in the field is replete with reference to interventions, value, and expected outcomes of therapeutic recreation services in mental health (Austin, 1982; Carter et al., 1985; Dickason, 1977; Gunn, 1977; Hitzhusen, 1977a; Johnson & Zoerink, 1977; Menninger, 1960; O'Morrow & Reynolds, 1989; Powell & Sable, 1990; Raynor, O'Shea, & Finch, 1990). Given the scope and quantity of research, a limited review of the relevant studies concerning the following interventions is presented: (a) motor skill development, (b) leisure education and leisure counseling, (c) social skills training, (d) adventure challenge, (e) stress management/relaxation, (f) family therapy, (g) expressive techniques, (h) activity/task applications, (i) reality orientation, (j) remotivation therapy, and (k) physical fitness/exercise. These interventions appear to be the primary treatment areas addressed by therapeutic recreation services in mental health. Many of these approaches are not necessarily unique to the therapeutic recreation field but are drawn from related disciplines and have been employed to improve a dysfunctional area, treat a problematic behavior, and/or enhance an existing skill or competency.

Motor skill development. The application of motor skill development strategies are common as an avenue for the enhancement of motor functioning, the expression of an independent lifestyle, and independent leisure functioning (Buettner, 1988; Carter et al., 1985; Peterson & Gunn, 1984; Wehman & Marchant, 1977; Wehman & Schleien, 1981). Specific interventions emphasize systematic instruction for the development of basic motor skills. Instruction for the enhancement of locomotion, fine and gross motor functioning, object manipulation, static and dynamic balance, and leisure activity participation are identified within the literature (Shoemaker & Kaplan, 1972). The ability of an individual to effectively interact within the environment effects their growth and personality development.

Leisure education and leisure counseling. Leisure education from a conceptual perspective is well documented within the therapeutic recreation literature. Leisure education must be viewed as a developmental process "through which individuals develop an understanding of self, leisure, and the relationship of leisure to their life-styles" (Mundy & Odum, 1979, p. 2). Literature on the use of systematic instruction for the development of skills for independent leisure functioning is rather pervasive (Schleien, Tucker, & Heyne, 1985; Schleien, Wehman, & Kiernan, 1981; Wehman, 1977; Wehman, 1978; Wuerch & Voeltz, 1982). In general, the term "leisure education" describes the entire process that encompasses broad categories of leisure skill development, life-style awareness, and leisure counseling approaches.

The application of leisure counseling as a separate entity was first introduced by Dr. W. E. Olson and Dr. J. B. McCormick in 1956. According to the authors, "The Recreation Counseling Program was designed to help the patients maintain the level of social contact reached while hospitalized and to guide them in the use of their leisure time" (Olson & McCormick, 1957, p. 238).

The use of leisure counseling interventions continues to be prevalent within the literature (Aguilar, 1987; Caldwell, Adolph, & Gilbert, 1989; Hultsman, Black, Seehafer, & Hovell, 1987). The focus of the intervention is determined by the needs of the client and may include one of several orientations: (a) Leisure-Related Behavioral Programs, (b) Leisure Lifestyle Awareness, (c) Leisure Resource Guidance, or (d) Leisure Skill Development (McDowell, 1977).

Social skills training. Social skills training encompasses a wide array of skills necessary for independent interaction within the environment. As suggested by Christoff and Kelly (1985), "The implementation of specific 'modules' is an effective way to incorporate social skills training in the overall treatment program of the institution" (p. 365). Instruction that emphasizes the acquisition of specific skills or content areas is suggested. Systematic skills training in personal hygiene, appearance, social etiquette, social interaction skills, cognition and problem solving, and leisure skills are potential target areas for instruction (Skalko, 1991). Therapeutic recreation specialists employ a range of instructional components that fall under the broad spectrum of social skills.

Adventure challenge approaches. Adventure challenge interventions use a series of challenging activities that offer elements of physical and emotional stress to promote change within the individual. This approach has been described as, ". . . The testing of an individual's skill in a natural environment where an element of risk is present and where there is doubt about the outcome of the experience" (Dattilo & Murphy, 1987, p. 15). Adventure challenge programs encompass a wide range of activities where individual and group problem solving, trust, awareness, and goal setting are important components (Roland, Summers, Friedman, Barton, & McCarthy, 1987). Such programs as day camping experiences (Holzworth, Grott, & Hippensteel, 1973; Stoudenmire, 1978); residential camping (Polenz & Rubitz, 1977; Rawson, 1978); survival training (Adams, 1969); ropes courses (Voight, 1988; Witman, 1987); and multiple individual and group initiative activities (Shank, 1975) are some of the applications employed in the treatment of individuals with mental disorders.

Stress management/relaxation. The application of techniques that promote the development of effective stress management and relaxation techniques is well documented within the literature (Austin, 1982; Carter et al., 1985; Girdano & Everly, 1979; Peterson & Gunn, 1984). Such interventions are frequently incorporated as an element of a larger program offering such as social skills training, exercise, or leisure education.

Family therapeutic interventions. Recent literature identifies a trend toward the application of family intervention strategies in the treatment of emotional disabilities (Levy, 1985; Monroe, 1987).

> Family therapeutic recreation is defined as the application of recreation activities (including reality-oriented discussions) in the treatment of family members as a unit to help them achieve better personal and group functioning.... (Clift, 1972, p. 25)

The involvement of the family in the treatment of emotional disability is increasing in popularity. The intent is to assist the family in developing effective patterns of interaction and to enhance the inclusion of all members into the family unit.

Expressive techniques. The use of art, drama, puppetry, film making, fantasy, and dance are all identified as therapeutic mediums used within therapeutic recreation services (Lovelace, 1972; Stensrud, Mishkin, Craft, & Pollack, 1987; Thompson & Wade, 1974; Williams, 1975). The goals of the techniques generally revolve around such areas as: (a) enhancement of self-awareness, (b) communication, (c) self-expression, (d) motor skill development, (e) creative play, and (f) cognition.

Activity/task applications. As with many approaches to therapeutic recreation, the use of task oriented activities to facilitate individual skill development, enhance locus of control and esteem, and mediate depressive symptoms has developed slowly (Carter et al., 1985; Raynor et al., 1990; Williams, 1975). Although the approach encompasses a wide range of activity applications, the means by which individuals are afforded opportunities to exercise control, develop competencies, practice skills, and successfully complete tasks are paramount.

Reality orientation. Reality Orientation programs assist cognitively impaired and disoriented individuals with re- orientation to person, time, and place. The intervention is a facility-wide commitment and must be incorporated as such in order to maximize benefits. Authors such as Kraus (1983) and Austin (1982) promote the use of formal reality orientation sessions to assist the client in relating meaningfully to their environment. The true therapeutic benefits of reality orientation as an intervention remain inconclusive. The intervention continues, however, to remain in the literature.

Remotivation. Remotivation, originated by Dorothy Haskins Smith, is used to assist labile individuals in stimulating healthy aspects of the individual's mind to facilitate and renew interests in daily activities (Austin, 1982). Levy (1971) and Stracke (1970) also discuss the application of motivation and remotivational techniques for the resumption of participation in life.

Physical fitness/exercise. Exercise and fitness training such as jogging, walking, swimming, and cycling are receiving more attention as effective modalities for the treatment and prevention of mental disorders. The adaptability of exercise to a variety of settings and persons with disabilities makes it an extremely attractive treatment for any therapeutic recreation program. Exercise that achieves 40 to 70% of the maximum heart rate, is sustained for 10 minutes or more, and is performed two or more times per week appears to provide the necessary treatment needed to modify mild depression and anxiety disorders (Morgan & Goldston, 1987). Since exercise does increase physical stress on the cardiovascular system, it is always necessary to include appropriate medical screening for participants prior to initiating a program, especially for those over 35 years of age or those with medical problems.

Outcomes and Benefits of Therapeutic Recreation in Mental Health

The preceding sections address the settings, populations, theoretical foundations, and interventions reported in the literature as they relate to the delivery of therapeutic recreation services in mental health. The majority of the material identifies purported benefits of services and dominant interventions. This section will provide the empirical evidence of the efficacy of therapeutic recreation services in mental health. Emphasis will be placed on research reported in the therapeutic recreation literature. However, where appropriate, representative efficacy research found in the literature from related disciplines will also be presented. In order to provide consistency with the previous sections, outcome-oriented empirical studies reported in the literature will be presented according to the previously identified interventions. Tables 3 to 13 summarize major studies identified.

A search of the Psych-Lit, ERIC, and Dissertation Abstracts from 1980 to 1990 was completed for therapeutic recreation (recreational therapy) and each of the intervention areas. The literature search identified documented research for therapeutic recreation and related disciplines.

Motor Skill Development

The literature indicates that therapeutic recreation specialists utilize motor skill development activities as an aspect of the treatment regime for individuals with emotional disabilities. A review of the literature with regard to the efficacy of motor skill development activities in mental health services, however, has demonstrated the limited attention given to this area of intervention for persons with emotional disabilities (see Table 3). Although there exist descriptive statistical studies that address the characteristics of individuals with emotional disabilities including motor skills (Anderson, Williams, McGee, & Silva, 1989; Whyte, 1981), empirical research on the efficacy of therapeutic recreation services on the motor development of persons with emotional disabilities is restricted.

Buettner (1988) and Wehman and Marchant (1977) address the application of motor skill activities and systematic intervention procedures for the development of motor skills for individuals with emotional disabilities. These studies demonstrate future areas of inquiry for the field.

Buettner (1988) introduced the use of exercise coupled with developmental theory to promote flexibility, strength, and ambulation with regressed geriatric patients. Through the use of adaptive equipment and progressive developmental exercise, the older adult with dementia demonstrated statistically significant improvement in the dependent variables of flexibility, strength, and ambulation.

Wehman and Marchant (1977) introduce the use of systematic instruction in the acquisition of recreational skills for children with severe behavioral disabilities. Utilizing a small case research design, the authors demonstrated that recreational skills can be developed through the use of a five stage instructional approach including: (a) Informal Assessment, (b) Task Analysis, (c) Task Analytic Assessment, (d) Instructional Procedures, and (e) Monitoring and Evaluation. Results indicated that the five stage approach proved effective in the development of simple motor skills for recreational participation.

Leisure Education/Leisure Counseling

Theoretical literature professing the values of leisure education and leisure counseling for improving leisure functioning is extensive (See Bibliography). However, the same cannot be said for empirical studies examining the effects of leisure education and leisure counseling in mental health. Such studies are quite limited. Table 4, "Efficacy of Therapeutic Recreation in Mental Health: Leisure Education/Leisure Counseling," provides a summary of empirically based research on leisure education and leisure counseling in mental health.

Tom (1981) examined the effects of a leisure education program on the leisure attitudes and behaviors of individuals with a history of substance abuse. Measures were taken using the Tennessee Self-Concept Scale (TSCS), Leisure Activities Blank (LAB), Leisure Attitude Dimension (LAD), Internal-External Locus of Control (I-ELC), and Behavior Checklist (BC). Results of the study showed positive effects as measured by the LAB and the related elements of anger and vigor of I-ELC measure. The author reported, however, no significant changes in the subjects with respect to the variables of self-concept, leisure attitude, or behavior.

An examination of the effects of a leisure education program on perceived leisure well-being of psychiatric adults was completed by Skalko (1982). The study used a pre-test and post-test design and measured perceived leisure well-being via the Leisure Well-Being Inventory (McDowell, 1978). Significant differences were reported between experimental and control groups on post-intervention measures of perceived leisure well-being. The author emphasized the exploratory nature of the study and cautioned the generalization of results due to lack of validity and reliability measures of the instrument.

Skalko (1990) also investigated the effects of leisure education and therapeutic recreation programming on the quality of discretionary time use of individuals with chronic mental illness. The results indicate that during intervention phases, the quality of discretionary time use of individuals with chronic mental illness can be altered in a positive direction. Upon withdrawal of intervention, however, subjects return to lower quality time usage.

In studying the effects of a leisure education program on expressed attitudes toward recreation and expressed attitude toward delinquency of adjudicated adolescents, Aguilar (1987) found marginal results. Although some changes were shown, none of were statistically significant. Several concerns were addressed that affected the results of the study including: (a) the average age of the participants, (b) the large group to which the instrument was administered, and (c) the length of the Leisure Education Program.

Wolfe and Riddick (1984) examined the effects of a leisure counseling program on the leisure attitude and self-esteem of adults with psychiatric disability. The authors report no significant change on any of the measures. The authors indicated, however, that a longer period of intervention may be required to realize significant gains.

Schleien (1982) found significant gains when examining the effects of a leisure education program on the leisure time use and nature of play of severely learning disabled children. The leisure education program produced gains in cooperative and constructive play and decreases in inappropriate and isolate play for the learning disabled subjects. The incorporation of a pre- post-social validation parent telephone questionnaire showed generalization of cooperative leisure skills to the home environment.

Research on the application of leisure education and leisure counseling techniques offers mixed reports on the efficacy of the approaches in mental health settings. The general consensus of the research indicates the need for further study and more systematic procedures over longer periods of time.

Social Skills Training

Social skills training has been recognized for its contribution to the acquisition of skills for social competence and community functioning (Test & Stein, 1978). Literature in social skills training contains numerous theoretical and empirical studies that demonstrate the efficacy of social skills training for persons with mental illness (see Table 5).

Liberman et al. (1984) found that through systematic social skills training, the psychiatric client could develop basic social skills. Observations indicate that trained behaviors could be generalized to untrained scenes (social situations not trained to interact within), and that the general acquisition of social skills were enhanced.

The application of role playing (Eisler, Blanchard, Fitts, & Williams, 1978; Eisler, Hersen, & Miller, 1973; Hersen & Bellack, 1976a) has been applied with success in promoting social skills. All of the above studies found that through a series of role playing situations, social and conversational skills could be enhanced. Generally, outcomes were measured through the use of frequency, duration, or observer ratings of behavior. Results indicate that the social skills intervention technique is effective with target behaviors such as eye contact, voice tone and volume, affect, and assertiveness.

Monti et al. (1979) completed a study comparing social skills training with a combined social skills/bibliotherapy intervention. The Rathus Assertiveness Scale, the Edwards Social Desirability Scale, plus clinical outcome measures were used to compare intervention effectiveness. Social skills training proved to be more effective than the combined training approach in social skill enhancement.

In a study by Wong in 1983 (cited in Liberman et al., 1986), the effects of supervised recreational activities on dysfunctional behaviors of persons with chronic mental illness were examined. It was found that a systematic recreational therapy services program reduced the frequency of hallucinatory speech behavior of a male subject with chronic schizophrenia. Unstructured time with access to leisure materials without prompting was compared to other times when the subjects were prompted and reinforced for participation in available activities.

> Obsessive-compulsive ruminations, posturings, inappropriate laughter, mumbling to self, and other bizarre behaviors were significantly reduced when patients were engaged in structured recreational activities. (Liberman et al., p. 642).

Therapeutic recreation literature related to the efficacy of social skills interventions in mental health is limited. Reynolds and Arthur (1982) studied the effects of peer modeling and cognitive self-guidance on the social play of children with emotional disabilities. The results indicated that, although an improvement in cooperative play was demonstrated, the changes were only temporary in nature.

Research in the area of social skills training includes studies that demonstrated no significant change or temporary change (McLatchie, 1981; Nagahiro, 1983). The majority of literature in subject behavior, however, supports the use of social skills training for the individual with mental illness. In general, the application of social skills training has demonstrated short-term merit and suggests that continued reinforcement may extend the longevity of the desired outcomes.

Adventure Challenge

One of the fastest growing and most popular mental health and correctional intervention programs within therapeutic recreation and related professions has been adventure challenge programming. According to Hunter (1987) there are well over 100 programs that use physically and psychologically demanding outdoor programs as a rehabilitative stimulus. Most are viewed as cost-effective alternatives to traditional clinical or institutional programs serving emotionally impaired and adjudicated youth (Arthur, 1976). Others are supplemental to more comprehensive treatment or educational programs.

Given the popularity of these programs, one would expect the support of a significant body of research. However, although many studies have been reported in the literature, most are pre-experimental designs and therefore lack validity beyond the study itself (Wright, 1983). Therefore, this review will be limited to more recent controlled studies that appear to contribute to an understanding of adventure challenge programs and their application in therapeutic recreation. (See Table 6.)

In a study designed to assess the importance of adventure programs on cooperation and trust, Witman (1987) assigned 17 emotionally impaired adolescents to one of three treatment groups: (a) control, (b) social recreation, or (c) adventure. The Cooperation and Trust Scale and a Behavior Rating Scale completed by their personal counselors were used to identify pre- and post-treatment responses to planned therapeutic interventions over a 3-day period in each of the three groups. Following treatment, the adventure group members were perceived by their counselors as having more cooperative, altruistic, trusting, caring, and group-oriented behavior. It was reported that members of the adventure group also appeared to tolerate and accept changes in their social community structure more easily than their peers, an unexpected outcome the investigator attributed to the effect of team-building experiences used during the adventure program. The author warns against over generalizing from these impressive outcomes, however, due to the variability of the measurement tools and the potential contamination of ancillary treatment effects in the comprehensive health care delivery system. The results of this study were also limited to a rather finite period and therefore may not be sustained beyond a few days or weeks following the intervention. This is a common problem with most if not all studies conducted in this area of investigation.

Another study, involving 10 adjudicated male youths (Hunter, 1987), used the constant comparative method of field-based recording and event analysis described by Glaser and Strauss (1967) to collect data from a 28-day Outward Bound training program. The results of this investigation suggest how and why adventure program participants change thus providing the basis for a substantive empirically-based theory on the nature and potential effect of these experiences. Specific results indicated that several of the participants became more open, reduced verbal abuse to others, increased willingness to assist others, and reduced complaining about activities. The author notes that since this program did not appear to have adverse effects on any of the participants, it could be viewed quite positively when compared to traditional forms of treatment for adjudicated youth. Although much remains to be known, this study suggests that adventure programs do contribute to positive behavior changes in some participants. However, Hunter and Purcell (1984) caution that since there are a multitude of variables that are difficult to control, changes that occur as a result of participation in adventure programs are probably program and subject-specific.

Using a quasi-experimental design, Wright (1983) studied the effect of a 26-day wilderness treatment program on 47 adjudicated youth. Analysis of the data revealed significant differences between the experimental and control groups with the experimental group showing an increase in self-esteem, self-efficacy, internality, and fitness following participation in the program. However, participants failed to develop cognitive problem-solving skills which suggests program changes would be required to effect similar positive changes in this area.

One of the major themes in the adventure challenge literature has been the focus on self-concept. An individual's view of himself/herself directly affects his/her ability to cope with the circumstances of life (Fitts, 1971). Therefore, this psychological construct has become a therapeutic goal for many educational and rehabilitation institutions (Ewert, 1983). Although some of the literature has shown the positive results of adventure programs on self-concept and related components (Ewert, 1988; Fletcher, 1970; Mathias, 1977) other studies have been inconclusive, suggesting the need for more rigorous research designs (Ewert, 1983).

In a related study, persons with disabilities were integrated with able-bodied individuals in a wilderness adventure program (McAvoy, Schatz, Stuts, Schleien, & Lais, 1989) to test the theoretical framework of anxiety and self-concept and to assess the effect of participation on various personal and lifestyle variables. Analysis of findings indicated a decrease in trait anxiety for all participants. The results also indicated a substantial positive change in personal lifestyle attributes including: (a) increased confidence, (b) greater willingness to take risks, (c) increased sense of physical strength, (d) heightened environmental concern, (e) better understanding of self, (f) increased tolerance of others, (g) and for stressful situations, increased ability to live independently, and (h) positive changes toward education and employment. Although this study did not include individuals diagnosed with emotional disabilities, the results suggest adventure recreation programs can have a significant positive impact on anxiety levels and related personality variables for persons with and without disabilities.

Finally, in a descriptive study involving 32 acute inpatients diagnosed as having an affective disorder, post-traumatic stress disorder, anxiety disorder, schizophrenia, or substance abuse, a modified adventure challenge program was used as one of several treatment components in a Veterans Hospital (Roland et al., 1987). Staff reported that clients who completed the adventure challenge program demonstrated improved self-esteem, sense of accomplishment, and communication skills. It was also noted that many clients did not respond to other treatment modalities until after they participated in the challenge program. Observations suggest that the experience served as a catalyst to traditional psycho-therapeutic interventions. The study is unique in that it documents the potential of adventure challenge programs for more seriously disturbed psychiatric inpatients who were previously thought to be inappropriate for such programs (Stitch, 1983).

Given the nature and complexity of attitudinal and behavioral change, it is extremely difficult to demonstrate the unequivocal success of adventure challenge programs in the rehabilitation of persons with emotional disabilities. However, the literature does seem to indicate the potential of this intervention strategy for use with certain types of clients, especially children and youth. Further outcome research with adventure challenge programs is certainly needed to confirm these results.

Stress Management/Relaxation

A review of the therapeutic recreation literature reveals a limited number of studies referencing stress management. However, in spite of this status, stress management is used by many therapeutic recreation professionals in a variety of settings: (a) pain clinics, (b) substance abuse treatment centers, (c) mental health centers, and/or (d) related service delivery areas. Therefore, this literature review will highlight studies from related disciplines that have significant implications and application to our field. (See Table 7.)

Physical activity has frequently been analyzed for its stress reducing properties. Recently, Berger and Owen (1988) proposed a stress reducing taxonomy that, according to the authors, would modify stress responses. The necessary properties for stress reducing activities would include physical activities that are (a) aerobic, (b) non-competitive, (c) predictable, and (d) rhythmical. Additionally, they suggest the activity should be: (a) a regularly scheduled weekly activity (frequency = 2 + times per week); (b) of moderate intensity (40 to 70% of maximum heart rate); and (c) at least 20 to 30 minutes in length (duration). Finally, they suggest the activity should be pleasing and enjoyable to the participant. To the degree that a given activity meets these criteria, one might expect short-term reduction in stress levels for the participant (Berger, 1983/1984, 1986, 1987). The beneficial psychological effects of physical activity can only be maintained through regular participation in those selected activities that meet the proposed criteria. Continuous weekly involvement is required to extend short-term positive effects into long-term gains.

In the study cited above, Berger and Owen (1988) found that yoga participants reported significant short-term reductions in acute anxiety measures while swimmers, body conditioning participants, fencers, and two control non-activity participant (lecture classes) groups did not. This data is somewhat inconsistent with previous studies that have demonstrated significant short-term reduction in stress as a result of aerobic conditioning in swimming (Berger, 1983/1984, 1986) and jogging (Long, 1984; Sachs, 1982; Sinyor, Schwartz, Peronnet, Brisson, & Seraganian, 1983).

Following a thorough review of the exercise literature, De Vries (1987) concludes that there is, "substantial agreement among investigators that exercise provides a 'tranquilizer' effect" (p. 104). He further states that exercise of an appropriate type, intensity, and duration may be equal to or possibly more effective than other popular antidotes to anxiety such as meditation or medication. This response to exercise appears to have an immediate as well as long-term effect for persons of all ages provided continued involvement in physically demanding activities is maintained.

In a slightly different approach to stress management, Barnett and Storm (1981) designed a laboratory experiment to test a psychoanalytic paradigm that might be observed through play behaviors of children following a stressful event. The investigators found support for the therapeutic role of play in facilitating expression and thereby reducing the anxiety related specifically to a traumatic event. According to the authors, play provides children the opportunity to restore "a sense of harmony and concordance to the environment when it has been temporarily disrupted" (p. 170). From this study, we learn that children often initiate play experiences to cope with unpleasant events. The perception of freedom, so critical to the nature of play itself, allows the experience to become therapeutic by self-directed expression of the emotional conflict. Given the revealing nature of play behaviors, they provide an excellent source of diagnostic information for therapeutic recreation personnel and therefore justify creating a variety of "free play" opportunities for children in treatment settings.

In an extensive review of the stress management literature, Matheny, Aycock, Pugh, Curlette, and Silva Cannella (1986) describe the most effective coping strategies for stressors. From an analysis of 54 research studies, the four techniques which showed the greatest potential for effective coping were: (a) cognitive restructuring, (b) relaxation, (c) social skills, and (d) negative diversion. In her analysis, and review of this article, Stumbo (1988) notes that a comprehensive leisure education program as outlined by Mundy and Odum (1979) and Peterson and Gunn (1984) appears to have great potential to address these particular coping strategies. Although this proposal is based on theoretical assumptions regarding the efficacy of leisure education to instill these coping techniques, it does provide support for the potential of therapeutic recreation programs that develop the specific skills involved in effective stress management.

The management of stress is a complex phenomena that extends far beyond the therapeutic recreation literature. However, there are many interventions techniques that have been effectively used by therapeutic recreation personnel to assist in the treatment of stress related problems. Since stress management techniques are most effective when they are carefully matched to the particular individual and situation, it is recommended that the specialist develop expertise in teaching and applying several coping strategies.

Family Therapeutic Applications

A relatively new treatment area in the field of therapeutic recreation is the application of therapeutic activity interventions in the treatment of the family unit. Due to the developing nature of this treatment, the information and literature concerning the treatment of families using therapeutically planned activities is limited. Although therapeutic recreation is becoming a viable treatment modality, most of the literature speaks more to descriptions of programs in operation than to empirical outcomes.

In general, the use of activities in the treatment of dysfunctional families can be categorized into two areas. The first area is activities used to assist a family to improve its leisure/recreation issues and general leisure functioning. The second area involves activities treating specific family issues such as communication, family structure, and limit setting.

In the treatment of leisure functioning, Fink and Beddall Fink (1986) developed a rationale for and a description of a family leisure program for inpatient psychiatric hospitals. The authors report the program was effective in enhancing family role definitions, in promoting cooperative interaction skills, and in the development of leisure skills and concepts. The program also served to stimulate better relationships between the hospital staff and family members, provided useful diagnostic information on family dynamics, and provided a setting to practice skills taught by other disciplines.

Hart (1984) reported that value laden activities, such as repelling, that develop trust were rated more highly by family members attending a family camp than were traditional activities such as talent shows. The author also reported anecdotal evidence to suggest that values-oriented activities promoted family unity, self-respect and confidence, increased willingness to play together, and spiritual growth.

Perceived constraints to leisure participation by families of children with emotional and behavioral disabilities were shown to be: (a) money, (b) time, (c) family responsibilities, (d) work, and (e) more important things to do (Levy, 1985). Interestingly, the child with the disability, per se, was not identified as a significant barrier to family leisure participation. The majority of the parents tended to view leisure activities as being important to their child and 88.6% indicated they would like to do more activities together.

There are also several examples of efforts to engage, treat, and evaluate families using prescribed activities in the literature. In a descriptive study, DeSalvatore and Roseman (1986) used activities such as new games, cooking sessions, and arts and crafts to engage hospitalized children with emotional impairments and their families in a process used to assess and treat family problems, particularly the relationship of various subsystems, communication, limit setting, family boundaries, and rules. Results indicate an increase in self-esteem for parents and children, an increase in positive communication among family members, and parents became more effective in behavior management. Simon (1982) used a similar therapeutic approach to effectively evaluate family structures and identify key issues.

Although no strong empirical evidence exists to support the often quoted axiom, "the family that plays together, stays together," a number of descriptive studies reviewed by Holman and Epperson (1984) seemed to suggest some rationale for this premise. Stinnett, Sanders, DeFrain, and Parkhurst (1982), for example, concluded that "vacation, recreation, and talking" (p. 12) were very important variables in strengthening the family. Similarly, a study commissioned by General Mills (General Mills American Family Report, 1981) indicated "going on vacation" and "talking with parents" were helpful in establishing congruence between teenagers and their parents. The implications of this research, as tenuous as it is, suggests that therapeutic recreation programs that include the examination and development of family leisure experiences would appear to make a significant contribution to the treatment and rehabilitation process.

Given the lack of empirical research in this area, it is difficult to develop substantive conclusions about the role of therapeutic recreation in the treatment of dysfunctional families. However, evidence from descriptive studies suggests potential areas of intervention including evaluation of family systems, development of communication and interpersonal relationships. (See Table 8.)

Expressive Therapy

Although several expressive therapies such as dance, horticulture, music, art, and psychodrama are used in mental health treatment programs, they typically require specialized training and/or certification outside the field of therapeutic recreation. As such, it does not seem appropriate to review the efficacy of these treatment modalities in the scope of this paper except for those studies that have been published in therapeutic recreation journals or are clearly associated with the field of therapeutic recreation. Depending on the setting, expressive therapies often overlap with therapeutic recreation or, in the absence of a trained professional such as a music, art, or dance therapist, these therapies often become regular components of the therapeutic recreation program.

Through the review of the therapeutic recreation literature, few recent studies and no empirical studies in expressive therapeutic techniques were identified. (See Table 9.) Articles in the Therapeutic Recreation Journal on dance (McGinnis, 1974); drama (Karpilow, 1970; Malatesta, 1972); horticulture (Hefley & Sperling, 1973); and film-making (Williams, 1975); as well as one on horticulture (Griffiths & Griffiths, 1976) in the Journal of Leisureability represent the bulk of the sources. Unfortunately, these articles simply describe expressive therapy programs and do not provide substantive support for potential outcomes that could be expected. Therefore, little evidence exists to demonstrate the efficacy of therapeutic recreation through expressive techniques.

Similarly, in spite of over 1,000 articles written on the topic of pet therapy, limited evidence exists to show its unequivocal effectiveness in the treatment of persons with mental illness (Draper, Gerber, & Layng, 1990). Yet, some authors have continued to make claims that pet therapy provides physiological, psychological, and social benefits to a variety of persons with disabilities (Cusack & Smith, 1984). As with other areas of the expressive therapies, most of the studies are anecdotal or descriptive in nature and therefore, are of limited value to efficacy research.

In summary, the research on expressive therapies is extremely limited and of little value in determining valid and reliable outcomes expected in therapeutic recreation programs of this nature. It would appear that at the present time, the field of therapeutic recreation must rely on research collected by the respective disciplines of art, music, dance, and psychodrama therapy to provide the rationale and support for these therapeutic interventions.

Activity/Task Applications

Action-oriented therapies (e.g., group task activities, adventure challenge, camping, physical activities) have made significant contributions in the treatment of persons with psychological impairments. Some of these contributions are documented in other sections of this paper (see adventure challenge and physical fitness/exercise). In addition, several unique treatment programs have recently presented descriptive reports of their work (Raynor, 1987; Raynor et al., 1990). Table 10 offers a convenient reference of these works.

In the first study, adult and adolescent patients in a short-term psychiatric hospital were involved in building a large, 3-person kayak. Although an analysis of the data revealed no statistically significant changes, anecdotal records indicate positive results such as improved cooperation and group interaction, a sense of pride and accomplishment in the product, and a variety of opportunities to relate individual clinical issues to performance in the group.

The second study included adult, adolescent, and child inpatient psychiatric units becoming involved in an archaeological dig on the site of a proposed new hospital complex (Raynor, 1987). Over the course of the study approximately 75 patients participated in the project. Again, the results were anecdotal but showed numerous positive responses to this treatment intervention strategy. Treatment goals with individual patients were facilitated by their involvement in the project.

Although the evidence is primarily anecdotal, involvement in activity/task interventions does appear to contribute to a variety of environmental, group, and individual outcomes that promote the goals of mental health. It is evident that continued empirical verification is needed.

Reality Orientation

Reality orientation is described in the literature as an intervention to reduce confusion and increase orientation of the mentally ill and confused elderly for over 2 decades. Historically, the early literature reports the efficacy of reality orientation intervention (Folsom, 1968) but examples of systematic inquiry are limited. Since the application of reality orientation strategies is quite dominant in the area of geriatrics, this report will concentrate on studies with disoriented and elderly subjects. It is important to recognize that the efficacy of reality orientation as an intervention is inconclusive. (See Table 11.)

In a study by Citrin and Dixon (1977), the effects of a formal 24 hour reality orientation program, as measured by subjects' recall on a Reality Orientation Information Sheet, was evaluated. Experimental group subjects were enrolled in a 24 hour reality orientation program which included classroom reinforcement. The control group subjects did not receive reality orientation reinforcements. Results indicated significant differences between the two groups in post-test measures on the Reality Orientation Information Sheet with the experimental group demonstrating significantly greater gains in information recall.

Baines, Saxby, and Ehlert (1987) found that the use of reality orientation prior to and in combination with remotivation therapy approaches. The combined intervention contributed to more significant gains in cognition and behaviors of experimental group subjects.

Other studies have also demonstrated the efficacy of reality orientation on specific behaviors and orientation. Miller (1987) compared the use of reality orientation to that of validation therapy upon the variable of orientation and morale and behavioral functioning. The author found that reality orientation intervention produced greater gains in orientation than did validation therapy. No significant changes were observed in morale or behavior.

Ivan (1982) compared the effects of reality orientation and re-socialization on the variable of cognition and social accessibility of confused elderly. Utilizing the Short Portable Mental Status Questionnaire at intervals during the study, the author concluded that the reality orientation program was more effective in producing positive change in cognitive accessibility while the re-socialization intervention was more effective in altering social accessibility. The changes were, however, short-term in nature.

Reality orientation techniques have also been applied to the reduction of hallucinatory and delusional behavior of psychiatric adults (North, 1987). Employing reality orientation information at the onset of hallucinations or delusional behavior, was found to be effective in reducing the frequency of the behaviors (North).

The efficacy of reality orientation in the treatment of individuals who exhibit confusion and disorientation has shown mixed results. Reality orientation, however, continues to be widely used to address symptoms of confusion and disorientation associated with a range of mental diagnoses.

Remotivation Therapy

The efficacy of remotivation therapy also appears to be inconclusive in the literature. Some studies, however, do offer positive indications of the efficacy of remotivation techniques (Bowers, Anderson, Blomeier, & Pelz, 1967; Long, 1961). (See Table 12.)

Bowers et al. (1967) found remotivation therapy to be effective in improving individual behavior and social functioning of geriatric patients. Three groups (Group 1--all male; Group 2--all female; and Group 3--male and female) were evaluated for individual in-group behavior and for social functioning. The authors indicated significant improvements were generated for in-group and social behavior functioning after 6 months of participation in the remotivation group for two of the three groups. The all male group showed improvements but the gains were not statistically significant.

Birkett and Boltuch (1973) did not find significant difference in the efficacy of remotivation therapy as compared to conventional group therapy. The patients were engaged in weekly, 1 hour sessions of remotivation. Both groups showed improvement but the differences were not statistically significant.

In a study comparing the use of children versus adults as facilitators in remotivation therapy with confused elderly individuals, Allred (1985) found no significant difference in scores as reflected by the Life Satisfaction Index-Z. No statistical difference was found between the life satisfaction scores in either of the remotivation intervention groups or control group scores.

Long (1961) presented a preliminary report on the effectiveness of remotivation techniques on the exhibited behavior of adults with psychiatric disabilities residing in a state hospital. Results from the L-M Fergus Falls Behavior Rating Scale (FFRS) and the Custodial Mental Illness Ideology Scale (CMI) showed significant differences between the wards receiving remotivation and those wards that did not receive remotivation.

The efficacy of remotivation therapy techniques seems inconclusive. The literature, however, purports that a wide range of values and remotivation techniques are utilized in numerous settings. The need for continued research on the use of remotivation therapy techniques in therapeutic recreation is evident.

Physical Fitness/Exercise

Exercise and physical activity have long been recognized for their contribution to physical well-being and their positive effect on specific physiological variables associated with health and wellness such as blood pressure and heart rate (McGlynn, 1987). More recently, researchers have sought to show a similar relationship between exercise and psychological variables such as mood state, stress reduction, and personality development (Morgan & Goldston, 1987).

Although over 1,100 studies have been reported in the literature regarding this subject, relatively few have demonstrated sound, reliable research methodology (Folkins & Sime, 1981; Morgan, 1984). Therefore, it has been difficult to show unequivocal positive relationships between exercise and mental health. There are however, several studies that used appropriate methods which contribute to our understanding of this phenomenon. Table 13 offers a summary of these studies.

Martinsen, Medhus, and Sandvik (1984) studied the effect of exercise training on 49 hospitalized male and female clients who met the DSM-III criteria for depression. Subjects ranged in age from 17 to 60 (mean = 40). Findings of the 9 week study, which randomly assigned patients to exercise and control groups, showed a significant difference in the reduction of depression scores with the most positive effect on the exercise group. Aerobic exercise reportedly contributed to a significant reduction in inner tension, depressive thinking, concentration difficulties, sleep disturbances, and observed muscular tension. These findings compare favorably with those of Reuter, Mutrie, and Harris (1984) who prescribed exercise and counseling respectively for two groups of nine depressed college students and Greist et al. (1979) who studied the effect of physical training on young, mildly depressed patients. Although it has been suggested that physical exercise serves primarily as a distraction from other personal problems (Bahrke & Morgan, 1978), the present study seems to indicate that aerobic exercise has an antidepressive effect as well as a positive effect on various psychosomatic disorders such as headaches, migraines, muscular tension, lumbar pain, obesity, and cardiac neurosis.

Sime (1987) used a multiple baseline study with cross-sectional time series analyses on a population of 15 moderately depressed subjects to demonstrate mood state changes following a 10 week aerobic exercise program. Depression scores, as recorded by the Beck Depression Inventory, were significantly lower following the exercise treatment and remained lower at the 6-month and 21-month follow-up for all those who continued to exercise on a regular basis. Such a long-term follow-up is rare in the exercise and mental health literature and the positive effect certainly supports the psychological benefits of vigorous exercise.

Following a comprehensive review of the most significant clinical studies, Martinsen (1990) concluded that, although much remains to be known, aerobic exercise is more effective than no treatment and not significantly different from other forms of treatment, including various forms of psychotherapy. This is particularly true for clients with mild to moderate forms of unipolar depressive illness. Martinsen also notes that depressed individuals have reduced levels of fitness caused by physical inactivity which contributes to their lack of physical and emotional health. These findings have been reported by others (Iso-Ahola & Mobily, 1982; Sime, Mayer, Witte, Ganster, & Tharp, 1985; Wassman & Iso-Ahola, 1985) and provide added support for physical fitness training in a comprehensive treatment program for non-bipolar depressive disorders.

From these few selected studies and others reviewed by the authors, it is apparent that the growing volume of research provides substantial evidence that physical activity can have a moderating effect on depressed mood states. There are numerous theories that have been suggested to explain these effects but most believe a variety of variables including biological, environmental, psychological, and social factors contribute to the eventual changes. Given the physiological and psychological benefits of exercise for people of all ages, it would seem appropriate for therapeutic recreation specialists to include physical exercise as a significant component of their programs.

A Final Thought About Outcome Research

A review of the literature on the efficacy of therapeutic recreation programs in mental health has shown the strengths and weaknesses of our research efforts. We have made progress in documenting the effectiveness of some aspects of our service but have a great deal to learn about other areas. The key to understanding our unique and special contribution to the rehabilitation of individuals who experience mental illness may however, in many cases, be overlooked or ignored because of its simplicity. A study by Vale and Mlott (1983) concluded that psychiatric inpatient adults reported a significant correlation between stated enjoyment and treatment effectiveness. Creating a positive environment by facilitating authentic interpersonal relations and offering opportunities to feel accepted and build self-confidence appear to contribute substantially to the outcomes of treatment. Spontaneity and playfulness, qualities that are often lacking or repressed in individuals undergoing psychiatric treatment, appears to be more important to maintaining a healthy, balanced life than is often thought. The findings of Reich and Zautra (1981, 1984, 1989) suggest that engagement in activities that produce a positive affect mitigates negative psychological distress and contributes to the participant's quality of life. This research, as well as that of others (Cousins, 1979; Nezu, Nezu, & Blissett, 1988; Porterfield, 1987; Ruben, 1980), suggests that the nature of the experience is critical to our health and therefore, those programs that promote and encourage laughter, enjoyment, and playfulness contribute to the efficacy of therapeutic recreation in mental health settings. In addition, Wassman and Iso-Ahola (1985) suggest structured activities or planned activities are more effective than self-initiated activities in modifying symptoms of depression. Therefore, research indicates that the most effective interventions will be those in which therapeutic recreation specialists systematically develop programs that promote interpersonal relationships, feelings of acceptance, and self-confidence.

Recommendations for Future Research

Overview

A review of research to date on the efficacy of therapeutic recreation in mental health settings and the methodologies employed, depicts a collection of studies conducted primarily through related disciplines. The research identified through the review of the literature emphasizes the continued need for systematic efficacy research and the development of effective methods to be used by therapeutic recreation professionals in mental health settings.

Efficacy research studies cited in this review of the literature involve a range of research methodologies. The application of small case research designs including task analytic skill evaluation, multiple base line design and behavioral observation, and pre-test/post-test designs were utilized.

A summary of the results of the limited number of current outcome oriented research studies indicates that the approaches used by therapeutic recreation specialists are effective in generating positive changes in physical, social, cognitive, and emotional states. In general, however, the need for continued research is emphasized throughout the review.

Recommendations

As a result of this review, there are a number of recommendations that can be made to address the current state-of-art of efficacy research for therapeutic recreation in mental health.

1. The field must develop systematic plans to improve the quality and quantity of research in the future. Descriptive and anecdotal studies should be de-emphasized and empirically based research studies increased. University curricula should begin to emphasize basic efficacy research skills at the undergraduate level with greater emphasis on research competencies at the master's level of preparation. In addition, doctoral preparation should strongly emphasize empirically based research competencies for all doctoral candidates.

2. There exists limited research on the efficacy of therapeutic recreation in mental health in the areas of motor skill development, expressive therapeutic interventions, leisure education and leisure counseling, and family interventions. Programs that employ one or more of these techniques should initiate research studies to determine the effectiveness of these approaches.

3. Some of the most promising mental health outcomes in therapeutic recreation programs appear to be in the area of physical fitness and exercise. Increasingly, therapeutic recreation professionals should institute sound exercise programs with data collection techniques that continue to demonstrate the efficacy of the approach.

4. Most of the research has focused on the short-term outcomes. Longitudinal studies on the effectiveness of therapeutic recreation services need to be implemented in almost all areas.

5. Qualitative research methodologies should be employed with greater frequency. Strong qualitative research studies on the perceived effects of therapeutic recreation should be implemented.

6. Cooperative research with other disciplines would seem appropriate and useful to the field. Therapeutic recreation professionals should increase efforts to engage in cooperative research efforts with related disciplines within their

facilities including occupational therapy, physical therapy, psychology, and social work.

7. The lack of sound empirical research in therapeutic recreation in mental health has significant implications to the growth and development of the profession. The need to justify services or demonstrate the value of the service is directly related to its acceptance as a prescribed and "billable" service through third party carriers. We must renew efforts to develop a solid research base for therapeutic recreation services in mental health. Greater communication, cooperation, and exchange must occur between practitioners and researchers/educators. This must be a shared charge by all parties concerned. The aggressive implementation of studies to determine the efficacy of therapeutic recreation in mental health is critical to the continued growth of the field.

8. Research that addresses the relationship between therapist qualities, interpersonal styles, the nature of the experience, and perceived confidence on the part of the consumer is needed. As implied by Vale and Mlott (1983), demonstrating therapeutic recreation's contribution to the enjoyment of life and those variables that affect individual perceptions should be investigated.

9. Finally, the continued move toward the deinstitutionalization of persons with mental illness places demands on the field for community-based research. Therapeutic recreation plays a unique role in the community adjustment of persons with mental illness. The efficacy of therapeutic recreation services on the acquisition of functional skills, skills for effective community integration, leisure skill acquisition, skills for community adjustment, and the role of therapeutic recreation in the maintenance of the individual with mental illness in the community thus preventing/reducing hospital recidivism must be addressed.

The field of therapeutic recreation continues to struggle with the quantity and quality of outcome oriented research (Compton, 1989). Among the primary charges for the field of therapeutic recreation continues to be the demonstration of the efficacy of our services (Compton; Witt, 1988).

Table 1. Adult Populations Served in Mental Health

Disorders	Essential and Associated Features
Organic Mental Disorders - Delirium & Dementia - Amnestic Syndrome - Organic Delusional Syndrome - Intoxication & Withdrawal	- Psychological or behavioral abnormality associated with transient or permanent brain dysfunction. - Different emotional, motivational, behavioral abnormalities; cognitive impairment, anxiety; depression; fear of the loss of control; decrease control of sexual and aggressive impulses.
Schizophrenia	- Disturbances in many psychological areas including content and form of thought, perception, affect, sense of self, volition, relationship to external world, and psychomotor behavior; poor self-care; poor social relations; delusions and hallucinations.
Delusional Disorder (Paranoid)	- Presence of persistent, non-bizarre delusions; possible hallucinations; possible mania and/or depression.
Somatoform - Conversion Disorder - Hypochondriasis - Somatization	- Physical symptoms suggesting physical disorder for which there are no clear organic findings. These symptoms are associated with psychological factors or conflicts.
Mood Disorders - Bipolar - Depressive	- Contains a number of different sub-classifications; essential feature is a disturbance of mood either an elevation, expansion, irritable mood, or depressed mood; other affected areas include activities of daily living; sleep; energy; self-esteem; thought and/or cognitive processes.
Anxiety Disorders	- Experience of unexpected panic attacks; shortness of breath; faintness; increased heart rate; shaking; sweating; choking; nausea; chest pains; various fears; chills or hot flashes.
Sexual Disorders	- Parahilias--recurrent sexual urges and sexually arousing fantasies involving non-human objects, suffering of one's self or one's partner, children or other non-consenting person. - Sexual Dysfunctions--inhibition in psychophysiological changes that characterize the sexual response cycle.
Adjustment Disorders	- Reaction to an identifiable psychosocial stressor; maladaptive nature of the reaction is indicated by the impairment of occupational functioning; symptoms that are in excess of a normal reaction to stressors.

Table 2. Child/Adolescent Populations Served in Mental Health

Disorders	Essential and Associated Features
Mental Retardation	- Significant subaverage general intellectual functioning; Deficits in adaptive functioning in the areas of social skills, communication, activities of daily living and/or self sufficiency; onset before the age of 18 years.
Pervasive Developmental Disorder	- Impairment in reciprocal social interaction, verbal and non-verbal communication, and fantasy/imagination.
	- Poor cognitive skills; abnormal motor behavior; sensory input problems; self-injurious behavior; poor sleep patterns and abnormal mood patterns.
Attention-Deficit Hyperactivity Disorder	- Inappropriate degree of attention; impulsiveness; hyperactivity; difficulty playing quietly; excessive gross motor activity; poor self-esteem; temper outbursts; mood lability; poor frustration tolerance; academic problems.
Conduct Disorder	- Persistent pattern of conduct in which basic rights of others and major age-appropriate societal norms or rules are violated; physical aggression is present; cruelty, destruction and violence may be present; lack of awareness of others' feelings; anxiety; depression; poor academic performance; lack of guilt.
Oppositional Defiant Disorder	- Negativistic, hostile, and defiant behavior; low self-esteem; mood lability; temper outbursts; frequently actively defies adult requests or rules and deliberately annoys others; 8 years old plus.
Separation Anxiety Disorder	- Excessive anxiety around separation from a significant person with whom the child is attached; fears of real or imagined objects; extreme homesickness; depressed mood; fears may appear bizarre.
Avoidant Disorder	- Shrinking from contact with unfamiliar people; social withdrawal; embarrassed; timid; lack of assertiveness; inhibition of normal psychosexual activity in adolescents.
Anorexia Nervosa	- Refusal to maintain body weight; intense fear of weight gain; distorted body image; amenorrhea; vomiting/purging; focus of food as a topic of thought or fantasy; unusual hoarding; denial of problem.
Bulimia Nervosa	- Recurrent episodes of binge eating; food eaten secretly followed by abdominal discomfort, sleep, and social interruption to induce vomiting; depressed mood; possible substance abuse.
Gender Identity Disorder	- Intense distress about own sex; persistence to be of opposite sex; preoccupation about all the features of the opposite sex; some may display social withdrawal and/or depression.
Tourette's Disorder	- Multiple motor and one or more vocal tics; social acceptance difficulties; obscene thoughts.

Table 2. (cont'd)

Disorders	Essential and Associated Features
Reactive Attachment Disorder of Infancy or Childhood	- Disturbance in of social relatedness of all on most social/interpersonal contexts; "failure to thrive" is associated with severe forms of the disorder; feeding disturbances; sleep problems; sensory hypersensitivity; apathetic in a number of areas such as weak cries and weak motor responses.

The American Psychiatric Association. (1987). <u>Diagnostic and statistical manual of mental disorders</u> (DSM III-R) (3rd ed.-Revised), Washington, DC: Author.

Table 3. Efficacy of Therapeutic Recreation in Mental Health: Motor Skills Development

Authors	Subjects	Measures	Outcomes
Buettner (1988)	Regressed geriatric	Measures of strength, flexibility, and ambulation	Exercise improved dependent variables of strength, flexibility, and ambulation.
Wehman & Marchant (1977)	Emotionally disabled children	Task analysis of skill acquisition	Demonstrated efficacy of task analytic instruction for recreation activity skill development.

Table 4. Efficacy of Therapeutic Recreation in Mental Health: Leisure Education/Leisure Counseling

Author	Subjects	Measures	Outcomes
Aguilar (1987)	Adolescent delinquents	Effects of leisure education on expressed attitude toward recreation and expressed attitude toward delinquency	No statistical difference in expressed attitude toward recreation or delinquency.
Schleien (1982)	Severely learning disabled children	Observation of cooperative and constructive play; questionnaire	Leisure education program produced gains in cooperation and constructive play. Generalization of skills to the home environment.
Skalko (1990)	Chronically mentally ill adults	Observation of discretionary time use	Improved quality of discretionary time use during intervention phases.
Skalko (1982)	Psychiatric adults	Leisure Well-Being Inventory; anecdotal notes	Leisure Education Program had positive effect for experimental group compared to control group post-test scores.
Tom (1981)	Substance abusers	Tennessee Self Concept Scale; Leisure Activities Blank; Leisure Attitude Dimension; Internal-External Locus of Control; Behavior checklist	Leisure awareness program had positive effect on LAB. Changes in anger and vigor profile of mood states were significant following treatment.
Wolfe & Riddick (1984)	Psychiatric adult	Leisure attitude; Self-esteem	No change.

Table 5. Efficacy of Therapeutic Recreation in Mental Health: Social Skills Training

Author	Subjects	Measures	Outcomes
Argyle, Tower, & Bryant (1976)	Psychiatric adult	Self reporting of anxiety and observation	Social skills training and desensitization training had a positive effect on social comfort.
Bellack, Hersen, & Turner (1976)	Chronic schizophrenic adults	Observation of target behaviors	Improved social functioning demonstrated the efficacy of social skills training for persons with schizophrenia.
Coyle (1988)	Schizophrenic adults	KATZ Adjustment Scale	No statistical difference by treatment approach.
Davis & Mathews (1980)	Chronic schizophrenic adults	KATZ Adjustment Scale; Conversation Rating Scale; Staff Rating Scale; Piagetion Tasks for Cognitive Functioning; Egocentricity of Thought Test; scales from the California Psychological Inventory	No significant difference between groups. Change in positive direction on "humor" and "Socially Skilled."
Dispenza & Nigro (1989)	Mentally ill	Observation of life skills and communication skills	Positive change in knowledge.
Federicksen, Jenkins, Foy, & Eisler (1976)	Small case psychiatric	Observation	Improved appropriate response.
Fryatt (1981)	Female psychiatric adults	Self report ratings of anxiety and depression; assessment of social adjustment	Approaches differed in effects. Treatment reduced anxiety and depression and improved social adjustment.

Table 5. (cont'd)

Author	Subjects	Measures	Outcomes
Gross, Bringham, Hooper, & Bologna (1980)	Delinquent youth	Observation	Reduction in problem behavior exhibited.
Hazel, Schumaker, Sherman, & Sheldon-Wildgen (1982)	Delinquent youth	Observation of social skills	Retention of social skills.
Holmes, Hansen, & Lawrence (1984)	Psychiatric adults	Observation of social skills	Improved performance.
Liberman, Lillie, Faloon, Harpin, Hutchison, & Stout (1984)	Psychiatric adults	Observation	Improved social skill competence.
Matson & Stephens (1978)	Small case psychiatric adults	Observation	Improved short-term social skill usage.
McLatchie (1981)	Psychiatric adults	Means-End Problem-Solving Procedure; Psychotic Inpatient Profile	No significant difference in effect.
Monti, et al. (1979)	Psychiatric adults	Observation; Ratus Self Assertiveness; Clinical Outcome Criteria Scale; self-reporting	Social skills training proved more effective than bibliotherapy in social skill acquisition.

Table 5. (cont'd)

Author	Subjects	Measures	Outcomes
Nagahiro (1983)	Aggressive children	Locus of Control Scale for Children; Piers-Harris Children Self Concept Scale; Walker Problem Behavior Identification Checklist	Change in predictive direction but no statistically significant changes in control, self-concept, or behavior.
Potelunas-Campbell (1982)	Female outpatient schizophrenic adults	Behavior Analytic Method for Assessing Social Competencies; Non-verbal Assertiveness Scale	Statistically significant improvement in self-efficacy, expectations, and social skills. Improved competence, and non-verbal assertiveness on trained items.
Reynolds & Arthur (1982)	Emotionally disturbed children	Observation of play behavior	Intervention resulted in temporary increases in cooperative play.
Rude (1983)	Depressed females	Beck Depression Inventory; MMPI criteria for for depression	Improvement in level of depression of treated subjects.
van Dam Baggen & Kraaimaat	Psychiatric adults	Observation; self reports	Social skills training program resulted in increased social skills and decreased social anxiety.

Table 6. Efficacy of Therapeutic Recreation in Mental Health: Adventure Challenge

Authors	Population	Measure	Outcomes
Hunter (1987)	Adjudicated male youth	Field observation and notes; Unstructured interviews	Improved self-confidence with mixed response (some profound changes while others exhibited no change).
McAvoy, Schatz, Stuts, Schleien, & Lais (1989)	Adults with and without physical disabilities	STATE-TRAIT Anxiety Inventory; Structured interview	Decrease in state anxiety; positive lifestyle changes.
Roland, Summers, Friedman, Barton, & McCarthy (1987)	Acute inpatients control (matched)	Critical Incident Participant Questionnaire	Improved self-esteem; sense of accomplishment; improved communication skills; catalyst to other therapeutic modalities. Significant improvement in depression scale reported; increased self-esteem and self-mastery.
Sime (1987)	Moderately depressed adults	Beck Depression Inventory; Profile of Mood States; Daily Mood Scale	
Witman (1987)	Hospitalized adolescents	Cooperation and Trust Scale; Observation	Positive attitudes toward cooperation and trust; increased tolerance for change.
Wright (1983)	Adjudicated youth	Tennessee Self Concept; Harvard Step Test; Rotter's Internal-External Scale; Generalized Expectancy for Success Scale (GESS); Means-Ends Problem-Solving Procedure (MEPS)	Improved short-term change in the delinquents' sense of self-acceptance of personal responsibility for behaviors; increased sense of personal capability; improved level of cardiovascular fitness.

Table 7. Efficacy of Therapeutic Recreation in Mental Health: Stress Management/Relaxation

Authors	Population	Measure	Outcomes
Barnett & Storm (1981)	Children	Behavioral observation in play lab	Play was effective coping mechanism for acute anxiety.
Berger & Owen (1988)	College students (swimming, yoga, fencing, lecture class)	Profile of Mood States	Yoga participants reduced short-term anxiety.
de Vries (1987)	General review of previous research	Variety of physiological and psychological measures	Exercise is an effective antidote to anxiety.

Table 8. Efficacy of Therapeutic Recreation in Mental Health: Family Therapeutic Applications

Authors	Population	Measures	Outcomes
De Salvatore & Roseman (1986)	Hospitalized children and and family	Behavioral observation	Anecdotal reports of increased self-esteem; positive communication.
Simon (1982)	Hospitalized children and families	Behavioral observation	Evaluation and assessment data collected.
Stinnett (1982)	General population families	Survey	Recreation/play is helpful in strengthening the family structure.

Table 9. Efficacy of Therapeutic Recreation in Mental Health: Expressive Therapies

Authors	Population	Measures	Outcomes
Cusack & Smith (1984)	Review list for elderly	Descriptive narrative	Mixed.
Draper, Gerber, & Layng (1990)	Review of pet therapy research	Descriptive study	Mixed. Some positive results but studies not empirical.
Kongable, Buckwalter, & Stolley (1989)	Alzheimer residents/pet therapy	Behavior observation checklist	Increased socialization with other residents.

Table 10. Efficacy of Therapeutic Recreation in Mental Health: Activity Task Applications

Authors	Populations	Measures	Outcomes
Raynor (1987)	Hospitalized adult, adolescent, and child psychiatric	Behavioral observation	Anecdotal notes report improvement on treatment goals.
Raynor, O'Shea, & Finch (1990)	Hospitalized adult and adolescent psychiatric	Behavioral observation	No statistical changes but anecdotal notes report positive behavioral change.

Table 11. Efficacy of Therapeutic Recreation in Mental Health: Reality Orientation

Author	Subjects	Measures	Outcomes
Baines, Saxby, & Ellert (1987)	Confused elderly	Observation orientation and behavior	Use of RO prior to and in combination with reminiscence therapy proved effective in improving cognition and behavior.
Bumanis & Yoder (1987)	Confused elderly	Reality orientation	No significant difference between groups.
Dvorkin (1980)	Confused elderly	Measure of confusion and orientation; observation	Functional reality orientation produced greater results than traditional RO on dependent measures.
Hart & Fleming (1985)	Confused elderly	Psychiatric Orientation Questionnaire	Modified reality orientation showed greater short-term improvements in orientation.
Holland (1984)	Confused elderly	Measure of orientation	RO communication training demonstrated improved orientation.
Ivan (1982)	Confused elderly	Short Portable Mental Status Questionnaire	RO produced significant gains in cognitive accessibility. Resocialization was found effective in social accessibility. Gains were short-term in nature.
North (1987)	Adult psychiatric	Observation of behavior	Reality orientation reinforcement upon exhibition of hallucinatory and delusional behavior reduced the frequency of the behaviors.
Quattrochi-Tubin (1984)	Confused elderly	Mental Status Questionnaire; Observation of self-feeding	Reality orientation improved orientation. Behavioral training had positive effect on self-feeding behavior.
Vogel (1989)	Confused	Assessment of Mental Status	No statistical difference in incidence of confusion. Difference in number of correct responses.

Table 11. (cont'd)

Author	Subjects	Measures	Outcomes
Wolfe (1983)	Regressed geriatric patients	Philadelphia Geriatric Center Mental Status Questionnaire	Treatment program produced marked improvement on dependent variables.

Table 12. Efficacy of Therapeutic Recreation in Mental Health: Remotivation Therapy

Author	Subjects	Measure	Outcomes
Allred (1985)	Frail elderly	Life Satisfaction Index-Z; Analysis of attitude toward students and elders	Positive change but not significant; Small positive shifts in attitudes toward elderly.
Birkett & Boltich (1973)	Geriatric	Observation of behavior	No statistical improvements.
Bowers, Anderson, Blomeier, & Pelz (1967)	Geriatric	Observation of behavior and social functioning	Significant improvement in individual behavior and social functioning for two of three groups.
Long (1961)	Psychiatric adult	L-M Fergus Falls Behavior Rating Scale; Custodial Mental Illness Ideology Scale	Significant difference between remotivation groups and control groups.

Table 13. Efficacy of Therapeutic Recreation in Mental Health: Physical Fitness/Exercise

Authors	Population	Measures	Outcomes
Fremont (1983)	Depressed adults	Profile of Mood States	Significant improvement in mood state scores.
Martinse, Medhus, & Sandvik (1985)	Hospitalized depressed patients	Beck Depression Inventory; Comprehensive Psychopathological Rating Scale	Significant reduction in depression scores as well as inner tension, depressive thinking, concentration difficulty, sleep disturbances, and muscular tension.
Reuter, Nutire, & Harris (1985)	Depressed university students	Beck Depression Inventory	Significant reduction in depression scores.
Sime (1987)	Moderately depressed adults	Beck Depression Inventory; Profile of Mood States; Daily Mood Scale	Significant reduction in depression score reported; increases in self-esteem and self-mastery.
Van Andel (1986)	University students	Profile of Mood States; Bipolar Scale; Multidimensional Health Locus of Control; Self-reported questionnaire	Significant improvement in mood state score for exercisers; improvement in "powerful others" locus of control score.

Bibliography and References

* Designates references cited in text.

Adventure Challenge

*Adams, D. (1969). <u>Survival training: Its effects on the self-concept and selected personality factors of emotionally disturbed adolescents.</u> Unpublished dissertation, Utah State University.

*Arthur, M. (1976). The survival experience as therapy: An appraisal. <u>Journal of Leisurability, 3,</u> 3-10.

Bernstein, A. (1972). Wilderness as a therapeutic behavior setting. <u>Therapeutic Recreation Journal, 6</u>(4), 160-161, 185.

*Ewert, A. (1983). <u>Outdoor adventure and self-concept: A research analysis.</u> Eugene, OR: Center of Leisure Studies.

*Ewert, A. (1988). Reduction of trait anxiety through participation in outward bound. <u>Leisure Sciences, 10,</u> 107-117.

*Fitts, W. H. (1971). <u>The self-concept and self-actualization.</u> Nashville, TN: Dede Wallace Center.

*Fletcher, B. A. (1970). <u>Outward bound students of outward bound schools in Great Britain: A follow-up study.</u> Bristol: University of Bristol.

Gibson, P. M. (1979). Therapeutic aspects of wilderness programs: A comprehensive literature review. <u>Therapeutic Recreation Journal, 13</u>(2), 21-33.

*Glaser, B. G., & Strauss, L. A. (1967). <u>The discovery of grounded theory.</u> Chicago: Aldine.

*Holzworth, W., Grott, J., & Hippensteel, N. (1973). Effects of day camp on adult psychiatric inpatients. <u>Therapeutic Recreation Journal, 7</u>(1), 37-40.

*Hunter, I. R. (1984). The impact of voluntary selection procedures on the reported success of outdoor rehabilitation programs. <u>Therapeutic Recreation Journal, 18</u>(3), 38-44.

*Hunter, I. R. (1987). The impact of an outdoor rehabilitation program for adjudicated juveniles. <u>Therapeutic Recreation Journal, 21</u>(3), 30-43.

*Hunter, I. R., & Purcell, K. D. (1984). Program characteristics and success in a resocialization program for adjudicated delinquents. <u>Corrective and Social Psychiatry, 10,</u> 25-34.

Jerstad, L., & Stelzer, J. (1973). Adventure experiences as treatment for residential mental patients. <u>Therapeutic Recreation Journal, 7</u>(3), 8-11.

Kimball, R. (1983). The wilderness as therapy. <u>Journal of Experiential Education, 3,</u> 6-9.

*McAvoy, L., Schatz, E. C., Stuts, M. E., Schleien, S. J., & Lais, G. (1989). Integrated wilderness adventure: Effects on personal and lifestyle traits of persons with and without disabilities. <u>Therapeutic Recreation Journal, 23</u>(3), 50-64.

*Mathias, D. W. (1977). <u>An evaluation of the outward bound solo experience as an agent in enhancing self concepts.</u> Master's thesis, University of Oregon. (University Microfilms No. 155.6).

*Polenz, D., & Rubitz, F. (1977). Staff perceptions of the effect of therapeutic camping upon psychiatric patients' affect. <u>Therapeutic Recreation Journal, 11</u>(2), 70-73.

*Rawson, H. E. (1978). Short-term residential therapeutic camping for behaviorally disordered children aged 6-12: An academic remediation and behavior modification approach. <u>Therapeutic Recreation Journal, 12</u>(4), 17-23.

*Roland, C. C., Summers, S., Friedman, M. J., Barton, G. M., & McCarthy, K. (1987). Creation of an experiential challenge program. <u>Therapeutic Recreation Journal, 21</u>(2), 54-63.

Ryan, J. L., & Johnson, D. T. (1972). Therapeutic camping: A comparative study. <u>Therapeutic Recreation Journal, 6</u>(4), 178-180.

Stoudenmire, J. (1977). Including educational and perceptual training in a therapeutic camp for emotionally disturbed children. Therapeutic Recreation Journal, 11(1), 12-15.

*Stoudenmire, J. (1978). Similarities between children's behavior at home and at a therapeutic summer camp. Therapeutic Recreation Journal, 12(2), 35-37.

*Stitch, T. (1983). Experiential therapy for psychiatric patients. Journal of Experiential Education, 3, 23-30.

*Voight, A. (1988). The use of ropes courses as a treatment modality for emotionally disturbed adolescents in hospitals. Therapeutic Recreation Journal, 22(2), 57-64.

*Witman, J. P. (1987). The efficacy of adventure programming in the development of cooperation and trust with adolescents in treatment. Therapeutic Recreation Journal, 21(3), 22-29.

*Wright, A. N. (1983). Therapeutic potential of the outward bound process: An evaluation of a treatment program for juvenile delinquents. Therapeutic Recreation Journal, 17(2), 33-42.

Expressive Techniques

Birtchnell, J. (1984). Art therapy as a form of psychotherapy. In T. Dalley (Ed.), Art as therapy: An introduction to the use of art as a therapeutic technique (pp. 30-44). London: Tavistock Publications.

Bonny, H. (1978). Facilitating guided imagery and music sessions. Baltimore: ICM Books.

Bonny, H. (1989). Sound as symbol: Guided imagery and music in clinical practice. Music Therapy Perspectives, 6.

Cassity, M. D. (1976). The influence of a music therapy upon peer acceptance, group cohesion, and interpersonal relationships of adult psychiatric patients. Journal of Music Therapy, 13, 66-76.

Cassity M. D. (1981). The influence of a socially valued skill on peer acceptance in a music therapy group. Journal of Music Therapy, 18, 148-154.

Cavallin, B. J., & Cavallin, H. W. (1968). Group music therapy to develop socially acceptable behavior among adolescent boys and girls. In E. T. Gaston (Ed.), Music in therapy. New York: MacMillan.

Cripe, F. F. (1986). Rock music as therapy for children with attention deficit disorder: An exploratory study. Journal of Music Therapy, 23, 30-37.

*Cusack, O., & Smith, E. (1984). Pets and the elderly: The therapeutic bond. New York: The Haworth Press.

Dalley, T. (Ed.). (1984). Art as therapy: An introduction to the use of art as a therapeutic technique. London: Tavistock.

*Draper, R. J., Gerber, G. J., & Layng, E. M. (1990). Defining the role of pet animals in psychotherapy. Psychiatric Journal of the University of Ottowa, 15(3), 169-172.

Eidson, C. (1989). The effect of behavioral music therapy on the generalization of interpersonal skills from sessions to the classroom by emotionally handicapped middle school students. Journal of Music Therapy, 26(4), 206-221.

Emunah, R. (1985). Drama therapy and adolescent resistance. The Arts in Psychotherapy, 12, 71-79.

Freeman, K. M., & Koegler, R. R. (1973). Psycho-therapeutic recreation: A new role for the recreation specialist. Therapeutic Recreation Journal, 7(1), 34-36.

Goodrich, J. (1982). Drama as a therapeutic tool in addiction. In E. C. Irwin & E. J. Portner (Eds.), Scope of drama therapy. Proceedings of the First Conference, National Association of Drama Therapy.

Goodrich, J., & Goodrich, W. (1986). Drama therapy with a learning disabled, personality disordered adolescent. The Arts in Psychotherapy, 13, 285-291.

*Griffiths, A. E., & Griffiths, L. W. (1976). Healing through horticulture. Journal of Leisurability, 3(1), 29.

*Hefley, P. D., & Sperling, A. (1973). Therapeutic recreation through horticulture. Therapeutic Recreation Journal, 7(3), 31-34.

Henderson, S. M. (1983). Effects of a music therapy program upon awareness of mood, group cohesion, and self-esteem among hospitalized adolescent patients. Journal of Music Therapy, 20, 14-20.

Henzell, J. (1984). Art, psychotherapy, and symbol systems. In T. Dalley (Ed.), Art as therapy: An introduction to the use of art as a therapeutic technique (pp. 15-29). London: Tavistock Publications.

Hickling, F. W. (1989). Sociodrama in the rehabilitation of chronic mentally ill patients. Hospital and Community Psychiatry, 40(4), 402-406.

Irwin, E. (1979). Play, fantasies, and symbols: Drama with emotionally disturbed children. American Journal of Psychotherapy, 34, 389-400.

Johnson E. R. (1981). The role of objective and concrete feedback in self-concept treatment of juvenile delinquents in music therapy. Journal of Music Therapy, 18, 137-147.

*Karpilow, B. (1970). Drama therapy. Therapeutic Recreation Journal, 4(1), 15-16.

*Kongable, L. G., Buckwalter, K. C., & Stolley, J. M. (1989). The effects of pet therapy on the social behavior of institutionalized Alzheimer's clients. Archives of Psychiatric Nursing, 3(4), 191-198.

*Lovelace, B. M. (1972). The use of puppetry with the hospitalized child in pediatric recreation. Therapeutic Recreation Journal, 6(1), 20-21, 37.

*Malatesta, D. (1972). The potential role of "theatre games" in a therapeutic recreation program for psychiatric patients. Therapeutic Recreation Journal, 6(4), 164-166, 190.

*McGinnis, R. W. (1974). Dance as a therapeutic process. Therapeutic Recreation Journal, 8(4), 181-186.

McGlashen, T., Wadeson, H., Carpenter, W., & Levy, S. (1977). Art and recovery style from psychosis. The Journal of Nervous and Mental Disease, 164, 182-190.

McKinney, C. (1990). The effect of music on imagery. Journal of Music Therapy, 27(1), 34-46.

Michel, D. E., & Martin, D. (1970). Music and self-esteem research with disadvantaged, problem boys in an elementary school. Journal of Music Therapy, 7, 124-127.

Murphy, J. (1984). The use of art therapy in the treatment of anorexia nervosa. In T. Dalley (Ed.), Art as therapy: An introduction to the use of art as a therapeutic technique (pp. 96-110). London: Tavistock.

Oster, G., & Gould P. (1987). Using drawings in assessment and therapy. New York: Brunner/Mazel.

*Strensrud, C., Mishkin, L., Craft, C., & Pollack, I. (1987). The use of drama techniques in cognitive rehabilitation. Therapeutic Recreation Journal, 21(2), 64-69.

*Thompson, A. R., & Wade, M. G. (1974). Real play and fantasy play as modified by social and environmental complexity in normal and hyperactive children. Therapeutic Recreation Journal, 8(4), 160-167.

Wadeson, H. (1975). Combining expressive therapies. American Journal of Art Therapy, 15, 43-46.

Wadeson, H. (1980). Art psychotherapy. New York: John Wiley and Sons.

Waller, D. (1984). A consideration of the similarities and differences between art teaching and art therapy. In T. Dalley (Ed.), Art as therapy: An introduction to the use of art as a therapeutic technique (pp. 96-110). London: Tavistock.

*Williams, S. A. (1975). Titles: Film-making as a therapeutic medium. Therapeutic Recreation Journal, 9(4), 158-160.

Family Treatment Approaches

*Clift, J. E. (1972). Family recreational therapy: A new treatment technique. Therapeutic Recreation Journal, 6(1), 25-27, 36.

Committee on the Family Group for Advancement of Psychiatry. (1985). The family, the patient, and the psychiatric hospital: Toward a new model, #117. New York: Brunner/Mazel.

*DeSalvatore, G., & Roseman, D. (1986). The parent-child activity group: Using activities to work with children and their families in residential treatment. Child Care Quarterly, 15(4), 213-222.

DeSalvatore, H. G. (1989). Therapeutic recreators as family therapists: Working with families on a children's psychiatric unit. Therapeutic Recreation Journal, 23(2), 23-29.

*Fink, J. B., & Beddall Fink, T. (1986). Implementation and rationale of family leisure programs for an inpatient psychiatric hospital. Trends III: Therapeutic recreation expressions and new dimensions (3rd ed.), pp. 52-59.

*General Mills American Family Report. (1981). Families at work. Minneapolis: General Mills.

*Hart, K. (1984, October). Values programming in family recreation. Journal of Health, Physical Education, Recreation, and Dance, 55, 8-10.

*Holman, T. B., & Epperson, A. (1984). Family and leisure: A review of the literature with research recommendations. Journal of Leisure Research, 16(4), 277-294.

*Levy, J. (1985). Families with disturbed children: Why don't they recreate? American Therapeutic Recreation Association Newsletter, 1, 15.

Malkin, M. (1990). Co-Dependency, family, and leisure issues in adolescent substance abuse treatment. Presented at the annual conference of the American Therapeutic Recreation Association, Kansas City, MO.

*Monroe, J. E. (1987). Family leisure programming. Therapeutic Recreation Journal, 11(3), 44-51.

Ohlson, E. L. (1976). Parental involvement in play therapy. Canadian Counselor, 19(4), 166-168.

Ross, P. (1977). A diagnostic technique for assessment of parent-child and family interaction patterns: The family puppet technique for therapy with families with young children. Family Therapy, 4(2), 129-142.

*Simon, E. (1982). Parent-child activity. In L. Hoffman (Ed.), The evaluation and care of severely disturbed children and their families. New York: SP Medical and Scientific Books.

*Stinnett, N., Sanders, G., DeFrain, J., & Parkhurst, A. (1982). A nationwide study of families who perceive themselves as strong. Family Perspective, 16, 15-22.

Leisure Education/Leisure Counseling

*Aguilar, T. E. (1987). Effects of a leisure education program on expressed attitudes of delinquent adolescents. Therapeutic Recreation Journal, 21(4), 43-51.

Bushell, S. (1973). Recreation group counseling with short-term psychiatric patients. Therapeutic Recreation Journal, 7(3), 26-30.

*Caldwell, L. L., Adolph, S., & Gilbert, A. (1989). Caution! Leisure counselors at work: Long term effects of leisure counseling. Therapeutic Recreation Journal, 23(3), 41-49.

Chase, D. R. (1977). Leisure counseling and leisure behavior research. Therapeutic Recreation Journal, 11(3), 94-102.

Compton, D. M., & Goldstein, J. E. (Eds.). (1979). Perspectives of leisure counseling. Arlington: National Recreation and Park Association.

*Connolly, M. L. (1977). Leisure counseling: A values clarification and assertive training approach. In A. Epperson, P. A. Witt, & G. Hitzhusen (Eds.), Leisure counseling: An aspect of leisure education (pp. 198-207). Springfield: Charles C. Thomas.

Dickason, J. G. (1972). Approaches and techniques of recreation counseling. Therapeutic Recreation Journal, 6(2), 74-78, 95.

*Dickason, J. G. (1977). Approaches and techniques of recreation counseling. In A. Epperson, P. A. Witt, & G. Hitzhusen (Eds.), Leisure counseling: An aspect of leisure education (pp. 54-63). Springfield: Charles C. Thomas.

Dunn, J. K. (1981). Leisure education: Meeting the challenge of increasing independence or residents in psychiatric transitional facilities. Therapeutic Recreation Journal, 15(4), 17-23.

*Edwards, P. B. (1977). The bridges of leisure counseling. In D. M. Compton & J. E. Goldstein (Eds.), Perspectives of leisure counseling. Arlington: National Recreation and Park Association.

Fain, G. S. (1977). Leisure counseling: Translating needs into action. In A. Epperson, P. A. Witt, & G. Hitzhusen (Eds.), Leisure counseling: An aspect of leisure education (pp. 45-53). Springfield: Charles C. Thomas.

*Gunn, S. L. (1977). Leisure counseling: An analysis of play behavior and attitudes using transactional analysis and gestalt awareness. In A. Epperson, P. A. Witt, & G. Hitzhusen (Eds.), Leisure counseling: An aspect of leisure education (pp. 161- 170). Springfield: Charles C. Thomas.

*Gunn, S. L. (1979). The relationship of leisure counseling to selected counseling theories. In D. M. Compton & J. E. Goldstein (Eds.), Perspectives of leisure counseling. Arlington: National Recreation and Park Association.

Gunn, S. L. (1981). Neurolinguistic programming: A new horizon in leisure counseling. Therapeutic Recreation Journal, 15(4), 36-43.

Hayes, G. A. (1977). Leisure education and recreation counseling. In A. Epperson, P. A. Witt, & G. Hitzhusen (Eds.), Leisure counseling: An aspect of leisure education (pp. 208-218). Springfield: Charles C. Thomas.

Hitzhusen, G. (1973). Recreation and leisure counseling for adult psychiatric and alcoholic patients. Therapeutic Recreation Journal, 7(1), 16-22.

*Hitzhusen, G. (1977a). Recreation and leisure counseling for adult psychiatric and alcoholic patients. In A. Epperson, P. A. Witt, & G. Hitzhusen (Eds.), Leisure counseling: An aspect of leisure education (pp. 225-235). Springfield: Charles C. Thomas.

Hitzhusen, G. (1977b). Youth recreation counseling: A necessity in therapeutic recreation. In A. Epperson, P. A. Witt, & G. Hitzhusen (Eds.), Leisure counseling: An aspect of leisure education (pp. 236-243). Springfield: Charles C. Thomas.

Hoffman, C. A., & Ely, B. D. (1973). Providing recreation counseling in a psychiatric hospital: A vital community link. Therapeutic Recreation Journal, 7(3), 3-7.

*Hultsman, J. T., Black, D. R., Seehafer, R. W., & Hovell, M. F. (1987). The purdue stepped approach model: Application to leisure counseling service delivery. Therapeutic Recreation Journal, 21(4), 9-22.

*Johnson, L. P., & Zoerink, D. A. (1977). The development and implementation of a leisure counseling program for female psychiatric patients based on values clarification techniques. In A. Epperson, P. A. Witt, & G. Hitzhusen (Eds.), Leisure counseling: An aspect of leisure education (pp. 171-197). Springfield: Charles C. Thomas.

Land, C. (1974). Recreation counseling for psychiatric patients in a day treatment setting. Therapeutic Recreation Journal, 8(4), 156-159.

Li, R. K. K. (1981). Activity therapy and leisure counseling for the schizophrenic population. Therapeutic Recreation Journal, 15(4), 44-49.

McDowell, C. F. (1974). Toward a health leisure mode: Leisure counseling. Therapeutic Recreation Journal, 8(3), 96-104.

*McDowell, C. F. (1976). Leisure counseling: Selective lifestyle processes. Eugene: University of Oregon.

342

*McDowell, C. F. (1977). Leisure counseling: A review of emerging concepts and orientations. In A. Epperson, P. A. Witt, & G. Hitzhusen (Eds.), Leisure counseling: An aspect of leisure education (pp. 137-148). Springfield: Charles C. Thomas.

*McDowell, C. F. (1978). Leisure well-being inventory. Eugene, OR: Leisure Lifestyle Consultants.

*McDowell, C. F. (1979). An analysis of leisure counseling orientations and models and their integrative possibilities. In D. M. Compton & J. E. Goldstein (Eds.), Perspectives of leisure counseling. Arlington: National Recreation and Park Association.

*McKechnie, G. E. (1977). Psychological foundations of leisure counseling: An empirical strategy. In A. Epperson, P. A. Witt, & G. Hitzhusen (Eds.), Leisure counseling: An aspect of leisure education (pp. 64-82). Springfield: Charles C. Thomas.

McLellan, R. W., & Pellett, L. (1975). Leisure counseling-the first step. Therapeutic Recreation Journal, 9(4), 161-165.

McMinn, S. B., & Lay, C. M. (1987, November). Leisure activity and hospital readmission of short-term psychiatric patients. Paper presented at the Annual Meeting of the Mid-South Educational Research Association, Mobile, AL. (ERIC Document Reproduction Service No. ED 293 019).

*Montagnes, J. M. (1977). Reality therapy approach to leisure counseling. In A. Epperson, P. A. Witt, & G. Hitzhusen (Eds.), Leisure counseling: An aspect of leisure education (pp. 149- 160). Springfield: Charles C. Thomas.

*Mundy, J., & Odum, L. (1979). Leisure education: Theory and practice. New York: Wiley & Sons.

*Olson, W. E., & McCormack, J. B. (1957). Recreational counseling in the psychiatric service of a general hospital. Journal of Nervous and Mental Diseases, 125, 237-239.

O'Morrow, G. S. (1972). Social recreational counseling for the ill and disabled. Therapeutic Recreation Journal, 6(2), 69-73.

O'Morrow, G. S. (1977). Recreation counseling: A challenge to rehabilitation. In A. Epperson, P. A. Witt, & G. Hitzhusen (Eds.), Leisure counseling: An aspect of leisure education (pp. 7-30). Springfield: Charles C. Thomas.

Overs, R. P., Taylor, S., & Adkins, C. (1977). Avocational counseling: A field trial. In A. Epperson, P. A. Witt, & G. Hitzhusen (Eds.), Leisure counseling: An aspect of leisure education (pp. 106-136). Springfield: Charles C. Thomas.

Rios, D. W. (1978). Leisure education and counseling with severely emotionally disturbed children. Therapeutic Recreation Journal, 12(2), 30-34.

Rule, W. R., & Stewart, M. W. (1977). Enhancing leisure counseling using an adlerian technique. Therapeutic Recreation Journal, 11(3), 87-93.

*Schleien, S. J. (1982). Effects of an individualized leisure education instructional program of cooperative leisure skill activities on severely learning disabled children. Dissertation Abstracts International, 43/12B, p. 3934.

*Schleien, S. J., Wehman, P., & Kiernan, J. (1981). Teaching leisure skills to severely handicapped adults: An age-appropriate darts game. Journal of Applied Behavioral Analysis, 14, 513-519.

*Schleien, S. J., Tucker, B., & Heyne, L. (1985). Leisure education programs for the severely disabled student. Parks and Recreation, 20, 74-78.

*Skalko, T. K. (1982). The effects of a leisure education program on the perceived leisure well-being of psychiatrically impaired active army personnel. Unpublished doctoral dissertation, University of Maryland, College Park, MD.

*Skalko, T. K. (1990). Discretionary time use and the chronically mentally ill. Therapeutic Recreation Annual, 1, 9-14.

Stacke, R. (1977). An overview of leisure counseling. In A. Epperson, P. A. Witt, & G. Hitzhusen (Eds.), Leisure counseling: An aspect of leisure education (pp. 31-44). Springfield: Charles C. Thomas.

Thompson, G. (1972). Outline for development of a recreational counseling program. Therapeutic Recreation Journal, 6(2), 83-85, 96.

*Tom, A. M. (1981). The effect of leisure awareness on the attitude and behavior of the substance abuser. Dissertation Abstracts International, 42/03A, p. 1017.

Walshe, W. A. (1977). Leisure with personality. In A. Epperson, P. A. Witt, & G. Hitzhusen (Eds.), Leisure counseling: An aspect of leisure education (pp. 83-105). Springfield: Charles C. Thomas.

*Wehman, P. (1978). Task analysis in recreation programs for mentally retarded persons. Journal of Leisurability, 5, 13-20.

*Wehman, P. (1977). Helping the mentally retarded acquire play skills: A behavioral approach. Springfield, IL: Charles C. Thomas.

*Wolfe, R. A., & Riddick, C. C. (1984). Effects of leisure counseling on adult psychiatric patients. Therapeutic Recreation Journal, 18(3), 30-37.

*Wuerch, B. B., & Voeltz, L. M. (1982). Longitudinal leisure skills for severely handicapped learners: The Ho'onanea curriculum. Baltimore: Paul H. Brookes.

Motor Development

*Anderson, J., Williams, S., McGee, R., & Silva, P. (1989, November). Cognitive and social correlates of DSM-III disorders in preadolescent children. Journal of the American Academy of Child and Adolescent Psychiatry, 28(6), 842-846.

*Buettner, L. L. (1988). Utilizing developmental theory and adaptive equipment with regressed geriatric patients in therapeutic recreation. Therapeutic Recreation Journal, 22(3), 72-79.

Khanna, S., Desai, N. G., & Channabasavanna, S. M. (1987, Spring). A treatment package for transsexualism. Behavior Therapy, 18(2), 193-199.

Kraft, R. E. (1983). Physical activity for the autistic child. Physical Educator, 40, 33-37.

Krug, J. L. (1979). A review of perceptual motor/sensory integrative measurement tools. Therapeutic Recreation Journal, 13(3), 41-43.

*Shoemaker, F., & Kaplan, H. (1972). Observations on physical fitness and developmental skills of emotionally disturbed boys. Therapeutic Recreation Journal, 6(1), 28-30, 35.

*Wehman, P., & Marchant, J. A. (1977). Developing gross motor recreational skills in children with severe behavioral handicaps. Therapeutic Recreation Journal, 11(2), 48-54.

*Whyte, L. (1981). Learning problems in children judged high-risk for handicapping conditions during the neonatal period. International Journal for the Advancement of Counselling, 4(4), 269-273.

Physical Fitness/Exercise

*Bahrke, M. S., & Morgan, W. P. (1978). Anxiety reduction following exercise and meditation. Cognitive Therapy and Research, 2, 323-333.

Doyne, E. J., Chambliss, D. L., & Beutler, L. E. (1983). Aerobic exercise as a treatment for depression in women. Behavioral Therapy, 14, 434-440.

*Folkins, C. H., & Sime, W. E. (1981). Physical fitness training and mental health. American Psychologist, 36, 373-389.

*Fremont, J. (1983). The separate and combined effects of cognitively based counseling aerobic exercise for the treatment of mild and moderate depression. Unpublished doctoral dissertation, The Pennsylvania State University.

*Greist, J. H., Klein, M. H., Eischens, R. R., Faris, J., Gurman, A. S., & Morgan, W. P. (1979). Running as a treatment for depression. Comprehensive Psychiatry, 20, 41-54.

344

*Iso-Ahola, S. E., & Mobily, K. E. (1982). Depression and recreation involvement. Therapeutic Recreation Journal, 16(3), 48-53.

Klein, M. H., Greist, J. H., Gurman, A. S., Neimeyer, R. A., Lesser, D. P. et al. (1985). A comparative outcome study of group psychotherapy vs exercise treatments for depression. International Journal of Mental Health, 13, 148-177.

*Martinsen, E. W. (1990). Benefits of exercise for the treatment of depression. Sports Medicine, 9(6), 380-389.

*Martinsen, E. W., Medhus, A., & Sandvik, L. (1984). The effect of aerobic exercise on depression: A controlled study. Unpublished manuscript. (p. 92 of Exercise & Mental Health).

McCann, I. L., & Holmes, D. S. (1984). Influence of aerobic exercise on depression. Journal of Personality and Social Psychology, 46, 1142-1147.

*McGlynn, G. (1987). Dynamics of fitness: A practical approach. Dubuque, IA: Wm. C. Brown.

*Morgan, W. P. (1984). Physical activity and mental health. In H. M. Eckert & H. J. Montoye (Eds.), Exercise and health. Champaign, IL: Human Kinetics.

*Morgan, W. P., & Goldston, S. E. (1987). Exercise and mental health. Washington, DC: Hemisphere Publishing.

*Reuter, M., Mutrie, N., & Harris, D. V. (1984). Running as an adjunct to counseling in the treatment of depression. Unpublished manuscript, The Pennsylvania State University.

*Sime, W. E. (1987). Exercise in the treatment and prevention of depression. In Morgan & Goldston (Eds.), Exercise and mental health. Washington: Hemisphere Publishing.

*Sime, W. E., Mayer, B., Witte, H., Ganster, D., & Tharp, G. (1985). Occupational stress testing in the real world. In F. J. McGuigan, W. E. Sime, & J. Wallace (Eds.), Stress and tension control (Vol II). New York: Plenum Press.

*Van Andel, G. (1986). Mood, health locus of control and physical activity. Unpublished doctoral dissertation, Indiana University.

*Wassman, K. B., & Iso-Ahola, S. E. (1985). The relationship between recreation participation and depression in psychiatric patients. Therapeutic Recreation Journal, 19(3), 63-70.

Reality Orientation

*Baines, S., Saxby, P., & Ehlert, K. (1987, August). Reality orientation and reminiscence therapy: A controlled cross-over study of elderly confused people. British Journal of Psychiatry, 151, 222-231.

*Bumanis, A., & Yoder, J. W. (1987, January). Music and dance: Tools for reality orientation. Activities, Adaptions, and Aging, 10(1-2), 23-35.

*Citrin, R., & Dixon, D. (1977). Reality orientation: A milieu therapy used in an institution for the aged. Gerontologist, 17, 39-43.

*Dvorkin, L. (1980). Functional reality orientation with cognitively and emotionally impaired institutionalized elderly. Dissertation Abstracts International, 41, 3909.

*Folsom, J. (1968). Reality orientation for the elderly mental patient. Journal of Psychiatry, 1, 291-307.

*Hart, J., & Fleming, R. (1985). An experimental evaluation of a modified reality orientation therapy. Clinical Gerontologist, 3(4), 35-44.

*Holland, L. J. C. (1984). Reality oriented communication training for senile dementia patients. Dissertation Abstracts International, 41, 2127.

*Ivan, M. R. (1982). Reality orientation and resocialization group treatments with the differentially confused institutionalized aged. Dissertation Abstracts International, 43, 2754.

*Miller, M. J. (1987). The effects of reality orientation and validation therapy with disoriented nursing home residents. Dissertation Abstracts International, 48, 2953.

*North, G. G. (1987). The treatment of hallucinatory and delusional behavior with reality orientation. Dissertation Abstracts International, 49, 918.

*Quattrochi-Tubin, S. J. (1984). Cognitive and behavioral strategies in enhancing functioning among elderly residents of a nursing home. Dissertation Abstracts International, 46, 334.

*Vogel, D. C. (1989). The effects of 24-hour reality orientation on patients in an ICU setting. Dissertation Abstracts International, 27, 497.

*Wolfe, J. R. (1983). The use of music in a group sensory training program for regressed geriatric patients. Activities, Adaptions, and Aging, 4(1), 49-62.

Remotivation Therapy

*Allred, G. B. (1985). The effects of intergenerational remotivation therapy on the life satisfaction of institutionalized elderly. Dissertation Abstracts International, 46, 2922.

*Birkett, D., & Boltuch, B. (1973). Remotivation therapy. Journal of the American Geriatric Society, 21, 368-371.

*Bowers, M., Anderson, G., Blomeire, E., & Pelz, K. (1967). Brain syndrome and behavior in geriatric remotivation groups. Journal of Gerontology, 22, 348-352.

*Long, R. S. (1961). Remotivation: Fact or artifact. Preliminary report, Remotivation Research Project. Washington, DC: American Psychiatric Association.

*Stracke, D. (1970). Climates in remotivation in therapeutic recreation. Therapeutic Recreation Journal, 4(1), 9-12.

Social Skills Training

*Argyle, M., Tower, P., & Bryant, B. (1976). Desensitization and social skills training for socially inadequate and socially phobic patients. Psychological Medicine, 4, 435-443.

Becker, R. E., & Heimberg, R. G. (1988). Assessment of social skills. In A. S. Bellack & M. Hersen (Eds.), Behavioral assessment: A practical handbook (3rd ed.). New York: Pergamon Press.

*Bellack, A. S., Hersen, M., & Turner, S. M. (1976). Generalization effects of social skills training with chronic schizophrenics: An experimental analysis. Behavior, Research, and Therapy, 14, 391-398.

Bellack, A. S., Turner, S. M., Hersen, M., & Luber, R. F. (1984). An examination of the efficacy of social skills training for chronic schizophrenic patients. Hospital and Community Psychiatry, 35, 1023-1028.

Brady, J. P. (1984). Social skills training for psychiatric patients. American Journal of Psychiatry, 141, 491-498.

*Christoff, K. A., & Kelly, J. A. (1985). A behavioral approach to social skills training with psychiatric patients. In L. L'Abate & M. A. Milan (Eds.), Handbook of social skills training and research (pp. 361-387). New York: John Wiley & Sons.

*Coyle, P. F. (1988). A comparative analysis of varying treatment approaches on the level of community adjustment among schizophrenic outpatients. Dissertation Abstracts International, 50/05A, 1438.

Curran, J. P., & Monti, P. M. (Eds.). (1982). Social skill training: A practical handbook for assessment and treatment. New York: Guilford Press.

*Davis N. J., & Mathews, A. T. (1980). An integrated approach to social skills training for schizophrenic clients in a day treatment setting. Dissertation Abstracts International, 41/08B, 3157.

*Dispenza, D. A., & Nigro, A. G. (1989). Life skills for the mentally ill: A program description. Journal of Applied Rehabilitation Counseling, 20(1) 47-49.

*Eisler, R. M., Blanchard, E. B., Fitts, H., & Williams, J. G. (1978). Social skills training with and without modeling for schizophrenic and non-psychotic hospitalized psychiatric patients. Behavior Modification, 2, 147-173.

*Eisler, R. M., Hersen, M., & Miller, P. M. (1973). Effects of modeling on components of assertiveness behavior. Journal of Behavior Therapy and Experimental Psychiatry, 4, 1-6.

Eisler, R. M., Hersen, M., & Miller, P. M. (1974). Shaping components of assertive behavior with instruction and feedback. American Journal of Psychiatry, 131, 1344-1347.

Finch, B. E., & Wallace, C. J. (1977). Successful interpersonal skills training with schizophrenic inpatients. Journal of Consulting and Clinical Psychology, 45, 885-890.

Fredericksen, L. W., Jenkins, J. O., Foy, D. W., & Eisler, R. M. (1976). Social skills training to modify abusive verbal outbursts in adults. Journal of Applied Behavioral Analysis, 9, 117-127.

*Fryatt, M. J. (1981). Comparative effects of small group social competence training for psychiatric patients. Dissertation Abstracts International, 42/10A, 4363.

Glickman, H. S., Margolies, P., Lash, S. S., Shah, G. V., Donaldson, B., & Lewandowski, J. (1986). Behavior analytic approach to placement of patients in community settings. Paper presented at the Annual Meeting of the American Psychological Association, Washington, DC.

Goldsmith, J. B., & McFall, R. M. (1975). Development and evaluation of an interpersonal skill-training program for psychiatric inpatient. Journal of Abnormal Psychology, 85, 51-58.

Goldstein, A. P. (1973). Structured learning therapy. New York: Academic Press.

Goldstein, A. P., Martens, J., Huben, J., Van Belle, H. A., Schaaf, W., Wiersima, H., & Goldhart, A. (1973). The use of modeling to increase independent behavior. Behavior Research and Therapy, 11, 31-43.

Gordon, R. E., & Gordon, K. K. (1985). A program of modular psychoeducational skills training for chronic mental patients. In L. L'Abate & M. A. Milan (Eds.), Handbook of social skills training and research (pp. 388-417). New York: John Wiley & Sons.

*Gross, A. M., Bringham, T. A., Hooper, C., & Bologna, N. C. (1980, June). Self-management and social skills training: A study with predelinquent and delinquent youths. Criminal Justice and Behavior, 7(2), 161-184.

*Hazel, J. S., Schumaker, J. B., Sherman, J. A., & Sheldon-Wildgen, J. (1982, March). Group training for social skills: A program for court-adjudicated probationary youths. Criminal Justice and Behavior, 9(1), 35-53.

*Hersen, M., & Bellack, A. S. (1976a). A multiple baseline analysis of social skills training in chronic schizophrenics. Journal of Applied Behavioral Analysis, 9, 239-245.

Hersen, M., & Bellack, A. S. (1976b). Social skills training for chronic psychiatric patients: Rationale, research findings, and future directions. Comprehensive Psychiatry, 17, 559-580.

Hersen, M., Eisler, R. M., Miller, P., Johnson, M., & Pinkston, S. (1973). Effect of practice, instruction, and modeling on components of assertive behavior. Behavior Research and Therapy, 11, 447-451.

Hersen, M., Turner, S. M., Edelstein, B. A., & Pinkston, S. G. (1975). Effect of phenothiazine and social skills training in chronic schizophrenics. Journal of Clinical Psychology, 31, 588-594.

*Holmes, M. R., Hansen, D. J., & St. Lawrence, J. S. (1984). Conversational skills training with aftercare patients in the community: Social validation and generalization. Behavior Therapy, 15, 84-100.

Jacobs, H. E., Kardashian, S., Kreinbring, R. K., Ponder, R., & Simpson, A. R. (1984). A skills-oriented model for facilitating employment among psychiatrically disabled persons. Rehabilitation Counseling Bulletin, 28, 87-96.

*Liberman, R. P., Lillie, F. J., Falloon, I. R. H., Harpin, E. J., Hutchison, W., & Stout, B. A. (1984). Social skills training for relapsing schizophrenics: An experimental analysis. Behavior Modification, 8, 155-179.

*Liberman, R. P., Mueser, K. T., Wallace, C. J., Jacobs, H. E., Eckman, T., & Massel, K. (1986). Training skills in the psychiatrically disabled: Learning coping and competence. Schizophrenia Bulletin, 12(4), 631-647.

Lukoff, D. G. (1981). Comparison of a holistic and a social skills training program for schizophrenics. Dissertation Abstracts International, 41/11B, 4268.

*Matson, J. L., & Stephens, R. M. (1978). Increasing appropriate behavior of explosive chronic psychiatric patients with a social-skills training package. Behavior Modification, 2, 61-77.

*Monti, P. M., Fink, E., Norman, W., Curran, J., Hayes, S., & Caldwell, A. (1979). Effect of social skills training groups and social skills bibliotherapy with psychiatric patients. Journal of Consulting and Clinical Psychology, 47(1), 189-191.

*McLatchie, L. R. (1981). Interpersonal problem solving group therapy: An evaluation of a potential method of social skills training for the chronic psychiatric patient. Dissertation Abstracts International, 42/07B, 2995.

*Nagahiro, W. T. (1983). Social role taking: A treatment model for aggressive children. Dissertation Abstracts International, 44/09A, 2717.

*Potelunas-Campbell, M. F. (1982). The development and evaluation of a social skills training program for supervisor/supervisee dyad interactions in a work adjustment program for female schizophrenic outpatients. Dissertation Abstracts International, 43/06A, 1899.

*Reynolds, R. P., & Arthur, M. H. (1982). Effects of peer modeling and cognitive self guidance on the social play of emotionally disturbed children. Therapeutic Recreation Journal, 16(1), 33-40.

*Rude, S. S. (1983). An investigation of differential response to two treatments for depression. Dissertation Abstracts International, 44/02B, 616.

*Skalko, T. K. (1991, April). Social skills training for persons with chronic mental illness. Journal of Physical Education, Recreation and Dance, 62(4), 31-33.

*Test, M. A., & Stein, L. I. (1978). Training in community living: Research design and results. In L. I. Stein & M. A. Test (Eds.), Alternatives to mental hospital treatment. New York: Plenum.

*Van Dam Baggen, R., & Kraaimaat, F. (1986). A group social skills training program with psychiatric patients: Outcome, drop-out rate and prediction. Behavior Research and Therapy, 24(2), 161-169.

Wallace, C. J., Nelson, C., Liberman, R. P., Aitchison, R., Lukoff, D., Elder, J., & Ferris, C. (1980). A review and critique of social skills training with schizophrenic patients. Schizophrenia Bulletin, (6), 42-64.

Wong, S. E., Terranova, M. D., Marshall, B. D., Banzett, L. K., & Liberman, R. P. (1983, May). Reducing bizarre stereotypic behavior in chronic psychiatric patients: Effects of supervised and independent recreational activities. Presented at the Ninth Annual Convention of the Association of Behavior Analysis, Milwaukee, WI.

Wong, S. E., Terranova, M. D., Bowen, L., & Zarate, R. (1987). Providing independent recreational activities to reduce stereotypic vocalizations in chronic schizophrenics. Journal of Applied Behavior Analysis, 20(1), 77-81.

Stress Management/Relaxation

*Barnett, L. A., & Storm, B. (1981). Play, pleasure, and pain: The reduction of anxiety through play, Leisure Sciences, 4(2), 161-175.

*Berger, B. G. (1983/1984). Stress reduction through exercise: The mind-body connection. Motor Skills: Theory into Practice, 7, 31-46.

*Berger, B. G. (1986). Use of jogging and swimming as stress reduction techniques. In J. H. Humphrey (Ed.), Current selected research in the psychology and sociology of sport, 1, 97-113. New York: AMS Press.

348

*Berger, B. G. (1987). Stress reduction following swimming. In W. P. Morgan & S. E. Goldston (Ed.), Exercise and mental health (pp. 139-143). Washington, DC: Hemisphere Publishing.

*Berger, B. G., & Owen, D. R. (1988). Stress reduction and mood enhancement in four exercise modes: Swimming, body conditioning, hatha yoga, and fencing. Research Quarterly for Exercise and Sport, 59(2), 148-159.

*De Vries, H. A. (1987). In W. P. Morgan & S. E. Goldston (Eds.), Exercise and mental health (pp. 99-104). Washington, DC: Hemisphere Publishing.

*Girdano, D., & Everly, G. (1979). Controlling stress and tension: A holistic approach. Englewood Cliffs, NJ: Prentice-Hall.

*Long, B. C. (1984). Aerobic conditioning and stress inoculation: A comparison of stress-management interventions. Cognitive Therapy Research, 8(5), 517-542.

*Martinsen, E. W. (1990). Benefits of exercise for the treatment of depression. Sports Medicine, 9(6), 380-389.

*Martinsen, E. W., Medhus, A., & Sandvik, L. (1984). The effect of aerobic exercise on depression: A controlled study. Unpublished manuscript. (p. 92 of Exercise & Mental Health).

*Matheny, K. B., Aycock, D. W., Pugh, J., Curlette, W. L., & Silva Cannella, K. A. (1986). Stress coping: A qualitative and quantitative synthesis for implication for treatment. The Counseling Psychologist, 14(4), 499-549.

*Reuter, M., Mutrie, N., & Harris, D. V. (1984). Running as an adjunct to counseling in the treatment of depression. Unpublished manuscript, The Pennsylvania State University.

*Sachs, M. L. (1982). Running therapy: Change agent in anxiety and stress management. Journal of Health, Physical Eduction, Recreation and Dance, 53(7), 44-45.

*Sinyor, D., Schwartz, S. G., Peronnet, F., Brisson, G., & Seraganian, P. (1983). Aerobic fitness level and reactivity to psychological stress: Physiological, biochemical, and subjective measures. Psychosomatic Medicine, 45, 215-217.

*Sime, W. E. (1987). Exercise in the prevention and treatment of depression. In W. P. Morgan and S. E. Goldston (Eds.), Exercise and mental health (pp. 145-152). Washington, DC: Hemisphere Publishing.

*Stumbo, J. J. (1988). Research on stress coping: Implications for therapeutic recreation practice. In C. A. Ashton-Shaeffer & C. A. Peterson (Eds.), Research into action: Applications for therapeutic recreation programming: Vol. 8 (pp. 2-12). Champaign, IL: Office of Research and Park Resources.

Therapeutic Activities

Bigelow, G. W. (1971). A comparison of active and passive recreational activities for psychotic patients. Therapeutic Recreation Journal, 5(4), 145-151, 191.

Card, J. A., & Schweer, J. M. (1989). A planned recreation intervention program: Its effect on perceived leisure freedom of mentally ill patients. Research Report, University of Missouri.

Card, J. A., & Chamberland, L. R. (1988). One-on-one therapeutic recreation intervention with elderly, mentally ill nursing home residents: Does it make a difference? Research Report, University of Missouri.

Grossman, A. H. (1976). Power of activity in a treatment setting. Therapeutic Recreation Journal, 10(4), 119-124.

*Raynor, B. (1987). An archaeological project for inpatient psychiatry. Therapeutic Recreation Journal, 11(2), 39-45.

*Raynor, B., O'Shea, J., & Finch, A. J. (1990). Building boats and character: The folbot project. Therapeutic Recreation Journal, 24(4), 23-31.

Retondo, T. (1972). The male heroin addict's participation in recreation activities. Therapeutic Recreation Journal, 6(4), 162-163, 177.

*Wassman, K. B., & Iso-Ahola, S. E. (1985). The relationship between recreation participation and depression in psychiatric patients. Therapeutic Recreation Journal, 19(3), 63-70.

Therapeutic Recreation General

*Austin, D. R. (1982). Therapeutic recreation: Processes and techniques. New York: Wiley & Sons.

*Carter, M. J., Van Andel, G. E., & Robb, G. M. (1985). Therapeutic recreation: A practical approach. St. Louis: Times Mirror/Mosby College Publishing.

*Compton, D. M. (1989). Research initiatives in therapeutic recreation. In D. M. Compton (Ed.), Issues in therapeutic recreation: A profession in transition (pp. 427-444). Champaign, IL: Sagamore Publishing.

*Cousins, N. (1979). Anatomy of an illness as perceived by the patient. New York: Bantom.

Kelley, J. D., & Smith, B. L. (1972). Standards for therapeutic recreation in psychiatric facilities. Therapeutic Recreation Journal, 6(2), 52-61, 93-94.

Kennedy, D. W. (1987). Leisure and mental illness: A literature review. Therapeutic Recreation Journal, 21(1), 45-50.

*Kraus, R. (1983). Therapeutic recreation services: Principles and practices (3rd ed.). New York: Saunders College Publishing.

*Levy, J. (1971). An intrinsic-extrinsic motivational framework for therapeutic recreation. Therapeutic Recreation Journal, 5(1), 32-38.

Levy, J. (1982). Behavioral observation techniques in assessing change in therapeutic recreation/play settings. Therapeutic Recreation Journal, 16(1), 25-32.

Linford, A. G., & Jeanrenaud, C. Y. (1972). Stimulation preferences between neurotics and psychopaths: A synthesis of current research and its application to therapeutic recreation programming. Therapeutic Recreation Journal, 6(1), 31-34.

Linford, A. G., & Kennedy, D. W. (1971). Research-the state of the art in therapeutic recreation. Therapeutic Recreation Journal, 5(4), 168-169, 190.

Malkin, M. J., Howe, C. Z., & Del Rey, P. (1989). Psychological disability and leisure dysfunction of female suicidal psychiatric clients. Therapeutic Recreation Journal, 23(1), 36-46.

McPherson, I. T. (1977). Control of hyperactive children in recreational activities. Therapeutic Recreation Journal, 11(2), 59-65.

*Menninger, W. C. (1960). Recreation and mental health. Recreation and Psychiatry. New York: National Recreation Association.

*Nezu, A. M., Nezu, C. M., & Blissett, S. E. (1988). Sense of humor as a moderator of the relation between stressful events and psychological distress: A prospective analysis. Journal of Personality and Social Psychology, 54(3), 520-525.

*O'Morrow, G. S., & Reynolds, R. P. (1989). Therapeutic recreation: A helping profession (3rd ed.). Englewood Cliffs: Prentice-Hall.

*Peterson, C. A., & Gunn, S. L. (1984). Therapeutic recreation program design: Principles and processes. Englewood Cliffs: Prentice-Hall.

*Porterfield, A. L. (1987). Does sense of humor moderate the impact of life stress on psychological and physical well-being? Journal of Research in Personality, 21(3), 305-317.

*Powell, L., & Sable, J. (1990). Application of holistic health techniques in therapeutic recreation. Therapeutic Recreation Journal, 24(4), 32-41.

*Reich, J. W., & Zautra, A. J. (1981). Life events and personal causation: Some relationship with satisfaction and distress. Journal of Personality and Social Psychology, 41, 1002-1012.

*Reich, J. W., & Zautra, A. J. (1984). Daily event causation: An approach to elderly life quality. Journal of Community Psychology, 12, 312-322.

*Reich, J. W., & Zautra, A. J. (1989). A perceived control intervention for at-risk older adults. Psychology and Aging, 4, 415-424.

Robb, G. (1970). A new dimension in treatment: Therapeutic recreation for the emotionally disturbed child. Therapeutic Recreation Journal, 4(1), 13-14.

*Ruben, H. (1980). Competing: Understanding and winning the games we all play. New York: Tippincott & Crowell.

Schleien, S. J., & Ray, M. T. (1988). Community recreation and persons with disabilities: Strategies for integration. Baltimore: Paul H. Brookes.

*Shank, J. (1975). Therapeutic recreation through contrived stress. Therapeutic Recreation Journal, 9(1), 21-25.

Shapiro, I. G. (1972). A rationale for the use of limits in the recreation programming for emotionally disturbed children. Therapeutic Recreation Journal, 6(4), 158-159.

Shary, J. M., & Iso-Ahola, S. E. (1989). Effects of a control-relevant intervention on nursing home residents' perceived competence and self-esteem. Therapeutic Recreation Journal, 23(1), 7-16.

Sheridan, P. M. (1976). Therapeutic recreation and the alcoholic. Therapeutic Recreation Journal, 10(1), 14-17.

*Thompson, A. R., & Wade, M. G. (1974). Real play and fantasy play as modified by social and environmental complexity in normal and hyperactive children. Therapeutic Recreation Journal, 8(4), 160-167.

Touchstone, W. A. (1975). The status of client evaluation within psychiatric settings. Therapeutic Recreation Journal, 9(4), 166-172.

*Vale, W. H., & Mlott, S. R. (1983). An assessment of treatment enjoyment and effectiveness in psychiatric hospitalization. Therapeutic Recreation Journal, 17(1), 26-32.

Vogler, E. W., Fenstermacher, G., & Bishop, P. (1982). Group-oriented behavior management systems to control disruptive behavior in therapeutic recreation settings. Therapeutic Recreation Journal, 16(1), 20-24.

*Wassman, K. B., & Iso-Ahola, S. E. (1985). The relationship between recreation participation and depression in psychiatric patients. Therapeutic Recreation Journal, 9(3), 63-70.

*Wehman, P., & Schleien, S. J. (1981). Leisure programs for handicapped persons: Adaptions, techniques, and curriculum. Baltimore: University Park.

Wertman, M., & Jaretzki, A. (1972). Recreation therapy in a children's residential psychiatric service. Therapeutic Recreation Journal, 6(4), 172-177.

*Witt, P. A. (1988). Therapeutic recreation research: Past, present, and future. Therapeutic Recreation Journal, 22(1), 14-23.

Theoretical Foundations

*Adler, A. (1956). The use of heredity and environment. In H. L. Ansbacher & R. R. Ansbacher (Eds.), The individual psychology of Alfred Adler. New York: Harper.

*Allport, G. W. (1955). Becoming: Basic considerations for a psychology of personality. New Haven, CT: Yale University Press.

*Allport, G. W. (1961). Pattern and growth in personality. New York: Holt, Rinehart & Winston.

*American Psychiatric Association. (1987). Diagnostic and statistical manual of mental disorders III-revised. (DSM III-R). Washington, DC: Author.

Austin, D. R. (1971). Catharsis theory: How valid in therapeutic recreation? Therapeutic Recreation Journal, 5(1), 30-31.

*Bandura, A., & Walters, R. H. (1963). Social learning and personality development. New York: Holt, Rinehart & Winston.

*Borgatta, E. F. (1968). Traits and persons. In E. F. Borgatta & W. W. Lambert (Eds.), Handbook of personality theory and research (pp. 510-528). Chicago: Rand McNally.

Borgatta, E. F., & Lambert, W. W. (Eds.). (1968). Handbook of personality theory and research. Chicago: Rand McNally.

*Cartwright, D. S. (1979). Theories and models of personality. Dubuque: Wm. C. Brown.

*Cattell, R. B. (1965). The scientific analysis of personality. Baltimore: Penguin Books.

Corsini, R. (Ed.). (1973). Current psychotherapies. Itasca: Peacock.

*Dattilo, J., & Murphy, W. D. (1987). Behavior modification in therapeutic recreation. State College: Venture.

*Ellis, M. J. (1973). Why people play. Englewood Cliffs, NJ: Prentice Hall.

*Erikson, E. H. (1950). Childhood and society. New York: Norton.

*Erikson, E. H. (1963). Childhood and society. New York: Norton.

Errickson, E. (1972). Practical consideration in the development of operant programs. Therapeutic Recreation Journal, 6(2), 66-68.

Fine, R. (1973). Psychoanalysis. In R. Corsini (Ed.), Current psychotherapies (pp. 1-33). Itasca: Peacock.

*Gerson, Jr., G., Ibrahim, H., DeVires, J., Eisen, G., & Lollar, S. (1991). Understanding leisure: An interdisciplinary approach (2nd ed.). Dubuque, IA: Kendall/Hunt.

Glasser, W. (1965). Reality therapy. New York: Harper Rowe.

Glasser, W., & Zunin, L. M. (1973). Reality therapy. In R. Corsini (Ed.), Current psychotherapies (pp. 287-316). Itasca: Peacock.

*Goldstein, A. (1973). Behavior therapy. In R. Corsini (Ed.), Current psychotherapies (pp. 207-250). Itasca: Peacock.

*Hergenhahn, B. R. (1980). An introduction to theories of personality. Englewood Cliffs: Prentice-Hall.

Holland, G. A. (1973). Transactional analysis. In R. Corsini (Ed.), Current psychotherapies (pp. 353-400). Itasca: Peacock.

*Horney, K. (1950). Neurosis and human growth. New York: Norton.

Huber, J. T., & Millman, H. L. (Eds.). (1972). Goals and behavior in psychotherapy and counseling. Columbus: Charles E. Merrill.

*Hunnicutt, B. (1979). The freudian and neo-freudian views of adult play and their implications for leisure research and therapeutic service delivery. Therapeutic Recreation Journal, 13(2), 3-13.

*Ismail, A. H. (1987). Psychological effects of exercise in the middle years. In W. P. Morgan & S. E. Goldstein (Eds.), Exercise and mental health. Washington, DC: Hemisphere Publishing.

Iso-Ahola, S. E. (1980). Perceived control and responsibility as mediators of the effects of therapeutic recreation on the institutionalized aged. Therapeutic Recreation Journal, 14(1), 36-43.

*Kelly, G. (1972). Personal constructs therapy. In J. T. Huber & H. L. Millman (Eds.), Goals and behavior in psychotherapy and counseling. Columbus: Charles E. Merrill.

Kemper, W. (1973). Gestalt therapy. In R. Corsini (Ed.), Current psychotherapies (pp. 251-286). Itasca: Peacock.

*Levy, J. (1978). Play behavior. New York: John Wiley & Sons.

*Lobstein, D. D. (1983). A multivariate study of exercise training effects on beta-endorphin and emotionality in psychologically normal, medically healthy men. Unpublished doctoral dissertation, Purdue University.

*Lundin, R. W. (1974). Personality: A behavioral analysis (2nd ed.). New York: McMillan.

*Maslow, A. H. (1970). Motivation and personality (2nd ed.). New York: Harper & Row.

Meador, B. D., & Rogers, C. A. (1973). Client-centered therapy. In R. Corsini (Ed.), Current psychotherapies (pp. 119-166). Itasca: Peacock.

Monte, C. F. (1977). Beneath the mask: An introduction to personalities. New York: Praeger.

*Mosak, H. H., & Dreikurs, R. (1973). Adlerian psychotherapy. In R. Corsini (Ed.), Current psychotherapies (pp. 1-33). Itasca: Peacock.

*Rogers, C. (1972). Client-centered therapy. In J. T. Huber & H. L. Millman (Eds.), Goals and behavior in psychotherapy and counseling. Columbus: Charles E. Merrill.

Rusalem, H. (1973). An alternative to the therapeutic model in therapeutic recreation. Therapeutic Recreation Journal, 7(1), 8-15.

*Thorne, F. C. (1973). Eclectic psychotherapy. In R. Corsini (Ed.), Current psychotherapies (pp. 445-486). Itasca: Peacock.

*Tinsley, H. E., & Tinsley, D. J. (1986). A theory of the attributes, benefits, and causes of leisure experience. Leisure Sciences, 8(1), 1-45.

CHAPTER 9

A SUMMARY OF BENEFITS COMMON TO
THERAPEUTIC RECREATION

Catherine P. Coyle, W. B. Kinney, & John W. Shank *

Introduction

This chapter is an attempt to synthesize common elements of the various position papers, the discussions at the conference, and information that has recently emerged since the conference. As is evident from reading the preceding chapters, each paper is based on at least three categorical structures: (a) the theoretical foundations on which clinical decisions and interventions in therapeutic recreation are based; (b) the actual outcomes that result from these interventions; and (c) recommendations for future efficacy research. It is these three categories that provide the structure for this summary.

Theoretical Foundations

Each of the preceding authors have illustrated the varied theoretical foundations from which the practice of therapeutic recreation is derived. There is no **single** theoretical framework which dominates the practice of therapeutic recreation. All of the authors suggest that theories pertaining to human development, cognition, social learning, and leisure are relevant to the discipline of therapeutic recreation, with many additional theoretical perspectives becoming relevant depending upon the disability group with which one is working.

It would appear that the discipline of therapeutic recreation clearly operates from an "eclectic" theoretical perspective. Eclecticism, according to Thorne (1973), ". . . involves consideration of all pertinent theories, methods, and standards for evaluating and manipulating clinical data according to the most advanced knowledge of time and place" (p. 451). However, it is unclear at this point whether the eclecticism in therapeutic recreation practice actually reflects the systematic evaluation of the most advanced knowledge of time and place (i.e., data-based knowledge). More likely, the practice of therapeutic recreation is

---

* *Authors are listed alphabetically. Contributions are considered to be equal.*

driven by an "intuitive practitioner-based eclecticism" derived from clinical trial and error that is often "situationally specific" (Barlow, Hayes, & Nelson, 1984). For instance, the provision of similarly named therapeutic recreation services such as leisure education often differ according to the setting, agency, therapist, and most importantly, the client.

The tendency to have an intuitive eclectic approach to practice is not unique to therapeutic recreation. In fact Barlow et al. (1984) state:

> . . . Despite the seemingly strict adherence to theoretical constructs and the allegiance to psychotherapeutic schools verbalized by most psychotherapists, there is a growing feeling among observers that most therapists are more similar than they are different in their practice. (p. 35)

An eclectic approach may be most effective for achieving rehabilitation outcomes as it allows therapeutic recreation specialists the freedom to choose which approach to use with each client. Unfortunately, as suggested by Barlow et al. (1984), widespread use of such an approach does not allow for systematic analysis of what interventions work in what settings and with what clients.

It is this specific knowledge that the therapeutic recreation discipline must document if they are to advance the knowledge base of the discipline. The use of intuitive eclecticism in the development and implementation of therapeutic recreation programs and in the actual processing of the therapeutic experience may be successful in practice. From a research perspective, however, it will be problematic, causing difficulties in replicating the actual applied intervention. The lack of theory driven practice may seriously hamper research efforts within the discipline and, therefore, needs to be given serious attention.

Benefits of Therapeutic Recreation

A number of benefits derived from involvement in therapeutic recreation were identified in both the preceding chapters and during the conference discussion. They can be broadly classified into six major areas related to *physical health and health maintenance, cognitive functioning, psychosocial health, growth and personal development, personal and life satisfaction, and finally, societal and health care system outcomes.* Although an extensive amount of literature was reviewed, undoubtedly there were some omissions of research studies documenting outcomes relevant to therapeutic recreation, especially in the area of unpublished dissertations and theses. This is unfortunate but unavoidable and highlights the need for academicians to mentor graduate students in the publishing process.

The following list of benefits should not be viewed as a comprehensive inventory. Nor should it be perceived as suggesting the only areas in which benefits can be derived from therapeutic recreation involvement. Rather, it represents those areas in which some preliminary evidence exists and which conference delegates believe further research efforts should be directed. It represents a sampling of the research reviewed in the various position papers, the discussions at the conference, and information that has recently emerged since the conference.

Physical Health and Health Maintenance

Involvement in Therapeutic Recreation Reduces Cardiovascular and Respiratory Risk

1. A water aerobics program two times a week for 16 weeks significantly reduced diastolic blood pressure, body fat, and body weight in 27 elderly community residents (Green, 1989). These findings were replicated in a second study with 24 elderly community residents (Keller, 1991).

2. Improved exercise stress test scores (METS, treadmill time, submaximal heart rate, resting heart rate) were demonstrated with older chronically ill patients at a VA outpatient clinic through a supervised exercise program (Morey et al., 1989).

3. In an experimental study conducted by Cutler Riddick (1985), an aquarium program conducted in elderly individual's homes significantly reduced their diastolic blood pressure.

4. Santiago, Coyle, and Troupe (1991) found adults with physical disabilities who were involved in community and individual aerobic exercise programs had significant improvements in cardiovascular and metabolic functional capacity (as measured by peak VO2) when compared to a non-exercising control group.

5. Research has indicated that involvement in exercise can significantly improve cardiorespiratory functioning among adults with physical disabilities (Figoni et al., 1988; Hoffman, 1986; Jocheim & Strohkendle, 1973; Koch et al., 1983; Miles et al., 1982; Van Loan et al., 1987; Zwiren et al., 1973).

6. A controlled study of exercise and asthma found that an exercise program involving physically active recreation (swimming and running) resulted in increased work tolerance and decreased heart rate for asthmatic children (Rothe et al., 1990).

7. Similarly, Szentagothai et al. (1987) reported that long term physical exercise programs (1 to 2 years of regular swimming and gymnastic activities involving 121 children between 5 and 14 years of age) were effective in reducing asthmatic symptoms, frequency of hospitalization, and use of medication.

8. Cerny (1989) found that an exercise program was equally as effective as a standard protocol of bronchial hygiene therapy in terms of the pulmonary function and exercise response of patients with cystic fibrosis.

Involvement in Therapeutic Recreation
Reduces the Risk of Physical
Complications Secondary
to Disability

1. Reduced incidences of decubiti and urinary tract infections were found among wheelchair athletes compared to wheelchair non-athletes (Stotts, 1986).

2. Increased activity has been shown to reduce medical complications and increase survival rate (Anson & Shepard, 1990; Krause & Crewe, 1987).

3. In a case study on adults with physical disabilities Coyle, Santiago, Kinney, and Blair (1991) reported improved cholesterol levels as a result of aerobic exercise. The improvements represented a potential reduction in the risk of coronary heart disease, a known secondary complication related to physical disability, of approximately 35%.

4. Videogames have been used to motivate young children with burns to exercise thus maintaining mobility and enhancing healing and counteracting the loss of function often associated with burns (Adriaenssens, Eggermont, Pyck, Boeckx, & Gilles, 1988).

5. Comparing 160 children (ages 3 to 13) in a control group with 68 children who received structured and comprehensive child life interventions, Wolfer et al. (1988) found that the treatment group had significantly greater rates of recovery from surgery.

6. Tipton et al. (1986) after a review of experimental studies on the influence of physical activity on ligaments, tendons, and joints suggested that physical activity may prevent the host of conditions which lead to chronic back pain.

Involvement in Therapeutic Recreation Improves the General Physical and Perceptual Motor Functioning of Individuals with a Disability

1. A horseback riding program has been shown to improve coordination of individuals with physical disabilities (Brock, 1988).

2. Strength and endurance of adults with disabilities have been shown to increase as a result of participation in physical recreation (Davis et al. 1981).

3. Increased flexibility, hand strength, and ambulation was demonstrated among older residents of a long-term care facility through a developmental fitness program two times per week (Buettner, 1988); and range of motion was improved in a quasi experimental design using a structured cooking group as the intervention (Yoder, Nelson, & Smith, 1989).

4. Improved perceptual-motor abilities, body perception, balance, locomotor agility, ball throwing, and tracking was reported among individuals with mental retardation who were involved in a physical recreation program (Marini, 1978).

Cognitive Functioning

Involvement in Therapeutic Recreation Increases General Cognitive Functioning

1. Involvement in a comprehensive recreation program significantly improved cognitive abilities as measured on the Clifton Cognitive Ability Assessment for 70% of the nursing home residents in the program (Conroy et al., 1988).

2. A quasi-experimental design using matched controls showed significantly improved functioning on the Mini-Mental State exam for elderly individuals who received dance and movement activities 1 hour per week for 8 months (Osgood, Meyers, & Orchowsky, 1990).

3. A plush animal program improved mental functioning for nursing home residents when compared to the controls (Francis & Baly, 1986).

4. Krebs et al. (1989) found signs of increased mental alertness and cognitive activity following exercise in individuals with spina bifida.

5. Peniston (1991), using an experimental pre-post test research design, reported that elderly individuals with mild and moderate memory loss who participated in a 6 week computer games program demonstrated significant improvement in cognitive strategies, attention, memory, and impulse control when compared to the control group who received no intervention.

Involvement in Therapeutic Recreation Increases Short- and Long-Term Memory

1. A unique program involving home visitations accompanied by rewards for seeking and remembering information between visits significantly improved both short- and long-term memory for nursing home residents in the randomly assigned treatment group (Beck, 1982).

2. The use of reality orientation prior to and in combination with remotivation therapy has been found to contribute significantly to cognitive functioning (Baines et al., 1987). An additional experimental study determined that reality orientation enables significantly greater gains in information recall (Citrin & Dixon, 1977).

Involvement in Therapeutic Recreation Decreases Confusion and Disorientation

1. Reality orientation for disoriented nursing home residents significantly improved with a music based reality orientation program. Randomly assigned controls who received a standard reality orientation program showed no improvement (Riegler, 1980).

2. A music based sensory stimulation program conducted 30 minutes per week, twice a week for 16 weeks significantly improved reality orientation of disoriented nursing home residents who were randomly assigned to treatment or control groups (Banziger & Rousch, 1983).

3. Comparing patients who received reality orientation with those receiving validation therapy, Miller (1987) found that the group receiving reality orientation showed greater gains in orientation than those who received validation therapy.

Psychosocial Health

Involvement in Therapeutic Recreation
Reduces Depression

1. Two separate quasi-experimental studies conducted by Francis and Baly (1986) and Francis and Munjas (1988) showed that a plush animal program significantly reduced depression for intermediate nursing home residents as measured on the Beck Depression Inventory.

2. A larger study, using 162 depressed nursing home residents randomly assigned to groups, revealed that reminiscence treatments significantly reduced depression as measured by the Beck Depression Inventory (Fry, 1983).

3. Katz et al. (1985) found that exercise reduced depression among individuals with a physical disability; Greenwood (1990) found that tennis resulted in significant reductions in depression; and Weiss and Jamieson's (1988) study with the same population found that water exercise effectively reduced depression among individuals with a physical disability.

4. Three separate experimental studies utilizing bibliotherapy with depressed elderly have significantly reduced depression--one for over 6 months (Scogin, Jamison, & Gochneaur, 1989); and one for over 2 years (Scogin, Jamison, & Davis, 1990). The third (Scogin, Hamblin, & Beutler, 1987) did not indicate the time period.

5. In a quasi-experimental study with adults with physical disabilities, Santiago et al. (1991) found a lessening of depressive symptoms in the exercise experimental group of 59.3% in comparison to an increase of 2.0% in the control group.

6. A 9-week aerobic exercise intervention contributed to a significant reduction in depressive symptomatology such as inner tension, sleep disturbance, concentration difficulties, and depressive thinking for adults hospitalized for depression who were randomly assigned to either the treatment or control group (Martinsen et al., 1984).

7. A physical exercise program has been found to be effective with mildly depressed adults (Greist, 1987; Greist et al., 1979; Taylor et al. 1985), as well as depressed university students (Reuter et al., 1985; Van Andel, 1986).

8. Sime (1987) found that depressed adults who completed an exercise treatment program not only had significantly lower depression scores compared to a control group, but those who continued to exercise after the treatment program were also found to have lower depression scores at 6 and 21 month follow-up points.

9. A structured activity treatment program has been found to be effective in reducing depressive symptomatology and can increase levels of active engagement with one's surroundings (Wassmann & Iso-Ahola, 1985).

10. Kavanagh et al. (1977) found a reduction in depression among past coronary patients who exercise.

Involvement in Therapeutic Recreation Reduces Anxiety

1. Carson et al. (1985) found that a comprehensive child life program significantly reduced the anxiety levels of hospitalized children.

2. Using a combination of behavioral indicators to create an overall anxiety score, Ipsa et al. (1988) reported on an experimental study in which a supervised play program offered to children 5 to 10 years of age receiving medical treatment in an outpatient clinic resulted in less anxiety among the children and less irritability among the parents who were waiting with their children.

3. The anxiety children normally experience due to hospitalization and related medical procedures can be significantly reduced through the provision of accurate, age appropriate information (Rasnake & Linscheid, 1989), although providing children with an opportunity to "play with" medical equipment and materials is more effective than merely providing information in reducing anxiety and helping children be prepared for surgery (Demarest et al., 1984).

4. A variety of studies have demonstrated the value of exercise in reducing anxiety associated with stress. Berger (1983, 1986) reported that physical conditioning through swimming produces significant, short-term reduction in stress, as does yoga and jogging (Long, 1984; Sachs, 1982).

5. A thorough review of the literature indicates substantial agreement among researchers that exercise provides a tranquilizer effect, and that exercise of the appropriate type, intensity, and duration appears to be equal to or more effective than medication for anxiety (de Vries, 1987).

6. In a quasi-experimental study with individuals hospitalized in a rehabilitation facility, Shank, Coyle, and Kinney (1991) found that persons receiving individual therapeutic recreation services were rated by nursing staff as having significantly lower levels of anxiety than control subjects.

Involvement in Therapeutic Recreation
Improves Coping Behavior

1. Art, journal writing, daydreaming, meditating, and travel have proved to be effective at improving coping among individuals with a physical disability (Baer, 1985; Dew et al., 1983; Lewis, 1985; Ulrich et al., 1990).

2. Hiking, camping, and adapted sports have produced significant increases in self-efficacy and self-confidence among individuals with a physical disability (Austin, 1987; Curtis et al., 1986; Robb & Evert, 1987; Stewart, 1981; Strucker & Barkus, 1986).

3. A music based reality orientation intervention with disoriented nursing home residents significantly increased sensory and environmental awareness for the randomly assigned experimental group (Wolf, 1983).

4. Participating in sports and nature/wilderness activities has significantly increased acceptance of disability (Jackson & Davis, 1983; McAvoy, 1989; Sherril, 1988).

5. Wolfer et al. (1988) compared hospitalized children (3 to 13 years) who received comprehensive child life services with those who did not and found that those who received the interventions had more effective coping mechanisms when faced with threatening or painful medical procedures.

6. Therapeutic play enables children to cope with unpleasant experiences such as a traumatic event (Barnett & Storm, 1981).

7. In a quasi-experimental study with individuals hospitalized in a rehabilitation facility, Shank, Coyle, and Kinney (1991) found that persons receiving individual therapeutic recreation services were significantly better able to use activities as a means of coping with the stress of hospitalization than were control subjects.

Involvement in Therapeutic Recreation
Reduces Stress Level

1. The use of humorous videos has shown to increase immune cell proliferation, which buffers stress, for individuals with a physical disability (Berk et al., 1988).

2. In an experimental study using "matched controls" therapeutic recreation treatments were shown to strengthen the individual's immune response by acting as a catalyst for decreases in ACTH and increases in the Growth Hormone (Russoniello, 1991).

3. A comprehensive leisure education program resulted in better stress management in research conducted by Rancourt (1991a, 1991b) with women who were in treatment for substance abuse; while McAuliffe and Ch'ien (1986) report that social and recreational activities were helpful for stress management among individuals with addictions.

4. Diversional recreation experiences have been shown to facilitate stress recovery, provided the experience is assessed positively by the individual (Heywood, 1978).

Involvement in Therapeutic Recreation
Improves Self-Control

1. Improvement in self-control was demonstrated in an experimental design in which elderly intermediate care residents were given bird feeders and instructed in the use and care of the feeders (Banziger & Rousch, 1983).

2. Dattilo and Barnett (1985) have demonstrated that therapeutic recreation interventions lead to increased spontaneous initiation of activity, engagement with the environment, and self-assertiveness for individuals with mental retardation. Another study by Lanagan and Dattilo (1989) resulted in increased choice making and preference with the same population.

3. An experimental design with 28 randomly assigned nursing home residents in a horticulture intervention resulted in significant improvement in perceived competence (Shary & Iso-Ahola, 1989).

Involvement in Therapeutic Recreation Increases Self-Concept, Self-Esteem, and Adjustment to Disability

1. Sports and athletics have been shown to significantly increase body perception and body image in individuals with a physical disability (Hopper, 1988; Ross & Zoccoppetti, 1979).

2. Hiking and camping have resulted in increased self-efficacy and self-confidence for individuals with a physical disability (Robb & Evert, 1987; Struckey & Barkus, 1986).

3. Healthy senior citizens in an experimental group receiving dance and movement activities for 90 minutes, two times per week over 8 months increased in self-concept on the Tennessee Self-Concept Scale significantly more than the control group (Berryman-Miller, 1988).

4. Sports and nature/wilderness activities have resulted in increased acceptance of disability among individuals with a physical disability (Jackson & Davis, 1983; McAvoy et al., 1989; Sherril et al., 1988).

5. Shank, Coyle, and Kinney (1991) found that persons in a rehabilitation hospital who received individual therapeutic recreation services reported significantly higher levels of self-esteem at discharge when compared with individuals who did not receive any therapeutic recreation intervention. This difference remained significant when initial differences in the pre-test levels of self-esteem were controlled.

6. Comparing hospitalized children who received structured play programs with those who did not, Gillis (1989) found that structured play resulted in significantly more positive self-esteem.

7. Sports and athletics have proven effective in increasing body perception and body image for individuals with a physical disability (Hopper, 1988; Ross & Zoccoppetti, 1979).

Involvement in Therapeutic Recreation Improves General Psychological Health

1. A comparison study showed improved psychological health on the Affect Balance Scale among the treatment group who received a music program 30 minutes per week for 12 weeks (Cutler Riddick & Dugan-Jendzejec, 1988).

2. A plush animal treatment improved psychological health of intermediate nursing home residents over 8 weeks when compared to a group that did not receive the treatment (Francis & Baly, 1986).

3. Involvement in a horticulture program showed significantly increased morale for nursing home residents randomly assigned to the treatment condition over those assigned to the control group (Shary & Iso-Ahola, 1989).

4. Shank, Coyle, and Kinney (1991b) surveyed individuals with a variety of disabilities who were involved in special recreation programs across the United States. Benefits derived from recreation participation in the areas of positive feelings about their self and maintaining and improving social and recreational activities were reported by these individuals.

Involvement in Therapeutic Recreation Improves Social Skills, Socialization, Cooperation, and Interpersonal Interactions

1. Improvement in social skills has been demonstrated through a variety of studies conducted with individuals with developmental disabilities (Matson & Adkins, 1984; Rynders, Schleien, & Mustonen, 1990; Schleien et al., 1987; Schleien et al., 1988; Strain, 1975).

2. Drama, camping, and athletic activities have been documented to improve socialization in a variety of studies conducted with individuals with a physical disability (Bodziock, 1986; Stensrud et al., 1987; Stuckey & Barkus, 1986).

3. Bullock and Howe (1991) have documented that a community transition program in North Carolina has decreased social isolation for adults with disabilities.

4. Experimental studies by Banziger and Rousch (1983) and Beck (1982) have documented increased sociability (utilizing ratings by nursing staff) among nursing home residents using two separate therapeutic recreation interventions.

5. Videogame play has been shown to increase social affiliation among nursing home residents when compared to another control facility (Cutler Riddick et al., 1986).

6. Rancourt (1991a, 1991b) has documented how individuals with substance abuse who were involved in a comprehensive leisure education program showed increased knowledge and skills in self-awareness, decision-making, social skills, and social interactions.

7. James and Townsley (1989), in a study investigating the contribution of activity therapies to comprehensive treatment programs involving chemical dependency, found that recreation therapy activities assisted in developing interpersonal trust and improving specific communication skills.

8. Systematic social skills training produced basic social skills (Holmes et al., 1984; Monti et al., 1979), and these skills have been shown to generalize to untrained social situations (Liberman et al., 1984).

9. Social skills training of female outpatient schizophrenic adults resulted in improved social competence, self-efficacy, and non-verbal assertiveness (Potelunas-Campbell, 1982).

10. Peer modeling has been used to increase the social-cooperative play of emotionally disturbed children (Reynolds & Arthur, 1982).

11. Efficacy studies on adventure programs have determined this type of intervention to be effective in increasing communication skills, (Roland et al., 1987) social cooperativeness, and trust among adolescents and adults receiving inpatient treatment for psychiatric disorders (Witman, 1987).

Involvement in Therapeutic Recreation Reduces Self-Abusive and Inappropriate Behaviors

1. Reductions in self-abusive and inappropriate behaviors were demonstrated through a jogging program with individuals with mental retardation (Alajajian, 1981).

2. Using case study methodology, it was demonstrated that systematic recreational therapy intervention reduced hallucinatory speech (Wong, 1983; Wong et al., 1987). Similarly, Liberman et al. (1986) determined that inappropriate laughter and bizarre behaviors were significantly reduced when psychiatric patients were engaged in structured recreational activities.

3. North (1987) found the use of reality orientation in the treatment of adults with psychiatric disorders reduced hallucinatory and delusional behavior.

Growth and Development

Involvement in Therapeutic Recreation Increases Communication and Language Skills

1. In an experiment utilizing audio tapes with rehearsal of social skills Matson and Adkins (1984) improved the social skills (i.e., initiating conversation, complimenting one another, appropriate requests, appropriate responses) of individuals with a developmental disability.

2. A quasi-experimental study in an integrated camp setting revealed increased social interaction, skill acquisition, and integrated friendships for individuals with a developmental disability who received the treatment program (Rynders, Schleien, & Mustonen, 1990).

3. Strain (1975) documented the positive effects of socio-dramatic activities on social play.

Involvement in Therapeutic Recreation Reduces Inappropriate Behavior and Encourages Age-Appropriate Behavior

1. Schleien et al. (1988) demonstrated that children with severe developmental disabilities could acquire and generalize recreation skills, social interactions, and cooperative play behavior.

2. A recreation skill training program, in addition to weekly counseling sessions on free time use, and reinforcement training resulted in reduced stereotypic and age-inappropriate behaviors for moderately mentally retarded individuals (Schleien, Keirnan, & Wehman, 1981).

3. Alajajian (1981) documented that a jogging program for individuals with a developmental disability reduced self-abusive and self-stimulatory behaviors.

4. Eason, White, and Newsom (1982) documented that self-stimulatory behavior could be reduced in autistic children with instruction in appropriate play.

Involvement in Therapeutic Play
Increases the Acquisition of
Developmental Milestones

1. Daily structured play interventions, beginning during hospitalization and continuing for 2 years after discharge, were found to significantly advance the developmental levels of severely malnourished children. The experimental group of malnourished children performed significantly better than the control group on locomotor, hearing and speech, eye and hand coordination. In fact, the malnourished group receiving the play interventions actually scored higher than the healthy control group on hearing and speech, and reached the same levels of eye coordination (Grantham-McGregor et al., 1983).

Personal and Life Satisfaction

Involvement in Therapeutic Recreation
Increases Life and Leisure
Satisfaction and Perceived
Quality of Life

1. McGuire (1984), utilizing two wings of a nursing facility as treatment and control groups, demonstrated increased happiness with use of videogames.

2. A community transition program has proven to increase perceived quality of life for individuals with a physical disability (Bullock & Howe, 1991).

3. Creative dance and movement activities resulted in significantly improved life satisfaction scores for the elderly individuals in the experimental group compared with the matched controls, according to Osgood, Meyers, and Orchowsky (1990).

4. A horticulture program resulted in significantly improved morale and improved perception of competence for nursing home residents who were randomly assigned to the treatment condition compared to the control group (Shary & Iso-Ahola, 1989).

5. Using a multiple baseline design Skalko's (1990) research with adults with chronic mental illness indicated that leisure education and therapeutic recreation programming increased the quality of discretionary time use. Earlier research (Skalko, 1982) compared experimental and control groups of psychiatrically impaired adults and demonstrated that those receiving leisure education interventions showed significantly greater degrees of perceived leisure well-being.

Involvement in Therapeutic Recreation
Increases Social Support

    1. Creative dance and movement activities for 1 hour per week for 8 months have been shown to reduce loneliness and dissatisfaction in a matched control experiment with elderly individuals (Osgood, Meyers, & Orchowsky, 1990).

    2. A community transition program for individuals with a physical disability proved to reduce social isolation (Bullock & Howe, 1991).

    3. An aquarium activity in elderly houses resulted in reduced loneliness as measured on the UCLA Loneliness Scale in a randomly assigned experiment (Cutler Riddick, 1985).

    4. A nature activity (bird feeding) resulted in increased sociability for intermediate care residents who were randomly assigned to the treatment condition (Banziger & Rousch, 1983).

    5. In two comparison group designs, a videogame program resulted in increased affiliation (Cutler Riddick et al., 1986) and music sessions resulted in increased verbal interactions (Cutler Riddick & Dugan-Jendzejec, 1986) for nursing home residents.

Involvement in Therapeutic Recreation
Increases Community Integration,
Community Satisfaction, and
Community Self-Efficacy

    1. Community outings have been shown to result in increased barrier management skills among individuals with spinal cord injury (Blass, 1985).

    2. A sensitivity training program for personnel and non-disabled students in a community creative arts program resulted in improved community integration for the individuals with a developmental disability who participated (Schleien & Larson, 1986).

    3. A tennis activity resulted in increased self-efficacy and increased wheelchair management skills according to Greenwood (1990) and Hedrick (1985).

    4. Bierenbaum and Re (1979) have documented the role that activity participation contributed to adjustment to community living for individuals with a developmental disability.

5. A community transition program for individuals with a physical disability proved to reduce social isolation (Bullock & Howe, 1991).

Involvement in Therapeutic Recreation Increases Family Unity and Communications

1. Hart (1987) described the impact of adventure programming with families in terms of increased sense of unity and self-respect.

2. Beddall and Fink (1986) described a family leisure program on a psychiatric inpatient unit as offering opportunities for increased cooperative interaction skills and improved relationships between family members and staff.

3. DeSalvatore and Roseman (1986) indicated that therapeutic recreation with families of emotionally disturbed hospitalized children resulted in increased self-esteem among family members, increased positive communication, and more effective parental skills in managing their children.

Societal and Health Care Systems

Involvement in Therapeutic Recreation Helps Prevent Complications Secondary to Disability

1. Reduced medical complications and enhanced survival have been positively correlated to activity level and community life in adults with physical disabilities (Anson & Shepard, 1990; Krause & Crewe, 1987). Both of these (activity level and community life) are identified goals of therapeutic recreation.

2. Trader and Anson (1991) reported significant health differences existed between individuals with a spinal cord injury who had a commitment to leisure involvement and those who did not. Individuals with a leisure commitment reported a higher mean score for sitting tolerance; had spent fewer days in the hospital in the previous year; and were two and one-half times less likely to have a pressure sore than individuals without a commitment to leisure involvement.

3. Szentagothai et al. (1987) reported that long-term physical exercise programs (1 to 2 years of regular swimming and gymnastic activities involving 121 children between 5 and 14 years of age) were effective in reducing asthmatic symptoms, frequency of hospitalization, and use of medication.

**Involvement in Therapeutic Recreation
Improves Patient Compliance (with
rehabilitation regimes), Patient
Satisfaction with Treatment,
and Self-Dedication to
Treatment**

1. Clients with dementia involved in therapeutic recreation programs showed reduction in need for medication (Schwab, Rader, & Doan, 1985).

**Involvement in Therapeutic Recreation
Increases Outpatient Involvement and
Post-Discharge Compliance with
Treatment Plans**

1. Simpson, Crandall, Savase, and Pavia-Kreuser (1981) found positive changes in leisure functioning were related to favorable outcomes on drug use and criminality.

General Recommendations for Outcome Based Research
in Therapeutic Recreation

This chapter has reviewed a number of research studies which imply that therapeutic recreation influences the attainment of rehabilitation outcomes. As can been seen from the preceding pages, some documented empirical evidence exists which demonstrates the role of therapeutic recreation within health care; however, it is scarce, often lacks scientific rigor, and is rarely systematically replicated within or across diagnostic groups or settings. Furthermore, much of the evidence cited in the preceding chapters and this chapter do not directly examine therapeutic recreation interventions provided by certified therapeutic recreation specialists. Many of the outcomes reviewed were not the direct results of therapeutic recreation interventions; rather, they document interventions and findings relevant to the practice of therapeutic recreation. As a result of the conference, a number of general research recommendations and priorities were proposed for the discipline of therapeutic recreation. The following pages will report on these recommendations.

General Research Strategies

A number of general research strategies which future research efforts in therapeutic recreation should consider were suggested by each of the consensus groups. The strategies suggested were varied but can be grouped under the following headings: (a) *networking*, (b) *graduate programs*, (c) *research design*, and (d) *research dissemination*.

Networking

Many of the consensus groups indicated a need existed for better communication and networking strategies directed at facilitating an efficacy-based research program in therapeutic recreation. Most recommendations centered on the need for collaboration between academicians and practitioners in therapeutic recreation as well as between academicians from different disciplines.

Researcher to practitioner. The issue of research and its relevance to practice is viewed and valued differently between practitioners and academicians. Academicians are happy when the results of their research suggest that significant group differences exist between individuals randomly assigned to treatment and control conditions. The fact that the therapeutic recreation intervention was administered in a highly controlled and systematic manner, across a homogeneous group of individuals only strengthens the validity and reliability of the findings. However, when practitioners read such research results their response is "that is absurd, when will these educators realize that the real world doesn't work that way! I'll never get a group of clients who all have experienced a right cerebral vascular accident, let alone see them for three 60 minute sessions each week for three weeks." And so because practitioners frequently deal with unexpected discharges and individual clients rather than groups of clients, the research results are viewed as irrelevant and not applicable to practice.

The differing perspectives on research are further accentuated when one examines the opposing incentive system within the two environments. Academicians are typically rewarded for research productivity with workload reductions, tenure, and promotion; practitioners, in contrast, are asked to collect additional data beyond that which is typically needed in the performance of their job without any decrease in their workloads. Few agencies are able to justify a reduced client load because practitioners are involved in a research effort, and so research in the practice arena is often met with reservations.

Despite these practical and procedural differences, both practitioners and academicians at the 3-day conference felt a need existed for better communication and collaboration between the two groups. Many of the practitioners and academicians at the conference recognized the need for efficacy research in order to enhance the likelihood of therapeutic recreation's continued existence as a recognized service in rehabilitation. Most had heard Mary Lee Seibert's words before:

> . . . Times are changing. . . . Our own declarations about the efficacy of our services are no longer being accepted at face value. No longer will it be taken for granted that the services we render are beneficial to patients because we, as professional in the field, possess a particular set of knowledge and skills and use them to <u>do</u> something for others. We must demonstrate that what we do for others results in a predictable, desirable <u>outcome</u>.

That such a message was heard again during the conference keynote only reinforced the recognition of the need for research studies that examine the outcomes of therapeutic recreation services. It also underscored the reality that such research is not the responsibility of academicians alone. The need for tested knowledge and demonstrated outcomes reflects a "real world" demand on all therapeutic recreation professionals regardless of roles.

Conference delegates also recommended that academicians and practitioners begin to collaborate and dialogue about efficacy research in new ways. Academicians were challenged to disseminate research findings in a manner that makes integration into practice feasible. Such a dissemination effort should include more than writing a discussion or implications section in a journal article or presenting findings at the Leisure Research Symposium; for example, if academicians presented research results in a new practice-based format in both journal articles and conference sessions with input and reaction from practitioners, existing barriers would be reduced.

Most importantly, conference delegates were recommending the need for the establishment of a research directory in which academicians and practitioners in therapeutic recreation who were interested in collaborative efforts in efficacy research could identify their areas of interests. The establishment of such a directory would strengthen the likelihood that individuals with similar research interests could collaborate and begin to bolster the research data base that documents the clinical effectiveness of therapeutic recreation. The strengthening of this data base is imperative to the future of therapeutic recreation. Without it, ". . . others will determine when and how we practice and will control whether we are compensated for the services we deliver" (Seibert, 1991).

<u>Researcher to researcher</u>. Many of the conference delegates suggested that a need existed for the academic members of the discipline to establish better communication and cooperative efforts. The typical academic orientation on "competition" must give way to a more cooperative orientation in which researchers in therapeutic recreation at various institutions of higher education work jointly on efficacy based research efforts. The need for empirically documented outcomes of therapeutic recreation services is too great for individual and institutional competition to hinder research efforts in the discipline.

One recommendation offered to facilitate this cooperation was a discussion which focused on establishing among a few institutions of higher education a cooperative "research agenda." In such a scenario, faculty members from a few schools would jointly focus their research efforts on outcome studies in a specific area. Practitioners and students interested in research in this area would be referred to them by colleagues throughout the discipline. For such an effort to be successful, a few cooperative research agendas would need to be established among a variety of schools.

The urgency for researchers in the discipline of therapeutic recreation to work cooperatively with individuals external to the discipline was also addressed at the conference. The need to conduct research studies from an interdisciplinary perspective was repeatedly suggested and is consistent with the research efforts in the health care arena. The utility of interdisciplinary research efforts were especially apparent in research studies which could examine physiological changes as a result of therapeutic recreation involvement. Often therapeutic recreation researchers fail to utilize physiological measures for lack of knowledge regarding the techniques used to assess variables such as vital capacity, B-endorphine, growth hormones, or cholesterol levels. Physiological outcomes of therapeutic recreation are an important area that has not receive much attention in therapeutic recreation, yet the few studies completed in this area have had extremely promising results and are more readily accepted by the health care community.

None of these suggestions were extraordinary. Some have been made many times in private conversations with colleagues. Although little action has been taken to address these issues, it would appear that the discipline must begin to take some specific action steps in this area to assure its continued survival in health care.

Graduate Training Programs

Graduate training programs at both the master's and doctoral level can make significant contributions to efficacy research. Graduate programs need, first, to make a commitment to an efficacy research agenda and then encourage students to conduct research in one area of that agenda. When one considers the vast number of theses and dissertations that are produced each year and then imagines that if only one-third of these were efficacy based research, the thought of an incredibly sizeable increase in our efficacy data base becomes easily attainable.

Replication studies, which we give credence to in our discussions of the scientific method, usually receive lip service when it comes to student research. Students want, and are generally supported by faculty, to do original research. All too frequently, this original research turns out to be a survey on some benign issue that does little or nothing to contribute to our scientific data base. Graduate students, particularly at the master's level, should be encouraged to conduct replication research, and we should lend more credibility to replication research by valuing it more.

Graduate programs at the doctoral level should intensify the research training experience in the curriculum. Students should be thoroughly familiar with various research methodologies that are amenable to the practical rigors of field settings, and they should be familiar and comfortable with the knowledge and use of a variety of statistical techniques. This is true even for the student who intends to focus on a phenomenological study for their dissertation. Even this student will eventually be in a position to consult with field settings where research questions are most suitably addressed by methodologies involving multivariate analysis.

Doctoral programs should consider adding a research apprenticeship to their curricular requirements where students run a small pilot of their intended dissertation design and, thus, gain greater awareness of possible complications which require further thought before proceeding with the dissertation. Such a requirement may add to the research expertise of the student and may also produce stronger and more significant dissertations. We should recognize that the doctoral degree is a research degree and put an end to the often heard statements that "I just want to be an advanced clinician..." or "I just want to be a good teacher, not a researcher." Practitioners generally consider someone with the doctorate to be an expert in research; it is time for university programs to reinforce that assumption through guaranteeing those experts.

Variety of Research Designs

Recommendations were made by the conference participants that research efforts in therapeutic recreation should seriously examine the use of a variety of research designs when designing research studies. The selection of research methodology that is compatible with practice was seen as important because of the need to make sure research reflects practice. Many of the studies summarized under the "benefits" section do not necessarily reflect the actual therapeutic recreation interventions that occur in practice.

In particular, suggestions were made regarding the consideration of single-subject and case study approaches to research. Each of these research approaches can be subsumed under the concept of "time-series methodology" (Barlow et al., 1984). Time-series methodology, according to Barlow et al., are research strategies that focus on the need to establish a series of measures on the same individual over a period of time.

Because of this individualistic focus, these designs are especially suited to clinical application as the emphasis is on the influence of a therapeutic recreation intervention on a particular client. This type of approach is much more consistent with the everyday practice of the therapeutic recreation specialist. Barlow et al. (1984) make a strong case for the goodness of fit between clinical practice and time-series methodology. They write:

> For example, the practical requirements that the professional systematically assess the client is translated into the research requirement that systematic, repeated measurements be taken of the client's problems. The practical suggestion that specific treatments be designed for the client is modified in time-series methodology only by the requirement that treatments be specified in such a way as to be replicable by other investigators. . . . (p. 158)

Appropriate use of time-series methodologies may significantly help bridge the practitioner-researcher gap in therapeutic recreation. A key issue which must be addressed when time-series methodologies are used is clinical replication. For this type of research to have any impact on the practice and recognition of therapeutic recreation clearly defined treatments or interventions will need to be used in a series of cases.

In addition to the use of alternate design strategies which are more suited for use in practice, delegates recommended the need to include a longitudinal perspective in much of the research efforts in therapeutic recreation. The general feeling at the conference was that it may not be until 3 to 6 months after discharge from a rehabilitation center that the influence of therapeutic recreation interventions surface and assist the client in maintaining independent functioning.

<u>Valuing the terms leisure and recreation</u>. The terms "recreation" and "leisure" are concepts and ideas that continue to evoke strong opinion about their influence on the advancement of therapeutic recreation's body of knowledge. Some contend that therapeutic recreation research ought to preserve the discipline's claimed uniqueness--the emphasis on recreation and leisure--and that researchers should focus on outcomes directly related to leisure functioning and an independent leisure lifestyle regardless of the value others associate with these outcomes. Individuals with this viewpoint argue that heath care policy makers and service agencies need to be educated about the importance of recreation and leisure to overall life quality. In short, recreation and leisure are important and valuable human endeavors and experiences in and of themselves and therapeutic recreation researchers should not apologize for a leisure-outcome focus. This perspective reflects an internally relevant rationale for the inclusion of therapeutic recreation in health care and human service systems.

Others contend that research ought to demonstrate the contributions therapeutic recreation services make to larger outcomes widely valued by health care and human service systems. This view seems to best reflect the suggestion of the Conference Keynoter, Dr. Mary Lee Seibert. She urged the therapeutic recreation discipline to demonstrate outcomes that are valued by the agencies that employ therapeutic recreation practitioners and the entities that pay for health care services. Thus, documented benefits of therapeutic recreation, such as increased involvement in recreation and leisure pursuits, are researched in terms of the influence on overall services outcomes such as reduced likelihood of secondary health complications, the maintenance of sobriety, or the increased and continuous use of socially active community opportunities. This perspective promotes an externally relevant rationale for inclusion of therapeutic recreation services in health care and human service systems, and demonstrates a congruency between the disciplines outcome focus with that of other health care disciplines.

The enormity of the need for efficacy research supports both views. The discipline needs to demonstrate the contribution of recreation and leisure, as treatment and as a human experience, to regaining and maintaining overall health and well-being. And, health care and social policy makers need to be educated to the importance of recreation and leisure in the total fabric of healthful living, including habilitation, rehabilitation, and independent living. Regardless of the justification one chooses, the need for empirical research is clear.

Need for Dissemination to a
Variety of Audiences

The knowledge and understanding created through therapeutic recreation research needs to be shared with other disciplines and agencies endeavoring to serve persons who are ill or have disabilities. It is particularly important to share this information in a context that is pertinent to others such that they are better able to see the relevance of therapeutic recreation services to health status, functional capacity, and quality of life. The discipline should make concerted and deliberate effort to foster and stimulate more cross-disciplinary collaboration and cooperation within training, research, and dissemination of mutually useful information. It would be particularly useful to increase efforts to publish therapeutic recreation research and practice in journals external to the discipline. Also, it would be beneficial to have the <u>Therapeutic Recreation Journal</u> and the <u>ATRA Annual</u> indexed in major health care indices (e.g. Psych Lit, Medline, Medlars, Index Medicus), and to explore similar possibilities with newer data base vendors such as Dialog and BRS.

Research Priorities in Therapeutic Recreation

As a result of the expert opinion of the conference delegates, some broad research themes were identified that future research in therapeutic recreation should address. Each of these research themes should be investigated in terms of the degree to which they influence/improve the health status, functional capacity, and/or quality of life for clients.

Implementing such a research agenda will not be easy. It involves, as many of the consensus groups suggested, a multiple tier approach to research. A multiple tier approach involves systematic efficacy evaluations of the direct results of therapeutic recreation interventions and then a determination of how these outcomes influence broader health care system concerns.

The challenge to the discipline is to determine the outcomes of therapeutic recreation services (despite its variability) and to identify the health care outcomes that these services may influence. The discipline must be not wary to limit its research to examining only those health-care outcomes that others have rightfully or wrongfully established as priorities for therapeutic recreation. Rather, therapeutic recreation researchers must stay open to envisioning other relevant and important health care outcomes that therapeutic recreation may influence (e.g., family cohesion or decreased dependency on services).

This was the challenge that the delegates struggled with during the 3-day conference. The general consensus among the delegates was that systematic efficacy research is needed that examines the role of therapeutic recreation in terms of *coping, health maintenance, independent living, vocational success, family support and cohesion,* and *life span transitions* and to relate changes in these areas (as a result of therapeutic recreation intervention) to health care concerns such as *recidivism, length of stay, medication use, compliance,* and most importantly, *cost-effectiveness.*

References

Adriaenssens, P., Eggermont, E., Pyck, K., Boeckx, W., & Gilles, B. (1988). The video invasion of rehabilitation, Burns, 14, 417-419.

Alajajian, L. (1981). Jogging program for deaf-blind students improves condition and reduces self-stimulation. News . . . About Deaf-Blind Student, Programmed Services in New England, 6(1), 3-4.

Anson, C., & Shepherd, C. (1990, March). A survey of post-acute spinal cord patients: Medical psychological, and social characteristics. Trends: Research News From Shepherd Spinal Center.

Austin, D. R. (1987). Recreation and persons with physical disabilities: A literature synthesis. Therapeutic Recreation Journal, 21, 36-44.

Baer, B. (1985). The rehabilitation influences of creative experience. The Journal of Creative Behavior, 19(3), 202-214.

Baines, S., Saxby, P., & Ehlert, K. (1987, August). Reality orientation and reminiscence therapy: A controlled cross-over study of elderly confused people. British Journal of Psychiatry, 151, 222-231.

Banziger, G., & Rousch, S. (1983). Nursing homes for the birds: A control-relevant intervention with bird feeders. The Gerontologist, 23,527-531.

Barlow, D. H., Hayes, S. C., & Nelson, R. O. (1984). The scientist practitioner. New York: Pergamon Press.

Beck, P. (1982). The successful interventions in nursing homes: The therapeutic effects of cognitive activity. The Gerontologist, 22, 389-383.

Berger, B. G. (1983/1984). Stress reduction through exercise: The mind-body connection. Motor Skills: Theory into Practice, 7, 31-46.

Berger, B. G. (1986). Use of jogging and swimming as stress reduction techniques. In J. H. Humphrey (Ed.), Current selected research in the psychology and sociology of sport, 1, 97-113. New York: AMS Press.

Berk, L., Tan, S., Nehlsen-Cannarella, S., Napier, B., Lee, J., Lewis, J., Hubbard, R., & Eby, W. (1988). Mirth modulates adrenocorticomedullary activity: Suppression of cortisol and epinephrine. Clinical Research, 36, 121.

Berk, L. et al. (1988). Humor associated laughter decreases cortisol and increases spontaneous lymphocyte blastogenesis. Clinical Research, 36, 435.

Berryman-Miller, S. (1988). Dance movement: Effects on elderly self concepts. Journal of Physical Education, Recreation & Dance, 59, 42-46.

Birenbaum, A., & Re, M. A. (1979). Resettling mentally retarded adults in the community--almost four years later. American Journal of Mental Deficiency, 83, 323-329.

Bodzioch, J., Roach, J. W., & Schkade, J. (1986). Promoting independence in adolescent paraplegics: A 2-week "camping experience." Journal of Pediatric Orthopedics, 6(2), 198-201.

Brock, B. J. (1988). Effects of horseback riding on physically disabled adults. Therapeutic Recreation Journal, 22(3), 34-43.

Buettner, L. (1988). Utilizing development theory and adaptive equipment with regressed geriatric patients in therapeutic recreation. Therapeutic Recreation Journal, 22(3), 72-79.

Bullock, C. C., & Howe, C. Z. (1991). A model therapeutic recreation program for the reintegration of persons with disabilities into the community. Therapeutic Recreation Journal, 25(1), 7-17.

Carson, D. K., Jenkins, J., & Stout, C. B. (1985). Assessing child life programs: Study model with a small number of subjects. Children's Health Care, 14, 123-125.

Cerny, F. J. (1989). Relative effects of bronchial drainage and exercise for in-hospital care of patients with cystic fibrosis. Physical Therapy, 69, 633-638.

Citrin, R., & Dixon, D. (1977). Reality orientation: A milieu therapy used in an institution for the aged. Gerontologist, 17, 39-43.

Conroy, M., Fincham, F., & Agard-Evans, C. (1988). Can they do anything? Ten single-subject studies of the engagement level of hospitalized demented patients. British Journal of Occupational Therapy, 51, 129-132.

Coyle, C. P., Santiago, M., Kinney, T., Blair, D. (1991, Fall). Benefits of physical exercise for individuals with a disability: Two case studies. Pennsylvania Recreation & Parks, pp. 4-8.

Cutler Riddick, C. (1985). Health, aquariums, and the non-institutionalized elderly. In M. Sussman (Ed.), Pets and the family (pp.63-173). New York: Haworth Press.

Cutler Riddick, C., & Dugan-Jendzejec, M. (1988). Health related impacts of a music program on nursing home residents. In F. Humphrey & J. Humphrey (Eds.), Recreation: Current selected research (pp. 155-166). New York: AMS Press.

Cutler Riddick, C., Spector, S., & Drogin, E. (1986). The effects of videogames play on the emotional states and affiliative behavior of nursing home residents. Activities, Adaptation & Aging, 8, 95-108.

Curtis, K. A., McClanahan, S., Hall, K. M., Dillon, D., & Brown, K. F. (1986). Health, vocational, and functional status in spinal cord injured athletes and nonathletes. Archives of Physical Medicine and Rehabilitation, 67, 862-867.

Dattilo, J., & Barnett, L. (1985). Therapeutic recreation for individuals with severe handicaps: Implications of chosen participation. Therapeutic Recreation Journal, 19, 79-91.

Davis, G. M., Shephard, R. J., & Jackson, R. W. (1981). Cardiorespiratory fitness and muscular strength in the lower-limb disabled. Canadian Journal of Applied Sport Sciences, 6, 159-177.

Demarest, D. S., Hooke, J. F., & Erickson, M. T. (1984). Preoperative intervention for the reduction of anxiety in pediatric surgery patients. Children's Health Care, 12, 179-183.

DeSalvatore, G., & Roseman, D. (1986). The parent-child activity group: Using activities to work with children and their families in residential treatment. Child Care Quarterly, 15(4), 213-222.

De Vries, H. A. (1987). In W. P. Morgan & S. E. Goldston (Eds.), Exercise and mental health (pp. 99-104). Washington, DC: Hemisphere Publishing.

Dew, M. A., Lynch, K., Ernst, J., & Rosenthal, R. (1983). Reaction and adjustments to spinal cord injury: A descriptive study. Journal of Applied Rehabilitation Counseling, 14(1), 32-39.

Duckert, F. (1987). Recruitment into treatment and effects of treatment for female problem drinkers. Addictive Behaviors, 12(2), 137-143.

Eason, L. J., White, M. J., & Newsom, C. (1982). Generalized reductions of self-stimulatory behavior: An effect of teaching appropriate play to autistic children. Analysis and Intervention in Developmental Disabilities, 2, 157-169.

Eriksen, L., Bjornstad, S., & Gotestam, K. G. (1986). Social skills training in groups for alcoholics: One-year treatment outcome for groups and individuals. Addictive Behaviors, 11, 309-329.

Figoni, S., Boileau, R., Massey, B., & Larsen, J. R. (1988). Physiological responses of quadriplegic and able-bodied men during exercise at the same VO2. Adapted Physical Activity Quarterly, 5, 130-139.

Francis, G., & Baly, A. (1986). Plush animals: Do they make a difference? Geriatric Nursing, 7, 140-142.

Francis, G., & Munjas, B. (1988). Plush animals and the elderly. Journal of Applied Gerontology, 7, 161-172.

Fry, P. (1983). Structured and unstructured reminiscence training and depression among the elderly. Clinical Gerontologist, 1(3), 15-37.

Gilbert, M. J. (1990-1991). The anthropologist as alcohologist: Qualitative perspectives and methods in alcohol research. The International Journal of the Addictions, 25(24), 127-148.

Grant, M., & Johnstone, B. M. (1990-1991). Research priorities for drug and alcohol studies: The next 25 years. The International Journal of the Addictions, 25(24), 201-219.

Grantham-McGregor, S., Schofield, W., & Harris, L. (1983). Effect of psychosocial stimulation on mental development of severely malnourished children: An interim report. Pediatrics, 72, 239-243.

Green, J. (1989). Effects of a water aerobics program on the blood pressure, percentage of body fat, weight, and resting pulse rate of senior citizens. Journal of Applied Gerontology, 8(1), 132-138.

Greenwood, C. M., Dzewattowski, D. A., & French, R. (1990). Self efficacy and psychological well-being of wheelchair tennis participants and wheelchair nontennis participants. Adapted Physical Activity Quarterly, 7(1), 12-21.

Greist, J. H. (1987). Exercise intervention with depressed outpatients. In W. P. Morgan & S. E. Goldston (Eds.), Exercise and mental health (pp. 117-121). Washington, DC: Hemisphere Publishing.

Greist, J. H., Klein, M. H., Eischens, R. R., Faris, J., Gurman, A. S., & Morgan, W. P. (1979). Running as a treatment for depression. Comprehensive Psychiatry, 20, 41-54.

Hawkins, J. D., & Fraser, M. W. (1987). The social networks of drug abusers before and after treatment. The International Journal of the Addictions, 22(4), 343-355.

Hedrick, B. N. (1985). The effect of wheelchair tennis participation and mainstreaming upon the perceptions of competence of physically disabled adolescents. Therapeutic Recreation Journal, 19(2), 34-46.

Heywood, L. A. (1978). Perceived recreation experience and the relief of tension. Journal of Leisure Research, 10, 86-97.

Hoffman, M. D. (1986). Cardiorespiratory fitness and training in quadriplegics and paraplegics. Sports Medicine, 3, 312-330.

Holmes, M. R., Hansen, D. J., & St. Lawrence, J. S. (1984). Conversational skills training with aftercare patients in the community: Social validation and generalization. Behavior Therapy, 15, 84-100.

Hopper, C. (1988). Self-concept and motor performance of hearing impaired boys and girls. Adapted Physical Activity Quarterly, 5, 293-304.

Ipsa, J., Barrett, B., & Kim, Y. (1988). Effects of supervised play in a hospital waiting room. Children's Health Care, 16, 195-200.

Jackson, R. W., & Davis, G. M. (1983). The value of sports and recreation for the physically disabled. Orthopedic Clinics of North America, 14, 301-315.

James, M. R., & Townsley, R. K. (1989). Activity therapy services and chemical dependency rehabilitation. Journal of Alcohol and Drug Education, 34(3), 48-53.

Jocheim, K. A., & Strohkendle, H. (1973). Value of particular sports of the wheelchair disabled in maintaining health of the paraplegic. Paraplegia, 11, 173-178.

Katz, J. F., Adler, J. C., Mazzarella, N. J., & Inck, L. P. (1985). Psychological consequences of an exercise training program for a paraplegic man: A case study. Rehabilitation Psychology, 30(1), 53-58.

Kavanagh, T., Shephard, R. J., Tuck, J. A., Qureshi, S. (1977). Depression following myocardial infarction: The effects of distance running. In R. Milvey (Ed.), Annals of the New York academy of sciences, 301 (pp. 1029-1038). New York: New York Academy of Sciences.

Keller, M. (1991). The impact of a water aerobics program on older adults. Unpublished manuscript.

Koch, I., Schlegel, M., Pirrwitz, A., Jaschke, B., & Schlegel, K. (1983). On objectivizing the training effect of sport therapy in wheelchair-users (In German). International Journal of Rehabilitation Research, 6, 439-448.

Krause, J. S., & Crewe, M. M. (1987). Prediction of long-term survival of persons with spinal cord injury. Rehabilitation Psychology, 32(4), 205-213.

Krebs, P., Eickelberg, W., Krobath, H., & Barch, I. (1989). Effects of physical exercise on peripheral vision and learning in children with spina bifida manifesta. Perceptual and Motor Skills, 68, 167-174.

Lanagan, D., & Dattilo, J. (1989). The effects of a leisure education program on individuals with mental retardation. Therapeutic Recreation Journal, 23(4), 62-72.

Lewis, K. (1985). Successful living with chronic illness. Wayne, NJ: Avery.

Liberman, R. P., Lillie, F. J., Falloon, I. R. H., Harpin, E. J., Hutchison, W., & Stout, B. A. (1984). Social skills training for relapsing schizophrenics: An experimental analysis. Behavior Modification, 8, 155-179.

Long, B. C. (1984). Aerobic conditioning and stress inoculation: A comparison of stress-management interventions. Cognitive Therapy Research, 8(5), 517-542.

Marini, D. G. (1978). Effects of additional physical and recreational curriculum on selected perceptual-motor abilities of educable mentally retarded children. Therapeutic Recreation Journal, 12(3), 31-38.

Martinsen, E. W., Medhus, A., & Sandvik, L. (1984). The effect of aerobic exercise on depression: A controlled study. Unpublished manuscript. (p. 92 of Exercise & Mental Health).

Matson, J., & Adkins, J. (1984). A self-instructional social skills training program for mentally retarded persons. Mental Retardation, 18, 245-248.

McAuliffe, W. E., & Ch'ien, J. M. N. (1986). Recovery training and self help: A relapse prevention program for treated opiate addicts. Journal of Substance Abuse Treatment, 3, 9-20.

McAvoy, L. H., Schatz, E. C., Stutz, M. E., Schlein, S. J., & Lais, G. (1989). Integrated wilderness adventure: Effects on personal and lifestyle traits of persons with and without disabilities. Therapeutic Recreation Journal, 23(3), 50-64.

McGuire, F. (1984). Improving the quality of life for residents of long term care facilities through video games. Activities, Adaptation & Aging, 6, 1-8.

Miles, D. S., Sawka, M. N., Wilde, S. W., Durbin, R. J., & Gotshall, R. W. (1982). Pulmonary function changes in wheelchair athletes subsequent to exercise training. Ergonomics, 25, 239-246.

Miller, M. J. (1987). The effects of reality orientation and validation therapy with disoriented nursing home residents. Dissertation Abstracts International, 48, 2953.

Monti, P. M., Fink, E., Norman, W., Curran, J., Hayes, S., & Caldwell, A. (1979). Effect of social skills training groups and social skills bibliotherapy with psychiatric patients. Journal of Consulting and Clinical Psychology, 47(1), 189-191.

Morey, M., Cowper, P., Feussner, J., DiPasquale, R., Crowley, G., Kitzman, D., & Sullivan, R. (1989). Evaluation of a supervised exercise program in a geriatric population. Journal of American Geriatrics Society, 37, 348-354.

North, G. G. (1987). The treatment of hallucinatory and delusional behavior with reality orientation. Dissertation Abstracts International, 49, 918.

Osgood, N., Meyers, B., & Orchowsky, S. (1990). The impact of creative dance and movement training on the life satisfaction of older adults. Journal of Applied Gerontology, 9, 255-265.

Peniston, L. (1991, September). The effects of a microcomputer training program on short-term memory in elderly individuals. A paper presented at the Benefits of Therapeutic Recreation in Rehabilitation Conference, Lafayette Hill, PA.

Potelunas-Campbell, M. F. (1982). The development and evaluation of a social skills training program for supervisor/supervisee dyad interactions in a work adjustment program for female schizophrenic outpatients. Dissertation Abstracts International, 43/06A, 1899.

Rancourt, A. M. (1991a). (in press). An exploration of the relationships among substance abuse, recreation, and leisure for women who abuse substances.

Rancourt, A. M. (1991b, April 7). Results of a past discharge survey of women who participated in a six month comprehensive leisure education program while in substance abuse treatment. Paper presented at the American Alliance of Health, Physical Education, Recreation, and Dance Symposium on Drugs and Drug Education, San Francisco, CA.

Rasnake, L. K., & Linscheid, T. R. (1989). Anxiety reduction in children receiving medical care: Developmental considerations. Developmental and Behavioral Pediatrics, 10, 169-175.

Reuter, M., Mutrie, N., & Harris, D. V. (1984). Running as an adjunct to counseling in the treatment of depression. Unpublished manuscript, The Pennsylvania State University.

Reynolds, R. P., & Arthur, M. H. (1982). Effects of peer modeling and cognitive self guidance on the social play of emotionally disturbed children. Therapeutic Recreation Journal, 16(1), 33-40.

Riegler, J. (1980). Comparison of a reality orientation program for geriatric patients with and without music. Journal of Music Therapy, 17, 26-33.

Robb, G. M., & Evert, A. (1987). Risk recreation and persons with disabilities. Therapeutic Recreation Journal, 21(1), 58-69.

Roland, C. C., Summers, S., Friedman, M. J., Barton, G. M., & McCarthy, K. (1987). Creation of an experiential challenge program. Therapeutic Recreation Journal, 21(2), 54-63.

Rothe, T., Kohl, C., & Mansfeld, H. J. (1990). Controlled study of the effect of sports training on cardiopulmonary functions in asthmatic children and adolescents. Pneumologie, 44, 1110-1114. (From Medline, 1991, UD 9104).

Russoniello, C. V. (1991, September). An exploratory study of physiological and psychological changes in alcoholic patients after recreation therapy treatments. Paper presented at the Benefits of Therapeutic Recreation in Rehabilitation Conference, Lafayette Hill, PA.

Rynders, J. E., Schleien, S. J., & Mustonen, T. (1990). Integrating children with severe disabilities for intensified outdoor education: Focus on feasibility. Mental Retardation, 28, 7-14.

Sachs, M. L. (1982). Running therapy: Change agent in anxiety and stress management. Journal of Health, Physical Eduction, Recreation and Dance, 53(7), 44-45.

Santiago, M. C., Coyle, C. P., & Troup, J. T. (1991, November). Effects of twelve weeks of aerobic exercise in individuals with physical disabilities. Paper presented at 8th International Symposium on Adapted Physical Activity, Miami, FL.

Schleien, S., Cameron, J., Rynders, J., & Slick, C. (1988). Acquisition and generalization of leisure skills from school to the home and community by learners with severe multihandicaps. Therapeutic Recreation Journal, 22(3), 53-71.

Schleien, S., Kiernan, J., & Wehman, P. (1981). Evaluation of an age-appropriate leisure skills program for moderately retarded adults. Education and Training of the Mentally Retarded, 16(1), 13-19.

Schleien, S. J., Krotee, M. L., Mustonen, T., Kelterborn, B., & Schermer, A. D. (1987). The effect of integrating children with autism into a physical activity and recreation setting. Therapeutic Recreation Journal, 21(4), 52-62.

Schleien, S. J., & Larson, A. (1986). Adult leisure education for the independent use of a community recreation center. The Journal of the Association of Persons with Severe Handicaps, 11(1), 39-44.

Schwab, M., Roder, J., Doan, J. (1985). Relieving the anxiety and fear in dementia. Journal of Gerontological Nursing, 11(5), 8-15.

Scogin, F., Hamblin, D., & Beutler, L. (1987). Bibliotherapy for depressed older adults: A self-help alternative. The Gerontologist, 27, 383-387.

Scogin, F., Jamison, C., & Davis, N. (1990). Two-year follow-up of bibliotherapy for depression in older adults. Journal of Consulting and Clinical Psychology, 58, 665-667.

Scogin, F., Jamison, C., & Gochneaur, K. (1989). Comparative efficacy of cognitive and behavioral bibliotherapy for mildly and moderately depressed older adults. Journal of Consulting and Clinical Psychology, 57, 403-407.

Seibert, M. L. (1991, September). Keynote presentation. Benefits of Therapeutic Recreation in Rehabilitation Conference, Lafayette Hill, PA.

Shank, J. W., Coyle, C. P., & Kinney, W. B. (1991a, September). A comparison of the effects of clinical versus diversional therapeutic recreation involvement on rehabilitation outcomes. Paper presented at Benefits of Therapeutic Recreation in Rehabilitation Conference, Lafayette Hill, PA.

Shank, J. W., Coyle, C. P., & Kinney, W. B. (1991b, September). Comparative effects of segregated and integrated recreation on persons with disabilities. Paper presented at Benefits of Therapeutic Recreation in Rehabilitation Conference, Lafayette Hill, PA.

Shary, J., & Iso-Ahola, S. (1989). Effects of a control relevant intervention program on nursing home residents' perceived competence and self-esteem. Therapeutic Recreation Journal, 23, 7-16.

Sherrill, C., & Rainbolt, W. (1988). Self-actualization profiles of male able-bodied and elite cerebral palsied athletes. Adapted Physical Activity Quarterly, 5, 108-119.

Sime, W. E. (1987). Exercise in the treatment and prevention of depression. In Morgan & Goldston (Eds.), Exercise and mental health. Washington: Hemisphere Publishing.

Simpson, D. D., Crandall, R., Savage, L. J., & Pavia-Krueser, E. (1981). Leisure of opiate addicts at posttreatment follow-up. Journal of Counseling Psychology, 28(1), 36-39.

Skalko, T. K. (1982). The effects of a leisure education program on the perceived leisure well-being of psychiatrically impaired active army personnel. Unpublished doctoral dissertation, University of Maryland, College Park, MD.

Skalko, T. K. (1990). Discretionary time use and the chronically mentally ill. Therapeutic Recreation Annual, 1, 9-14.

Stensrude, C., Mishkin, L., Craft, C., & Pollock, I. (1987). The use of drama techniques in cognitive rehabilitation. Therapeutic Recreation Journal, 21(2), 64-69.

Stewart, N. (1981). The value of sport in the rehabilitation of the physically disabled. Canadian Journal of Applied Sport Science, 6(4), 166-167.

Stotts, K. M. (1986). Health maintenance: Paraplegic athletes and nonathletes. Archives of Physical Medicine and Rehabilitation, 67, 109-114.

Strain, P. (1975). Increasing social play of severely retarded preschoolers with socio-dramatic activities. Mental Retardation, 13, 7-9.

Stuckey, K., & Barkus, C. (1986). Visually Impaired scouts meet the Philmont challenge. Journal of Visual Impairment and Blindness, 80(5), 750-751.

Szentagothai, K., Gyene, I., Szocska, M., & Osvath, P. (1987). Physical exercise program for children with bronchial asthma. Pediatric Pulmonology, 3, 166-172.

Taylor, C. B., Sallis, J. F., Needle, R. (1985). The relation of physical activity and exercise to mental health. Public Health Reports, 100, 195-202.

Thorne, F. C. (1973). Eclectic psychotherapy. In R. Corsini (Ed.), Current psychotherapies (pp. 445-486). Itasca: Peacock.

Tipton, C. M., Vailas, A. C., & Matthes, R. D. (1986). Experimental studies on the influences of physical activity on ligaments, tendons and joints: A brief review. Acta Medica Scandinavica Supplement, 711, 157-168.

Trader, B., & Anson, C. (1991, September). The relationship of leisure commitment to health in individuals following spinal cord injury. Paper presented at the Benefits of Therapeutic Recreation in Rehabilitation Conference, Lafayette Hill, PA.

Ulrich, R. S., Dimberg, V., & Driver, B. L. (1990). Psycho- physiological indicators of leisure consequences. Journal of Leisure Research, 22(2), 154-166.

Van Andel, G. (1986). Mood, health locus of control and physical activity. Unpublished doctoral dissertation, Indiana

University.

Van Loan, M. D., McCluer, S., Loftin, J. M., & Boileau, R. A. (1987). Comparison of physiological responses to maximal arm exercise among able-bodied, paraplegics and quadriplegics. International Medical Society of Paraplegia, 25, 397-405.

Wassman, K. B., & Iso-Ahola, S. E. (1985). The relationship between recreation participation and depression in psychiatric patients. Therapeutic Recreation Journal, 19(3), 63-70.

Weiss, C., & Jamieson, N. (1988). Hidden disabilities: A new enterprise for therapeutic recreation. Therapeutic Recreation Journal, 22(4), 9-17.

Witman, J. P. (1987). The efficacy of adventure programming in the development of cooperation and trust with adolescents in treatment. Therapeutic Recreation Journal, 21(3), 22-29.

Wolfe, J. (1983). The use of music in a group sensory training program for regressed geriatric patients. Activities, Adaptation & Aging, 4(1), 49-62.

Wolfer, J., Gaynard, L., Goldberger, J., Laidley, L. N., & Thompson, R. (1988). An experimental evaluation of a model child life program. Children's Health Care, 16, 244-254.

Wong, S. E., Terranova, M. D., Bowen, L., et al. (1987). Providing independent recreational activities to reduce stereotypic vocalizations in chronic schizophrenics. Journal of Applied Behavior Analysis, 20, 77-81.

Wong, S. E., Terranova, M. D., Marshall, B. D., Banzett, L. K., & Liberman, R. P. (1983, May). Reducing bizarre stereotypic behavior in chronic psychiatric patients: Effects of supervised and independent recreational activities. Presented at the Ninth Annual Convention of the Association of Behavior Analysis, Milwaukee, WI.

Yoder, R., Nelson, D., & Smith, D. (1989). Added purpose versus rote exercise in female nursing home residents. American Journal of Occupational Therapy, 43(9), 581-586.

Zwiren, L., Huberman, G., & Bar-Or, O. (1973). Cardiopulmonary functions of sedentary and highly active paraplegics. Medicine and Science in Sport, 5, 683-686.

CHAPTER 10

REACTION PAPERS

SUMMARY OF CHEMICAL DEPENDENCY
CONSENSUS GROUP

Colleen Hood & Mark Mattiko

Preliminary Discussion

A group of 11 individuals in the field of therapeutic recreation were brought together to come to consensus on the benefits of therapeutic recreation with addictive populations. This group consisted of educators and practitioners with expertise, experience, and interest in the area of addictions and a group facilitator who was used to assist in the consensus building process.

The initial step in this consensus building process was to review an extensive position paper which summarized current research findings related to addictions. The following is a synopsis of the discussions and findings of this group as they relate to the position paper, research, and clinical practice. This summary will present both the content and process which occurred during the consensus group meetings.

The initial step in this process was to identify specifically which aspects of the addictions population were to be discussed. Though addictive behaviors encompass a wide range of behaviors, only those addictive behaviors related to alcohol and other drug abuse were discussed. Thus, the population being addressed was those individuals who abuse alcohol and other drugs.

The group generated and identified benefits which are associated with therapeutic recreation in the treatment of addictions. This original list included both those benefits which were supported by research and those benefits which were primarily supported by experience and practice. The group decided that these benefits should be organized or grouped into a systematic framework. Within this framework, three major treatment components were identified: (a) social functioning, (b) stress management, and (c) leisure and recovering lifestyle. Specific benefits fell within one of these three broad treatment categories. The categories and the specific benefits are presented in Table 1.

After a discussion of the possible benefits of therapeutic recreation for this population, the group then re-examined the benefits to determine which were supported by research. In spite of a scarcity of empirical research in this area, the group was able to identify research that did address certain benefits. Table 1 identifies which benefits are supported by empirical research and by which sources, when possible.

Once benefits had been identified, it seemed useful to examine the overall goals of the treatment process from the perspective of health care providers. The rationale for this process was to attempt to relate the therapeutic recreation benefits to the overall anticipated treatment outcomes, thus providing a rationale for the inclusion of therapeutic recreation. The four generic goals of addictions treatment were identified as: (a) achieving abstinence, (b) maintaining sobriety, (c) reducing recidivism, and (d) increasing quality of life post-discharge.

Priorities for Outcomes Research in Substance Abuse

A discussion followed as to how to translate these benefits or goals into research priorities. Once again, a conceptual framework was identified and discussed to assist in the process of identifying research priorities. This efficacy research framework consisted of three stages:

1. Systematic empirical studies which demonstrate that therapeutic recreation programs are being designed and implemented to produce desired outcomes (knowledge and behavioral change) while in treatment. Specifically, these studies will document the effectiveness of therapeutic recreation programs and interventions in the areas of social functioning, stress management, and leisure and recovering lifestyle.

2. Systematic empirical studies which demonstrate the relationship between social functioning, stress management, and recovery lifestyle to the overall treatment goals of achieving abstinence, maintaining sobriety, reducing recidivism, and increasing quality of life.

3. Systematic empirical studies which demonstrate the relationship between the therapeutic recreation interventions and the overall goals of treatment, and specific NIDRR priorities (including prevention, diagnosis, treatment, management, cost containment, length of stay, recidivism, etc.).

Research Questions

This framework and prioritization of research issues was then used with a nominal group technique to develop examples of specific research questions which could be addressed. Before the research questions were developed, an assumption was made that the programs examined will be designed systematically, with explicit client goals, and content and process descriptions. Examples of research questions which could be included in the first stage of the efficacy research framework include:

1. Does a stress management program which addresses specific issues (both knowledge and behaviors, identified by the researcher) and uses specific intervention techniques (identified by the researcher) result in increased ability to cope with stress?

2. More specifically, does a stress management program which addresses the following topics: (a) definition of stress, (b) symptoms of stress, (c) impact of stress on recovery, (d) cognitive restructuring, and (e) relaxation techniques, result in increased ability to cope with stress in various situations?

Research questions for the other two areas--social functioning and leisure and recovering lifestyle--would follow a similar format and wording. A complete list of research questions developed is included at the end of this chapter.

The second level of the efficacy research framework related the specific therapeutic recreation interventions and content to the overall treatment goals. Examples of these research questions include:

1. Do clients who have been involved in a stress management program have longer periods of sobriety after discharge than clients who have not had stress management training?

2. Do individuals who have knowledge of and are using basic communication skills have longer periods of abstinence than those individuals who do not have these skills/interventions?

3. Do individuals who have strong social support networks have a higher quality of life than those individuals who do not?

4. Does the provision of therapeutic recreation services during treatment enable the enhancement of pleasure during post-treatment sobriety?

5. What is the relationship between abstinence and quality sobriety, and participation in recreation activities and leisure experiences?

Research Issues

The final challenge addressed by the group was to identify specific strategies to achieve the research goals and to disseminate the information. The first suggestion related to attaining the research goals was to develop a type of clearinghouse of information (both research based and programmatic) related to addictions and leisure. This clearinghouse would have a complete bibliography, including research related to the research priorities that would not be limited to leisure sources.

The second major suggestion was to develop a research protocol which would provide direction and standardization for practitioners and graduate students conducting efficacy research. The third suggestion was to develop an additional review panel to assist with the research agenda and to encourage collaborative studies. The fourth suggestion was to conduct longitudinal research designed to follow clients post-discharge. These projects could be interdisciplinary in nature and could include community recreation personnel. The final two suggestions were to encourage the development of research programs and the development of reliable assessment instruments to assist in the evaluation of client outcomes.

In terms of specific action plans identified by the group, several suggestions were made. The first suggestion was to attempt to reconvene this working group at the ATRA midyear forum in Chicago in March. The group would review the action plan and identify more specific actions, including the proposed research protocol. It was also suggested that a survey be conducted in the field to gather information regarding existing therapeutic recreation programs in addictions treatment, looking specifically at program content, interventions, expected client outcomes, and client evaluation procedures. The final suggestion was to disseminate programs which are already developed and packaged for use.

The final task was to identify target audiences for the information generated at this conference and/or the results of efficacy research. The audiences identified were: (a) doctorate granting universities; (b) practitioners in the area of addictions; (c) professional organizations; (d) allied health care researchers; (e) data bases which collect information related to addictions treatment; (f) addictions treatment facilities; (g) funding agencies; (h) health care insurance carriers; (i) health care professionals, including allied health care, physicians, and so forth; and (j) external accrediting bodies of health care facilities.

Concluding Remarks

A group of 11 therapeutic recreators met to come to consensus on the benefits of therapeutic recreation for addictions treatment. Utilizing nominal techniques, they arrived at a consensus that therapeutic recreation benefits clients/patients by addressing problems in the areas of stress management, social functioning, and leisure and recovering lifestyle. Benefits were derived from published and non-published research, clinical practice, and clinical experience and would potentially affect achieving abstinence, maintaining sobriety, reducing recidivism, and increasing quality of life.

Research Questions Suggested

This attachment includes a list of the research questions generated at this working conference. This list is intended to provide the reader with ideas and suggestions for thinking about the future research needs of the field of therapeutic recreation with respect to addictions treatment--it is not a comprehensive list of all possible research questions.

1. Does assertiveness training increase assertiveness?

2. Does a social skills training program teach the intended skills (e.g., conversational ability, ability to make requests)?

3. Does a community resource class have an impact on ability to identify places to meet people?

4. Does a family leisure education program increase shared family leisure experiences?

5. To what extent do therapeutic recreation programs meet the conceptual framework they are supposed to present? (Compare this information with outcomes for different conceptual models, to determine if the best conceptual framework is being used.)

6. To what extent does knowledge and use of chemical free alternatives (activities, resources, partners) affect sobriety?

7. To what extent does the provision of therapeutic recreation services influence post-treatment leisure lifestyle in relation to time, number and type of activities, leisure partners, and community resources?

8. Does the existence of a balanced leisure lifestyle affect recidivism?

9. To what extent do therapeutic recreation leisure education programs focusing on: (a) knowledge of leisure, (b) acquisition of new leisure skills, (c) learning new problem solving methods, and/or (d) increased social support, assist in the alleviation of boredom?

10. Does the provision of therapeutic recreation services during treatment enhance the experience of pleasure during post-treatment sobriety?

11. Does the ability to engage in enjoyable activities facilitate sobriety?

12. Does a program on social support/resources lead to the development of social support networks?

13. Is boredom alleviated by leisure involvement?

14. Which social skills are most important in recovery?

15. Which therapeutic recreation interventions have the most impact on denial?

16. Do individuals who learn but do not practice stress management techniques utilize them as effectively as persons who practice techniques while in treatment? Does either approach impact relapse rates?

Table 1. Research Priorities

Generic Goals of Treatment

I.	Achieve abstinence	Pavia & Kreuser (1981)
II.	Maintain sobriety	Franklin, Kidrich, Thrasher
III.	Reduce recidivism	(1974)
IV.	Increase quality of life	

Benefits of Therapeutic Recreation

I.	Social Functioning		
	(A)	Enhancement of social skills	McAuliffe & Ch'ien (1986)
			Rancourt (1991)
	(B)	Development of social support networks	McAuliffe & Ch'ien (1986)
			Rancourt (1991)
	(C)	Enhance basic communication skills	James & Townsley (1989)
II.	Stress Management		
	(A)	Relaxation	McAuliffe & Ch'ien (1986)
	(B)	Physical Exercise & Fitness	
	(C)	Anxiety management	
III.	Leisure and Recovering Lifestyle		
	(A)	Coping skills	Rancourt (1991)
	(B)	Chemical free alternatives	James & Townsley (1989)
	(C)	Balanced lifestyle	Rancourt (1991)
	(D)	Structuring free time	Rancourt (1991)
	(E)	Alleviate boredom and/or provide alternatives to boredom	McAuliffe & Ch'ien (1986)
	(F)	Experience pleasure and enjoyment	– depression – Frankel & Murphy (1974)
	(G)	Develop leisure skills	
	(H)	Develop problem solving and decision-making skills	
	(I)	Community reintegration	Rancourt (1991)

SUMMARY OF GERONTOLOGY CONSENSUS GROUP

Linda Troyer

Client and Health Care System Outcomes

A review of morbidity and mortality data, by Riddick and Keller (1991), provided a basis for the identification of health problems related to the aging process. Major geriatric health problems that were identified were: (a) cardiovascular disease, (b) orthopedic disabilities, (c) senile dementia, (d) loneliness, (e) depression, (f) cancer, and (g) substance abuse.

Upon discussion, the group felt that the therapeutic recreation profession should focus their intervention techniques among the four generic functional domains of health: (a) social, (b) emotional, (c) cognitive, and (d) physical. It was felt that these domains represent areas where therapeutic recreation interventions could provide major benefits to the older individual's functional status.

Group members also agreed that research should further explore the impact of therapeutic recreation as it relates to the health care delivery system or how therapeutic recreation interventions influence: (a) decreased need for various health care services, (b) decreased medical and/or health costs, (c) decreased staffing ratios, (d) decreased dependency on prescriptive medications, (e) decreased length of stay in health care facilities, (f) decreased use of all treatment and nursing services, (g) decreased recidivism, and (h) decreased use of inappropriate community resources.

Proposed Model Research Framework:
An Application

In order to work through an example of how one could assess the impacts of a therapeutic recreation intervention on client and health care system outcomes, and with a bias towards rehabilitation/treatment, the group chose (using the Nominal Group Process) to focus on emotional functioning. It should be noted that throughout the consensus building process, the members were challenged to show direct and indirect relationships between a suggested intervention(s), client benefit(s), and health care delivery system impact(s).

Thus, focusing on the domain of emotional functioning, the group identified what it considered feasible client outcome goals for therapeutic recreation or directing efforts at: (a) empowerment, (b) subjective well-being, (c) adjustment/stress management, (d) self-esteem/self-concepts, (e) appropriate affect, (f) perceived control/internal locus of control, (g) flow state, and (h) perceived competence. These health outcomes were deemed important areas where therapeutic recreation could have major benefits for the older individual.

Finally, once an interrelationship has been demonstrated between a specific therapeutic recreation intervention and a specific emotion outcome(s), the next step in the research would be to link the specific therapeutic recreation interventions to (see page 1, second paragraph, last sentence of this document, for some examples).

In summary, the framework, outlined by the group, could be replicated in all four of the identified generic functional health domains. The suggested research framework would serve to clearly delineate the potential contributions of the therapeutic interventions to older client outcomes as well as to health care system's outcome(s).

Strategic Approaches for Identifying Research Priorities

A variety of strategic approaches, for addressing the research priorities related to examining the efficacy of therapeutic recreation for use with the geriatric populations, exist. Among these approaches are to:

1. Utilize an interdisciplinary approach for assessing therapeutic recreation efficacy.

2. Employ methodologically sound research designs with emphasis on the use of: (a) a theoretical foundation, (b) a control group, (c) appropriate statistics, and (d) valid and reliable measurements.

3. Test interventions already in place that are thought to positively impact the health and functioning of older adults. In particular, the group identified two therapeutic recreation interventions that appear to be promising and, therefore, should be examined further--that is, relaxation and reminiscence activities.

4. Focus on assessing efficacy of therapeutic recreation processes related to health promotion/ prevention/wellness.

5. Examine the efficacy of therapeutic recreation programs in a variety of geriatric health care settings.

6. Increase the circulation of unpublished therapeutic recreation and gerontological based dissertations and/or theses to practitioners.

7. Emphasize the teaching of research skills to undergraduates during professional preparation and practitioners through continuing education.

8. Establish incentives for improving collaboration between practitioners and university faculty members for the development of research and protocols.

9. Assess the cost effectiveness of specific therapeutic interventions on client and health care system outcomes.

10. Review business/health care literature related to cost containment and cost effectiveness.

11. Examine effects of therapeutic recreation intervention on life satisfaction and how this, in turn, influences health care costs.

12. Identify ways to structure sabbaticals so university researchers can work with practitioners.

13. Address symptomatology versus pathology secondary to disabilities.

14. Examine how certification requirements could be modified to include three to six credit hours in research methods.

15. Educate practitioners on how to access/use valid instruments appropriate to clients and settings but not necessarily designed by therapeutic recreation professionals.

16. Explore alternative placement of the therapeutic recreation curriculum in colleges and universities.

17. Look at research internship models utilized by other allied health care professionals to improve therapeutic recreation professionals' research skills.

18. Develop a research agenda to promote the continuity of investigation.

19. Encourage, formally and informally, graduate students to undertake or participate in therapeutic recreation research efficacy endeavors.

20. Establish guidelines for case study reporting. Qualitative and quantative studies are needed to determine the benefits of therapeutic recreation both to geriatric client populations and the health care system.

Dissemination of Research Findings

The findings of methodologically sound research, which demonstrates the benefits of therapeutic recreation within the geriatric population, should be disseminated to a multitude of individuals and groups. More specifically, the findings of therapeutic recreation efficacy research should be disseminated to: (a) legislators, (b) practitioners, (c) payor sources, (d) higher education/university libraries, (e) certifying and accrediting bodies, (f) various journals of other disciplines, (g) consumer groups, (h) research data bases (e.g., ERIC), (i) foundations, and (j) appropriate federal agencies.

Reference

Riddick, C., & Keller, J. (1991, September). Benefits of therapeutic recreation as a treatment modality in geriatrics. National Conference on the Benefits of Therapeutic Recreation in Rehabilitation, Philadelphia.

SUMMARY OF PEDIATRICS CONSENSUS GROUP

Linda Caldwell

Preliminary Discussion

Prior to the consensus building discussions, the Pediatrics Consensus Group (PCG) reviewed its mandate as described Friday evening by the organizers of the Conference (Kinney, Shank, and Coyle). The group also revisited Dr. Mary Lee Seibert's comments.

The PCG began its deliberations by hearing a summary report from the authors of the pre-conference paper. The authors described the process they used to develop the paper and identified not only major issues relevant to the day's discussions, but also some of the stumbling blocks they encountered. To assist the PCG, the authors made the following observations. Terminology and defining the area of pediatrics *for the purposes of this endeavor* were the two main issues with which the authors grappled. Pediatrics is an area of concern similar to geriatrics; both areas cover a wide range of illnesses, developmental stages, and disabling conditions. Therefore, it took some time to explicitly delimit what should be in the realm of the mandate of this group. Terminology was a problem as it was confused by the language of Child Life specialists. Regarding the state of knowledge of therapeutic recreation and pediatrics, the authors concluded that there was more pertinent information in the psycho-social realm of pediatrics than in the physiological area.

The PCG thanked the authors for providing an insightful account of their paper writing project and for supplying an outstanding and comprehensive springboard for discussion. The PCG felt that there was no need to further discuss the issues regarding terminology and definition of pediatrics and agreed to accept and work with definitions and delimitations of the authors. It was noted by the PCG, however, that precision of terminology was critical in communications of the efforts of the group.

Outcomes Supported with Evidence

It was difficult to arrive at consensus as to what was known about therapeutic recreation benefits in pediatrics. The difficulty did not lie from lack of agreement but rather lack of material. There appears to be little truly known in this area. After a brief discussion about what "to know" means (e.g., levels of confidence of knowledge), the group developed a preliminary list of what could be labeled as being known with some confidence. This preliminary list was put aside for the remainder of the day, and was tackled again Sunday morning. At this time, the PCG developed a list of four items which it felt represented what is known with some confidence about therapeutic recreation and pediatrics:

1. Age appropriate play can reduce psychological upset caused by the delivery of health care services.

2. Family involvement has an influence on the child with an illness or disability. This influence may be positive or negative. The group believes therapeutic recreation mitigates the negative influences and enhances the positive influences of family involvement.

3. Engagement in play/recreation can reduce symptomatology and enhance functional capacity.

4. The group knows there is a strong relationship between recreation/play and quality of life. Therefore, development of age appropriate, independent play and recreation skills are necessary for quality of life (in hospital and upon return to community).

Outcomes Requiring Documentation

There were a number of undocumented [1] or poorly documented believed benefits of therapeutic recreation held by the PCG. The PCG focused on those beliefs that it felt reasonably comfortable with, despite lack of evidence. After brainstorming what undocumented beliefs the PCG had, the group turned to Dr. Seibert's presentation to offer a conceptual framework with which to organize these beliefs. The PCG chose to utilize the health care and treatment categories of: (a) prevention, (b) diagnosis, (c) treatment, and (d) management. The group's goal was to identify fairly specific outcomes under each of those categories and link them with therapeutic recreation interventions. In order to accomplish this, a matrix was developed (see Table 1). Each cell represents a believed outcome as a result of the corresponding therapeutic recreation intervention.

---

[1] Documented refers to scientific, empirical evidence, regardless of method used--e.g.,experimental design or phenomenological study).

Because these are undocumented or poorly documented outcomes, the cells represent areas where research is needed. For example, one would interpret the first cell (corresponding to Treatment and Structured Enrichment Program) which states "*decrease developmental delay*" as indicating research is needed to understand the relationship of structured enrichment programs (SEPs) and developmental delay. The connotation is that SEPs *decrease* developmental delay; thus a directional hypothesis is implied. In each cell, the relationship under question could be researched from a number of perspectives and in a number of ways. It is not possible nor appropriate to describe these here. Rather, these studies would be dependent upon the particular situation and environment of the research site, as well as the availability of practitioner and researcher support. This matrix is provided as a beginning to understand areas where research is needed and may prove productive to understanding therapeutic recreation outcomes in pediatrics.

The next task of the group was to identify priority areas for research based on the expected outcomes contained in the matrix. Obviously, some of the areas for potential research are more important than others. Utilizing a pseudo-nominal group process technique, the PCG identified the following major outcome areas as priorities for research. These are listed in descending order of importance.

Priorities for Outcomes Research in Pediatrics

1. Adjustment to disability/illness/health impairments.

2. Development of age appropriate, independent play and recreation skills (leisure lifestyle).

3. Enhancement of quality of life, in particular regarding pursuit of leisure lifestyle.

4. Enhancement of social skills.

5. Increased compliance.

6. Promotion of wellness.

7. Facilitation of community reintegration.

8. Prevention of secondary disabilities.

9. Prevention of boredom and demoralization.

10. Physical outcomes.

Research Questions

To provide further guidance in the development of a research strategy to understand the outcomes of therapeutic recreation in pediatrics, the PCG developed specific research questions pertinent to this area. At this juncture, the PCG again utilized an organizing framework offered by Dr. Seibert. The PCG organized its research questions under the following areas: (a) functional capacity, (b) health status, and (c) quality of life.

Specific Research Questions

Functional Capacity

1. What are the comparative effects of specific therapeutic recreation interventions (e.g., structured vs. unstructured vs. medical play) in reducing developmental delay due to illness or hospitalization?

2. What are the comparative effects of disability/diagnosis specific therapeutic recreation interventions on secondary disability (e.g., range of motion)?

3. What are the comparative effects of disability/diagnosis specific therapeutic recreation interventions on functional capacity?

4. What are the comparative effects of disability/diagnosis specific therapeutic recreation interventions on symptomatology?

Health Status

1. What are the effects of therapeutic recreation interventions on length of stay?

2. What are the effects of therapeutic recreation interventions on recidivism?

3. What are the comparative effects of specific family therapeutic recreation programs on length of stay?

4. What are the comparative effects of specific family therapeutic recreation programs (e.g., family education) on recidivism?

Quality of Life

1. What is the effect of leisure education on achieving community reintegration?

2. What is the effect of therapeutic recreation intervention (e.g., leisure education) on adjustment to disability?

3. What are the effects of re-socialization on adjustment to disability?

4. Does adjustment to disability reduce length of stay?

5. What is the effect of therapeutic recreation intervention on receptivity to treatment (e.g., medical compliance)?

6. What are the effects of recreational choice on the child's sense of control?

7. What are the comparative effects of specific therapeutic recreation interventions on a child's sense of boredom and demoralization?

Addressing Research Needs

Rather than discuss and develop specific research strategies and protocols, the PCG deemed it more productive to discuss general research issues that would be relevant to the task at hand. It should be noted, however, that issues of measurement (a major concern), research design, research sophistication, and academic/practitioner cooperation were of paramount concern to the PCG. Following are enumerated basic issues which the PCG felt pertinent to the area of pediatrics.

Research Issues

1. Therapeutic recreation specialists must receive training to understand the research process, regardless of whether they actually conduct the research or do it in cooperation with someone else.

2. Cooperation and communication must be strengthened between academics and practitioners. Specific strategies should be developed to facilitate this process.

3. Professors should foster an appreciation of research and teach research skills at all levels of university instruction. Students should be included in on-going research projects of professors. Students should be encouraged or required to conduct their own research at all levels of university education.

4. Professors in therapeutic recreation must become more committed to research. This commitment should include mentoring students and mentoring practitioners. Furthermore, professors must continue their own skill development in research and enhance their ability to utilize methods and statistics.

5. The conduct of longitudinal studies is essential.

6. Replication of studies should occur to validate research across disability/diagnostic groups and settings.

7. Follow-up to therapeutic recreation interventions should be conducted.

8. Control studies are needed.

9. Greater sophistication is required in assessment, measurement of variables used in research studies, statistical ability, and design of studies. In addition, more creative and non-traditional approaches are needed (e.g., phenomenological studies, experience sampling studies).

10. Research should focus on identifying relationships between/among **specific** interventions and techniques and **specific** outcomes. Therapeutic recreation should not be viewed as a global variable to be used in these studies.

Concluding Remarks

The PCG felt **strongly** that it was important for therapeutic recreation specialists working in pediatrics to work effectively with other treatment modalities and health care professionals and that **THE CHILD** is the most important consideration. Furthermore, the PCG felt **strongly** that in whatever information is communicated to various health care groups and policy makers, it is essential to discuss the leisure and recreation philosophical underpinnings which form the foundation of the field. Recreation and leisure are basic and necessary rights of everyone, and are **in and of themselves** critical to the quality of life. The group realizes that this is not a language or concept readily understood or accepted in the health care arena, yet the PCG felt it essential to educate health care professionals and policy makers.

Table 1: Therapeutic Recreation Interventions and Related Outcomes (con't.)

THERAPEUTIC RECREATION INTERVENTION

MAJOR OUTCOMES	Diagnosis/Disability Specific Play	Recreation/ Leisure Education	Physical Activity	Environmental Manipulation	Indirect vs. Direct Services	Patient & Family Education
Prevention	Prevent secondary disability (e.g., increase range of motion)	Decrease or prevent regressive behaviors Decrease or prevent boredom & demoralization	Decrease or prevent secondary disability	Decrease stress of child and family		Prevention of recidivism
Diagnosis			Provide functional assessment in real life context			
Treatment			Reduce symptomotology Increase physical development	Increase receptivity to treatment		
Management	Increase adjustment to disability Increase compliance Decrease length of stay	Provide ability to pursue leisure lifestyle Increase quality of life Enhance normalization/ adjustment	Wellness maintenance Decrease recidivism Decrease length of stay	Increase quality of life	Increase cost effectiveness	Increase compliance Increase adjustment to disability Increase quality of life Decrease length of stay

Table 1: Therapeutic Recreation Interventions and Related Outcomes

THERAPEUTIC RECREATION INTERVENTION

MAJOR OUTCOME	Structured Enrichment Program	Community Reintegration	Family Recreation	Social Activities and Play	Choice Enhancement	Medical Play
Prevention	Decrease or prevent developmental delay		Decrease dysfunctional families Decrease Over Benevolent Family Syndrome	Decrease social isolation	Prevent learned helplessness	Reduce tertiary stress related to hospitalization and procedures
Diagnosis			Augment diagnostic information			Augment diagnosis
Treatment	Enhance developmental skills			Enhance age appropriate social skills Increase resocialization Enhance relationship building		
Management	Decrease length of stay	Increase adjustment to disability Decrease length of stay	Increase compliance (family involvment in total care) Decrease length of stay	Decrease length of stay		Decrease length of stay Increase compliance

SUMMARY OF PHYSICAL MEDICINE CONSENSUS GROUP

Renee Lyons

Preliminary Discussion

The physical medicine and rehabilitation group was composed of 18 participants representing both academic and clinical perspectives in therapeutic recreation, and concerned with a broad range of physically disabling conditions, including: (a) AIDS, (b) amputation, (c) arthritis, (d) back injury, (e) blindness, (f) burns, (g) cancer, (h) cardiac conditions, (i) chronic pain, (j) deafness, (k) neuromuscular conditions, (l) post-surgery, (m) respiratory conditions, (n) spinal injury, (o) stroke, and (p) traumatic brain injury, and so forth. The group's discussions <u>primarily</u> addressed the needs of adults with acquired chronic physical disabilities versus congenital or acute disabilities. The group used salient needs of persons with disabilities and, relevance to therapeutic recreation roles as the primary factors in determining its list of recommendations. Issues were raised from the perspectives of assessment, treatment/intervention, maintenance, and prevention (exacerbation, recurrence, secondary disabilities such as bed sores), although these were treated by the group as interrelated and continuous processes for persons with chronic illness and disability. It is also important to note that the whole field of modern physical medicine, now based on an interdisciplinary team approach, is just beginning to develop research which can accommodate the multivariate rehabilitation goals and multidisciplinary treatment modalities that are required for this field.

Process and Framework Development

After the introduction of participants, Dr. Doris Berryman, Dr. Ann James, and Barbara Trader provided an overview of the working paper they had written for the meeting, entitled "Consensus Conference on the Benefits of Therapeutic Recreation: A Perspective on Physical Disabilities." The group members each gave a personal perspective on the paper and raised particular issues which they felt would be central to the group's discussions. (As it turned out, the majority of these issues have been integrated into the final recommendations.)

It was suggested that the group begin to develop the framework for its analysis of therapeutic recreation outcomes by first identifying what the literature indicates to be salient needs of persons with physical disabilities. These were compiled by four small groups under the themes: (a) psychosocial needs, (b) physical needs, (c) cognitive needs, and (d) recreation and leisure needs.

The psychosocial needs group identified the following key psychosocial issues which therapeutic recreation could influence: (a) hope, (b) positive affect, (c) self-worth, (d) mastery, (e) reframing of the self, (f) social isolation, (g) coping, (h) boredom, and (i) motivation. The primary strategies that therapeutic recreation employs (or might employ) to address these issues were: (a) to enhance the quality and quantity of activity involvement, and (b) to facilitate social interaction and social relationships.

The cognitive group concluded that the main focus of therapeutic recreation is to improve cognitive functioning in the following: (a) memory, (b) attention, (c) concentration, (d) problem solving, (e) perception, (f) awareness, (g) insight, (h) impulse control, (i) judgment, and (j) sequencing.

The physical performance needs group identified the following four areas where involvement in recreation activities can make contributions: (a) vital capacity--strength, balance, endurance, flexibility, cardiovascular performance, coordinator/dexterity, locomotion; (b) physiological needs--pain management, speech, hearing, tactile; (c) kinesthetic needs--body image, attitude, motivation, and adjustment; and (d) weight management.

The leisure functioning needs group covered two main areas of need: (a) the development of strategies to enhance leisure, and (b) the need for an adequate caregiver/support system to facilitate coping and to increase life satisfaction.

These issues were presented to the whole group, refined, and assessed in terms of specific roles of therapeutic recreation, the group's knowledge of outcomes, and what research needs doing. In considering the recommendations of the group, the following model was developed by the facilitator to demonstrate how the use of activities for specific rehabilitation outcomes, and leisure enhancement, both result in the benefits of improved life quality.

Therapeutic Recreation Outcomes Model:
Physical Medicine and Rehabilitation

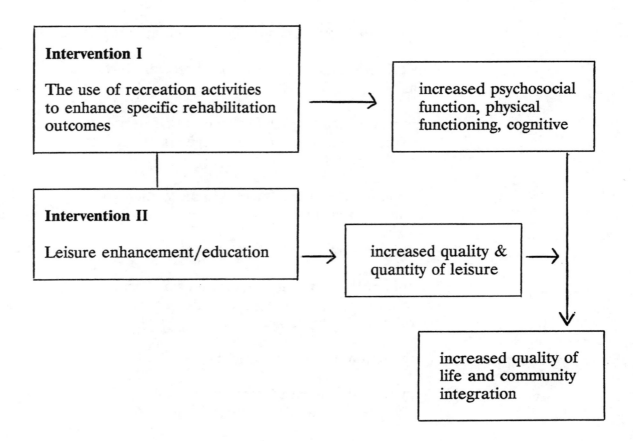

Recommendations from the physical medicine and rehabilitation group are given under the following headings: (a) important roles for therapeutic recreation in physical medicine and rehabilitation where some evidence of the outcomes is known; (b) important roles for therapeutic recreation in physical medicine and rehabilitation for which little or no evidence of outcomes or benefits is known; and (c) recommendations which arise from research and practice in therapeutic recreation for persons with physical disabilities but which were perceived to be general issues for the field of therapeutic recreation. It is important to note that evidence of specific therapeutic recreation interventions is still <u>scarce</u>; however, the research in therapeutic recreation <u>combined with</u> that of other disciplines provide preliminary evidence of the <u>needs of persons with a disability, the effects of involvement in recreation, and the effects of specific therapeutic recreation interventions on rehabilitation outcomes, and quality of life</u>.

I.   Areas of Research Which are Important and Where There Exists Some Evidence of Research Outcomes in Therapeutic Recreation

(A)   The use of recreation to enhance specific rehabilitation outcomes:

1.   Therapeutic recreation enhances psychosocial functioning, including:

(a)   increased mastery (self-efficacy, self-determination, decreased dependency on caregivers and health professionals);

(b)   hope for the future (increased motivation and increased energy);

(c)   reduced stress;

(d)   enhancement and maintenance of personal relationships, including facilitation of increased relational competence;

(e)   reduction of social isolation;

(f)   increased self-esteem (reframing of the self, acceptance and adjustment, and increased self-worth);

(g)   reduced boredom through increased activity; and, more meaningful, healthy activity;

(h)   increased positive affect (decreased depression, suicide ideation, and self-neglect).

2.   Therapeutic recreation facilitates cognitive outcomes (although very little research evidences currently exists).

3.   Therapeutic recreation enhances physical performance:

(a)   increased general health status, including increasing/maintaining endurance, strength, and range of motion;

(b)   fitness, and its outcome of stress reduction has positive effects on the immune system.

(B)   The use of leisure enhancement strategies and leisure education to improve leisure functioning, including:

      1.   facilitation of community integration/ reintegration;

      2.   amelioration/prevention of social isolation;

      3.   development and maintenance of social skills;

      4.   development of skills to counteract social stigma;

      5.   increased activity adjustment competencies;

      6.   increased knowledge of and use of community resources;

      7.   increased activity, more meaningful, enjoyable activity;

      8.   increased family recreation and reduction of family breakdown;

      9.   assertiveness training for community reintegration;

      10. facilitation of skill transfer to community settings.

(C)   By facilitating psychosocial, physical, and cognitive functioning, and increased leisure functioning, the contribution of therapeutic recreation interventions on overall rehabilitation outcomes include:

      1.   prevention/reduction of secondary disabilities;

      2.   reduced recidivism;

      3.   reduced exacerbations of symptoms (e.g., MS);

      4.   increased self-efficacy;

      5.   reduced length of stay in hospital;

      6.   enhanced work readiness;

      7.   enhanced use of community supports;

      8.   increased well-being and quality of life.

II.   Areas Where Research is Needed but Where Little Evidence of Therapeutic Recreation Outcomes Currently Exist

(A)   The comparison of types of activities and interventions in producing rehabilitation outcomes and enhancing quality of life.

(B)   The effect of organized community integration strategies on social isolation, loneliness, and depression.

(C)   The utilization of skills in community settings (e.g., Do participants in a structured community reintegration or leisure eduction program retain and utilize the skills/competencies taught? How are these competencies utilized in real life situations?).

(D)   The role and effectiveness of therapeutic recreation interventions to enhance family functioning which has been affected by disability, and the testing strategies which influence the effectiveness of significant others (family, friends, caregivers) in the rehabilitation process.

(E)   The impact of disability on the leisure and lifestyle behavior of particular groups where little information is currently available (e.g., persons with AIDS; persons with hearing handicaps; high quads; low level head injuries). This must include investigation of salient needs in order to produce the most effective services.

(F)   Cost-benefit analyses of therapeutic recreation (i.e., What are the most cost effective interventions for the benefits?). Such questions as the nature of service, duration, and location are all important elements. There should be comparative analysis with other health interventions. Are there efficiencies which can result in reduced costs for the individual, for society, for third party payers? Which is the best setting to provide which types of therapeutic recreation services--the community, the hospital, or other clinical settings?

(G)   The value of diversion in stress reduction.

(H)   Therapeutic recreation's role in cognitive enhancement in both diagnosis and intervention. How can we collaborate effectively with other disciplines in this area?

(I) The effect of using pre-morbid leisure activities as therapeutic recreation interventions, and on rehabilitation outcomes (e.g., Does the utilization of pre-morbid leisure behavior improve cognitive deficits such as memory, attention, problem solving?).

(J) Client readiness for therapeutic recreation interventions.

(K) The impact of pleasurable experiences on the immune system.

III. General Recommendations

The group recommends the following general strategies to enhance therapeutic recreation outcomes research:

(A) The issue of using the terms recreation and leisure in research which is often avoided and couched under a more acceptable label (acceptable may not only apply to status, but reimbursement of ?) such as increased health, quality of life, or physical activity.

(B) The development of a comprehensive data base on therapeutic recreation to accurately assess the status of outcome measures in therapeutic recreation.

(C) The establishment of a network of researchers who can collaborate around specific research/clinical problems, develop research ideas, enhance resources, conduct feasibility studies, and communicate about concepts, designs, and methods.

(D) Increased cooperation and sharing of information with other disciplines and multidisciplinary groups.

(E) The establishment of longitudinal studies in therapeutic recreation, particularly because the populations that are addressed most often are dealing with chronic health problems, where the course of the condition may be unpredictable and/or degenerative. Quick fixes are not particularly beneficial. There also must be continuity of service from the hospital to the community.

(F) The sharing of therapeutic recreation findings with other groups (disciplines) and agencies serving persons with disabilities, particularly influences on aspects of psychosocial, physical, and cognitive functioning, and on life quality.

(G)   The identification of new research designs which accommodate clinical field studies and the group's research questions. Address the issue of prescribed versus free choice in terms of rehabilitation outcomes--the appropriateness of each.

(H)   The systematic assessment of current assessment/outcome instrumentation (what exists, how/with whom it is feasible, what needs development).

(I)   The use of cultural and gender sensitive research methods.

(J)   The assessment of the influence of staff training on service provision (studies of paraprofessional and professional roles). Issues raised by participants included the evaluation of the efficacy of university training programs, the training of therapeutic recreation specialists at the graduate versus undergraduate level in terms of impact on the quality of therapeutic recreation services and the growth of research, and techniques for developing a cadre of skilled therapeutic recreation researchers.

SUMMARY OF PSYCHIATRY CONSENSUS GROUP

David Austin

Preliminary Discussion

Preliminary discussion identified three major categories of concern for therapeutic recreation research in mental health. These were: (a) prevention, (b) diagnosis/treatment, and (c) functional behaviors (i.e., rehabilitation/ management).

Outcomes Supported with Evidence

1. Engagement in constructive pleasurable activity increases psychological well-being, reduces symptomatology, and contributes to treatment outcomes.

2. Prescribed physical activity of appropriate type, intensity, and duration reduces anxiety, stress, and depression.

Outcomes Requiring Documentation

1. Enjoyment and satisfaction with treatment is enhanced through prescribed therapeutic recreation services.

2. Activities and environments that are structured to encourage and promote playfulness, enjoyment, and laughter contribute to desirable treatment outcomes.

3. The acquisition and utilization of appropriate recreation behaviors and skills increases personal coping.

4. Prescribed therapeutic recreation interventions can be used to enhance functional independence.

5. Participation in recreation activities provides opportunities for mastery and control leading to feelings of enjoyment, self-efficacy, and empowerment.

6. Pleasurable activity can be used to increase the frequency of positive social behavior.

7. Prescribed therapeutic recreation interventions reduce stress and anxiety.

Priorities for Outcomes Research in Mental Health

1. What is the role of therapeutic recreation in the development of functional independence skills?

2. What is the effect of leisure education/leisure counseling on improving the leisure behavior and psychological well-being of various diagnostic groups?

3. What is the effect of therapeutic recreation interventions on client length of stay?

4. What is the relationship of therapeutic recreation to DSM III-R symptoms?

5. What is the needed frequency, intensity, and duration of therapeutic recreation interventions needed to affect symptoms?

6. What are the physiological effects of participation in therapeutic recreation activities?

7. What is the optimal timing of interventions in the phases of illnesses or disorders?

Other Research Questions
(presented in random order)

1. Does increased leisure knowledge lead to appropriate decision-making?

2. How is leisure knowledge best acquired?

3. What are the effects of leisure counseling on life transitions (e.g., retirement, leaving home)?

4. What are criteria for determining pleasurable activity or what is rewarding?

5. What is the perception of leisure time by various diagnostic groups?

6. What is the effect of the provision of "structured time" on psychiatric symptoms?

7. Is client orientation to free time related to the therapist's perceptions?

8. Does incased leisure satisfaction decrease symptoms?

9. Do self-initiated activities have more impact than other-initiated activities?

10. Do individuals who score high in leisure functioning have lower recidivism rates?

11. Which prevention methods (e.g., workshops) have the most impact on recidivism rates?

12. Is the leisure social network related to recidivism?

13. Which specific therapeutic recreation approaches are most effective in developing client investment in treatment?

14. How does therapeutic recreation relate to the critical first 72 hours of treatment?

15. What is the impact of the therapeutic recreation assessment process on clients?

16. What are the relative effects of individual versus group interventions?

17. What is the effect of environmental manipulation on treatment?

18. What is the relevance of the provision of "normalized" therapeutic recreation activities in diagnostic assessment?

19. How do various types of clients use discretionary time?

20. What are the short- and long-term effects of therapeutic recreation interventions on problem solving?

21. How does therapeutic recreation participation relate to social networks?

22. What is the effect of therapeutic recreation on longer community stays?

23. What is the role of therapeutic recreation in aftercare?

24. What is the role of therapeutic recreation in developing/maintaining self-esteem?

25. What is the role of therapeutic recreation in self-advocacy?

26. How does therapeutic recreation assist clients to maintain and strengthen affiliations with family, friends, and community groups?

27. How does therapeutic recreation help clients to form new ties with individuals and groups?

28. What are the best means to teach clients how to make use of available community recreation resources?

29. By what means can therapeutic recreation stimulate client's awareness of his or her leisure needs?

30. What are attitudes held about leisure by various diagnostic groups?

31. Does mainstreaming psychiatric clients into community recreation programs produce positive effects?

32. How can experiences be designed to increase motivation for participation?

33. Is there an ideal ratio of staff to clients in order to bring about optimal treatment outcomes?

34. Do the characteristics of the therapist's style affect the outcomes of interventions?

Identification of Factors that Influence
the Selection of Research
Priority Areas

1. Priorities set by research funding sources.

2. A growing aging population.

3. Client satisfaction and demands.

4. Interest by disciplines that may cooperate in interdisciplinary research efforts.

5. Interests of university researchers.

6. Philosophy and theory development in mental health and therapeutic recreation.

7. Interests of those providing reimbursement.

8. Research agenda set by therapeutic recreation profession.

Other Areas

Time did not allow the mental health group to discuss recommendations regarding the most sensible and strategic approaches to addressing the research priorities. Nor was there time to discuss dissemination methods.

SUMMARY OF DEVELOPMENTAL DISABILITIES CONSENSUS GROUP

Julie Dunn

Preliminary Discussion

Because of the large scope of disabling conditions included under the umbrella of developmental disabilities, the consensus group elected to delimit the definition of the target group. Thus, for this area, the target group was considered to be those individuals with mental retardation of all ages, including individuals with multiple disabling conditions, if one of those conditions was mental retardation.

The known benefits of therapeutic recreation intervention and the future research needs were organized on a matrix representing the major areas of client status (health status, functional capacity and quality of life) and type of service (intervention, diagnosis and prevention).

Known Benefits

Therapeutic recreation interventions have been demonstrated to contribute to the health status of individuals with developmental disabilities. Specifically, interventions have been shown to enhance fitness, facilitate the perception of pleasure, contribute to survival and the ability of the individual to thrive. Diagnosis and prevention related to improved health status needs to be investigated through future research.

In the area of functional capacity, therapeutic recreation intervention was found to affect motor development, social skill development (including social interaction skills), cognitive development, communication behavior, enhancement of play and recreation skills repertoire, and vocational competence. Diagnostic procedures and prevention efforts related to functional capacity are in need of future research efforts.

Benefits of therapeutic recreation intervention related to quality of life included: the development of leisure lifestyle, enhancement of autonomy (freedom, choice, self determination), awareness of community resources, and increased positive attitudes as a result of integrated programs. In the area of diagnosis, leisure functioning has been measured for some individuals of higher functioning levels. Additional research is needed in the assessment of other quality of life variables for individuals of all ability levels. Prevention efforts which would contribute to an enhanced quality of life also need further research.

Though many benefits have been demonstrated, it is believed that they need to be replicated to support their existence and generalized to other individuals with mental retardation. The large majority of benefits were identified to be the result of therapeutic recreation intervention. Thus, in addition to the expansion of research in this area, considerable wok needs to be accomplished to identify contributions of therapeutic recreation in diagnosis and prevention.

Research Questions

From the same conceptual matrix fifteen general areas of research were identified with specific research questions defining each area.

Health Status

1. What impact do therapeutic recreation interventions have on personal health maintenance and reduction of illness? More specifically, how does therapeutic recreation impact; personal health responsibility, the practice of healthy nutrition, prevention of rehospitalization, prevention of chemical dependency, chronic conditions and other disease? Can therapeutic recreation assist families in the prevention of further dysfunction of the family member who is developmentally disabled?

2. What effect do therapeutic recreation services have on consumption of primary medical services? Specifically, can therapeutic recreation affect a reduction in: the amount of medication needed, the length of hospitalization, anxiety, the number of auxiliary services needed, and the symptoms of depression and anxiety which would contribute to an increase in illness?

3. What effect does therapeutic recreation have on physiological/psychological conditions? Specifically, can therapeutic recreation intervention reduce symptoms, contribute to successful adjustment to chronic conditions, and increase coping mechanisms to facilitate rehabilitation efforts?

4. What effect does therapeutic recreation have on longevity?

5. What effect does therapeutic recreation have on coping behaviors related to ongoing health status? More specifically, can therapeutic recreation intervention assist an individual in successfully managing the effects of stress, aging, disability and life change events?

6. What role does therapeutic recreation play in minimizing further disability throughout the lifespan? Can it minimize the potential for developmental delay, the need for related services at school age? Can it decrease socially unacceptable behavior and need for involvement in the correctional system?

Functional Capacity

7. Can the application of therapeutic recreation to improve functional capacity reduce the ongoing dependence on specialized and related service needs of individuals with mental retardation and their families? Specifically, can it reduce educational costs to society, enhance adjustment to changing life roles, and lower recidivism rates?

8. Can the application of therapeutic recreation interventions improve the family's ability to support/contribute to the individual's vocational, social, educational, leisure, community involvement success? Examples of potential areas of intervention research are sex education and expression, activities of daily living, community living skills, and repertoire development?

9. What is the role of therapeutic recreation in diagnostic services for individuals with mental retardation? Specifically can naturally occurring inappropriate behaviors, or school related problems be assessed by therapeutic recreation services?

10. Can recreation behaviors predict success throughout one's life across school, vocational, home and community settings? Can assessment of leisure functioning and decision making contribute to an understanding of the client's functional capacity?

Quality of Life

11. To what degree do therapeutic recreation interventions and outcomes contribute to vocational success?

12. To what degree do therapeutic recreation interventions and outcomes contribute to lifespan transitions such as; effective adjustment throughout the lifespan, improved choice, increased effectiveness in decision making, adjustment to least restrictive or changing environments, increased leisure satisfaction (subjective well-being as contribution to transition)?

13. To what degree do therapeutic recreation interventions and outcomes contribute to social and family cohesiveness and integration? Specifically, does therapeutic recreation contribute to increased community acceptance, increased friendship, social networks and community connectedness, education of families and significant others, prediction of family risk factors, sexuality, and sexual expression, and family stability.

14. Can therapeutic recreation assist families and significant others in the understanding of the leisure needs of persons with developmental disabilities?

15. Can therapeutic recreation programs, specifically, leisure education increase the quality of life for transition into adulthood?

General Guidelines for Research

The following general guidelines are suggested to direct research in efficacy of therapeutic recreation services for individuals with developmental disabilities.

1. All of the "known" findings require further research both in depth and breadth of research.

2. The effect of "Leisure" (therapeutic recreation intervention) from the lifespan perspective needs investigation.

3. Research needs to take into consideration the individual within the context of the various systems in which the individual has membership and therefore other components of those systems must be involved in the interventions.

4. Research is needed to generalize findings from nondisabled individuals to individuals who are developmentally disabled, and between different types of disabling conditions.

5. The therapeutic recreation profession needs to agree on what constitute therapeutic recreation so to prove its efficacy.

6. Research methodology used to study the suggested questions needs to be driven by the questions, subjects and settings.

7. Research should be applied and field based.

8. Multiple methods should be used in investigations.

Conclusion

A variety of studies have been conducted which demonstrate the efficacy of therapeutic recreation intervention. Largely, these studies have investigated the impact of specific interventions of the improvement of functional capacity of individuals or small groups of subjects. Little overall effort has been applied to examine larger groups of individuals either as groups or through replication of studies over individuals. Additionally, coordinated effort is needed to examine integrated effects of multiple interventions, across age ranges and functional levels. As a profession, therapeutic recreation has begun the task of demonstrating the efficacy of its interventions for individuals with developmental disabilities, but a major research concentration is still needed in this area.